THE SOCIOLOGY OF KNOWLEDGE

THE SOCIOLOGY OF
KNOWLEDGE

AN ESSAY IN AID
OF A DEEPER UNDERSTANDING OF THE
HISTORY OF IDEAS

BY

W. STARK

M.A., Dr. rer. pol., Dr. jur.,
Reader in the History of Economic Thought,
University of Manchester

THE FREE PRESS
Glencoe, Illinois

First published in the U.S.A. 1958
by The Free Press,
a corporation.

© *1958 by Werner Stark*

By the same author

The Ideal Foundations
of Economic Thought

The History of Economics in
its Relation to Social Development

America: Ideal and Reality

Printed in Great Britain
by Butler and Tanner Ltd.
Frome and London

It is only through the conversation of man with man that ideas come into existence. Two human beings are as necessary for the generation of the human mind as they are for the generation of the human body.

FEUERBACH

It is not given to us to grasp the truth, which is identical with the divine, directly. We perceive it only in reflection, in example and symbol, in singular and related appearances. It meets us as a kind of life which is incomprehensible to us, and yet we cannot free ourselves from the desire to comprehend it.

GOETHE

CONTENTS

PREFACE

THE present book is in the first place an introduction to the subject whose name it bears, the so-called 'sociology of knowledge'. Anyone who reads it right through from beginning to end will, it is hoped, have some idea of the themes with which this study has been concerned and of the main solutions to its problems which have been attempted. I have endeavoured to give an account both of permanent trends and recent developments.

But I have tried to provide more than a mere summary; I have done my best to re-think the whole subject and to clarify its issues. There was great need of such clarification. In the past, two rather disparate, nay irreconcilable, preoccupations have coexisted within the sociology of knowledge and constantly cut across each other: the study of the political element in thought, of what is commonly called 'ideology', and the investigation of the social element in thinking, the influence of the social groundwork of life on the formation of a determinate mental image of reality. The one has sought to lay bare hidden factors which turn us away from the truth, the other to identify forces which tend to impart a definite direction to our search for it. I have radically separated the two subjects, as will be seen from chapter 2, and have then concentrated on the latter; thus laying the foundations of what might be called a 'pure' theory of the social determination of thought, or, alternatively, a social theory of knowledge. Nor is this the only clarifying distinction which I have striven to introduce; others are contained in the middle section of the first chapter and in chapters 4–8.

The picture of the sociology of knowledge which has emerged from my considerations is in some essential points different from that traditionally entertained. So far, the names which have loomed largest have been those of Marx and Mannheim on the one hand, Nietzsche and Pareto on the other. In consequence of my strict distinction between social determination and ideological distortion of thought, they have unavoidably been dislodged from the centre, and pushed outward towards the perimeter, of the stage, and their place has been taken by Max Weber, in whose spirit (I hope I may say) the present treatise has been conceived. In so far as Max Weber was a disciple of Heinrich

Rickert, and Heinrich Rickert was a member of the neo-Kantian school, this essay is a humble attempt to carry on one of the major lines of modern philosophical speculation. It must be said at once, however, that my book is the work of one who is an historian of ideas and a sociologist, rather than a professional philosopher; and that I am very conscious of my limitations in this respect. Still, my forays into the realm of philosophy will not, I trust, be held against me, for neither the social theorist nor the historian of ideas can do his job properly unless he tries to think out the deeper implications of the phenomena with which he has to deal.

Unavoidably, my pages contain a good deal of polemic, and I have had some hard things to say especially about the Nietzsche–Pareto tradition. Nevertheless, I have found to my astonishment that a fair measure of agreement exists in the literature, and I should like to record my pleasure at this fact. Complete unanimity between opinions inspired by and derived from Max Weber, and convictions entertained by such thinkers as Karl Marx or Mannheim is, of course, out of the question, but the two positions, at least as far as detail is concerned, are not so wide apart that a meaningful conversation between them would appear impossible.

In writing this book, I have had in view, not only the obvious immediate purpose, but also a second more distant one, namely to prepare the way for a detailed investigation of the *history* of the sociology of knowledge. Most of the leading social philosophers have had definite, and often fascinating, ideas on the subject, which it would be a highly important and attractive task to scrutinize. Not only the five great men already mentioned, but also Vico, Montesquieu, Comte, Spencer, Durkheim, Veblen, Tönnies, Cooley, Sumner, Bergson, Alfred Weber and Sorokin, would, among others, richly repay intensive study. It is in particular the second part of the present book which is meant to serve as a basis for such an historical investigation; it seeks to provide some concepts which will enable us to characterize and compare the various distinctive theories that have been put forward in the past. In order to make sure that the categories I have elaborated will be really helpful when it comes to the analysis and assessment of any individual contribution, I have, before giving final form to this book, subjected Montesquieu, by way of experiment (so to speak), to a closer consideration, extracted from his writings his scattered but definite opinions on the social element in the genesis of ideas and assembled them into a coherent picture. The study which has resulted is, I venture to hope, not uninstructive, and I intend, in due course, to incorporate it in a further volume on 'The Origins of the Sociology of Knowledge'.

A special word should perhaps be said at this point to those who may chance to come across this book without having as yet any previous

Preface

knowledge of its subject. The very label by which the subject is commonly known is apt to arouse, and has in fact more than once aroused, prejudice in those who have approached it for the first time. If individual ideas are put into connection with social forces, does this not necessarily involve a depreciation of the individual and his mind? Is he not reduced thereby to the position of a mere mouthpiece of collective or even impersonal tendencies? To those who may raise these questions, or rather entertain these suspicions, I must say already here with all emphasis that they are wrong. The present writer has all due respect for the spontaneity and even the greatness of the individual personality; he wholeheartedly subscribes to the adage: *individuum est ineffabile*. The sociology of knowledge as he sees it does not undertake to argue away the creativeness of the individual mind: if it did, it would be hopelessly unrealistic and useless from the very start; it merely attempts to shed some light on it, to render its operation intelligible, and that is an entirely different matter. It takes only one single fact for granted, namely that no one is an island, and that to be a man of culture is to be a creature of society. This, surely, is no extravagant assumption. Nobody but a solipsist could arraign the soundness of it, and solipsism is not a philosophy which ever has been, or indeed needs to be, taken seriously.

It goes without saying that it has been my ambition to present my ideas in a stylistic form which is not altogether unworthy to be called English. In this difficult task I have had the invaluable assistance of my friend Peter Heath; he has gone over my text and drawn my attention to all the sins, great and small, which I had committed against the spirit of the language. It is impossible for me to thank him adequately for what he has done. Another friend of mine, Professor George Kerferd, has allowed me to discuss with him the special terminology, based on Greek, which I have employed in the second part of the book. To him also I am greatly indebted. But neither Kerferd nor Heath must be held responsible for anything that may arouse misgivings or justify criticism in the ensuing pages.

Help on the bibliographical side, which I am happy to acknowledge, has been generously extended to me by Professor George Gurvitch of the Sorbonne, Professor René König of the University of Cologne, and Professor Carlo Antoni of the University of Rome. My wife has furthered my work in more ways than I can mention and helped me immeasurably in my task.

W. STARK

Manchester,
December 22nd, 1956

xi

PART ONE

THE PROVINCE OF THE
SOCIOLOGY OF KNOWLEDGE

CHAPTER ONE

PRELIMINARY ORIENTATION

(a) INTRODUCTION

THERE can be few to whom it has not happened at one time or another to attend a concert, the programme of which included, first a symphony of the eighteenth century, perhaps Haydn's 'Military' or Mozart's 'Haffner', and then a symphony of the nineteenth century, say, Beethoven's 'Eroica' or Bruckner's 'Romantic'. Conductors love contrasts of this kind, and rightly so, for nothing serves better to bring out the specific excellences of a work of art than its juxtaposition with another work of art comparable in stature but different in content and in style. Now, anyone who has become aware of the great dissimilarity between the music of a Haydn or a Mozart on the one hand, and the music of a Beethoven or a Bruckner on the other, and who begins to speculate about the nature and the implications of this dissimilarity, will soon discover that it is nowhere more immediately manifest than in the third movements of the respective symphonies. Both the older and the younger composers follow the traditional *andante*, the slow and serious music, with light relief, to bring back a more smiling and contented mood: but whereas an eighteenth-century audience expected, and was served with, a sprightly minuet, the minuet has given place, a few decades later, to the scherzo, a movement similar in aim and inspiration, but different in form. This disappearance of the minuet which took place around the year 1800 —one might almost be tempted to say, around the year 1789—points beyond the confines of musical creation and musical thought to the wider sphere of social life and social strife. The minuet was, as everyone knows, an expression of *ancien régime* society and sociability; it could not survive the social order of which it was part, parcel and product; it had to vanish as soon as its historical basis dissolved and disappeared. And thus it is that a social and political revolution draws after it certain kindred developments in the realm of culture, and even in so apparently remote and independent a province of this realm as music, the most abstract of all arts, the art furthest removed from the hurly-burly of everyday events.

3

But the replacement of the minuet by the scherzo is only a comparatively superficial difference between the eighteenth-century symphony and its nineteenth-century successor. The dissimilarity goes a good deal deeper than that. It concerns not only pure form, but, what is much more important, the relation of form and content as well. When we call Haydn and Mozart representatives of classicism, what we mean is that with them form is throughout in control of content, passion is firmly contained by the spirit. Certainly, deep forces are sometimes stirring in the music of a Mozart, for instance in his symphony in G minor (number 40): they struggle upward and outward, as it were, and clamour for freer expression. 'But however poignant these expressions may become at this or that point . . . they are still presented with an incomparable classical poise and restraint; nor does the composer find it necessary to lay stress on distress by committing drastic breaches of form anywhere.' [1] With Beethoven, things are different. Not that he ever allows the content to burst the form or passion to escape control altogether. But what a contest between the two, what a struggle! Furious forces beat against the barriers that hem them in, as a raging sea may foam against the rocks along the shore-line. 'The main difference between Beethoven's conception and his predecessors' is not the actual form but, so to speak, the voltage, the degree of tension between the component musical characters or ideas. . . . What in Haydn's sonata had been a spirited conversation, and in Mozart's a picturesque adventure, becomes with him a dramatic scene of terrific tension.' [2] Let us concede at once that a great deal of this must be attributed to personal characteristics: it is simply a fact that Beethoven was a much more choleric individual than either the more placid Haydn or the more sanguine Mozart. But is it not also clear and undeniable that something of contemporary social reality is mirrored and expressed, not only in the settled formality of the eighteenth-century symphony, but also in the passionate and painful attempt to realize a greater freedom in art as in life which is characteristic of a Beethoven and a Berlioz? Can we imagine an 'Eroica' or a 'Fantastique' written in 1780 and performed in the *salle des glaces* at Versailles? We cannot. It was only the cataclysm of the French Revolution which released and unleashed the forces, at once destructive and creative, demoniacal and angelic, which inform the music of a Ludwig van Beethoven.

But we can go even further. The music of the pre- and the post-revolutionary periods are different, not only because they are different in form, and not only because they show differences in the relationship of form and content: they are different even in content itself, quite apart

---

[1] Eric Blom in Hill, *The Symphony*, 1949, 88. Cf. also Turner, *Mozart, the Man and his Works*, 1938, 321 *seq*.

[2] Hans Gal, *The Golden Age of Vienna*, 1948, 51.

from any formalistic aspect of the matter—different in thought and feeling and experience. If the contrast between Beethoven and Haydn in the underlying philosophy is not greater than we actually find it, the reason is merely that the spiritual revolution of Europe had taken place much earlier than the political—in the middle of the eighteenth century rather than at the end. When Rousseau uttered his soul-stirring cry: *Retournons à la nature*, he expressed a mood which was felt by musicians as much as it was by political pamphleteers. It was people like Carl Philipp Emanuel Bach who, in the forties of the century, broke away from the severe contrapuntal style of their elders and, in Dr. Gal's graphic phrase, worked 'for the emancipation of melody from its tight constrictive bodice'.[1] The intellectual revolution was already over when Haydn appeared on the scene. He certainly preserved the traditional forms of musical composition; these were only discarded after the whirlwind of 1789 had swept the boards clean; but he poured new wine into the old bottles. 'A certain type of minuet in his symphonies, sturdy and stamping like a peasant at a dance, is definitely the earliest appearance of low-class music, shaped and idealized by a great master.'[2] Thus Haydn, like Beethoven, belongs already to what might loosely be called the bourgeois age.[3]

But that does not mean that a comparison of the thought-content of their music does not yield interesting and enlightening results, for the two composers represent successive and contrasting phases in the development of the bourgeois mind. Haydn shows it in the ascendant, in its optimistic stage, when all is confidence, expectation and anticipation. 'There is no profounder expression of the philosophical ideals of eighteenth-century rationalism than the perfect logical order of a string quartet or a symphony of Haydn's. Our world, created by God on a prestabilized harmony, is the best of all possible worlds. This, the quintessence of Leibniz's philosophy, is not only the clearly stated main idea of Haydn's greatest work, *The Creation*. It stands, an unwritten motto, on every page of his music, a creed based on the sublime confidence that if only Reason would prevail, universal happiness would be round the next corner.' Rightly does Dr. Gal in this passage[4] link Haydn and Leibniz: their spiritual kinship must be obvious to all who know them. But Leibniz was also the philosopher of François Quesnay and Adam Smith,[5] of economists and politicians and world-reformers in general:

[1] *Loc. cit.*, 18.
[2] Cf. *ibid.*, 21. Cf. also Gray in Hill, *The Symphony*, 1949, 26 *seq.*, 32.
[3] The same applies to Mozart. Cf. the very clear indications in Turner, *Mozart, the Man and his Works*, 1938, 58 *seq.* Cf. also 199: 'He belongs to the age of revolution in Europe, not to the earlier Augustan age.'
[4] *Loc. cit.*, 25. Cf. also Gray's most interesting remark concerning Haydn's use of the bassoon (whose tragic possibilities of expression he entirely neglects) in Hill, *loc. cit.*, 32.   [5] Cf. my *Ideal Foundations of Economic Thought*, 1943, Essay I.

he was the philosopher who assured the world that the *ordre positif* of Europe, the traditional feudal order, could and should be wiped away, because underneath it there is the much better *ordre naturel* preordained by the all-wise and all-loving deity whose work men can easily mar but never mend—the philosopher, in a word, who gave the revolutionary forces that supreme self-confidence which they needed in order to accomplish their task.

In a sense, even Beethoven's mind still has its roots in this world-view —but how dark a shadow has been cast over it, how deeply has it been tinged with doubt, how painfully has it been touched by despair! In the second, fourth and eighth symphonies it still asserts itself, but how different is the mood of the third and fifth! And the ninth, does it not read like a creed of defiance, an assertion of optimism in the face of a world that is going from bad to worse? [1] Shattered is the facile belief of the eighteenth century that a society of liberty and equality (the twin principles in which Beethoven passionately believed) will also be a society of fraternity and bliss. 'In "Egmont", in "Coriolanus", in the third, fifth, seventh, ninth, and even the eighth symphony you find Beethoven at the very moments of his most delirious, most ecstatic exultation in his triumphant strength suddenly interrupting himself with a question.' [2] The French Revolution is over: the magic formula has been tried, but the experiment has miscarried. Certainly, it would be foolish to deny the purely personal element in Beethoven's music; it would be foolish even to belittle it and play it down. Certainly, he is all the time talking about his own fate: but he is also talking, and talking quite consciously, of the fate of his age, of the fate of his kind. 'Beethoven's "favourite theme", we are told, was politics', writes one who knows him intimately. 'It was not the politics of the politician intriguing for party, place and power to aggrandize self and friends; it was "politics" as the art of creating society, a society that will express a richer and fuller life.' [3] The developments of the Napoleonic age made it increasingly clear that the sufferings of the revolutionary era had not been the birth-pangs of a better world; that what had come into being was a monstrosity as evil and repulsive as the feudalism which it had driven out. The bitter realization of this fact filled Beethoven's mind and personality to its remotest nook and cranny. A purely individualistic reading of his artistic work will never reveal all the meaning of his music. *He* never thought of himself as an isolated man or mind, however much others may have done so. He belonged to his period and was its mouthpiece, voicing the anxieties of a class and generation which had seen its ideals tested and found wanting. We must see, not only the

[1] Cf. Turner, *Beethoven: The Search for Reality*, 1927, esp. 317.
[2] Turner, *loc. cit.*, 263.
[3] Turner, *loc. cit.*, 261. Cf. also Gal, *loc. cit.*, 44.

'Eroica', but all his art against the backcloth of the French Revolution and its aftermath, and only if we do so shall we be able to enter into its depths. In this way even the content of music is vitally connected with its subsoil in contemporary social reality and understandable in terms of it.

Now, this connection between the mental and the extra-mental, between thought and society, is traceable not only in the higher reaches of creative art, but also in the higher reaches of philosophical speculation. It is a well-known fact that, throughout the ages, British philosophy has been predominantly realistic, sober and down-to-earth, whereas German philosophy has been predominantly, not to say exclusively, metaphysical and divorced from everyday reality. We need only group together some eminent contemporaries to see this: Leibniz and Locke, Kant and Bentham, Hegel and John Stuart Mill. The German academic philosopher has always been a little like Carlyle's Professor Diogenes Teufelsdröckh in *Sartor Resartus*, living high above the city in his lonely garret, locked up with his profound thoughts, and appearing to the common multitude as a true but impenetrable sage. It cannot be taken for granted that there can really be an 'explanation' of the contrasting character of these two dissimilar national traditions in philosophy, but if something like an explanation is sought, one direction which must obviously be explored is the great difference of socio-political development in the two countries. Britain achieved a working democracy early in her history: however imperfect that democracy may have been prior to 1832, the political arena stood open to the intellectual and could be entered freely and without fear. There were opportunities even for the petty bourgeois, and men like Hobbes, Locke, Bentham and John Stuart Mill grasped at them in their different ways. Germany, on the other hand, was and has remained almost to the present day, a country of authoritarianism. To talk about politics was dangerous, to write about it more or less impossible; so that to think about practical affairs, about problems of the day, was a rather thankless and useless task. Understandably, the greatest minds turned away from reality and towards the ideal, towards the realm of the 'pure spirit' in which the intellect could freely spread its wings and soar up to the heights.[1] Candidly did Hegel declare in his inaugural lecture at Heidelberg that philosophy should avoid political entanglements, and few of his tribe have thought otherwise in the matter.[2] Who will explore an avenue that leads only to a dead end, to complete frustration, and perhaps even to loss of livelihood and freedom? Thus political circumstances imparted opposite directions to philosophical speculation in Britain and in Germany, and though there may also be other factors in

[1] Cf. Mannheim, *Ideology and Utopia*, ed. 1952, 197 *seq.*, 213 *seq.*
[2] Cf. Löwith, *Von Hegel zu Nietzsche*, ed. 1953, 103 *seq.*, 317 *seq.*

the situation, one feature in the complex of causes which have made German and British philosophy what they are must be seen in the extra-philosophical, extra-mental, social constellation under which philosophers lived and worked on the Thames and on the Spree. 'The German philosophy of modern times', Max Scheler has written, 'was in the first place an achievement of the educated protestant middle class, above all of the manse, a fact which explains not only many aspects of form, style, terminology (the latter in contrast to current usage and often gruesome), and its strong tendency to become enclosed in rigid schools which hardly manage to understand each other, but also various material characteristics, as for example its relatively tenuous connection with mathematics and the exact sciences, its unpolitical, contemplative animus, its comparative lack of radicalism (which becomes particularly obvious in a comparison between the German and Western philoso-phies of enlightenment), its almost complete mental aloofness [1] from the "spirit" of industry and technology . . . These important facts have created in Germany entirely different fronts in the struggle of philo-sophical opinions from those that exist in the Romance countries.' In Germany, Scheler concludes, 'the philosopher is mostly quite divorced from practical life' [2]—a statement which is very true of Kant, Hegel, Schopenhauer and Nietzsche, but which nobody will be inclined to make of the leading English philosophers, a Hobbes, a Locke, a Bentham or a John Stuart Mill.

Perhaps it will be objected to this interpretation that the real reason why British philosophy always remained close to reality is after all a purely intellectual one, namely the fact that both the English and the Scots embraced Calvinism, whereas that creed left no deeper traces on the German mind. Calvinism, with its doctrine of man's total perversion, maintained that metaphysical speculation can never be more than a sad waste of time since the truth must for ever be hidden from us poor fallen creatures—a waste of time, or, even worse, an insolent and rebellious grasping at a forbidden fruit which the Lord has manifestly reserved unto Himself. Was it not this *belief* which turned the British away from metaphysics, rather than the openness and attractiveness of the political arena? Far be it from the present writer to impugn the truth contained in this argument. But if it is taken to imply that intellectual develop-ments can only be explained by other intellectual developments, then it must be declared insufficient to prove the contention. For the question at once arises: why did the British embrace Calvinism in the first place? And if an answer is sought to this query, we shall soon find ourselves at and beyond the confines of the intellectual field. Calvinism was carried to power by certain social, political and even economic move-

[1] *'fast vollständige innere Ferne . . .'*
[2] *Die Wissensformen und die Gesellschaft*, 1926, 97.

ments—movements at any rate which can never be adequately understood if we study them exclusively from the point of view of the history
of ideas. Thus the conclusion seems inescapable that even the nature of
British philosophy, its un-metaphysical and anti-metaphysical bent, is
somehow connected with the evolutions and revolutions through which
British society has had to pursue its way.

The point we are trying to make, namely, that cultural phenomena are
interconnected with social ones and fully understandable only if they
are seen within this nexus, is nowadays very widely accepted, although
its acceptance seems often only implied and sub- or semi-conscious.
One meets it frequently in daily and periodical publications. Writing
not long ago in the *Manchester Guardian*, Neville Cardus had this to
say on Igor Stravinsky: 'At bottom, he is a Russian, uprooted and
rendered by circumstance the cosmopolitan prophet of the latest meta-
morphosis of what is known as the "contemporary scene" . . . A
composer is related to and under the influence of his social and
economic environment. Different conditions produce or encourage the
production of a Haydn and a Bruckner. The more closely he is connected with his public, the more obliged a composer is to address himself to his listeners in a language he knows they will understand. The
musical scene or habitat has disintegrated in recent years; there is no
main contemporary musical language, familiar at once to a public at
large.' [1] In the same week, Geoffrey Barraclough, reviewing *German
History—Some New German Views*, said, according to *The Listener*:
'An examination of recent trends in German post-war history . . .
reveals all the ambiguities and cross-currents of German post-war
policy. . . . The present German adhesion to the West seems to me as
factitious as the former German rejection of Western values. It is the
reaction of a bourgeois intelligentsia, anxious, in a world of "mass-
democracy", for its inherited standards; and it is characteristic not only
of the present book, but of post-war German historiography as a
whole, that it represents only a middle-class outlook, and that the views
of the German working-classes remain unexpressed. History in any
society reflects the prevailing social forces; and we shall do well to
remember that in 1945, as in 1918, there was no shift in social forces in
Western Germany, only a political change imposed from above and
outside, which left big business and its adherents firmly entrenched in
power. This fact is reflected both in German history and in German
policy.' [2] These are only two examples out of many which might be
cited, and they show how common the conviction is that forms of
thought and feeling depend on the social situation within which they
have come to birth.

It is even more significant that the same conviction can also be seen

[1] May 29, 1954, 3.   [2] May 27, 1954, 923.

operative on a higher, more sophisticated level. Bruno Erdmann and Kuno Fischer are among the most distinguished historians of philosophic thought, and both have seen the commanding figure of Hegel in its interplay with the socio-political forces of his day. For Erdmann, Hegel is essentially the thinker of the period of restoration, the man who, in opposition to Kant and Fichte, whose systems correspond to the successive phases of the French Revolution, brings back an intellectual *ancien régime*, an old metaphysical and religious dogmatism. For Fischer, on the other hand, he is the herald of the idea of evolution, a forward-looking rather than a backward-looking figure, the product of a world in flux. Given the complexity of the Hegelian system, it is not surprising that both these interpretations should have in them a kernel of truth, as Arnold Ruge was later to emphasize. The detail is not important at this point: [1] what we have sought to demonstrate here is merely that even the technical philosopher is at times conscious of the social involvement of technical philosophy, especially when he tries to fathom the thought of a really important personality.

So far as art and the thinking on art are concerned, the opinions of Richard Wagner, who was almost as great a theoretician in his chosen field as he was a practitioner, may well claim our attention in this context. In his view, the problems of creative art are in the last analysis identical with the problems of public life. The tragedies of Aeschylus and Sophocles, for instance, were essentially 'the work of Athens', and the decay of Greek tragedy the immediate result of the dissolution of the Greek *polis*. In the same way modern art reflects, as he says, the spirit of the industrial undertakings of our great cities; the modern theatre in particular is 'a flower grown out of the swamp of the modern bourgeoisie'. Better art can only spring from a better society. 'From its state of civilized barbarism true art can only raise itself to its dignity on the shoulders of our great social movement: it shares the same aim and both can reach it only if they recognize it together.' [2]

Thus the conviction that social substructure and cultural superstructure are a unity, held together by ties which are more than external and accidental, is very widespread on all levels of thought and scholarly consideration. But if the question is asked whether this conviction rests on any well-pondered and clear-cut ideas, the answer must, unfortunately, be in the negative. People believe that there is *some* connection between the specific configuration of human relationships in a given society on the one hand, and the characteristic forms of thinking and feeling prevalent in that same society on the other; but what *exactly* this connection is, they do not know and they do not even seem

---

[1] Cf. Löwith, *Von Hegel zu Nietzsche*, 1953, 74 *seq.*, 98 *seq.* For Kuno Fischer cf. also *ibid.*, 198.

[2] *Die Kunst und die Revolution.* Cf. Löwith, *loc. cit.*, 202.

interested enough to ask. Nobody will venture to say that John Stuart
Mill's was a superficial mind, a mind easily satisfied with vague generali-
ties. But this is what he has to say on the problem under discussion here:
'The opinions and feelings of mankind, doubtless, are not a matter of
chance. They are consequences of the fundamental laws of human
nature, combined with the existing state of knowledge and experience,
and the existing condition of social institutions and intellectual and
moral culture.' [1] It would be unfair to scrutinize too closely or criticize
too severely what is obviously only an incidental remark. Nevertheless,
what a hopeless jumble of disparate ideas this statement is! It mentions
at least four factors that determine, or rather co-determine, the outlook,
philosophical and artistic, of a given community; these four factors are
only indistinctly indicated, not clearly described; each of them is manifestly highly complex in itself; and how they co-operate, for instance,
how much influence they respectively wield, is not even hinted. Moreover, the whole passage intimates that there is really nothing
problematical in the matter; it implies, and almost openly asserts, that
everybody 'doubtless' knows the truth about the social origin of the
'opinions and feelings of mankind'. What is so surprising is not that
Mill does not stay to clear the matter up; that is understandable, since
he is concerned with other things and hurries on to meet them; but what
is surprising, and not a little characteristic, is that he does not seem to
realize that he is by-passing a very great problem indeed.

Since Mill's day, more than a hundred years have passed, and yet the
state of affairs seems hardly different now from what it was then, so
far as the common opinion of the bulk of the educated is concerned.
The *Journal of the History of Ideas* started its existence [2] with the
following lines on its opening page: 'Whatever other definitions of man
be true or false, it is generally admitted that he is distinguished among
the creatures by the habit of entertaining general ideas. Like Br'er
Rabbit he has always kept up a heap o' thinking; and it has usually
been assumed—though the assumption has been nominally disputed
by some schools of philosophers—that his thoughts have at all times
had a good deal to do with his behaviour, his institutions, his material
achievements in technology and the arts, and his fortunes.' [3] This
statement is at least as vague and unsatisfactory as Mill's parallel effort
in 1848, and, as far as it goes, it helps to show that the problems raised
by the generally admitted interconnection of human thought and social
life have not yet been properly focused and defined, let alone clarified
and conquered.

Still, a beginning has been made. There has arisen, inside the wider

[1] *Principles of Political Economy*, Bk. II, ch. 1, § i.   [2] Jan. 1940.
[3] A. O. Lovejoy, *loc. cit.* It should hardly be necessary to point out that the above
passage expresses the common idea on the issue in hand, and not Professor Lovejoy's!

kingdom of the social sciences, a special discipline which has come to be called 'the sociology of knowledge.' [1] Many regard it as essentially a product of the twentieth century, but its roots go much further back than that. It does not try to make out that the carrier of culture—the thinker of thoughts and the creator of artistic values—is anybody but the individual (though some of its more foolish protagonists have pushed in that direction). But it insists that the individual himself cannot be understood unless he be seen in his social setting, in the living interplay of his self with other selves. It claims that, if we want to comprehend the full meaning of any cultural phenomenon, we must go beyond it and study the social circumstances with which it is genetically connected; or, to be even more careful and to avoid all possible overstatement, that it is fruitful for the understanding of cultural phenomena to explore the social setting within which they have been conceived and born. Its ultimate aim is both a doctrine and a method: a doctrine or theory which will show exactly what the interrelations of social substructure and intellectual superstructure are: whether they are close or loose, one-sided or mutual, etc. etc.; and a method or mode of procedure which will enable us to uncover the social—the 'existential'—roots of any concrete mental structure or artistic achievement and thereby to gain more insight into its making and meaning, its essence and existence, than we should have or could have otherwise.

It may be useful at this point to put before the reader, without much comment, a few of the definitions of the subject that have been attempted. They will speak for themselves. 'The sociology of knowledge', says Karl Mannheim in a terse programmatic sentence, 'seeks to analyse the relationship between knowledge and existence.' [2] It endeavours 'to comprehend the theories and their mutations in close relation to the collective groups and typical total situations out of which they arose and whose exponents they are. The inner connections between thought and social existence must . . . be reconstructed'. And, in another connection: 'The proper theme of our study is to observe how and in what form intellectual life at a given historical moment is related to the existing social and political forces.' [3] These pronouncements all recall Karl Marx's famous formula: 'It is not the consciousness of men that determines their existence, but, on the contrary, their social existence which determines their consciousness.' [4] According to Sprott, 'the sociology of knowledge . . . is concerned with the way in which systems of thought, whether cognitive or evaluative or both, are conditioned by

[1] Why the sociology of *knowledge* and not of ideas, of thoughts, or of mental life will be explained later. Cf. below, p. 122 *seq.*

[2] *Ideology and Utopia*, Engl. ed., 1952, 237.

[3] *Loc. cit.*, 156, 60. Cf. also 277 *seq. ibid.*

[4] *A Contribution to the Critique of Political Economy*, trans. Stone, 1913, 11 *seq.*

other social facts'.[1] For Dahlke and Becker, 'sociology of knowledge is the analysis of the functional interrelations of social processes and structures on the one hand and the patterns of intellectual life, including the modes of knowing, on the other', whereby 'logical priority is assigned neither to "society" nor to "mind" '.[2] An interesting and well-conceived definition has also been put forward by Helmut Schoeck: 'The question is, whether and in what degree man's quality as a social being can be discovered in his mental acts.'[3] Sometimes the characterization of the subject is couched in less general terms. So, for instance, when Mannheim says: 'The aim ... is ... to distinguish and isolate diverse styles of thinking and to relate them to the groups from which they spring'; sometimes the individual is moved into the centre of the picture, and then, according to the same authority, it is asserted by the sociology of knowledge that 'the ideas expressed by the subject are ... [to be] regarded as functions of his [social] existence.'[4] All these formulations have their own little problems: to mention but one, the use of the word 'function' or 'functional' raises important issues which must be cleared up; some of these formulations, too, are frankly question-begging and can easily be attacked on that score; but at the moment we need not stay to discuss these difficulties, and it would be wrong at this early stage to over-complicate the matter. Much will be said on all the relevant points later on. Here all that we have wanted to achieve is a clear indication of the field within which the sociologist of knowledge goes to work.

The very term 'sociology of knowledge' brings to mind the parallel term 'theory of knowledge' used in philosophy, and it may be very helpful for the understanding of the former discipline if we briefly compare it to the latter. The theory of knowledge—or epistemology, as it is also called—is concerned with the relation between the knowing or perceiving subject on the one hand, and the world of objects which he sets out to perceive and know on the other. How is it that the objective world enters into subjective consciousness, and that an ordered, structured and unified image of that world appears therein? The classical epistemologists, when they set about answering this question, understood by 'subject' in this connection the individual— the individual seen in isolation, Man with a capital M as it were. It is this conception, typical of thinkers like Kant for example, which the sociologist of knowledge desires to see reconsidered. There is no such thing as an isolated man; men who have grown up outside the social bond— feral men—have been met with now and then, but they were anything

[1] *Science and Social Action*, 1954, 141.
[2] *Philosophy and Phenomenological Research*, vol. 1941/2, 310.
[3] *Zeitschrift für die gesamte Staatswissenschaft*, vol. 1950, 37.
[4] *Ideology and Utopia*, 45, 50.

but clear intellects, anything but the rational human being whom Kant regards as the prototype of humanity and the characteristic subject of knowing; they were rather half- or three-quarter animals who certainly had a vague and confined awareness of external things, but decidedly no knowledge of them, if the word knowledge be taken in the Kantian, or even in the current sense of a mental picture illumined by the powerful arc-lamps of the human *ratio* or Reason. The sociologist of knowledge would urge that the idea with which Kant was operating was a construct rather than a reality. In reality we find no abstract man (singular) but only concrete men (plural)—men, that is, who have been shaped by diverse social influences and educated into definite and specific beings differing from age to age, from country to country, and from society to society. What such a being feels, what he thinks, and, indeed, what he becomes conscious of, must, or at any rate may, depend on the shape which his mind has acquired in the process of social living. In other words, according to the sociology of knowledge, it is illegitimate and even absurd to divorce man *quâ* perceiver and knower of the external world from man *quâ* member of a concrete society. Nobody can acquire knowledge without being alive; but to be alive means, in the case of man, to be part and parcel of ongoing social processes—processes which are not just a background of his personal consciousness, but, in a very definite sense of the word, operative within it, and constitutive of it. From this point of view the sociology of knowledge may appear as a complement to, or perhaps even as a corrective of, the traditional approach to the problem of epistemology.[1]

It may be urged against this line of argumentation that the social entanglements of man and his mind are real enough, but that they are irrelevant to the process of knowing all the same. Idealists like Kant might assert that human reason is identical in all human beings, and that they all approach the world with the same mental categories, with the same 'transcendental consciousness'. Materialists like Bentham might argue that the human senses operate identically in all human beings, and that they all see reality with the same eyes. Perhaps they do; it is not for the sociologist of knowledge to teach the epistemologist his business. But a distinction may and must be introduced here which will push the argument further along. Both Kant and Bentham, both idealists and materialists, have traditionally concentrated their attention on the ingathering by the human mind of knowledge concerning *physical* reality: and it is clear that where purely *physical* knowledge is concerned, man's *social* consciousness may not be very relevant. (The same also applies to purely formal knowledge, that knowledge of the formal or mathematical aspect of things according to number, weight

[1] We shall later reduce this somewhat exaggerated statement to its proper dimensions.

and measure, which looms so large within the Kantian system of philosophy.) But is it not also clear, and that immediately, without much need for reflection, that things are very different when we come to specifically *social* knowledge, to men's experience of the human realm, of historical reality in the widest sense of the term? Take a crude example: any of the great battles which shook the world, such as those of Marathon or Sedan. Such an event has certain physical and formal characteristics: the number of troops engaged on either side; the number of arrows or shells fired; the amount of pain generated in the affray; the economic value of the property destroyed, and so on, and so forth. All these features—all these *facts*—can be apprehended without the intervention (if we may so express it) of the specifically socialized sector of the mind, purely intellectually as it were, and with the help of the senses. And, indeed, all men will have to agree so far as such factual points are concerned. But all is changed when we try to perceive, beyond the physical and formal facts, the *meaning* of such events. Surely, that meaning will look different to Persians and Greeks, to Germans and French,—different also to different historians according to the point of view they occupy, which, in turn, will depend on the social education they have received and the social situation in which they find themselves.

We have no wish to imply here that prejudice will enter into the assessment of meaning; prejudice is conquerable and should be conquered. But even where complete candour prevails and perfect objectivity is guaranteed, the apprehension of meaning will be an act of the *whole* personality including the specifically social sector of the mind; indeed, it is not absurd to claim that the specifically social sector of the mind will have a larger say in the matter than either the sensual apparatus or the formal intellect. Philosophically speaking, it is not a transcendental consciousness which takes in the meaning, i.e. the essence, of a social fact, but an immanent consciousness, a socially determined, socially specified, socially filled consciousness, the consciousness of a man who lives within a certain social order and apprehends all social events in terms of it. Of course, it will be objected here that a *judgment* concerning meaning is not *knowledge* at all but something different, namely *valuation*. The decisive idea behind this objection will be the conviction, or rather the assumption, that we first take cognizance of the facts (even in matters social), and then afterwards come to some assessment of meaning which is in this way an adventitious and secondary act. But this belief is nothing but a piece of what Kant used to describe as naïve dogmatism—the very sort of idea which a critical epistemology must set out to show up and correct. In matters social at any rate, valuation—valuation of a specific kind, entirely unlike what is commonly called prejudice—does not follow upon, but must

15

precede the act of cognition. Out of the welter and boundless variety of social facts we only study—indeed, we only notice—those which have significance according to the system of values with which we approach them. We see the broad and deep acres of history through a mental grid as it were—through a system of values which is established in our minds *before* we look out on to it—and it is this grid which decides on the one hand what will fall into our field of perception, and on the other will make it possible for us to co-ordinate our cognitions and form them into a coherent image, comparable, in its unity and clarity, to the picture which our categories or our senses enable our minds to form of the subhuman, material universe. If it be said that we must get rid of that grid, that we should approach the study of the human, social universe simply with our minds' eyes open but nothing before them, then we shall indeed get a quasi-scientific picture of social happenings, we shall see their physical characteristics and formal dimensions, but we shall be for ever unable to discover their human implications, i.e. their social characteristics and historical dimensions. This is an inescapable truth, as inescapable as the cogencies of logic.

Those who have fancied it possible to perceive the facts of history without any antecedently formed system of valuations established in their minds, have invariably been simply unaware of that system of valuations. And, indeed, such a system of valuations has all through the ages been beneath the threshold of consciousness for the student of social facts. That is the reason why the sociologist of knowledge who brings it out into the open is in a very real sense of the word the heir of the critical epistemology of a Kant: he, too, draws attention to an *a priori*, though it is very different from the one exposed by the sage of Königsberg. But the social *a priori* is as real and as basic to the functioning of the process of social knowing as the Kantian is to the process of physical and formal knowing. Why is it in the first place that we fix our eyes on what happened at Marathon in 490 B.C. or at Sedan in A.D. 1871 or 1914 or 1940, rather than on any of the countless other events which took place at the same time? Only because we have decided antecedently that such-like happenings are more significant than the rest; only because we have in our minds a prior judgment to this effect. Without such prior judgments, without, in other words, a system of values, we should never be able even to focus any social fact: our attention would roam helplessly and hopelessly over the boundless plains of history and human geography, coming to rest nowhere, receiving no tangible or definite impressions anywhere.

And not only would our mental eye be unable to come to rest on any complex of impressions, our intellect could not possibly conceive of the coherence and the unity of that complex either. *Prima facie,* physically, formally, a battle like that of Marathon or Sedan is a vast series, or rather a vast congeries, of acts—an indefinite, almost infinite number of individual happenings, all of which are in themselves complete, disconnected and meaningless. What makes of them a social event, a unitary fact which we apprehend and comprehend as a unity? It is only their common meaning which constitutes them what we call a battle. Now meaning is not inherent in things: it is supplied by the human mind which sees them, and sees them as a whole. We supply— we impart—co-significance to the elements of the picture—indeed, we only make these elements *into* a picture by supplying and imparting that co-significance, and we are enabled to provide it, not by the categorial apparatus of our intellect, nor yet by the brain-function which co-ordinates the operation of our sense-organs (both of which have very little, though certainly something, to do with it), but essentially by the system of values which we already possess when we go to meet them. Hence without a prior notion of what is more or less significant, and also at the same time of what is more or less co-significant, we could at best become aware of certain social facts, but we could not *know* any. For knowledge is clear and conscious, and, above all, structured knowledge. But the structuring of knowledge is dependent on a principle of selection and a principle of order, and both are to be seen exclusively in what we have called the 'grid' before the eye of the student of history, the *a priori* in his mind, in short—his basic system of values. Now this system of values differs from society to society. Societies are unlike each other precisely in this, that they have different preconceptions concerning what is good and bad, right and wrong, what is worthy to be pursued or better eschewed. And the process of socialization to which every new human being is subjected and which transforms him from a bundle of empty possibilities into a man of full powers, from a nondescript baby into a personality capable of knowledge—into a potential Thucydides or Livy or Otto von Freising or Machiavelli or Ranke—is precisely the instilling into his mind of such characteristic value-conceptions, of such principles of selection and ordering.

This does not mean, by itself, that everybody is for ever committed to the pre-judgments of the society which has made him; it does not mean either that the differences in their world-views and views of history which result from the underlying contrasting valuations of the different societies are something that we cannot conquer and overcome. Nothing in that direction can *ab initio* be declared impossible. But it does mean that a naïve and unreflecting approach to the field of social experience, such as is characteristic of 999 out of a thousand historians and students of human affairs in general—that a 'natural' view of history and the contemporary social world—needs 'critical' analysis, needs to be shown to be based on, and determined by, an antecedent system of valuations which is likely to be identical with the system by which the seeker after social knowledge and his society live. It does mean that extra-theoretical—'existential'—factors are present, unrecognized, even in a view of history and society which, on the conscious level, is altogether 'pure' and wholly 'theoretical'; that, even where individual prejudice has no place, there yet obtain certain basic social pre-valuations of which we ought to take note. It therefore means above all that there is need of a social theory of knowledge (which will essentially be a theory of social knowledge)—a theory which critically examines the genesis and the nature of our knowledge of the human universe. And this theory will be important, not only for the understanding of the initial process by which our world-view in the narrower sense of the word—our way of actually *seeing* the world—is constituted and becomes what it is, but also for the understanding of the subsequent processes by which our world-view in the wider, more metaphorical, sense of the word—our basic philosophy, our specific way of thinking and feeling —is shaped and brought into being. For it is plain that *all* thought, whether it takes form in a philosophical or an artistic guise, whether its precipitate is a metaphysic or a symphony, must depend upon, and be so to speak defined by, the underlying way of experiencing reality which works itself out therein and without which it could never become and be what it actually is. The sociology of knowledge therefore seeks to provide the key—or to be more modest, a key—for the understanding of all cultural phenomena.

All this will be set forth in greater detail and in a more systematic manner later on, especially in our third chapter. Here we have only attempted to indicate what the definitions we have quoted are apt to mean when they speak of a 'social conditioning of knowledge', an 'interrelation of knowing and living', and so on.

Our next step should logically be the presentation of a sample of analysis in the spirit and with the tools of the sociology of knowledge. This example will show much better what the nature and mission and ambition of our discipline are than even the best abstract definition or discussion can ever hope to do. We have just now explained what the sociology of knowledge is with the help of the parallel but contrasting concept 'theory of knowledge'. But we do not thereby wish to intimate or claim that the sociology of knowledge, as it has so far developed, is predominantly a philosophical discipline. That it has a philosophical reference and philosophical implications, is clear. But its protagonists have always regarded it as a positive rather than a philosophical study.[1] They have tried their hand at various concrete problems and endeavoured to show how this or that specific complex of ideas, or individual artistic style, have *in fact*, as a superstructure, reflected the social sub-

[1] Cf. e.g. Mannheim, *Ideology and Utopia*, ed. 1952, 239; Maquet, *Sociologie de la Connaissance*, 1949, 30.

structure on which they rested. This emphasis on empirical research is obviously altogether sound. Philosophical conclusions should come after the investigation of reality, not before it. First we must get proof that thought-processes do in fact depend on life-processes, on processes of social living, for their colour and content, and only then can we sensibly raise the question what the epistemological consequences of this dependence are. Any other procedure would amount to putting the cart before the horse. Let us see, then, in the light of a concrete instance, how the school has gone about its business. However, before we can turn to this illustration of the theme, we must clear up one point which has so far, in the whole literature, remained wrapped in cloud and confusion. If we say that, according to the theory, human thought is in some way dependent on its existential or social substructure, this concept of 'social substructure' has about it an unfortunate ambiguity which must be removed if any further progress in the development of the theory is to be sound and free from uncertainty.

(b) THE TWO VARIETIES OF THE SOCIOLOGY OF KNOWLEDGE

An example will show very quickly what the ambiguity involved is. From 1880 onward, American philosophy was deeply influenced by the movement called pragmatism, and the question arises whether the origin and the spread of that movement cannot in part be explained in the light of contemporary social reality. This is indeed so. Pragmatism preaches a consistently activistic doctrine of man: man, even when he fancies himself to be wrapped up in pure contemplation, for instance in the pursuit of truth for truth's sake, is yet in reality bound to his habitual modes of action. For the propositions which appear to him as true are simply those which have in practice proved themselves workable, effective, successful. Even mental life is a struggle for survival in which the purposive, the practicable, the pragmatic is selected, and the not so purposive, the impracticable, the pragmatically useless is detected and discarded. Thoughts are thus essentially instruments for the control of the objective world, not ideas about it: a system of metaphysics is not so different from a shovel or a spade as men have imagined throughout the centuries. Surely, this whole complex of ideas is strikingly in line with the American way of life: the Americans are doers, not dreamers; their society has from the beginning been confronted with the supreme task of subjugating a vast continent, a task essentially technical in nature, and this all-pervading and all-determining endeavour has informed not only their economy, but also their culture. This over-all direction of social life must have suggested and stimulated an all-round pragmatism. And American society was also super-individualistic. Like no other, it resembled, in the eighties of which we are speaking, a war of all against all, in which the strong could rise to the top and the weak were doomed to go under. A man had to 'prove himself' in practical life if he was to become 'established' in society. Is it surprising that philosophers should have developed a parallel theory concerning propositions and judgments? These, too, were expected to 'prove themselves' in practical life before they could gain admission to the body of 'established truths'. It can be said, then, that pragmatism as a system of ideas rested on the contemporary social reality of the United States as its substructure.

But the origin and spread of pragmatism can perhaps be explained in a second way. Philosophy is made predominantly, if not exclusively, by professors; professors work in, and draw their subsistence from, universities; universities are run by men with certain principles in mind and purposes in view; may not these principles and purposes behind the universities influence, or even determine, the mental life that is going on within their walls? The universities of the United States are most of them controlled by members of the business community, whether this control is overt and direct, or more covert and indirect. Now business men do not understand, and consequently are unwilling to finance, enterprises which seem pointless and useless; they will constantly ask: what is this university, what is this school, what is this professor doing for the community? The policy of appointments and promotion will be of a piece with this fundamental attitude. Those will get in, and those will get on, who 'justify' their appointments and promotions and salaries. University teachers would be less than human if they did not, within limits at any rate, adjust the direction of their work to these hard realities. Who would not rather do what helps him up the ladder of worldly success than the opposite? Thus the whole endeavour of the academic community will be linked, by subtle influences, to the pragmatical outlook of the founder-fathers and foster-fathers of the universities and academies, and a philosophical movement like pragmatism may well be, to some extent and in some part, the fruit of such influences. But in so far as it is the remote working-out of tendencies of this kind, its 'substructure' is not social life in general, but rather a specific set of social institutions and organizations—those institutions and organizations by and in which knowledge is professionally produced and administered.

Hence two rather different sorts of sociology of knowledge are possible. In order clearly to distinguish them, it might be useful at this juncture to call the one the macrosociology of knowledge, because it fixes its attention on the inclusive society and its influence, the social macrocosm as it were, and the other the microsociology of knowledge, because it is concerned with the narrower world of scholarship and art, with the domestic world, so to speak, of the man of scholarship and artistic creation.[1]

What we have just called the microsociology of knowledge is likely to come up against even stronger resistances than its sister, macro-sociology. Not only are people in general unwilling to hear that 'pure' thought is connected with any extra-mental factors, but they are likely to become openly resentful when told that scholars often take their cue from their employers and accommodate their scholarship to the pre-occupations and prejudices of those who hold the purse-strings.[2] And, indeed, the basic thesis of the microsociology of knowledge must never be formulated in such crude terms. Apart from everything else, it would be unrealistic to say that considerations and conditions of employment have in fact a strong influence on scholarship and its contents: academic freedom and dignity are happily well established in the western world. But while there is as a rule no conscious connection between the thought of a thinker and the organization with which and within which he lives —while there is no need to shout 'corruption!'—there are some hidden (and on the whole respectable) interrelations between mental super-structure and organizational substructure which should be as objectively and fearlessly investigated as all other aspects of reality.

It is not the purpose of the present book to go deeply into this matter. Its subject is the macrosociology, not the microsociology, of knowledge. Nevertheless, a short review of some of the relevant themes may be of use here. One illustration near at hand is the development of sociology as an academic subject. In France it has made considerable progress, in Britain hardly any so far. The main explanation of this difference must needs be macrosociological. France has, since the great Revolution, been a divided country; two irreconcilable value-systems are constantly at war with each other; in the last village, the last *abbé* is likely to clash with the last *instituteur*. Hence social life is a problem. It is not a problem—it is not seen as a problem—in Britain, a largely pacified society with a tolerably uniform value-system at its basis, where com-promise is the accepted method for the settlement of all conflicts. Thus, north of the Channel, a vital stimulus is missing to the development of social theory. But the organization of the universities also has some-thing to do with the difference. In France, sociology has been lucky to

[1] I feel like apologizing for the introduction of these ugly neologisms. The social sciences are already being ridiculed for their uncouth terminologies, and it is a great responsibility further to add to them. Nevertheless, clarity, the prime concern of the scholar, demands that he should distinguish *distinguenda* by as clear and unambiguous labels as he possibly can.

[2] The special case of commercially motivated and financed research (e.g. the listener research of radio and television organizations or the market research of advertising agencies) is left out of consideration here. Cf. Merton, *Social Theory and Social Structure*, 1949, esp. pp. 210–13 and ch. X.

21

find a home in the philosophical faculties: conflict with economics, and the economists, has thereby been obviated. And the philosophers, with their well-established subject, had no need to hold down a new-comer who was, after all, essentially a younger sister. In Britain, resist-ance to the introduction of sociology into academic life has often come from economists (and the same has also been true, to some extent, of Germany): to them the upstart was a useless competitor for funds, and some of them resented the idea that there should be a social science of more general nature than their own, a science which might claim to be 'higher' than theirs. It is by no means suggested here that this was a major factor: that it was a factor of some consequence is, however, undeniable. Of course, there was a time when economics itself was forced to fight hard for a foothold in the academic citadel; [1] and it is no illicit generalization to assert that practically all new disciplines have had to face some difficulties of this sort—difficulties which have not only concerned their worldly prospects but have tended to affect even their intellectual content and development.

How deeply a system of ideas may be influenced by the academic set-up and its power-politics can be seen from Georg Simmel's life-work. When he tried to introduce sociology into the university curriculum he was told that there could be no such science since there was no conceiv-able subject-matter with which it could concern itself. If it were defined as the study of human interaction (a definition which Simmel pressed), then, it was argued, sociology was both everything and nothing: it was everything because all cultural phenomena are due to human inter-action (language, history, economic life and all the rest), and nothing because the special disciplines (linguistics, historiography, economics and so on) between them adequately covered the whole field and there simply was no vacant spot which sociology could aspire to fill. Simmel might have argued that it is absurd to think of reality as a field which is parcelled out into little plots or kitchen-gardens, each cultivated by a particular group of researchers who can rightly regard it as their preserve and warn off all newcomers; and that, in reality, *all* sciences study, at least potentially, *all* facts, only from different angles and aspects. Granted that linguists investigate a social phenomenon, namely language, they approach it from the linguistic and not from the social side, and so there is room for, and indeed need of, a special discipline which will tackle the same phenomena from the specifically sociological standpoint. Simmel *might* have argued along these lines, but as a matter of fact he did not. He accepted his adversaries' argument and countered

---

[1] An interesting example of this is F. G. Daries's book, *Erste Gründe der Cameral-Wissenschaften*, 1756, which strives hard to demonstrate the 'respectability' of economic science. Some of the arguments the author endeavours to invalidate have also been brought forward against sociology.

it by developing the formalistic system of sociology with which his name is habitually associated. If there is no free subject-*matter* with which a science of sociology can deal, he pleaded, there is always the *form* of human interaction which is not yet anybody's preserve—indeed, is a broad acre still waiting for the ploughman and the harvester. In this way he made sociology into the study of social forms—into a socio-geometry as it were. Several motives must have induced Simmel to strike out in this particular direction,[1] but one of them was, without a doubt, the desire to overcome (irrational) academic resistances, and in so far as Simmel's total world-view was determined by such conscious, semi-conscious or subconscious strivings, we have before us an instance of the influence of organizational facts and factors on mental processes—an instance which can fruitfully be analysed by the microsociology of knowledge.

If this is a rather special case, much more general tendencies of a kindred nature can easily be adduced. Departmentalism is an unavoidable feature of all large-scale organizations, and universities do not escape this necessity. But departmentalism breeds the departmental mind, a mind possessed by the principles of the pigeon-hole. There will be a tendency—often unperceived, but none the less real for that—to formulate all research-projects in terms of the established specialisms. But reality is not a collection of special subjects. It is much rather an unbroken totality, a seamless robe. For this reason great new insights have often come from the man who has disregarded the fences which organizational needs have artificially erected, who has jumped over, or broken through, borders and boundary-walls. Nobody is strategically so well placed for an advance in knowledge as the scholar who sees underground connections between phenomena which have so far never been seen together. But this very type of scholar is likely to be academically a misfit, an awkward fellow. He belongs in several departments or faculties, and at the same time none will claim him as their own (so long, at any rate, as he has not made good). The fate of the man who cuts across the pigeon-holes is never comfortable. He will be penalized for his boldness. At the very least he will be denied recognition and promotion.[2] Thus there rise up, from the organizational pattern at the bottom of our academic institutions, tendencies which act as a brake on intellectual progress, and which help to canalize it in certain ways and preserve the channels once dug across the landscape.

It would also be interesting to compare, from the point of view of the microsociology of knowledge, the thought-processes in, and achievements of, private scholars on the one hand, and academically employed

---

[1] An important element in the situation was Simmel's desire to get away from historicism and historical relativity. Forms are eternal, however much contents may change.
[2] Lovejoy has said many apposite things on this theme in his article in the first issue of the *Journal of the History of Ideas*, 1940, pp. 4 and 5.

scholars on the other. It would probably be found that the differences between them are by no means restricted to the obvious fact that the one has more time for research and writing than the other. We may guess at any rate that the private scholar will be bolder in pursuit of his ideas— we may think here of Nietzsche after he had left Basle, or of Spengler, but also of Bentham or Spencer—whereas the academic teacher will be clearer in his exposition, forced as he is in his daily work to talk intelligibly to those who are not always intelligent.[1] But if this cannot be taken for granted without further investigation, experience has shed a good deal of light on a kindred problem. In Britain and the United States, national emergencies have regularly drawn academic personnel into the temporary civil service, and as regularly it has been discovered that their approach to problems was not the same as that of the permanent civil servants whose ranks they were called upon to reinforce. The reader will find much that is enlightening on this point in Robert Merton's admirable book *Social Theory and Social Structure* (1949). The professional bureaucrat has learnt to be content with a humble rôle. He is asked precise questions by his ministers who are politicians, and who decide on policies, and he is so conditioned as to give precise answers and not to talk out of turn. He is concerned with techniques, not with values. He will, in the ideal, and even in the typical case, work as assiduously at the implementation of a decision that goes against his valuations and private convictions as he will at the carrying-out of one that is in line with them. It is not for nothing that a civil servant is called a 'servant', and his 'service' will be to him a matter of pride rather than humiliation. Many academic people, accustomed as they are to relative autonomy, or at least to the absence of open controls, have found it impossible to click into that mentality. They are used to taking a more independent and comprehensive view of problems and things, to consider values as well as techniques, to pronounce on the *what* as much as on the *how*. They don't want to be told, they want to tell the politicians what line it is right and proper to pursue in a situation. Indeed, they are quite likely to be doctrinaire; there is something in the professorial mode of life which tends to make professors (even English and American ones) into men of principle. Bureaucrats, on the other hand, are forced to be realistic: they are near the seat of power and must produce feasible solutions to practical problems. In a word, the thought-processes of the academic man are entirely different from those of the permanent civil servant, and they are so different because they have gone through a different organizational mill.

[1] Some good material is to be found in Justus Hashagen's contribution to *Versuche zu einer Soziologie des Wissens*, 1924, esp. 240–4. The subject under discussion is historical scholarship. Wider aspects of the same kind are considered in Helmut Plessner's paper in the same publication, esp. 417–23.

The matter may at times become so significant as to assume historic importance. Max Weber was convinced that Germany's catastrophe in 1918 was to a large extent due to the dominant part which the civil service played in German public life. Independent politicians, and even professors like himself, might have told the Kaiser that he was acting foolishly and might have stopped him in his nefarious career. But the bureaucrats who surrounded him thought this outside their brief (as good bureaucrats in fact should) and so there was nobody and nothing —after Bismarck, the pilot, had been dropped—to prevent the ship of state from smashing against the rocks.

Another important contrast in intellectual work due to organizational factors, which Merton brings up for consideration, is that between the lone scholar and the team. The lone scholar, who collects all his own material, need not work out a concrete schedule of definitions and categories before he starts: he knows what he is after, and can rely on his own findings. But where many are to share in the gathering of the basic information, it is absolutely necessary that they should all follow the same principles. There must, as Merton formulates it, be 'reliability, by which is meant roughly, the consistency between independent observations of the same material' (207). We are not concerned here with the relative merits of the two techniques: probably each has its own advantages and disadvantages. The team is more likely to be disciplined in the search for facts, the lone scholar more imaginative. The point that needs stressing is that the two modes of procedure will produce two dissimilar sets of mental habits, two ways of researching and, in consequence, up to a point, of thinking also. Merton is inclined to assume that the logic of teamwork will drive the team-workers towards the technique of the exact sciences, in which the objectification of methods as well as results is so traditional and so vital, whereas the lone scholar will move nearer to the artistic type of mind where individual vision counts for much and no misgivings are aroused if different men look at the same facts with different eyes.

We have so far taken our illustrations from the sphere of scholarly work, but it is not difficult to complete the picture by a look at parallel phenomena in the field of artistic creation. The great change-over from eighteenth to nineteenth century art, from classicism to romanticism, is accompanied by a change in the social position of the artist. Working, as a rule, before the French Revolution, for an individual nobleman-employer, we find that after the great upheaval in all typical cases he is producing for an anonymous public, for an impersonal market.[1] Haydn was still a *domestique* of Count Esterhazy, wore his livery and took his

---

[1] Beethoven characterized the new situation very well when he said, in his day 'one must be half a business man' if one wants to be an artist. Turner, *Beethoven, The Search for Reality*, ed. 1954, 58.

meals with the master's maids and stablegrooms; Mozart, too, was in the same position while he lived in Salzburg, but after 1781 could stand it no longer and became a free-lance at Vienna; Beethoven was already an independent artist and, as many incidents in his life testify, fiercely proud of his independence.[1] Nobody but the most unrealistic aesthete will deny that this total transformation in the life-conditions of the artist had some influence on the nature of his output. Dr. Gal has freely acknowledged it. 'The first work', he writes of Beethoven, 'in which he fully realizes his own vision of a monumental conception, *Sinfonia Eroica*, was probably the most staggering novelty in the history of music. There is not only a new style, a new sound, a new greatness of form and design, but a completely new attitude to the world. . . . No obedient servant of his liege-lord had ever been able to conceive such music. Here the artist feels himself an equal to the greatest of this world.' [2] Gone are the days when a man like Leopold Mozart had to accept 'the double rôle, as was customary, . . . of valet and musician': [3] but the shackles have not only fallen from the body; they have also dropped from the mind and set free a new vision and a new universe of music.

It is at this point that we can see particularly clearly what great service the microsociology of knowledge can render the historian of ideas—how deeply it allows us to look into the artist's and the thinker's mind. It throws, if one may so express it, much social light on individual development. A man's condition in life is, for better or worse, his fate: his soul cannot escape its imprint. Many features in a work of art are rightly ascribed to the artist's personality: but this personality is formed in and by its clash with circumstances, and among these circumstances status, and even the conditions of employment, are very potent factors. Franz Schubert was born into a smiling world and reflected it in such jolly music as that of his fifth symphony: but soon tragedy looms up and sheds deep, dark shadows over his work, giving it a poignancy that is at times positively painful. This turn towards unhappiness is not unconnected with Schubert's inability to fit into the society that surrounded him, and even, quite simply, with the impossibility of securing a job. After 1814, Dr. Gal tells us, 'the young, prosperous middle class took over [in Austria], and the first result was a calamity for the musician. For the time being, there was no proper place for him in this thriving civic world. What it could provide for him was a scanty, very haphazard living as a teacher, rare occasions for public performances and a rather modestly developed publishing trade. . . . When as a youth of nineteen he [Schubert] threw up his job as a schoolmaster . . . that vigorous, robust modern society would have let him starve to death but

[1] Cf. Turner, 35, 38, 39, 54, 55, 57, 219.   [2] *Loc. cit.*, 52.
[3] Turner, *Mozart, The Man and his Works*, 1938, 14.

26

for the constant help of some devoted friends who supported him, still more or less at starvation level.' [1] No wonder that the smile departed from his face and a look of pain settled upon his features—and upon his scores.

Mozart's case had been very similar. The 'black thoughts' which sometimes appear in his music, the moods of despair, for instance in his String Quintet in G minor and in the Kyrie of his Requiem, are to a large extent a reflection of the fact that he knocked at many doors in search of bread, and none was opened. By bracketing together Mozart and Schubert we are by no means trying to reduce them to a type. Dr. Gal's book reveals how complex are the relations which both the macro- and the microsociology of ideas have to investigate. 'It is interesting', he writes, 'that in Haydn's and Mozart's music their conscious attitude towards the feudal order under which they lived is reversed. Haydn accepted it without question. But in his music he is an unashamed plebeian, who never disdains any sort of popular melodic material and feels marvellously at his ease even in an atmosphere of rustic vulgarity. With Mozart it is just the other way round . . . Mozart, with his middle-class upbringing and sensitiveness, suffered terribly under the humiliations . . . in the service of the Archbishop of Salzburg. He loathed the coarse language, the insolent intimacy of the servants' hall [whereas] Haydn was one of their sort and did not mind.' Mozart '[in consequence] revolted against aristocratic tyranny, but'—and this is the interesting point here—'in his music he reveals himself as the most high-bred aristocrat who ever lived with all the sensitiveness of a supercivilized ancestry. Haydn's delightful vulgarity is simply inaccessible to him. He remains an aristocrat even in his most popular melodies.' [2] 'Typical', objectifiable circumstances may explain a good deal of this contrast— for instance the fact that Haydn was born in 1732 and Mozart only in 1756, i.e. much nearer the dissolution of the feudal order and the bourgeois revolt; or that Haydn was a child of village life where the old dispensation was still well established, and Mozart a child of the town where feudalism had always been something resented. It may even be apposite to point out that a peasant, in virtue of his whole psychology, will be much less likely to accept or to ape the standards and tastes of the aristocracy than a petty bourgeois—imitating those above them being a well-known and well-proved as well as understandable desire on the part of the petty bourgeoisie. Nevertheless, one feels in this discussion that the limits of sociological interpretation are here in sight. When all social circumstances are taken fully into account and the sociology of knowledge is driven as far as it can reasonably be, there remains the irreducible fact that different personalities react differently to the same conditions—there remains the ineffable spontaneity of the

[1] *Loc. cit.*, 61 *seq.*   [2] *Loc. cit.*, 28, 22.

individual. Perhaps psychology can carry on from here; the sociology of knowledge may well have reached its *Ultima Thule*.

But wherever we draw the borderline around the subject which we have called the microsociology of knowledge, whether we include a large area or a small, one thing is certain, namely that, within its proper field, it has a contribution to make to the analysis of the origins and contents of mental processes. There has even been a tendency to equate microsociology of knowledge and sociology of knowledge itself, to say that the latter should consist exclusively of the former. J. Kraft, for instance, has denied that there can be such a thing as the macrosociology of knowledge, the derivation of thought-contents from social reality at large. Knowledge, he argues, is a psychical phenomenon—it is in people's heads as it were; so it cannot well be explained by what goes on outside those heads (a *non-sequitur* of the purest water); furthermore, we cannot connect thoughts with social entities, for social entities are not 'real' in any material sense, they are merely linguistic fictions and thus nothing—nothing at any rate that could explain anything else (a materialism so crude as to rule itself out of court). But Kraft admits that there may be a sociology of the organizations of knowledge (churches, schools etc.)—that there may be a microsociology of knowledge, as part of special and applied sociology.[1]

A similar position has more recently been taken up by a social scientist of far heavier calibre, Florian Znaniecki, especially in his book *The Social Rôle of the Man of Knowledge* (1940). Znaniecki considers knowledge in itself as a realm altogether divorced from social reality, as the possession of and participation in a truth which is suspended, as it were, far above us in the skies, but which we can see as we do the stars. There can be no sociology of knowledge, but only a sociology of the carriers of knowledge, of those who elaborate, preserve and teach it. They, the men of knowledge, have a function to fulfil in social life; they enter into social relationships and are shaped by them, and it is this latter fact from which any study of the social nature of knowledge should start and to which it should stick. The very title of Znaniecki's book shows what he has in mind. The sociology of knowledge is to be restricted to the study of a certain area or complex of human interaction —to 'studying the social rôle of pragmatic and moralistic leaders, theologians, philosophers, scholars and scientists', and of their 'schools, as social groups organized for the special task of perpetuating and popularizing existing knowledge, and . . . associations functioning to promote the development of new knowledge'.[2] 'Systems of knowledge —viewed in their objective composition, structure and validity—cannot be reduced to social facts', Znaniecki says, begging a very large question.

[1] Cf. Grünwald, *Das Problem der Soziologie des Wissens*, 1934, 115.
[2] Cf. *Soziologische Forschung in unserer Zeit*, 1951, 250.

'Yet their historical existence within the empirical world of culture, in so far as it depends upon the men who construct them, maintain them by transmission and application, develop them or neglect them, must in a large measure be explained sociologically.' Accordingly, the main questions which he asks are these: 'Are there any relationships of functional dependence between the social rôles which scientists perform and the kind of knowledge which they cultivate? More specifically: Are the systems of knowledge which scientists build and their methods of building them influenced by the social patterns with which scientists are expected to conform as participants in a certain social order and by the ways in which they actually realize those patterns?' [1]

From this particular angle (which is sociological in a much narrower and more stringent sense than the macrosociology of knowledge ever can be), Znaniecki attempts to throw some light even on the content of culture as it has recently developed, or tended to develop. 'The content of theological knowledge', he writes, 'is becoming less and less inclusive: much pragmatic and scientific knowledge has been excluded from theological doctrines. Compare, for instance, the modern theologies of Western religions with the old theology of Brahmanism, where every-thing—even material technique—had a religious meaning. This', Znaniecki continues, coming to his explanation, 'may be due to the gradual narrowing of the total functions of religious groups as a result of competition with various specialized secular groups—political, technical, economic, scientific, artistic.' [2] Like the involution of theo-logy, the evolution of science, and its growing preponderance over the cultural disciplines, is seen by Znaniecki as a reflex of certain processes of social interaction. 'We would like to mention the possibility of a sociological explanation of this historical precedence of natural sciences', he says rather modestly. 'We believe that it may be found in compara-tive study of functional relationships between the social rôles of natural scientists and those of cultural scientists . . . The essential point is that scientists dealing with natural phenomena, once they got rid of magical and religious interpretations of the natural world, had no difficulty in accepting the general principle of theoretic objectivity. . . . It was much more difficult to attain theoretic objectivity in studying cultural pheno-mena, because the scientist could not easily separate his rôle as an investigator from that of an active participant in a particular culture. If he did so, he provoked negative reactions from his fellow-participants, if he did not, he became involved in insoluble . . . controversies with scientists who participated in foreign cultures with divergent systems of values. . . . Obviously, such controversies impeded, and still impede, scientific progress.' [3]

[1] *The Social Rôle of the Man of Knowledge*, 1940, 10 and 22.
[2] *Soziologische Forschung*, 253.   [3] *Ibid.*, 254.

The point here made, it must be admitted, is an important one. Nevertheless, the quotation just given shows up the narrow limitations of Znaniecki's approach. The relative clause 'once they got rid of magical and religious interpretations of the natural world . . .' bypasses, in all too cavalier a fashion, the central problem of the whole development which the sociology of knowledge should try to tackle. And if it be pointed out that Znaniecki has provided a kind of explanation by referring to the loss of ground suffered in the struggle of competition by the various priestly and semi-priestly groups in society, then we are only led into a vicious circle. For why have the practitioners of the black arts and even the priests lost ground? Surely, because society has 'got rid of magical and religious interpretations of the natural world'. The fact of the matter is that Znaniecki takes as a *datum* what is really an *explicandum*. His method, confined as it is to microsociological considerations, comes to a stop at the point where it ought to begin.

This is *not* to say that, rightly handled, his method is not of value. If it be recognized for what it is, a secondary tool which should come into operation after the total intellectual atmosphere of society has been explained, as explained it must be, with reference to the total historical movement of the social system, if its microsociology of knowledge be fitted into a wider, more inclusive, macrosociological frame, then it can lead to much insight and illumination. For it is a fact whose relevance cannot be gainsaid that the *république des professeurs*, as Thibaudet called it, is a society, or at the very least a quasi-society, with social relations and even a power-structure inside it, as well as social and power-relations to the global society outside it. Merton has rightly spoken of an ethos, and a mores, of science: [1] anyone who wishes to take part in scientific work as it is collectively carried on and institutionally organized in Western society must conform to certain norms, just as a member of any society is compelled to do, and this conformity, reinforced by powerful sanctions both negative and positive, by punishment and reward, will help to shape the scientists' mind. It is clear that what Merton calls 'the ultimate accountability of scientists to their compeers' [2]—the need to submit research-findings to general scrutiny —has given them certain mental characteristics which are absent, for microsociological reasons, from other types, e.g., to cite an extreme example, mystics. But the scientific outlook can never be completely explained in this way for its roots lie in the total world-view of modern man, and this in turn stems from even deeper currents in the social life of the last few centuries.

That the social and organizational structure of the learned community inside Western society (and *a fortiori* all that flows from it) is a secondary, not a primary phenomenon, can be seen from the fact

[1] *Loc. cit.*, 309.   [2] 314.

that it has always tended to fit itself harmoniously into the framework of the contemporary inclusive social order. Such as the wider society was, such the narrower society of learning tended to be. In the Middle Ages, for instance, the university showed many traits of 'community' (in the sense given to the word by Ferdinand Tönnies), whereas in the last three centuries it has increasingly assumed characteristically 'associational' features. So long as Aristotelianism remained predominant and expressed, on the intellectual level, the unity and closedness of medieval life, *all* departments and institutes co-operated in terms of the same mental structure. Starting all from the same basic assumptions and principles, and working all towards the same final results, they tended to form up into a hierarchical order in which everyone commanded the prestige of his subject, according to the layer of being, high or low, with which it was concerned. Few people would have doubted in 1348, when the University of Prague was founded, that a professor of theology was 'higher' in position than a teacher of veterinary science. Even in the seventeenth century, the science faculties were still often called the 'lower' faculties, whereas those of theology and law were called the 'upper' faculties.[1] Such conceptions have departed from the modern academy for it is now a *république des professeurs*. All subjects and all professors are regarded as equals. The pristine communal basis of scholarly work is replaced by certain loose conventions regarding procedure, and they are all that there is in common. Otherwise all specialisms are in principle autonomous, and within them intellectual competition with a definite bent towards originality and progressiveness prevails. Rightly therefore does Plessner speak of a medieval *Werkgemeinschaft* or community of work, and of a modern *Werkgesellschaft* or association for work in research and teaching,[2] the one reflecting the *Gemeinschaft* of medieval, the other the *Gesellschaft* of modern times.

It seems, then, that Znaniecki has greatly overestimated the importance of the microsociology of knowledge. Not only is it unable to replace the macrosociology of knowledge, but it cannot even claim parity with it, since microsociological, i.e. professional and organizational factors, can only operate within the limits of macrosociological determinants. Perhaps we can best characterize the relation of the two sub-disciplines to each other with the help of a pair of concepts used by G. C. Homans in his work *The Human Group*. He distinguishes the external and the internal systems of a group, the group in our case being the intellectuals and artists in a given country at a given time. Their contemporary society is the external system; their professional and organizational subsociety is the internal system. Both develop

[1] Scheler, *Die Wissensformen und die Gesellschaft*, 1926, 211.
[2] *Versuche zu einer Soziologie des Wissens*, ed. Scheler, 1924, 424.

31

cultures, as well as habits and norms of action etc. Now the internal system will certainly add something to the external system, it will perhaps evolve specific variations on the themes provided by the external system, it may even twist parts of the external culture system into new shapes, but it is difficult to imagine that it will rise superior to the latter in influence on the individuals concerned and their modes of thought and life.

A few examples will, it is hoped, clinch our argument. Summing up the researches of Needham and Farrington, Sprott has expressed himself as follows: 'Scientific inquiry . . . may be ruled out by an incompatible climate of opinion. It may be stifled . . . when the creative artificers, from whose activities science springs, are replaced by slaves, whose work is held to be beneath notice by the slave-owning class. These then indulge in what is, by contrast, deemed to be pure thought. When, however, the bourgeoisie break the bonds of feudalism . . ., when individual initiative is prized and individual freedom . . . is claimed, and when new opportunities of industry and commerce present themselves, then the institutionalization of science becomes possible.' [1] Here the very appearance of organizational influences on thought is shown to be dependent on definite social conditions. Another characteristic instance is offered by the development of medieval philosophy. As is generally known, it moved from a typically realistic theory of knowledge to a more nominalistic attitude which foreshadowed the consistent nominalism of later centuries. As we shall see in the latter part of this chapter, this development becomes intelligible in the light of macro-sociological considerations; but microsociological influences are by no means wanting. Paul Landsberg has pointed out that realism survived longer in the monasteries than in the universities staffed by secular priests, but that full nominalism only gained the victory when lay professors drawn from bourgeois families began to dominate teaching and learning. [2] The trend and content of intellectual development was thus determined by the transformation of the inclusive society, but its tempo depended also on the academic personnel and its organization.

A last illustration may fitly be drawn from the sphere of art. The dainty music of a Mozart or Haydn gives way, in the nineteenth century, to the colossal clangour of a Berlioz or Wagner. While the two former composers were satisfied with a platoon of performers, the two latter demanded battalions, including as it were an artillery detachment. This great change may have something to do with the musicians' conditions of employment: the individual patron has gone out, the great public has come in; enormous concert halls must now be filled—filled by people, and filled with sound. But the real reason for the development

---

[1] *Science and Social Action*, 1954, 147.
[2] *Schmollers Jahrbuch für Gesetzgebung*, etc., 1931, 786 *seq.*

is not microsociological. Berlioz and Wagner were protagonists of an individualistic and iconoclastic generation, revolutionaries filled with fantastic, even megalomaniac ambitions for whom all restrictions were cramping, who wanted to demonstrate, by their music, that the age of anarchy was at hand and man was soaring high above the pettiness of the *ancien régime* which had held their predecessors captive: they are understandable only in terms of general social historical trends, and not in terms of concert-organization and cash-box worries or the like. Of course, they did wish to see the masses at their feet, and in so far as they allowed this desire to influence their music-making, the micro-sociological principle of explanation may rightly be invoked; but even in this desire itself, there is still a macrosociological element, for, with Berlioz and Wagner, we are inside an era which was democratic as well as individualist, and both fancied themselves in the mantle of the democrat.

The whole problem under discussion has not received the attention in the literature which it deserves. Max Scheler has come nearest to confronting it directly (although even he does not draw the essential distinction between the two branches of the sociology of knowledge elaborated here). His idea is that the substructural forces (biological, political and economic) create certain possibilities for, or even suggest the development of, definite mental superstructures or culture-complexes appropriate to them: but that these possibilities will only become actualities, that these developments will only take place, if there are leaders, models, pioneers, who get hold of them and carry them out. To use and elaborate his own simile: the substructural tendencies open the sluice-gates of the spirit, but there must be mentally creative men—aggressive men as it were—who see the gaps opened up and press forward through them, carrying a possible cultural achievement or set of achievements from the sphere of mere potentiality forward into the sphere of actualization and actuality. One of his examples is the rise of modern science. At a given stage of history the world calls, so to speak, for scientific ideas; forces and needs such as the growth of population and the necessity of feeding the increased numbers of men (to mention but one strand in the tangled skein of substructural tendencies) set free the potentialities contained in the human mind for the evolution of a scientific world-view. The response to these inviting possibilities comes from two types of élites: the metaphysicians and the entrepreneurs and engineers. Science, as we find it in the modern world of the West, is both a detached and theoretical explanation of nature, and at the same time a tool for its utilization and control. Hence the co-operation of both the groups mentioned was essential to make it what in fact it has become. 'Positive science is and was everywhere where it arose . . . the child of a marriage of philosophy and practical experience.' [1] But this marriage could only come about under certain social preconditions, in a certain biological, political and economic milieu. In this theory of Scheler's, macrosociology and microsociology of knowledge are fairly harmoniously united. The former explains potentiality of realization, the latter actual realization, actualization; the former determines what cannot be done (for the stream of the spirit can only pour through the channels, narrow or wide, which the macrosociological forces have permitted to open); the latter determines what will actually be done (for the use of the potentialities which have arisen is in the hands of certain types of men, certain élites). The theory as it stands seems attractive enough. Yet the belief in the co-operation of objective and subjective tendencies, necessity and freedom, which it implies is connected with a definite metaphysic which few will be quite ready to accept without misgivings.

As for Scheler himself, he sketches out, on the basis of his general theory, a comprehensive microsociology of thought within which the whole intellectual history of the human race is to be accommodated. There are, according to him, three distinct forms of knowing which, though they all have a permanent ground in life and coexist in all societies, none the less exist or predominate at different times and places in different proportions: religious knowledge; metaphysical knowledge; and scientific knowledge. To these three forms of knowing correspond three types of man who act as their carriers: the *homo religiosus*, seer or saint; the sage or thinker or philosopher; and the scientist or researcher. Again, to these three types of man there correspond three specific social forms of co-operation: church and sect; school of wisdom in the ancient sense; and school in the technical sense, or research institute. It is not necessary to expend many words in defence of this teaching: here, if anywhere, we see clearly that there really and truly exists what the Germans call a *Sinnzusammenhang*, an affinity in mental content or meaning, between a certain type of knowledge, a certain type of man, and a certain type of organization. Metaphysics cannot be carried on by visionaries because it is a rational pursuit; nor can it be practised in laboratories because it is not an observational or experimental science. Religious knowledge cannot be furthered in discussion classes like those carried on in the Akademe for it involves a going-out to meet God, not rational conversation confined to a circle of men; still less is it likely to be helped on by scientific research techniques. Science again involves an impersonal, critical and even sceptical attitude which contrasts most impressively with the master-and-disciple relationship so characteristic of the religious sphere and, in a different sense, of the school of wisdom, and so on, and so forth.

Scheler has many splendid examples to give of the social and

[1] *Die Wissensformen und die Gesellschaft*, 1926, 100. Cf. also 104/105.

organizational manifestations of the forms of knowing. Pantheism, for instance, as a typically metaphysical outlook, creates not only schools, but even implies a definite aristocratic tendency. The deep wisdom of the master is not for the masses but for his personal followers only: for the masses a popular religion must be enough.[1] The scientific world-view, on the other hand, is democratic in tendency: the knowledge it produces is not supported by authority but by such proof as is, in principle, open to, and testable by, all men. This is an insight lately stressed and elaborated by a good many other writers, notably Merton and Sprott,[2] and in so far as a democratic political system is, by reason of its general affinity to scientific procedures, a better fostering-ground for scientific achievements and advances than a dictatorship, we have before us a microsociological source of thought-processes which is worthy of the closest consideration.

However, what strikes one in looking at Scheler's argument and the arguments of those who have followed him in this particular, is the fact that he regards the form of social co-operation involved in the creation, preservation and propagation of knowledge as thought-determined rather than as thought-determining. This is what he says: 'It is always essential to consider the relation of the *contents* of know-ledge, e.g. the contents of faith, whether dogmatically defined or not, to the *forms* of organization themselves. Thus, for example, the very content of the Jewish religion of Jahweh, which constitutes it the religion of a chosen race and makes it averse to proselytizing, demands a "people" as its bearer; the content of all poly- and henotheistic forms of religion excludes a universal church (even as an aim); the content of Plato's doctrine of ideas conditions to a large extent the form and organization of the Platonic Academy. So too the organization of the Protestant churches and sects is primarily determined by the *content* of the creed which can exist only in this and in no other social form. And so the subject and method of the positive sciences necessarily requires the *international* form of impersonal co-operation and organizations; whereas the content and even the task of a metaphysic requires on the other hand the *cosmopolitical* form of collaboration between individu-ally different and irreplaceable national philosophies, or rather of their representatives. . . . Metaphysics, because of its very subject-matter, cannot be organized under the same scheme of a division of labour as positive science, for a total vision of the world [as metaphysics tries to

[1] Cf. on all this my introduction to Scheler, *The Nature of Sympathy*, 1954, esp. XXXII and XXVI.

[2] Merton, *Social Theory and Social Structure*, 1949, esp. ch. XII; Sprott, *Science and Social Action*, 1954, esp. 150 *seq.*, where it is shown, with the help of a concrete example, how authoritarian régimes tend to press authoritarianism and mental conformity even on the scientists.

achieve it] can only be realized by *one*, and that a *wholly* concrete person. For this reason, and not because of any historical accident, the *"school"* with a centre, the *"sage"*, is its materially necessary sociological form of existence.' [1] This, then, is Scheler's view: given certain ideas, ideas of a certain nature, religious, philosophical or scientific, it follows that, if they are to flourish, they must create for themselves appropriate forms of life in which they can so to speak feel themselves at home. Consequently, as we have already explained, the microsociological aspects are secondary only, not primary. The ideas are primary here, the organizational and institutional arrangements in which they are embodied flow from them, and the prime task is to see them in their social origination. But that, if we follow the logic implied in Scheler's argument, is a task of what we have termed the macrosociology of knowledge, of the study of the relationships between social life as a whole and the human modes of thinking and feeling engendered in it and by it.

To sum up, then, we by no means disparage or belittle what Znaniecki's approach has to offer. The social rôle of the man of knowledge (and of beauty) must be studied. The work of such pioneers as Thorstein Veblen with his challenging book, written in 1918, *The Higher Learning in America* (whose characteristic subtitle reads: 'A Memorandum on the Conduct of Universities by Businessmen') must be carried on, though in a spirit of complete candour and detachment, for the first and most important task is to gain theoretical insights, not to win political battles. 'One of the primary obligations of the sociology of knowledge consists, therefore,' as Louis Wirth has written, 'in a systematic analysis of the institutional organization within the framework of which intellectual activity is carried on. This involves, among other items, the study of schools, universities, academies, learned societies, museums, libraries, research institutes and laboratories, foundations, and publishing facilities. It is important to know how and by whom these institutions are supported, the types of activity they carry on, their policies, their internal organization and inter-relations, and their place in the social organization as a whole.' Moreover, 'the sociology of knowledge is concerned with the persons who are the bearers of intellectual activity, namely the intellectuals. . . . The composition of this group, their social derivation and the method by which they are recruited, their organization, their class affiliation, the rewards and prestige they receive, their participation in other spheres of social life, constitute some of the more crucial questions to which the sociology

[1] *Die Wissensformen und die Gesellschaft*, 1926, 22, 91 *seq.* (The emphases in our quotation are Scheler's.) Cf. also the very interesting passage on p. 210 *et seq.* Re the Platonic Academy and the Aristotelian School cf. Landsberg in *Versuche zu einer Soziologie des Wissens*, 1924, 297–301.

of knowledge seeks answers. The manner in which these factors express themselves in the products of intellectual activity provide the central theme in all studies which are pursued in the name of the sociology [we should say: the microsociology] of knowledge.' [1]

All these investigations are important and even necessary: nevertheless, we cannot reasonably hope that, in and by themselves, they will ever give us a full understanding of the genesis of whole cultures or culture-complexes, and as it is this genesis, in so far as it is social in character and hence amenable to sociological treatment, which constitutes the subject-matter of the sociology of knowledge, we must set our hopes on the macrosociology rather than on the microsociology of ideas. The present book will therefore be exclusively devoted to the former.

(c) THE SOCIOLOGY OF KNOWLEDGE AT WORK: A CONCRETE EXAMPLE

After this lengthy but necessary detour, we can return to our main business, the discussion of the sociology of knowledge in the narrower or proper sense of the word. What we now want to show is, how it operates when it comes to tackle a concrete piece of analysis, and we have selected for the purpose Paul Landsberg's investigation of the historical development of the theory, or rather theories, of knowledge as set out in his article 'Zur Soziologie der Erkenntnistheorie', published in *Schmollers Jahrbuch für Gesetzgebung, Verwaltung und Volkswirtschaft* in 1931.

The logic underlying Landsberg's argument is fairly simple. The philosophical theory of knowledge, whose social roots he wishes to lay bare, is the self-analysis of man as a perceiving, knowledge-gathering being. But this self-analysis will be deeply influenced by, and must at least harmonize with, the general picture of his self which man happens to entertain at the time and place in question. Now this general picture in turn will be tied to the ideas which man has formed concerning himself as a social being, i.e. concerning the relation of selfhood and society, and these ideas, lastly, will reflect the social reality—the real relation between the individual and the community—under which he lives. In this way there is a chain of interconnection which reaches upward from social life through social conceptions to what Kant used to call 'anthropology', man's doctrine of man, into such technical fields as epistemology, or the philosophical study of man as the subject of knowledge.

This is Landsberg's general programme as it were, and he seeks to implement it by showing how the historical transformations of

---

[1] Preface to Mannheim's *Ideology and Utopia*, ed. 1952, XXX *seq.*

epistemological thinking are explicable in terms of it. In twentieth, and even more in nineteenth-century philosophy, the word here taken in a wide sense which includes the naïve world-view of ordinary men and women, this thinking is characterized by a consistent and extreme nominalism. A general concept is formed, according to this order of ideas, by mentally gathering together a number of individual entities (which alone are real) under one verbal expression, under one linguistic umbrella. To this technical epistemology there corresponds a generally accepted sociology which is of exactly the same complexion. A society is simply the summing-up of so many individuals (who alone are real) under one formal definition. But this social theory is itself no more than an intellectual working-out of an appropriate social experience. For under modern conditions man is not born into a pre-existent social pattern as he was in tribal and feudal times: he has to find his own way in life, and he only binds himself to life by entering into contracts with other people. And even in so far as he binds himself into social entities which he finds already in existence when he appears upon the scene, these are very often obviously contractual in nature. A joint-stock company, a co-operative society, a trade union is a creation of its members, merely the creature of their joint wills. Society appears, and must appear under this dispensation, as something secondary, something that is, in a very real sense of the word, *made* by the independent individuals who enter into it. Now, this process of society-making, as it goes on in the outer world, is plainly parallel to the process of general-concept-making as it goes on in the inner world of man, in the human mind: [1] in either case the many are summed up under one collective term, and this collective term does not, as a collectivity, represent a real entity, but rather a label, a convenience, a fiction. But we need not rest content with the vague and tame observation that the two processes, social and mental, are parallel to each other: we can boldly proclaim that the former is basic to, and inspires, the latter. For few will deny that, in the order of being, reality precedes thought —especially if by reality is meant social reality, a reality, that is, which already contains a mental component, even though it be a characteristically para-theoretical, activistic mentality.

The extreme opposite to this comprehensive and consistent nominalism of modern man is the equally comprehensive and consistent realism of the primitive world-view. Though Lévy-Bruhl's *L'Ame*

[1] Landsberg tries to make this parallel even more concrete and impressive by comparing some mental processes of modern science with some contemporary real processes of the modern economy: in either case the summing-up of individuals in collective concepts or associations is determined by considerations of utility etc. We cannot follow him into all this detail and refer the reader to pp. 774 *seq.*, *loc. cit.*

Primitive, on which Landsberg's observations are mainly based, has in the meantime been corrected in many ways by social anthropologists in the course of their field research, the bulk of his discussion can stand. For the primitive, a snake is not so much *this* snake as an incarnation of 'snakehood': in his thinking the *genus* is prior to the individual. If a man or an animal has been killed, the whole tribe or clan or animal species are at once involved and need propitiation as totalities. Many ceremonies have precisely this in view. Indeed, the very happenings which we are wont to regard as the prime happenings in our individual lives, are to the primitive happenings affecting the body social: birth is the putting-forth of a new shoot by the family tree, an embodiment of the common *mana*; death is the dropping off of a dry branch, the return of a divided particle into the common *mana*. All these conceptions are, of course, manifestations of the solidarity of social life on the tribal level, of the close-knit character of the clan or sib. The picture the clansman forms of a snake is determined by the idea he has of himself: every MacDonald is to himself an incarnation of Donald life before he is—even to himself—Ian or Angus or Seumas. Totemism is only the most consistent form—the focus as it were—in and through which this world-view becomes clear and conscious. To be is to be a member—the member of a whole which is a substantial unity or unitary substance.

Landsberg touches in this connection (though all too lightly) upon the great problem of relativity implied in this dichotomy of world-views. Is not our (nominalistic) world-view more sensible, reasonable, realistic than the primitive? Is it not much more 'natural' to say that the individual is a substantial unity and society a mere name than *vice versa*? As modern men we are undoubtedly tempted to answer these questions in the affirmative: but as philosophers we must be careful not to fall victims to current prejudice. When we call a stone an individual thing, we are merely putting a unitary label on what is, in itself, essentially a sum of atoms, protons and electrons. Indeed, our individual self may—some would say, must—in the same fashion be broken down into constituent elements which only 'make' it by their association: witness the important psychological tradition called associationism; witness James Joyce and his atomized individual. Our way of handling reality is for this reason *prima facie* neither more realistic nor less fictional than that of the primitive. And there is the further question whether conscious nominalism does not necessarily presuppose a certain measure of subconscious realism: it is difficult to imagine any induction that does not take place within a definite framework of distinctions and order already existing in the observing mind when the process of induction starts, so that the universal categories are not really attained by going *ab ovo* from the individual instance to the common class, but rather by doing so within a conceptualization and classification already pre-existent and pre-formed.

The most valuable and suggestive part of Landsberg's essay is his exploration of the theory of knowledge of the Platonic age and the discussions and dissensions accompanying it. When that splendid epoch in the history of human thinking dawned, the Greeks had already far outgrown the primitive stage of social life; community was receding, individualism advancing. No wonder that we find forward-looking philosophers like Democritos who show in their whole mental outlook a definite likeness to what has come to be known as enlightenment, and at the same time backward-looking philosophers such as the great Plato. Landsberg sees these two men as antagonists, Democritos standing for the new-found freedom of the individual and all it implied, Plato longing for the vanished or vanishing integration of the community in close-knit forms of life, but already forced, in his system of ideas, to come to a compromise with the new realities.

Democritos, as a representative and mouthpiece of the progressive social forces of the day, develops a far-reaching nominalism. (His atomism is essentially a higher form of the nominalistic principle.) With it go a strong emphasis on democratic and cosmopolitan ideals, an ethic of individualistic cast which counsels the individual to pursue his own happiness by living according to reason and is thus a-political, and a sharp nominalism in linguistic philosophy. 'He was most likely the first to coin the decisive saying: names are accidental—not from nature' (779). In Epicurus the a-political and anti-political ideal of a private life is then combined with the contractual theory of the state, and so many if not all of the elements are collected which are characteristic of modern nominalism and contractualism, of Hobbes, Locke and Rousseau, the specific philosophers of the rising bourgeoisie. 'This whole mode of thinking and the ethic corresponding to it could only arise in times of individual striving for freedom in the face of older social ties' (780).

Very different is the striving, and consequently also the thinking, of the aristocratic Plato. The well-ordered *polis* under the rule of the *optimati* is his aim, not a democratic society of free individuals. Yet the loosening up of the social structure has gone so far that it is no longer possible to think in terms of the integral epistemological realism natural to the tribal ages. The category of the 'individual' has emerged in (social) life and can no longer be kept out of the philosophical world-view. Social and natural species can no longer be conceived as unities but must be acknowledged to be multiplicities. Yet Plato, rooted as his mind is in the reality and the ideal of a community life, cannot and will not jettison the old philosophical realism, the realistic principle in epistemology. And thus there forms in his mind the specifically Platonic

doctrine of ideas. Ideas are real in the sense that they are endowed with being. General concepts are not arrived at by induction
or constituted by definition but reflect the realm of reality called 'ideas'.
Ideas are thus given to the mental eye in a manner analogous to that
in which things are seen by the physical eye. Now it was the specific
difficulty of this theory of knowledge, in the historical situation in which
it was put forward, that it had to come to terms with the individuality
of individual objects which could no longer be gainsaid. This individuality, discovered as it had been by this semi-individualistic age, made it
impossible to conceive the relation of the concrete and individual to the
abstract and universal as a relation of part to whole, or member to
body. The concrete and individual was felt to be too 'real', too independent of the category, the class, the genus, to be treated in this way.
Plato solved the difficulty by replacing the conception of the part as a
member of the whole by the (to his age) more satisfactory concept of
its *participation*—or rather the participation of the individual and
concrete—in the idea ($\mu\acute{\epsilon}\theta\epsilon\xi\iota\varsigma$). There is individual existence, but it is
what it is essentially by its participation in the ideas which, immovable
and immortal, constitute true being, being in all its purity. 'In the same
way, the [human] individual is indeed an individual, but he *is* only (in
the ontological sense of the word) if he finds his place in the state and
receives from it his true being by participation. In this clear-cut sense
of the word, the existence of man is political. The ethos of the Platonic
writings concerning the state, the realistic philosophy of concept-
formation contained in the doctrine of ideas, and the reality of the
Greek *polis* form a structural whole as indivisible as that of nominalistic
individualism or of primitive realistic solidarism' (778).

After following this line of investigation further down the centuries,
Landsberg turns, in the second part of his essay, to a second aspect of
the history of epistemological theory, starting again with the common
opinion of modern times. Today it is the general conviction that all
knowledge is open to all men. Either this conviction is incorporated in a
sensualistic form and then it is emphasized that all human beings
possess the same physical apparatus and can thus gather knowledge like
all other human beings, or it is wrapped up in a rationalistic doctrine,
and then the basic assumption and assertion is that all human beings
are equally endowed with reason and that reason functions, by and
large, in the same fashion in all human beings and again puts them on
a level with each other as far as the acquisition of truth is concerned.
In either case, there is a far-reaching egalitarianism in regard to
epistemology. It is, of course, admitted that some people have more
detailed and technical knowledge than others, but this knowledge is, by
that very definition, regarded as *merely* detailed and technical and the
general belief is in any case that even this sort of knowing is, in principle,

open to all men and could be acquired by anybody, provided only he were trained in the appropriate way. For instance, 'Einstein's relativity theory finds credence . . . because people are convinced that its theorems were obtained from sense-experience, thinking and calculation, hence from the operation of common human . . . capabilities, only in an unusual degree and in extreme complication' (793 *seq.*).

Not so the Platonic philosophy. It is not egalitarian but aristocratic. Knowledge is not at the beck and call of all human beings, but can only be acquired by those whose being is akin to the being which is to be the object of knowledge. 'It is impossible that the multitude should philosophize. It lacks kinship with the gods and with the ideas' (791), teaches Plato. 'Only he who is capable of divinity, can recognize the divine' (795). The formula that true insight is an *adaequatio rei et intellectus*, a correspondence of thing and thought, has here a very specific and stringent meaning, a meaning which is human as well as technical. Not all eyes and not all intellects can see equally well, but some see and understand better than others, though the truth is and remains the same for all. 'Far-reaching differences in knowledge are due to differences in being, not to mere differences in the training and application of a common reason' (790 *seq.*). The truth can only be perceived and grasped by those who, in addition to the normal human equipment of sense and reason, have a specific charisma: by the philosophers who are a class, a status group, a caste, and who are predisposed, as it were, for the successful pursuit of the higher truths. (Landsberg points out here that Platonism again shows itself at this point as a theory which has outgrown primitive modes of thought but is still near to them. On the tribal level, the shaman or 'seer' has a magical privilege with regard to knowing, especially the knowing of transcendental reality; Plato gives his place to the more secular and rational class of philosophers but retains the idea of their privileged status.)

Very characteristically, this aristocratic conception is diametrically opposed to the democratic one with regard to the relation of fundamental knowledge on the one hand, and specialized knowledge on the other. Detailed and technical knowledge, it allows, may indeed be widespread; the cobbler knows what to do with his awl and last; but fundamental knowledge, the knowledge of the first and last things, will for ever be the privilege of a few. For the democratic theory, on the other hand, technical knowledge is the province of the few, but philosophical knowledge—for instance, the knowledge of God, of the conditions of salvation, of the difference between right and wrong—is within the grasp of all—see Protestantism, see Immanuel Kant. In this respect, sensualism is even more radically egalitarian than rationalism (which preceded it in the order of development), for rationalism must at any rate acknowledge one (attenuated) aristocratic principle—the demand for the control of the lower passions by the higher passion for truth, that self-control without which the mind is clouded and cannot perceive the facts as they are, and without distortion.

If we ask why there should be these differences in epistemological thought, why Plato, say, and Kant or Condillac should appear as opposite poles as distant from each other as north and south, the answer must be sought, to a very large extent, in social reality. Plato sees man first and foremost as the member of a specific status group, as warrior or ruler or artisan, and the common quality of citizenship is no more than a shadowy backcloth that does not count. For Kant and Condillac, on the other hand, man is above all a citizen, and his specific place in the social hierarchy is only an accident that signifies, or ought to signify, little. Hence a Plato will, quite naturally, conceive the acquisition of knowledge, too, as a specific task of a specific class, whereas a Kant or a Condillac will regard it as a possibility and a mission for all, denying even 'genius' a place in the advancement of science. And behind the contrasting conceptions of man as a being bound to status in the one case, and essentially an equal among equals in the other, stands the contrasting reality of the respective ages: the decaying, but still highly valued class or caste division of the Ionian *polis*, the budding and eagerly anticipated equality of the bourgeois state. 'No estate in society, no estates in knowledge' is its principle (796). To the democratic conception of knowing corresponds, as fact or as aim, a democratic conception of social life, and *vice versa*. We see here once again how epistemology, even in its most speculative and abstract shape, has roots which reach down, through the intermediate layer of a general doctrine of man, deep into the sub-soil of social reality which is thus, in the last analysis, one of the determining elements of philosophical speculation.

The sociology of knowledge here leads to insights which are of more than historical interest. Where the democratic conception prevails, we shall find predominating to the exclusion of all others those forms of knowing and knowledge-gathering which are really open to all men: mathematics and mathematical technique; observation with or without special instruments of observation. Concentration on these, so characteristic of the modern—the bourgeois—age, has paid a high economic dividend in the advancement of science and technology. But there has also been loss, as well as gain. All those channels of experience and hence of possible insight into reality which presuppose some special quality or qualification, have become blocked up and closed: the mystical vision, for instance, or any other special form of revelation, whether instinctual, artistic, ecstatic, or born of especial sympathy and empathy, but also the more sober philosophic intuition so dear to a Plato or a Plotinus. Such explorations of the realm of being are no longer understood by the common herd; indeed, they are very often met with downright ridicule. Where the attempt is made to reopen avenues of this kind, as for instance in the philosophy of Husserl or Scheler with their doctrine of *Wesensschau*, we have before us opposition movements against the spirit and the social order of the age, and it is certainly no accident that a Scheler, for instance, shows aristocratic traits in all his thought and action, so that he must be seen as part and parcel of the stream of social and political development which produced the anti-democratic propaganda of a Nietzsche and ultimately led to the anti-democratic reality of twentieth-century fascism.

These last considerations allow us a first fleeting glimpse of the deeper importance which may conceivably attach to the sociology of knowledge; perhaps its methods may not only throw light on the origins and content of succeeding world-views but also on their inherent limitations. For the moment, we shall only attempt to sum up what has been said so far. Perhaps we can do this best with the help of the concept of style so familiar from the field of fine art. In architecture, in printing, in music, each artist has indeed his own individual mark and manner; but beyond these, his work regularly exhibits features which link it with the works of other artists of his school or class or culture or age, and these collective characteristics we call a style. The common and the personal modes of expression do not normally stand in contrast to each other, but rather in the relationship of theme and variation. Now the basic theme, the common style of an art, again as a rule points outward beyond itself towards a wider thematic and stylistic unity: there are not only ties in taste and expression which bind together all the painters within a given social constellation (whatever that constellation may be), but also ties which connect them with the musicians, the architects, the sculptors, and so on, who live side by side with them. Yet even here the unifying characteristics of style do not come to a dead end. As many observers—most of them unaware even of the possibility of the analytical study which we have come to call the sociology of knowledge, and concentrating only in a positive, descriptive manner on the observable phenomena—have seen and explained, the artistic style of a period is usually matched by, and kindred to, the contemporary style of thought as it exhibits itself in an analogous fashion in literature, in scholarship, in philosophy and in religion. Many historians have elaborated fascinating inclusive pictures of such total mental styles or culture-mentalities. The sociologist of knowledge goes with them, but—and this is characteristic of his specific approach —he goes beyond them. He thinks in terms of a still wider totality or unity of life, a unity which binds together, not only mental phenomena as such, but mind and its manifestations (the superstructure) on the one hand, and social relationships with all that they involve (the substructure) on the other. Like Descartes, he connects *'cogito'* and *'sum'*, thought and being, but 'being' means to him, in accordance with the definition of man indispensable to all the social sciences, not isolated, but social existence, 'being in society'. What he suggests is that ideas are engendered in, and grow out of, social interaction, and that they show, in their concrete content, the reflected image of the social reality within which they have come to life.

CHAPTER TWO

THE ANTECEDENTS OF THE SOCIOLOGY OF KNOWLEDGE

(a) SOCIAL DETERMINATION VERSUS IDEOLOGICAL DISTORTION OF THOUGHT

THOSE who know the literature of the sociology of knowledge already, may have been surprised to find that the first chapter of this book, which was designed to provide a preliminary orientation in the subject, does not even mention the concept which, with many authors, occupies a key position: the concept of ideology. The reason for this conscious avoidance both of the word itself and of the phenomenon it signifies is the conviction of the present writer, that the doctrine of ideology is no more than a historical antecedent of the sociology of knowledge; that its centre of interest lies in a different level of mental life; that it is also different in its nature because it is a psychological rather than a sociological discipline; and that the sooner the traditional connection of the two studies is severed, the better it will be for both of them.

What is meant by an ideology? Following our usual practice, we shall try to answer this question with the help of a concrete example. In the early thirties of the present century, when the world was groaning under the load of misery brought on by the economic crisis, two different diagnoses were offered, and two different remedies were pressed. One school of thought maintained that the economic order had been thrown out of gear because the wage-level had been raised too high and fixed there. Everything, it was argued, has its due market price; so long as this economically correct price prevails, disequilibrium need not be feared; but as soon as any one price is artificially distorted, disequilibrium must ensue and trouble follow. Since Trade Unionism had achieved a position of power in society (power which was largely based on extra-economic, political factors), the market-system had not been able to work properly, for one of its elements was constantly prevented from adjusting itself to the given situation, and unemployment was the

46

logical result. The poverty of the underprivileged workless was merely the necessary counterpart to the affluence of the overprivileged workers. A more 'realistic' wage policy would right what had come to be wrong. This was not how the other school argued. They saw the crisis in terms of underconsumption rather than in terms of artificial wage-maintenance. The warehouses were bursting with wealth; need was great; yet supply and demand were unable to come together. Might not the reason for this absurd position be that demand was powerless to absorb the supply? Was there not simply too little purchasing power about, and was not the obvious remedy to put more rather than less money into the wage-earners' pay-packets of a Friday morning?

Nobody will be surprised to hear that the former opinion was strongly pressed by the employers' organizations and those journalists who had ranged themselves on their side, whereas the latter was championed by the Trade Unions and their sympathizers up and down the country. But this fact must necessarily arouse a certain suspicion —the suspicion that neither side was really interested in the truth, and that both parties simply tried to exploit the situation for their own purposes. Now, there may have been hack-writers on either side of the fence who did, cynically, build up a case for their side without any inner conviction of its justice, as a barrister works out a case according to his brief. But if such men existed, they present no problem either to the sociology of knowledge or to the doctrine of ideology. For their thought-processes were not conditioned by the situation: what they said was not what they thought; in their heart of hearts they were free men, able to follow the truth whither it might lead them. But there were other men—probably the vast majority—who, whether they were paid for it or not, honestly fell in with the school which favoured the social class and income-group to which they, or at least their sympathies, belonged: there was the trade unionist who was firmly convinced that he was not after higher wages, but after economic health; there was the employer who was equally convinced that he was not after larger profits, but after general prosperity. The minds of these men manifestly offered a serious problem: granted that their thought was, on the conscious level, entirely candid, was it not likely, was it not, to say the very least, possible, that subconscious desires had manœuvred them into the mode of thinking—into the theoretical fold—in which they found themselves? Julius Caesar once uttered the wise and realistic words: *quae volumus, ea credimus libenter*,[1] we readily believe what we wish to be true. Was this not a case in point? In other words, to give the matter a somewhat more refined philosophical formulation, were not meta-theoretical pre-occupations present, unrecognized, in the theoretical world-view of the people concerned? And was it not the task of scholarship, of science,

---

[1] *De Bello Civili*, II, 27. Cf. also Demosthenes, *Olynthiacs*, 3, 19.

the guardians of objective truth, to show them up in all such cases, and to bring them to light? And was there anybody at all whose ideas were free from this taint? Certainly, both economic theories were upheld by academic economists whose objectivity was beyond reproach. But even an academic man can be objective only on the conscious level; he may test and re-test himself, he may test himself for the third time, yet he will still be at the mercy of his subconscious urges because these are, by definition, hidden from his scrutiny and yet—alas!—so powerful, so insinuating, so imperative.

If and in so far, then, as a man entertains an idea or system of ideas in the psychological origin of which some selfish or sectional interest or desire has played a part [1] and which would have been different if that interest or desire had not entered in, his thought is to be characterized as problematic, or, to use the technical term now universally applied for the description of such states of mind, ideological. The word interest must be taken here in a fairly narrow connotation, in the sense of egotistical, professional or class (and possibly national) interest: it has nothing to do with that detached interest which we feel when we say, for example, that we are interested in Beethoven's choral symphony or in Leibniz's particular approach to the infinitesimal calculus. From this it follows that ideological thought is, *a limine*, something tainted, something shady, something that ought to be overcome and banished from our mind. [2]

We see here already the decisive difference between the doctrine of ideology and the sociology of knowledge. The former deals with a mode of thinking which is thrown off its proper course, the latter with all modes of thinking, and especially with those which form the intellectual

[1] Geiger, in his *Ideologie und Wahrheit* (cf. esp. 96), has pleaded that the difficult word 'interest' be discarded, and that we should speak instead of the 'involvement of a man's will' in his thought when we wish to characterize that thought as ideological. To the present writer it seems that the characterization of ideological thought as 'interested' or 'interest-begotten' or 'interest-determined' has more punch about it than Geiger's terminology (which is also problematic from another point of view since it is questionable whether there is any mental act at all which does not, in some way, involve willing). But I should like to emphasize that I use the term 'interest' in the sense of 'bringing into play man's conations and volitions and aversions and ambitions, etc.'—hence in the same spirit as Geiger uses his own parallel term.

[2] Cf. Geiger, *loc. cit.*, esp. 67 *seq. Gegenwartsprobleme der Soziologie*, 1949, esp. 147 *et seq.* Geiger's most pungent formulation occurs in the latter publication, p. 153: 'All ideology rests on the conversion of emotional attachments into para-theoretical conceptions . . . A says this or that about the object n. What he says is false or half-true'.—Geiger also emphasizes, what hardly needs further elaboration here, that ideology is one thing, lying another. Both are concerned with untruth, but whereas the liar tries to falsify the thought of others while his own private thought is correct, while he himself knows full well what the truth is, a person who falls for an ideology is himself deluded in his private thought, and if he misleads others, does so unwillingly and unwittingly. Cf. *Ideologie und Wahrheit*, 26 *seq.*

framework of our whole world-view and which exist long before any falsifying interest-begotten tendency can assert itself. If all men could and would come to control their subconscious and rise superior to the insinuations of selfish or sectional interests, the doctrine of ideology would die off, because there would be no more raw material left in the contemporary world for it to study. But the sociology of knowledge would be as important as before. No society can see the vastnesses of reality at the same time from all conceivable angles; only the divine mind can be imagined to be capable of this possibility; every society must take up some concrete vantage-point from which to survey the broad—the unbounded—acres of that which is, and every society will therefore have its own particular picture of reality because it sees reality, and must see it, in one particular perspective. The thesis of the sociology of knowledge is that the choice of the vantage-point from which the *ens universale* is envisaged, depends in every concrete society on the human relationships which make that society what it is; but it is not asserted that selfish or sectional interests enter into the matter already at the point where the fundamental vision first springs into being. That they may come in later on and assert themselves is not to be denied; but that is an entirely different problem. The sociology of knowledge does not deal with warped thought; rather it deals with the crystallization or 'concretization' of thought [1] in the sense that countless different

---

[1] The word 'crystallization', introduced here as a convenient shorthand expression for the facts set forth in our opening pages, and, by anticipation, for the contents of ch. 3, needs careful explanation; being metaphorical, it has its semantic pitfalls which must be guarded against. In and by itself, it is an altogether proper term to use, for, according to the *Oxford English Dictionary* (II, 1933, 1231), 'to crystallize' means, in figurative use, 'to give a definite or concrete and permanent form or shape to something of an undefined, vague, or floating character', and this is precisely what the value-system of society, introduced into the individual mind by the social forces (or, philosophically speaking, the mind's socially determined axiological *a priori*), does to human thought. But one possible misunderstanding must be avoided. By saying that a crystallization is effected, we mean that the contents of the mind become clear, and also that they become organized or structured, but not that they become stiff, set, or rigid. It is not as if there were first of all individual thought independent of social pre-conditions or axiological elements, which only then hardens, under social influences, into more abiding forms; no, the crystallization of which we are speaking stands at the very inception of thought in the sense of a conscious mental process with definite and tangible ideal contents; it is the *making* of thought, the making of the *mind*, which we have in view, not any kind of subsequent deadening or ossification. Before 'crystallization' we can imagine undefined, wayward, dream-like images floating through the mind, freely coming and going and leaving little or nothing behind, but we cannot imagine *knowledge* properly so called as typified in human, as opposed to animal, consciousness. 'Crystallization' thus describes a becoming concrete of the contents of the mind, and in so far as all human thought, even the most primitive and unsophisticated, is concrete—is concerned with assignable things, things in focus—it is a *sine qua non* to the functioning of the intellect. If there were such a word in the English language as 'concretization',

constructions and interpretations of reality are in principle equally possible, while only one of them can be implemented and elaborated at any one time, and the selection of the one out of the many is, in its submission, always so made that a mental universe emerges which will fit in with the pattern of human relationships characteristic and constitutive of the society concerned.

It is true that 'society' need not necessarily mean, in this context, inclusive society: in certain situations, a class may form its own worldview at variance with that of other classes, or a sect may form its own mental framework in defiance of the basic assumptions and interpretations of the orthodox majority. In such cases (of which it would not be difficult to furnish examples) interest-begotten modes of thinking may arise earlier and exert greater influence than is commonly the case. But the separation between ideology and socially determined thought will exist none the less. Before other 'interests' can claim satisfaction, one basic 'interest' must be satisfied—namely, the necessity to live in an understandable universe; without it, no concrete thought is possible at all, not even selfish thought; ideologies can only arise where there are already ideas; but the universe does not become understandable unless it is conceived and construed in terms which harmonize with—which, so to speak, are of one piece with—the terms in which social life is carried on. And therefore the sociology of knowledge, as a study, must logically precede, and be kept apart from, the doctrine of, and the hunt for, ideologies.

By making this sharp distinction between the doctrine of ideology on the one hand and the sociology of knowledge on the other, we do not for one moment wish to create the impression that the latter is important and the former not. On the contrary; the search for ideological influences which vitiate our thinking is of vital concern. Nowhere are they more dangerous than where they make use of, and abuse, undeniable scientific truths. A good example is Social Darwinism.[1] The Malthusian-Darwinian doctrine of the survival of the fittest in the natural war of all against all reflects a demonstrably occurrent process in the animal world and is the appropriate explanation of many factual phenomena. And there are also societies in which the law of the jungle reigns supreme, and which can truthfully be described in terms of it. But if those with the strongest elbows in a society, those who have been most successful in the struggle for the trough, proclaim that the elimination or exploitation of the weak by the strong is necessary, natural, or

it would be even better than 'crystallization', but it does not seem to exist, and one hesitates to introduce it. It may at the very most be permissible to use it—with apologies—in inverted commas, as above.

[1] For another example akin to this cf. Ziegenfuss, *Gesellschaftsphilosophie*, 1954, 2 *seq.*

at least desirable, then we are confronted with a distortion of thinking in those who believe this pseudo-science which it is all-important to rectify. For a human society is not under the laws of nature but under its own laws, and it can in freedom decide to what degree it wishes to admit or suspend the principle, operative in the lower creation, of the war of all against all. To expose the selfish roots of Social Darwinism in some of its representatives, to prove that it is a piece of propaganda and self-justification, and not a scientific truth, is a task of the doctrine of ideology which nobody should belittle. The distinction which we make between this and the sociology of knowledge is not one of value, but one of essence. The sociology of knowledge deals with the formation of a specific world-view, the doctrine of ideology with its deformation; the former is concerned with a positive, the latter with a negative phenomenon; and, as we shall presently see, only the former is a truly social science, whereas the latter belongs much rather to the sphere of psychology.

That the doctrine of ideology is not really a sociological or socio-philosophical discipline, can be demonstrated with the help of a concrete example. Throughout history, we find philosophies which assert that permanence is real and change a delusion—philosophies whose detail is vastly different, but whose kernel is simple and can be formulated in a very few words such as those just used. There is, near the beginning of the story, Plato with the assertion that rest is the perfection of being and movement only an impoverished form of it; there is, towards the end, Pareto with his 'scientific' 'proof' that social life is the same at all times and places since it is controlled by the unchanging 'residues' while only the surface seems to show development—a development which is not really development at all because it consists only in the replacement of one kind of idle talk (or 'derivation') by another. Now both Plato and Pareto were aristocrats who lived in an age which was very unkind to aristocracy. Both saw an upsurge of egalitarianism; both disliked what they saw and turned away from contemporary reality in disgust and dismay. Both fled from the real world with its changes into an unreal world of permanencies: their theories are ideological in origin and content. At their (subconscious) inception stood a practical and political preoccupation and prejudice. Underneath the threshold of consciousness there worked the anguished sentiment and desire that the world *should* not change; above the threshold of consciousness there formed—nourished from its subterranean root—the conviction, the delusive conviction, that the world *does* not change, does not *really* change, that change is only a ripple on the surface of the ocean which leaves the deeper layers of the water calm and unmoved.

We are not concerned here with the question whether it is possible or even reasonable to derive imposing structures of philosophy from

51

such petty causes. We are prepared to leave this issue entirely open at the moment. We only wish to show that this whole analysis (if analysis it can be called)—that this whole way of thinking is not sociological but psychological in origin. It certainly looks sociological: an aristocracy is a class; in Plato's and Pareto's day it was a class losing ground rapidly in the class struggle; it needed an 'ideology' which would sustain it in that struggle and offer a weapon, however blunt, against the attacking class enemy. (Pareto's assertion that underneath the power-distribution in society, and even underneath the given income-distribution, there lurks a more basic ability-distribution which is due to inborn and genetically transmitted features and thus could at best be temporarily overlaid but never permanently abolished by a social revolution, is particularly characteristic of this latter aspect of the formation of ideological conceptions.)[1] Nothing would, at first sight, seem to be more the concern of the social sciences than 'ideologies' sprung from such sources and situations. But appearances are deceptive: we are, in point of fact, confronted with a psychological adjustment to the situation, and not with a social process properly so called.

We see this at once if we set against the example just discussed an instance which is manifestly and undeniably merely an incident in a private life. A doctor-friend told the late Professor Geiger the following story: 'His colleague and patient N. N. complained even in the last stage of lung cancer of the persistence of his "bronchitis". The symptoms of cancer of the lung were unmistakable. N. N. could not but know what his situation was. If, as the medical man in charge of the case, he had observed the same symptoms in one of his patients, he would not have doubted for a single second what the diagnosis was. What he observed in his special case, however, was not the symptoms of one of his patients, but his own state. And that he did not wish to acknowledge for what it was . . . he lived and died in a fool's paradise.'[2] If we follow this delusion from the conscious down into the subconscious realm, we find again at the root of it an anguished wish and desire. Everything in the poor sufferer cried out: no! no! no! I must not have a mortal disease! But this outcry transformed itself, in the open mind, into a delusive conviction, into a fake-factual thought-content. The stages of the man's subconscious, semi-conscious, conscious thinking can perhaps be formulated in the following three sentences: I am afraid I have cancer of the lung; I wish I did not have cancer of the lung; surely—surely!—I do not have cancer of the lung! All human beings flee sometimes from the disappointments and miseries of this life into some such mental haven, trying to lock out what they cannot change and do not

---

[1] Cf. Gurvitch, *Le Concept de Classes Sociales de Marx à Nos Jours*, 1954, 78 and 87 *seq.*

[2] *Ideologie und Wahrheit*, 1953, 96 *seq.*

care to see, and for this reason the psychological mechanism concerned is common human knowledge.

In our present context the salient point is that the structure of the case of Dr. N. N. is not only parallel to, but essentially identical with, that of Plato and Pareto and other disappointed decaying noblemen. True, their trouble was not physical, but social. But in either case the basic state of anxiety is merely a remote cause of an adjustive thought-process, whereas this thought-process in itself is psychological. The doctrine of ideology thus deals with a cause of intellectual error, rather than with the social element in the pursuit and perception of the truth.

One might have expected, then, that the two disciplines would have run side by side in the past, stimulating each other perhaps, but never crossing or merging. Unfortunately, however, this has not been so. On the contrary, great confusion has reigned in the field.[1] There has been a tendency to identify the sociology of knowledge with what one might call a pan-ideological conception of thought—in other words, to make out that all thought is interest-inspired and interest-dominated, and that it is socially determined only in so far as the inspiring and dominating interest is social in character. A recent example of this is Stanislaw Warynski's stimulating book *Die Wissenschaft von der Gesellschaft* (1944). Warynski denies that interest in the sense of material interest—interest as it arises from, and shows itself in, the struggle of the social and economic classes for the control of the means of production—is at the root of some thought only; he asserts it to be at the root of all thought. And he also denies that interestedness in the sense defined will always lead to error, or even threaten to lead to error; he asserts that there are kinds of interestedness which will, on the contrary, lead on to truth. Granted that a decaying class will flee from the facts into a land of make-believe, will not a rising class have every reason to be realistic in outlook and none to falsify and transmogrify its impressions and insights? We are here manifestly in the Marxist camp: classes on the way out think wrongly; classes on the way in think rightly; but both think ideologically.

It is doubtful whether Marx and Engels themselves saw the matter in quite the same way. Warynski himself quotes one of Engels's letters

---

[1] An example of this confusion is Raymond Aron's terminology: In *Die Deutsche Soziologie der Gegenwart* (otherwise a most meritorious book) he refers on p. 71 (German ed., 1953) to ideologies as 'ideas which are determined by (social) reality'. On p. 86, however, he says: 'We can regard as ideologies in the first place the (false) ideas which serve the social classes for their self-justification or as weapons.' The latter definition is sound, but the former is misleading. The word ideology is a pejorative word; it describes unrealistic, prejudice-begotten thought. But 'ideas which are determined by social reality' are not, because they are so determined, necessarily erroneous. On the contrary; determination by—i.e. agreement with—the social bases of life is manifestly a factor making for realism and truth.

in which he equates ideological consciousness with false consciousness,[1] thus severely restricting the field of ideology; and *Die deutsche Ideologie* deals with, and exposes, the delusory character of much of German philosophical speculation in the forties of the nineteenth century, thus implying that ideology is in essence unrealistic thought, and unrealistic thought alone. But we must be careful here not to fall into the ditch of a purely verbal squabble, a squabble about the definition of ideology. We may and must concede to Warynski that Marxism contains a tendency at any rate towards pan-ideologism. The real question is whether Warynski's brand of Marxism is sound when it asserts the ideological—i.e. interest-determined—nature of all thought.

In order to answer this question, let us take up our position in the camp of the rising class, the class in whose favour the wind of history is blowing at the moment and which consequently has no incentive to see the world in any but realistic terms. Unless we are to assume that the thinkers of this class cannot err (a ridiculous assumption in itself, and one disproved by all the bitter disagreements inside rising classes throughout history), we are again confronted with a dichotomy. There will be thought falsified by some emotion, whether hate or desire or fear, and there will be thought not so falsified. For instance, the ideologist of a rising class may get a warped picture of the facts because in his disgust with the existing régime he suppresses or underrates (not only in word, but even in thought) its more positive aspects; or because in his yearning for the anticipated future he overestimates its proximity. Thus his position will not be different, *in principle*, from that of the ideologist of the sinking class. It will at best be different, that is to say better, in *degree* because one strong incentive to form delusions will be absent from his mind which will be present in the mind of the disappointed and dislodged. In other words, it will at best offer a greater chance of truth, but it can never afford a guarantee of truth. And so ideological and non-ideological thought must be as carefully separated here as everywhere else. And here, as everywhere else, ideological thought can only arise—indeed, interests can only be felt, strivings formed—after a meaningful universe has already been constituted, and its constitution may indeed be determined by the social and historical circumstances of the class (or other subsociety) concerned, but not by its economic or power-political or other sectional interests because these can never come into focus, however indistinctly, however darkly and dimly, until there is a general frame of reference, a basic *imago mundi*.

[1] *Loc. cit.*, 212. Engels writes: 'Ideology is a [mental] process which is indeed carried on by the so-called thinkers with consciousness, but with a false consciousness. The real determining forces which move him remain unknown to him, otherwise it would not be an ideological process . . .'

We can see what is apt to happen when sociology of knowledge and the search for ideologies are not consciously kept apart, by looking at Gunnar Myrdal's in many ways admirable book, *The Political Element in the Development of Economic Theory* (1929; English ed., 1953). Myrdal recognizes only two types of thought: scientific thought, which is absolutely right, and ideological thought, which is absolutely wrong. He has not discovered the fact that a system of ideas, including economics, may rest on certain basic assumptions and convictions which are characteristic of, and exclusive to, a definite society, which inhere, as it were, in its life-structure and life-process, which make the total picture of reality dominating that society its very own, an expression of its very self, which cannot, in consequence, be easily transferred to other societies, and which make the ideas included in that system less absolutely right than, say, purely formal propositions, and yet do not, at the same time, make them absolutely wrong in the sense in which delusive or ideological thought is wrong. He fancies that if only the ideological element can be eliminated, a set of assertions will emerge which will be as scientific in nature and as unconditional in validity as the assertion that twice two is four and thrice three is nine. So far as one can tell from his text, Myrdal had not, by 1929, heard of the sociology of knowledge; but he had heard of ideology, and he was determined to drive it for ever from the temple of economic science. His book is a typical example of the literature that has sprung from the desire, which asserts itself again and again and runs like a succession of waves through whole sciences, to 'unmask' ideologies and to cleanse thought from this evil contamination.

It is a sad story which Myrdal has to tell. He finds 'normative bias' throughout the length and breadth of traditional economics; 'the elements of political doctrine' are everywhere 'lurking in accepted solutions'; 'Ricardo's theoretical work' in particular 'was largely a rationalization of his practical political convictions' (53, X, 114). There has been, all along, widespread 'use of normative ideas as links in a scientific argument', and the consequence is that many a chain of reasoning which started in sound truth ended in foul error without the deviation from the straight and narrow path being so much as suspected, let alone detected. An example of this is the egalitarianism of people like Jevons which is indeed clad in the trappings of science but has as little claim to them as any political slogan. His theory of value is impeccable so long as it applies the hedonistic calculus to the individual. It is true—absolutely true—that the second pear or the second pound gives its owner less pleasure than the first pear and the first pound, and that, if he wishes to maximize his enjoyment, he must so arrange things that all consumptions and gratifications are broken off at the point where they give the same amount of benefit. But is it equally legitimate to push on from this sound insight and conclude, as so many utilitarians have done, that *social* utility will be maximized if all members of the community have the same income, if all are put into a position where they can proceed in their consumptions and gratifications to the same margin? No, says Myrdal. The link between the individualistic and the social theory of diminishing marginal utility is unsound, for it rests on an assumption, not a fact. The assumption is that all people's utility functions are the same, that Jack will feel in matters of utility very much like John and Jill. But it can never be convincingly demonstrated that this is so; in the nature of things, proof is out of the question as we have no method for the interpersonal comparison of sentiments or psychic experiences. What induces the utilitarians to proceed as if we did have such a method, and as if that method had proved their assumption scientifically, is simply a political prejudice of theirs. All men *ought* to be equal, they feel; all men *are* equal, they say. A *non sequitur* this of the first order. 'The subjective theory of value,' Myrdal writes, 'like other theories with a normative intention, makes it appear possible to deduce, by logical process, rational political principles [here egalitarianism in distribution] from its analysis of social phenomena [here the theorem of diminishing marginal utility]. . . . Such a deduction must involve a fallacy somewhere; some link must be omitted in the chain of reasoning from positive analysis to normative conclusions. In this case, the fallacy is the assumption of interpersonal comparisons of feelings. Analysis is based on incomparability, conclusions on comparability' (88). Jevons allows a political tendency to enter into his argument, and he makes it do service for a scientific axiom. And thus it is that the ideological element, the normative bias, becomes the undoing of science.

But the trouble just exposed is not the worst. Jevons's doctrine is at any rate half true; it travels along the scientific highway for a good distance, and only then deviates into the ideological byway which it should have avoided. Yet sometimes the ideological element is at the very root of an argument and informs it all through like a poison which spreads from the subsoil through a whole tree: 'The basic concepts are frequently charged with normative implications. Time and again attempts have been made to by-pass interest conflicts by the manner in which those basic concepts are defined. A precise definition of those concepts would, however, reveal that they are logically conditional. No definition can claim absolute and *a priori* validity. All definitions are tools which we construct in order to observe and analyse reality. . . . By operating with definitions which purport to be universally valid, people have often succeeded in making an implied political principle appear logically "correct". Psychologically, it is the other way round. The emotive force which is rationalized in the implied principle makes

56

the normative element that has been disguised in the definition appear to be absolute and "correct". The perpetual game of hide-and-seek in economics consists in concealing the norm in the concept. It is thus imperative to eradicate not only the explicit principles but above all the valuations tacitly implied by the basic concepts. Being concealed, they are more insidious and more elusive, and hence more likely to breed confusion' (192).

The very juxtaposition of these two passages shows where the weakness of Myrdal's analysis lies. He fails to distinguish between the entry of a normative element into a chain of reasoning (whether this entry be at an early point or later on), and the enclosure of this whole chain of reasoning within certain basic definitions which appear 'natural' and utterly unproblematic to the men who use them—or rather to the society in which they are used—and which no amount of honesty and no effort, however great, towards objectivity, towards liberation from preconception and prejudice could expose as unsound to the men whose world-view is couched in their terms and caught in their grip. The former case is the case of ideology; the latter is the province of the sociology of knowledge. Even the ideas enclosed in the latter may come to be impugned by societies other than the one which holds them; but they cannot be sensibly denied validity—validity as a matter of course —by the society which does hold them for they are in agreement with, and indeed an expression of, its very life-principle. Non-conformists there may be who will attack them even while they are holding sway; but such non-conformists will be *in* the society concerned rather than *of* it. They will logically have to take up their position, for the purposes of criticism, outside the inclusive social whole whose mental bases they wish to condemn. The men on the other hand who accept a certain social order and implement it by their mode of action must not be blamed for thinking in the mental modes which are implied in that order and reflect that mode, for this is but 'natural'. One might just as well ask them to jump over their own shadows.

There are then two tasks to be performed in studying, for instance, classical economics, not one only as Myrdal assumes: to find the ideologies that have crept into it, and to understand the intellectual bases on which it is built and which would remain—and remain unacceptable to an outside critic—even after the last ideology has been successfully removed. These bases are not simply 'scientific truths', i.e. absolute truths in the sense in which the propositions of the multiplication table are, but rather exemplify one particular world-view which is possible alongside others and which happened to fit in with, and to arise from, the principle or principles constitutive of the society which gave birth, *inter alia*, to classical economics. For both lines of investigation there is ample raw material.

57

Ideologies properly so called lie in general rather near the surface and can be easily detected by those whose eyes have been opened in the matter. If, for instance, the Physiocrats make propaganda for a *taxe unique* and say that it should fall on the land-owning nobles, whereas the farming community should be free from all fiscal burdens, the ideological element in and behind this doctrine stands out for all to see. Dr. Quesnay came from a family of commoner-gentleman-farmers, and he did not see why this class should find all the money to keep going the terrific waste of Paris and Versailles, or why the aristocracy should go scot-free. Similarly, there is a noticeable anti-landlordism in Ricardo. One need not be a Marxist to suspect that Ricardo's plea for free trade in bread-corn had something to do with the fact that he was a city-man in the double sense of a town-dweller (who wanted cheap bread for himself) and a city-of-London man, a capitalist (who wanted cheap bread for the workers). And it is pertinent to ask and important to investigate how far these ideological biases penetrated beyond such practical problems as tax and tariff-policy into the deeper, more theoretical layers of Quesnay's and Ricardo's thought.

However much one may desire to limit the operation of the ideological factor, the upshot of such an investigation would certainly not be a nil-report. Myrdal's book provides an instructive example. Few economists have been intellectually so honest as John Stuart Mill, a man of good will in every sense of the term. Now 'Mill rejected with indignation progressive taxation as a penalty on hard work and thrift, a pure theft and a glaring iniquity, but advocated in the same breath radical death duties, taxation of gifts, of unearned value increments, etc.' (170). So far as current earnings were concerned, then, Mill was in favour of inequality: proportional, not progressive taxation; so far as accumulated property was concerned, he was in favour of equalization: progressive, not merely proportional taxation, if not downright confiscation. Myrdal sees here (in our opinion rightly) 'the expression of political convictions', 'a bourgeois irritation' at work (168). Mill had ranged himself with the rising middle class. That middle class wanted to build up its wealth and resented any kind of taxation that would hinder them in their policy of *enrichissez-vous, messieurs*. But it also wanted to pull down the power-position of the landowning class, a position which rested partly, perhaps even mainly, on the large masses of property which the gentry had received from their parents and were anxious to hand on to their children, and so the bourgeoisie clamoured for high death-duties which would hurt the first estate rather than the third. Mill's policy can be summarized by saying that he wanted to favour wealth in construction, but not wealth in existence; hence his 'demand that that part of income which is saved should be exempted from taxation' (166)—perhaps the most tell-tale facet of his argument.

Myrdal pillories him for his inconsistency. 'Although he justified death duties with Bentham's argument of the diminishing marginal utility of income and of the desirability of a more equal income distribution, it never occurred to him that progressive taxation could be advocated on the same grounds.' But it is not as a theoretician that Mill thinks and speaks in all this; it is as a politician, a man with an axe to grind. 'His proposals for distributional reforms through certain tax measures . . . are directed against certain incomes' regarded as 'unjust' (171). There are, then, definite value-judgments at the basis of this part of Mill's economics, value-judgments which one party is as entitled to accept as another to reject. The conclusions derived from these valuations are not scientific but ideological—ideologically tainted. If the doctrine of ideology is brought to bear on such ideas, it is within its rights; it is doing the job which it is called upon to do.

But it is not true, as Myrdal assumed in 1929, that when the hunt for ideologies is brought to a successful conclusion and all the noxious influences are tracked down and driven out, there will remain in economics a pure, unproblematical, quasi-scientific truth akin to the truths of Euclidean geometry or textbook logic. For in the depths there works a principle of social determination [1] which has nothing whatsoever to do with resentments or aspirations or other interests of any kind. Joseph Schumpeter had an inkling of this when, in a passage of his *History of Economic Analysis*, he suggested that certain policies are expressions of bourgeois *interest*, while others are rather conceived '*in the bourgeois sense*',[2] i.e. flow from the bourgeois vision of the world. But if this is true of political ideas, it is still more true of theoretical conceptions. The best example is perhaps the deep-seated individualism of the classical economists, what some German authors have called, rather graphically, their atomism. The market is a meeting-place of isolated individuals who create an order by contract-making. Order is not a pattern pre-existent; it is a pattern emergent. Here we have an *is*-sentence which does not come from an *ought*-sentence; a crystallization of social and economic thinking in one particular sense, the bourgeois sense.

Perhaps it will be said by the pan-ideologists that there is, after all, an ought-sentence in the background of this purely factual assertion of

---

[1] In speaking, for convenience sake, of a 'principle of social determination', we do *not* mean to introduce, either openly or by covert suggestion, the idea of determinism in the philosophical connotation of the term. We mean at this point (as also in the sequel) neither unilateral nor univocal nor absolute or inescapable determination, but are merely suggesting that some sort of connection exists between social life on the one hand and thought-contents and thought-processes on the other. It is of course a problem of prime importance to determine the nature and stringency of this connection, and ch. 6 will be devoted to the discussion and solution of this question. [2] 1954, 406.

the atomistic character of the social order: the bourgeoisie felt that they ought to be free (e.g. free to maximize their profits), and so they pressed the view that the market-participants must be free if the market is to function. But this seems rather far-fetched. The 'ideologists' of the bourgeoisie were very often intellectuals who did not feel that way and, according to pan-ideologism itself, could not feel that way—unless, of course, one dismisses them all as mere hack-writers, an opinion which would be utterly unrealistic. No, Adam Smith was not a hack-writer; he was not anybody's hack-writer. But he happened to live in an age when the dominant world-view was going through one particular phase of concrete specification which implied, among other things, a conscious sociological atomism. Maybe another illustration will show this even better. The classical economists defined man, explicitly or implicitly, as a pleasure-seeking, pain-avoiding animal, a pleasure-maximizer and pain-minimizer. This is not an 'absolutely' true image of man: the type of man who is under the spell of traditionalism, for instance, will tend to maximize rest rather than enjoyment. But it is equally not an 'ideological' image of man. There is no selfish or sectional interest behind it. When Adam Smith says that all human beings are born with a quasi-instinctual drive to better their condition, he is making a pure *is*-statement; it is absurd to suspect that he or any of his disciples for some reason *desired* man to be a born utilitarian, that there was in his subconscious mind an *ought*-drive of this kind. In actual fact, the great economist was rather hostile to self-seeking. Now if it be argued that the hidden interest consisted in the attempt to justify bourgeois money-grabbing, that Smith said in effect: what is, must be, and is therefore natural, then we are attributing to him a mental life (conscious *or* subconscious) which he never had.

No, it was not interest, personal or transferred, that inspired his doctrine of man: it was rather the fact that in his day man's character had taken shape in a certain way, that out of the innumerable possibilities inherent in human nature one had come to pass and achieved actuality, that *homo sapiens* had narrowed himself down into *homo rationalis* and *homo oeconomicus* rather than into *homo traditionalis*, *homo poeticus*, or *religiosus*, or any other of his possible configurations. It was precisely Smith's freedom from pre-conceptions which determined him to write of man as he did—to conceive him as one who wanted to 'better his condition', as one inclined to 'truck and barter'. For such was the reality which he saw before his eyes—a reality which he neither tried to justify nor yet to condemn, but simply to understand.

One last example will perhaps clinch our argument. One finds in many authors of the age of Adam Smith, in Archdeacon Paley for instance, the opinion that monogamy is 'natural', that it rests, even in man, not on convention but on instinct, as it does among rabbits or robins. Whence this opinion accepted at the time as a scientific truth? The pan-ideologists, especially those from the pseudo-Marxist fold, will be quick to argue that when property-rights are of paramount importance, the desire for a legitimate heir will be equally strong, and the sanctity of marriage will become an appropriate ideology. But it is ludicrous to credit the good Archdeacon with preoccupations of this kind—they were absent both from his conscious and his unconscious mind. But, living as he did, in an individualistic-atomistic society, it was 'natural' for him to conceive of the marriage contract as a contract between two individuals—a contract for which everyone in society could be presumed eligible in view of the fact that Nature or Providence had decreed that boys and girls should be born in approximately equal numbers. This view was as 'natural' for him, and as free from ideology, in a setting which had in fact made monogamy the norm as a different view is 'natural' and normal for the Kikuyu.

The trouble with Myrdal's discussion is that many of the characteristics of classical economics in which he smells ideological bias, have not sprung from 'the political element' in it but from a basic intellectual construct which was merely a reflection, and on the whole an honest and realistic reflection, of the world as people in 1776 or thereabouts in fact perceived it. It is not so true as he would have us believe that 'analytical ideal types' (in the sense of thought-models) are apt to be connected with 'political ideals' (in the sense of interest-inspired daydreams); nor indeed is it fair to say that 'there has always been a tendency in economics to gloss over interest conflicts' (104, 193). It certainly cannot be denied that economic thought, like all thought, is subject to the pervasive influence of contemporary society, but it is constrained and bound by its facts as much as by any practical or political aims it may inspire in those who belong to it, whether individuals or classes. In other words, social influences condense themselves into genuine *is*-sentences born of a pure desire to see the truth and nothing but the truth, as well as into spurious *is*-sentences behind which there lurks a half-hidden or wholly-hidden *ought*.

Let us be brave and take for our *objectum demonstrationis* the very concept which Myrdal pillories most as wish-determined—the belief that maximum welfare will be achieved in a society under conditions of unrestricted, unstinted liberty. If we want to find out whether a theory of this complexion could have been formed under the guidance of factual impressions as well as under the stimulus of interested tendencies, we must ask two questions: firstly whether we are able, in the abstract, to imagine a social order in which this theorem would be true; and, secondly, whether in the concrete the society in which this theorem was formed, elaborated and propagated, i.e. French-English-Scottish society *circa* 1776, had in fact succeeded, to some extent at any rate, in realizing a pattern of this kind. To the first question, a positive answer can clearly be given; and we can also say what prime condition would have to be fulfilled in order to give the society concerned the chance of maximizing material satisfaction. It is the realization of equality. If we imagine, by way of thought-experiment, a society of this kind—a society in which, as Rousseau expressed it, nobody is strong enough to exploit his neighbour, and nobody so weak as to be forced to submit to exploitation—we see that such a society would be characterized by an equilibrium of individual forces, and from this equilibrium of individual forces there would spring a harmony of interests. A man could only gain business and enrich himself in a world so conceived and constituted if he offered the best wares at a given price, or the cheapest wares of a given quality, and hence his enrichment would flow from, and could only flow from, genuine service to the rest of the community.

Myrdal himself admits that in this hypothetical situation most of the propositions of classical economics which he seeks to 'unmask' as 'ideological' would in fact be realistic, in particular the central assertion of the spontaneous maximization of social utility which would not even need psychological and mathematical demonstration. 'If it were true', he says, 'that the interests of individuals are always and everywhere harmonious, so that everyone, by promoting his own interests, promotes automatically the interests of all, there would be no need for a [specious theorem concerning the] social summation [of individual happiness]. It would not be required for the determination of social utility. . . . However the computation is carried out [under the assumptions made], maximum social welfare would be obtained simply by a complete realization of laissez-faire' (43 *seq.*). But, he argues, the assumptions made are simply projections of the pipe-dreams of the classical economists; they rest on their idea of the world as it ought to be, not on their observation of the world as it is; and hence the whole deduction is politics rather than economics, propaganda rather than science, ideology rather than factual analysis.

This brings us to our second question—indeed, to our crucial question. Is it really true that around 1760–70, when Quesnay and Smith stood forth as the champions of a doctrine of the natural harmony of economic interests, their theory was utterly unrealistic because equality was an ideal rather than a fact, a political demand rather than an observable datum? Let us admit without demur that the society in which the classical economists moved was not egalitarian, that it showed great differences in wealth as well as great differences in power. But that is not the point. Theorists have never dealt with the complex reality lying before their eyes; they have always analysed a model abstracted from that reality, a model in which the essential features of reality are magnified and the accidental ones minimized or even omitted. Max Weber, when he elaborated his concept of ideal types, did not introduce a new idea which had just come to him; what he did was to formulate the theory of a methodological device which had always been applied in practice. Now the features which Quesnay and Smith concentrated on in elaborating their own 'ideal type' for analysis were, not surprisingly, the elements in reality struggling up into prominence, rather than those in prominence but ostensibly doomed to decay and extinction. Certainly, there were enormous masses of property concentrated in individual hands, giving those who held them the whip-hand over their neighbours and making nonsense of the theorem of maximum social utility. Even so, the assumption of equality in wealth and position which this theorem presupposes for its validity, was more than just a utopian dream. If it was not reality, it was reality in the making. The huge estates still in existence were all due to feudalism, either directly, as in the case of the aristocratic land-owners, the offspring of the warrior-nobles of the Norman or Frankish hosts, or indirectly, as in the case of the commoner stock-owners who had climbed into their privileged position through the grant of patents and other exclusive rights on the part of kings. But feudalism was manifestly on the way out; everybody could see that in 1760 or 1770. And what would the world be like when it had faded away? It was on the answer to this question that the classical economists (those of the eighteenth century at least) based the ideal type of social organization which they analysed and discussed in their books. After feudal rights and exclusive privileges had ceased to exist, they felt, society would become a society of peasants or independent farmers and artisans—a society of petty existences which would offer a near approach to the ideal of equality.

As for the *anciens riches*, Quesnay's ideas differed from those of Adam Smith. Quesnay's France had not yet moved as near to democracy as had Smith's Britain; he could not yet imagine a world ruled and run by the middle class; he still thought that the aristocracy was necessary as a *classe disponible*, a class 'at the disposal' of the community for the purposes of government and administration; and his sight was also distorted by the lopsided nature of the contemporary French economy which, under Colbert's influence, had developed a flourishing luxury industry but no appropriately strong and modernized agriculture, a fact which dominated the thought of the Physiocrats and gave it its characteristic one-sidedness. Quesnay therefore presents a picture in which political inequality at any rate is still taken as normal. But in Smith, we find the same or a similar picture without this asymmetry. A rough-and-ready equality among the independent individuals who compose society is the norm; deviations are just deviations. The society of peasants or farmers and artisans which is round the corner is a legitimate object of discussion for the economist. Why should he speak of what is, when in reality it is already a thing of the past? Why should he not speak of it, rather, in terms of what is to come?

Much of the technical detail of classical economics can easily be explained by reference to this basic construct which it has in view and to which it is referring throughout, the labour theory of value for instance, which gives Myrdal such frequent occasion for caustic criticism. Why is labour singled out as the only value-creating factor? Because in a society of peasants and artisans, land is the property of, and merely an appendage to, the peasant, and tools are the property of, and merely an appendage to, the artisan; in other words, because rent and interest have no independent existence in such a society and are, *quâ* cost-items and income-categories, totally submerged in labour. Myrdal thinks he can show up the unrealistic nature of the doctrine of Adam Smith by referring to the fact that he 'had to draw for a justification of his labour-cost principle on an ideal state of nature in which there was neither accumulated capital nor private property in land' (72), i.e. on a never-never land like the town of Titipu. Two answers can be made to such a taunt. Firstly, Smith did not 'have to' make use of the state-of-nature fiction; he did so in the style of his time because the fiction was a convenient expository device. And secondly—what is much more important—the assumed society without private property in land and capital was merely a simpler and more transparent case of the same sort of society as the anticipated society of peasants and artisans. In that primitive society, land and capital did not *exist*, so to speak, as cost-items and income-categories; in the society of peasants and artisans they did not *appear* as independent cost-items and income-categories because they were merged with, and sunk in, labour. And, in particular, they did not appear as substantive elements on the market and in the determination of exchange-ratios because they cancelled out, as it were. When a shoemaker had his shoes to offer and a tailor his clothes, and they argued about the proper way of exchanging their wares, they would both understandably concentrate in argument on the labour contained in them. 'You must give me two pairs of shoes for one suit: it takes six days to make a suit, but only three to make a pair of shoes.' It would have been no use insisting on the cost of needles and pressing irons, for the shoemaker would have countered by referring (and with equal justification) to the cost of hammers and lasts. (It is still some such consideration which is behind Ricardo's basic assumption that the capital equipment per worker is the same in all industries, and that capital is for that reason without influence on exchange-ratios and exchange-values.) The fact is that in a market on which only artisans are operating, gear (capital goods) is *nothing* apart from labour. Hence the labour theory of value, and much besides, is simply an implication of, and a logical deduction from, the social order reflected in

64

the image with which the classical economists are operating—a society of petty producers, of peasants or farmers, and artisans.

It cannot be held against this mental construct that it proved in the end to be a delusion; that capitalism produced a degree of inequality no less extreme, and no less fatal to the theorem of maximum social utility, than feudalism. For these developments were as yet in the future and unforeseeable. Nor can it be said—and this is the decisive point for our discussion—that Quesnay and Smith were taken in and thrown off the narrow path of realism by self- or class-interest or political wishes and day-dreams. Certainly, they had somewhat sanguine expectations of the bourgeois future, but these were inspired by the common human quality of hope rather than by any partial interest or political prejudice. It is most important to remember here that those who had no liking for the anticipated bourgeois future (either because they thought it would be one of low culture, as did the Marquis de Chastellux, or because they had an idea that it would produce its own brand of social disharmony, as did the Abbé Mably) also based their judgment on an 'ideal type' of society of the same kind as that established in the mind of Quesnay and Smith.[1] No, the vision of Adam Smith was not ideologically distorted. Its fault was not that it fused together observation and wish-image, but that it allowed anticipation too large a share in comparison with cool hardheadedness. In so far as it talked about an expected future rather than about the immediate present, it was certainly unrealistic; but it was not the un-realism of the ideologist. Extrapolation is a sin, but it is not necessarily the sin of the man who has an axe to grind.

However, we must try not to exaggerate. We hope to have proved that the mental construct at the basis of Smithian economics could and would have been reached by all observers with minds turned towards the future in 1770, even if their conscious and subconscious minds had been completely free of distorting influences. But we have not said, and will not say, that ideological elements were completely absent from contemporary thought. We are trying to rebut the claims of pan-ideologism, not to defeat the legitimate claim of the doctrine of ideology. Even Quesnay, as the son of a gentleman farmer, even Smith, as the son of a man of moderate means, may have had in their heads highly flavoured resentments against the aristocracy or highly coloured aspirations for the future. It is the task of the historian of ideas to find out whether they did or not, and to what extent their world-view was formed and deformed by such ideological influences. According to his factual findings, these thinkers will then have to be handed over to the unmaskers of ideological thought for condemnation, or to the sociologists of

---

[1] Some light is thrown on all this, though somewhat obliquely, in my book *America: Ideal and Reality* of 1947.

knowledge for defence. But one thing is certain: that such an issue must not be prejudged. Nobody can say without the most searching inquiry how far any concrete thought-structure is due to the rationalization of selfish or sectional interests, and how far to that contemporary crystallization (or near-crystallization) of social life in certain forms which will determine human ideas as well as human actions, and which is the proper subject-matter of the sociology of knowledge in contradistinction to the doctrine of ideology. But it is perhaps not too wild a guess to say that there have at all times been men who have served the truth rather than any other interest, and whose subconscious was nearly as empty of poisonous matter as their conscious minds. Perhaps they have even been the majority of those who have put pen to paper and produced books. In any case, it is they and they alone who are of focal interest to the sociology of knowledge. As for the others, those who are politicians rather than seekers of the truth, they will enter into the picture only after their mental products have been cleansed of all ideological dross—if and in so far as anything remains after that cleansing operation.

It is a fact to be recorded with the greatest possible pleasure that Gunnar Myrdal seems himself to have come round to this point of view since 1929, when *The Political Element in the Development of Economic Theory* was first published. 'The radical cure must lie in research without preconceived normative ideas', he had written in the Preface to the first (Swedish) edition. But the Preface to the English edition of 1953 shows a different attitude: 'Throughout the book', he says in candid and commendable self-criticism, 'there lurks the idea that when all metaphysical elements are radically cut away, a healthy body of positive economic theory will remain, which is altogether independent of valuations. . . . This implicit belief in the existence of a body of scientific knowledge acquired independently of all valuations is, as I now see it, naïve empiricism. Facts do not organize themselves into concepts and theories just by being looked at; indeed, except within the framework of concepts and theories, there are no scientific facts but only chaos. There is an inescapable *a priori* element in all scientific work. Questions must be asked before answers can be given. The questions are an expression of our interest in the world, they are at bottom valuations. Valuations are thus necessarily involved already at the stage when we observe facts and carry on theoretical analysis, and not only at the stage when we draw political inferences from facts and valuations' (VII, XV). These sentences, as the reader will see in due course, are a most happy and striking anticipation of the point of view which will be systematically developed in the third chapter of this book. Here it need only be pointed out that the *a priori* of which Myrdal speaks is not a personal but a social *a priori*—one that belongs, not to the individual mind, but to the social framework within which the individual mind is functioning. The 'valuations' to which he is referring are not those value-judgments of which we are thinking when we speak of prejudices due to selfish or sectional preoccupations; they are the value-system which precedes all selfish and sectional preoccupations and indeed all thought and action, they are the organizing principles at the basis of contemporary society, they are what makes the society in question what it is and thereby determines its practice as well as its theory. But more of this in its proper place.

The separation of the ideological element from the area of social determination is probably much more difficult to carry out in a science such as economics than in some other branches of learning, for economics is prominently concerned with such highly 'interesting' matters as the distribution of the national income, the incidence of taxation, etc. In history, for instance, where we are one more step removed from the battles of the day, it should be easier to discern what is propaganda (conscious or unconsciously inspired) and what is not, what is due to the socially determined viewpoint of the historian concerned. Not that the ideological element is any weaker in historiography; unfortunately it is not. History books have, throughout the ages, been favourite vehicles for all sorts of prejudices and ideals. But the ideological element is more manifest, more naked. Sometimes, indeed, a historian comes to notice it himself. Thus Heeren has written of his *Geschichte des europäischen Staatensystems und seiner Kolonien* of 1809 that 'on its appearance . . . the circumstances of the times had a great influence. It came out at the moment when Europe was in chains. Yet it nevertheless presented itself from the beginning as the history of a system of free states. To keep its memory alive, . . . seemed to me important.' And he added, well aware of the fact that his work had something of the political pamphlet about it: 'The first edition was sold out within a year.' In 1819 he wrote in the third edition: 'In the meantime I have seen the victory of the opinions which I had the intention of upholding.' [1] Such direct avowals are, of course, rare. Heeren's contemporary Niebuhr, for instance, would probably have been surprised if anyone had told him that ideological influences were noticeable in his *Römische Geschichte* of 1811/12. Yet something of the nationalistic ferment of the day and of the hate of Napoleon's tyranny is there and can be clearly seen.

Indeed, so strong is the ideological element in historiography, that it colours whole stretches of its development. In Germany, the struggle between *grossdeutsch* and *kleindeutsch*, i.e. between those who wanted a *Reich* including, or alternatively excluding, Austria asserted itself in many ways and spoilt many a good book. Heeren disliked not only

[1] Hashagen in *Versuche zu einer Soziologie des Wissens*, 1924, 249 *seq.*

Napoleon but also the Middle Ages; but when he ran down the Middle Ages he often meant Austria and her Catholicism rather than the Holy Roman Empire. This line of thought later reached its acme in Heinrich von Sybel. On the other side of the fence Ficker's eulogy of the Middle Ages implied the assertion that there could be no deeper meaning to German history unless it tended towards the south and found its true vocation around and beyond the Alps. Here again ideology can be seen to penetrate deeply into the study of seemingly remote subjects. Droysen's book on Alexander the Great (1833) draws a politically inspired parallel between the 'historic mission' of the kingdom of Macedonia and the 'historic mission' of the kingdom of Prussia. Sometimes the ideological element is social rather than narrowly political in character. Not only Marxist, but even typically 'academic' historians have allowed class consciousness to enter into and colour their history. The Italian Carlo Antoni has noted a case in point. 'What distinguished the historians of Rome, Niebuhr and Mommsen, from the other German historians of the nineteenth century,' he writes, 'was their interest in matters social. Their history of Rome was the history of a land-conquering peasant race which was being exploited and paralysed in its military potency by a rapacious aristocracy. But both of them, in recalling the fate of the plebs under the Gracchi, have raised an indirect accusation against the agrarian grandees of their own age and country, the Prussian Junkers . . . Niebuhr tries to show the close connection between the form and distribution of property and the organization of the foot soldiers, the nerve of Roman military power . . . Mommsen, for his part, justified the monarchy of the Caesars by the need to wrest the direction of the state from an aristocracy which, in its class egoism, had become unfit for ruling and pernicious.' [1]

French historiography has been equally subject to political and social influences of an ideological nature; it has always been divided, the line of division being the French Revolution and its Napoleonic aftermath. To some the events of 1789–1815 were the dawn of a great age, to others its twilight.[2] 'Nearly all French political parties from the extreme right to the extreme left . . . have carried on contemporary and day-to-day politics under the mask of historians of the Revolution.'[3] In England, the conflict and contrast between Whigs and Tories has also left its mark on the writing of history, as Butterfield has shown in *The Englishman and His History* (1945). Indeed, it was not only over English history that their clash became noticeable, but even Greek history. To be for or against the people—or populace—of Athens—that was the question which divided the two camps.

[1] *Vom Historismus zur Soziologie*, 1952, 168 *seq.*
[2] Cf. The thesis of Kate Stark, *Louis Blanc als Historiker der Französischen Revolution*, Hamburg, 1934.   [3] Hashagen, *loc. cit.*, 249.

In all these cases, the ideological element is nearly as plain as a pikestaff and correspondingly easy to touch, to hold and to throw off. But historiography also shows us the non-ideological element of social determination. Ranke is a good example here. Though by no means free from all practical preoccupations—he was a *Kleindeutscher* and a Protestant and consequently had no love of Catholicism or of the House of Habsburg—these are not highly coloured and always well controlled. And if it is said that his *History of the Popes* owed its quiet mood to the fact that it was written in the period of calm after the confessional conflict of 1837,[1] it can be asserted with even more justification that it was as irenic as it was because it was the work of a quiet man. Indeed, it has been said that Ranke was essentially a frigid person to whom political ideas and ideals meant very little—a man whose subconscious as well as conscious mind was largely undisturbed by the play of passion. Anyone who has read his tomes will be inclined to agree with this estimate of Ranke's personal psychology. But his whole work is based on one unconscious, subliminal conviction, namely, his conviction of the primacy of foreign affairs over domestic developments. What has happened in history is due less to the struggle for power inside states than to the struggles for power between them. His whole picture of the past is determined by this basic assumption or attitude. In it we see, not a political or interested prejudice (for what can it be to a man, in terms of politics or interest, whether the one sphere had had the ascendancy in the past or the other?), but rather a social pre-judgment, a preconceived but merely implied conviction that had been inspired by the contemporary facts of social reality.

Any study of the background of Ranke's thought will reveal that the scene was dominated by the search of the European powers for some sort of equilibrium. The great problem of survival lay there, not in domestic tensions. It was because the states of Europe, each a society closed up in itself and antagonistic to the others, were *in fact* absorbed by their painful manœuvring for position in the eternal struggle for power (absorbed in an inescapable and engrossing task which forced them to shelve the solution of internal difficulties, the questions of social reform) that Ranke developed the matter-of-fact conviction that history must *in theory* be seen and analysed in terms of foreign rather than of home policy. We simply behold in Ranke the intellectual reflection of the centuries of social and political practice which Ranke's disciple Friedrich Meinecke characterizes as the age of *raison d'état*, of Machiavellism, the age *par excellence* of power politics.

As a last example of pure social determination of thinking without ideological bias at its root we can quote the case of Freudianism. 'The Freudian theory', Sprott has written, 'is applicable, in so far as it is

[1] Hashagen, *loc. cit.*, 246.

applicable at all, to a patrilineal culture with relatively small household units and a long and close dependence of children on the care and approbation of only one or two persons. It is not applicable to many matrilineal societies, nor to societies where a child is attended to by a larger number of adults indifferently.' [1] If one takes the Freudian system as a whole, then the presence in it of ideological matter cannot be doubted; indeed, this matter is fairly deep-seated, for the desire to throw off inhibiting, often disease-generating repressions arising from the authoritarian element in social life is present throughout. Yet these wish-determined thought-processes start out from a picture of reality which is not, in and by itself, wish-determined—which is not para-theoretical, but genuine. In the late-Victorian Vienna where Freud grew up, life had realized, out of the indefinite number of potential family forms, one pattern in particular—the small family dominated by the male element, the breadwinner,—imbued with the characteristic high-powered internal pressure-system which we find reflected, not only in Freud's world-picture, but generally in contemporary literature, scientific and artistic. In so far as Freud thinks in terms of this set-up, his thought is indeed socially determined (for no Zuni would think as he did), but it is not ideologically deflected from the truth; indeed, it *is* the truth precisely *because* of its social determination. No other categories of thought would have been appropriate, in the concrete social situation in which he found himself, than the very categories from which he started—the categories of life.

(*b*) SOCIAL DETERMINATION AND IDEOLOGICAL DISTORTION: THE CASE OF COEXISTENCE

We hope to have established, by the preceding argument, that social determination of thought is one thing, and ideological determination quite another. This conviction is basic to the present book, and not one jot or tittle of it will, in principle, be abated. But the social scientist, unlike his colleague from the science faculty, is not confronted with an easily and neatly analysable reality, a reality which will allow itself to be cut up, docketed and accommodated in pigeon-holes; on the contrary, his field of observation shows, as one of its most prominent features, the process of syncretism—the flowing together of innumerable discrete tendencies whose respective causative influence on the observable phenomena can hardly ever be determined with any exactness. He is like the man in John Stuart Mill's famous example who, when he has cut a piece of paper with the help of a pair of scissors, is unable to say which blade has actually done the cutting—the upper or the lower, and must be satisfied with stating that both have been jointly responsible

[1] *Science and Social Action*, 1954, 24.

for the result. In the same way the historian of ideas, when he wants to investigate any particular system of thought put forward in the past and shed light on its origins, will find it difficult or even impossible to say whether its concrete form and content was determined more by the social perspective from which its author looked upon the world, or by wish-images, resentments or other psychological impedimenta which he carried in his heart or in his head.

But unfortunately the confusion does not end there. However neatly we may construct our categories, they cut across each other not only in practice, but in principle also. There is a sense in which it can be said that ideological thought springs from a value-judgment and is thus prejudiced, whereas socially determined thought does not and hence is free from taint; but there is another sense in which it must be admitted that socially determined thought, too, is based on an antecedently existing order of values. The very concept of social determination implies such a tie. Social determination means that thought is determined by the contemporary pattern of social life; but the latter in turn is determined by the fundamental values which the society concerned is pursuing. Indeed, the whole thesis of the sociology of knowledge, namely, that there is a vital correspondence between the substructure of practice and the superstructure of theory, between life and thought, rests on the (assumed) fact that the same order of values works itself out, both in action and in speculation. This will become much clearer in chapter 3, where the theoretical gist of the sociology of knowledge will be systematically exposed. Here it is our duty to show wherein the similarity and the dissimilarity of ideological and socially determined thought consists. It does not consist in the fact that ideological thought is value-bound and socially determined thought is value-free. Value-free thinking may be an ideal, but it is certainly nowhere a reality. The most cold-hearted and cool-headed scientist, as he measures rainfall densities or ascertains specific weights, is still actuated by some wish-image, some emotion, some more than scholarly preoccupation—be it only the desire to understand and thereby to master the world (an eminently practical inspiration!). Just as *l'art pour l'art* is still the pursuit of a value, namely beauty, so 'science for its own sake' is still science for the sake of a value, namely truth—and all the power which it can give. A completely value-free universe would be a universe without thought and without action; a world in which human beings could not exist.

No, the difference does not lie there. It lies in the fact that the valuations at the root of ideologies are only psychologically subliminal, whereas the valuations at the basis of socially determined ideas are both psychologically and socially subliminal. We can, in principle, get rid of the former; the socially completely adjusted and integrated individual (a type whom we can at least imagine in all purity, and to which some

71

people at any rate come fairly close) would have a mind unclouded by ideological influences. But his thought would all the more plainly reflect the social order (and through it its implied value-system) in its contents and in its processes. And of this social determination we cannot empty the mind at all; for if we did, we should only succeed in emptying it completely, rendering it a blank, that is—dissolving it. Our mind can as little function in a social vacuum as our body can in a physical vacuum. But the normal social space is as much pervaded by social valuations, as the normal physical space is pervaded by air.

But if this is so, are we not then compelled to conclude that socially determined thought is just as prejudiced as ideological thought? The answer is: no. And this for the simple reason that ideological thought is determined by a striving for what ought to be and hence is not, whereas socially determined thought is determined by a recognition of that which is—one might almost say, by the mind's functioning within the framework of that which is—and hence is in agreement with reality. Both ideological and socially determined thought are based on antecedently conceived value-systems, but whereas the values behind ideologies are values yet to be realized, values still in the air, the values behind socially determined thought are values already realized, values that have come down to earth, values incarnate—in a word, as the philosophers have it, value-facts. This should be clear. But a difficulty remains. Or rather, a new difficulty crops up when we go over from the consideration of a closed and simple social system to the study of the interrelations between social systems or to that of internally riven, complex super-systems.

Socially determined thought is not delusive, but it is a crystallized kind of thought; it is in the grip of a principle of historical specifica-tion. This has important consequences. We easily understand what is said and done within the universe of meaning to which we belong (which is also our universe of practical action and experience, our social world); but, just because our minds have been thus conditioned, we do not find it at all easy to understand what is said and done within another universe of meaning (within another social world)—by the African bushman, for instance, or medieval man. What is meaningful to other societies, is meaningless to ours. We lack the key, as it were, in which other lives and thoughts are set. To this problem, much of chapter 4 will be devoted. But here we must note that it *is* a problem only to the man who is determined to rise superior—if he can, and in so far as he can—to human limitations. For most people, there is no problem at all. They meet the mental products of other societies with uncomprehending hostility. The rites most sacred to the bushman are to them empty hocus pocus, the rites most sacred to the medieval period sheer obscurantism. The reason is that our thought is not only determined by, but also committed to, our own society. We are emotionally as well as intellectually involved in the social life that has bred and made us, we are—in a way—prejudiced in its favour, prejudiced in favour of the terms of life and thought and value in which our social life is ordered and organized.

Thus the difference between socially determined thought and ideology is not as great as it appeared at first, once we overstep the borderline around a closed social circle. And yet our analysis has been confirmed rather than controverted by the argument of the last two or three pages. For the 'natural' prejudice against the other social order, its code and its mentality, is, in principle, as conquerable as any ideological bias. The only question is: how? how can we rise superior to our limitations? In other words: what is it that happens when we try honestly to fathom the meaning of the thought-products of other societies? Surely, what happens is that we abandon, *pro tanto*, the social order to which we belong, that we are so to speak stepping out of it and entering into a wider social framework which embraces both 'our own' and the 'alien' social life. We are moving away from the stricter embodiments of our life- and thought-pattern towards a vaguer structure which can contain in itself more than one potentiality or half-actuality. We are loosening our adherence to our original value-system and begin to admit another value-system alongside it as, in principle, equally legitimate. If we refuse to do so, i.e. to leave our own social matrix and all it stands for, if we look at alien life (and thought) in terms of our own unmodified social determinations, we shall never understand it; in fact, we shall never be properly in contact with it. For what we shall be dealing with will be our society's view of the alien society, rather than that alien society itself.

In order to comprehend the alien society as it really is, human contact must first be established. But the establishing of human contact is really the taking up of a new kind of social life—a social life extremely slight, shadowy, tenuous, but yet a kind of social life. It will resemble social life in those societies of which the constituent parts, for instance the constituent social classes, have drifted so far away from each other in their lives that there is hardly any mutual understanding left (only that in this latter case the tendency is negative, i.e. towards a dissolution of the social bond, whereas in the former case it is positive, i.e. towards the development of social integration). Now in such a constellation, the two social and thought systems that have come into contact may enter into competition with each other. Both may claim the allegiance of the individuals concerned; both may inspire hopes and fears, infatuations and resentments; and if so, both may give rise to ideologies, just as competing political parties do or warring social classes in an integrated society; and through such ideologies the thought of both connected societies and of the individuals respectively comprised by them may be distorted and deflected from the truth.

But—and that is the point—this need not happen. Ideologies need not enter the picture at all. We may get a complex society with a double or treble or multiple social determination of thought, and this multiple determination will be possible because, and in so far as, the composite society here will be made up of subsocieties which really qualify as societies, which are endowed with all, or most of, the features which constitute and carry a social cosmos. Admittedly it is difficult to imagine that the member-societies of such a social supersystem will not be living in tension with each other, will not generate enmities and ideals, negative and positive, which in turn will evoke ideological growths. But even if they do, this will not engulf all thinking, any more than it does in a non-complex society.

In the composite society of which we are thinking, three elements will have to be distinguished in the mental superstructure: (1) the area of social determination by the inclusive whole. This is essential if there is to be a functioning together of the subsocieties in practice and mutual understanding so far as thoughts and feelings are concerned (these two aspects of integration are really indivisible). The area of mutuality need not be large, but a minimum is necessary if the super-system concerned is to survive; (2) the area of social determination by the constituent subsocieties. We must think of the relation between (1) and (2) as a relationship of theme and variations. The variations may all be close to the theme, and then we have a well-integrated supersystem. Medieval society may serve as an approximate example. Or the variations may be far from the theme, so far that only the keenest ear can discover the linking pattern underneath the disharmonious strains, and then we have an ill-integrated supersystem. Modern society is none too far from this state of affairs. We are living, as Raymond Aron has expressed it, in a polytheistic world.[1] Some of us worship at one altar; others at quite different ones; there is a great confusion of tongues. There is a polymorphous value-system at the bottom of our social life, even though all the different values find accommodation within a common framework. The theme in this late-capitalistic world is still the twin-preoccupation with material values and the rationalization of existence; ascetic and ecstatic movements are still beyond our horizon. But how great are the variations within the capacious limits of the theme! People strive for such different aims, live such different lives and consequently think such different thoughts that social unity has become rather shadowy. Other societies have been much better integrated—both in fact and in thought. But even in a loosely-knit and ill-integrated supersystem such as our own some underlying unity of theme must

[1] *Die deutsche Soziologie der Gegenwart*, 1953, 118.

remain to correspond to the existing reality of social coexistence and co-operation. Even the Marxists have never denied this. 'For dialectical sociology', Warynski writes, 'the entities opposed to each other in society are more than mere causal contrasts: they are at the same time correlations within a superordinated whole . . . In spite of their antagonistic character, they are still at the same time functional elements, correlatively conditioning each other, of one and the same totality. Its laws are simultaneously laws of correlation as well as of contradiction.'[1]

On the other hand, even in a well-integrated supersystem, some mutual distance between the constituent parts will remain, and the members of its subsocieties will continue to be both mentally and emotionally committed to their own life and its appropriate thought. Mutual understanding inside them will be easier than across the borderlines; their own categories will be experienced as more 'natural' than those regarded as 'natural' by the associated neighbouring groups. This fact leads us close to, but not into, (3) the area of ideological determination, the thought-contents due to the political struggle and the class war and all the rest of it, together with the prejudices, in the narrower sense of the word, to which these contests between the subsocieties of an inclusive supersystem may give rise.

All this confronts us with a further problem. Which concrete subsocieties of a complex inclusive society will be able to produce their own social determination of thought, in other words, a concrete pattern of thought in accordance with their own specific point of view, which, for its part, will be determined by the group's own social life and its position inside the common social life of the supersystem?

In answering this question, let us note first of all that this is a problem which does not arise in connection with ideological thought. Many ideological distortions of the truth are due to purely private obsessions, ambitions, apprehensions and so on; naturally so, for we are here (as we must always remember) in the realm of psychology, individual or collective. Every man, every family, every village community, in short everybody can have an engrossing interest which may enter into their world-view and thought-processes and come to dominate them. But not everybody can achieve a 'concretization' of thought as the term is understood by the sociology of knowledge. The individual is clearly excluded from the very beginning; he cannot make his own mental universe *ab ovo*. When he is born, his mind is all potentiality, with no actuality.[2] Before it can function at all, it must be made concrete in some way: actualization and the attainment of concreteness are the

---

[1] *Die Wissenschaft von der Gesellschaft*, 1944, 88 *seq.*

[2] The text presupposes the empiricist position, to which we are on the whole inclined. But even if it were true that the human mind is endowed with certain

same process. Hence before an individual has a chance to form his own view of the world—indeed, before he conceives his first clear idea [1]— social determination has already done its work. Whether there is a possibility that he may later on stir out of the pattern thus imposed on him is a separate issue which will be considered in due course; we have already, by implication, answered it in the affirmative. But if the mind's structure is later recast in a different or an ampler mould, the mould will always be some form of social life, some social order which has set its mark upon the individual concerned. But it is not the individual only who is incapable of independently framing a concrete universe of thought in a private way of his own; many social formations, too, will be in the same position. Can we really imagine a firm or a family developing their own determination of ideas? Surely not, for these groupings function in life, and consequently in thought as well, within a social situation which is defined *for* them and not *by* them. We begin here to get a first glimpse of the answer to the question we have posed: only those social formations will be able to develop their own specific universes of thought by giving concrete form to human thinking which are—at least potentially—ways of life as well as ways of thought, which have it in them, so to speak, to mould and control human action and human interrelations as well as human ideas. This preliminary result is not, of course, surprising. It is implied, from the very beginning, in the basic idea of the sociology of knowledge.

These considerations open up vast territories for the history of ideas to conquer. Where, in fact, do we find those 'concretizations', those concrete patterns, of thought which define a specific way of thinking, a widely inclusive *imago mundi*, and what social groupings are behind them? For the present a general knowledge of historical development, and the speculative interpretation thereof, must do service for want of more satisfactory information. Few scholars would probably be inclined to deny that social classes qualify as subsocieties having enough reality-forming power in them to be able to achieve their own crystallization or social determination of thought. They have this power *in esse* in so far as they mould and control the lives of their members. The proletarian lives from early youth under a different pressure-system, a different system of social control, from that of his upper class contemporary; no wonder that his whole way of thinking differs accordingly. But social classes also have reality-forming power *in posse*, in so far, that is, as

---

innate ideas, not much would need to be changed in our argument. Innate ideas would indeed restrict the social determination of thought, but they would not do away with it in so far as the free and adjustable sector of the intellect is concerned.

[1] Vague awarenesses, such as are characteristic of the cerebral life of animals, are, of course, possible prior to the concrete moulding of thought of which we are speaking. They presuppose no structured mind, only a physical apparatus.

they also have a tendency to become more than moulders of the lives of their members and set out to shape the form of the inclusive society itself, the whole social universe. This latter point is important, as we shall see presently. In principle, it is the privilege of the inclusive, i.e. life-controlling society to make its own determination of thought; it is only when a class comes within striking distance of becoming the life-controlling power in the inclusive society that its specific mode of thinking ceases to be a minor variation of a major theme and assumes that closed and substantive character which we are wont to think of when speaking in terms of the sociology of knowledge. The development of a characteristically bourgeois world-view throughout the eighteenth century and its virtual perfection even before the French Revolution is the prime example we have in mind. The bourgeois way of *life* was ready beneath the aristocratic life which formed, in 1790, no more than a thin and brittle crust above it and was in consequence easily cracked and cast off; and so were the bourgeois ways of *thought*.

But our purpose here is not with relatively simple, but with essentially complex societies; hence our proper topic of discussion here should be a supersystem within which partial systems are permanently co-existent and in some degree co-ordinated. We must think of French society in 1740 rather than in 1790; or, better still, of capitalism or feudalism at the height of their evolution, when different classes and status groups were able to dwell together under a common roof. Without attempting to prejudge the results of historical inquiry into the actual thought-structures observable in such societies, let us ask what we might expect to find, on general grounds and from a theoretical point of view. The answer is given by Max Scheler in an interesting paradigm to be found in his book *Die Wissensformen und die Gesellschaft:* [1]

Lower class	Upper class
1. Tendency to look forward (prospectivism)	Tendency to look backward (retrospectivism)
2. Emphasis on becoming	Emphasis on being
3. Mechanistic conception of the world	Teleological conception of the world
4. Realism in philosophy; the world as 'resistance'	Idealism in philosophy; the world as a 'realm of ideas'
5. Materialism	Spiritualism
6. Induction, empiricism	*A priori* knowledge, rationalism
7. Pragmatism	Intellectualism

[1] 1926, 204 *seq.* What follows is a paraphrase, not a literal translation of the table. It may be to the point to emphasize that Scheler was not a Marxist.

Lower class	*Upper class*
8. Optimism with regard to the future; the past as the 'bad old days'	Pessimism with regard to the future; the past as the 'good old days'
9. A dialectical mode of thinking; search for contradictions	Search for identities and harmonies
10. Emphasis on environmental influences	Emphasis on heredity and tradition

Much could be said in detailed criticism of this scheme from the empirical point of view. Rationalism, for instance, would seem to be much more appropriate to a lower (dissatisfied) class than to an upper (contented) one. 'Let us remake the world in the image of reason, according to a rational blueprint'—this is a text preached on by many revolutionaries down the ages. But it will be more rewarding to concentrate on the truth contained in the table, of which there is a very great deal.

Clearly, Scheler is thinking of tendencies only. He does not say that we must expect all members of the third estate in 1740 to have a world-view centred around becoming, and all aristocrats and abbés a world-view centred on being. This would be utterly unrealistic, indeed nonsense. What he does suggest is that if a man belongs to a class that is on a rising tide, so to speak, it will be more appropriate—more 'natural'—for him to think in terms of movement than of rest, and conversely in the case of one who belongs to a decaying class. In other words, he has modal rather than actual thinking in mind. In so far as a man is typical of his class; in so far as he achieves complete integration between himself and his subsociety, and between his thought and his life-conditions, his ontology (if we may use this big word) will be conceived in terms of movement rather than rest, of change rather than permanence.

But, a critic may ask here, are we still thinking of social determination of thought? have we not insensibly gone over to the discussion of ideologies? Not at all. Neither the one world-view nor the other need be vitiated by the intrusion of interest-begotten ideologies; both can be realistic. We must not forget that we are, by definition, speaking of a complex society, a society of many facets. Karl Mannheim often used the term aspect in this context. A complex society has many aspects; it shows a different side as it were to different classes, and these different side-views of it mirror themselves in men's minds as different aspect-structures—as different world-views. Social determination, let us remind ourselves, is a crystallization of thought, a narrowing down of it, a concentration on selected features of reality. It implies a limitation of our vision, perhaps even an impoverishment of it. But such limitation, such impoverishment, is not only to some extent inescapable for a being whose mind can only function if it is organized in a certain way; it is not even a necessary hindrance in the pursuit of truth.

If two geologists, one a petrologist and the other a hydrographer, look at the same mountain, their mental picture of it will not be the same. The petrologist's impression will be dominated by the rocky surface; his knowledge will be centred around the qualities of the rock materials; the hydrographer's impression will be dominated by the streamlets running down the mountain side; his knowledge will be centred around the system of drainage which he has before his eyes. Both will gather true knowledge; nothing will be amiss with the scientific nature of their work. Yet the area of agreement between them may be very small, so small indeed that they can hardly understand each other so that a meaningful conversation may be virtually impossible. Whether it will be possible or not, will depend on the degree to which the minds of the two men are determined by the inclusive science of geology which embraces both petrology and hydrography.

It is the same, in principle, with the way in which co-ordinated classes in a common inclusive society see the world (particularly the social world) and form their impressions into a coherent system of knowledge. A lower class which is, as we have expressed it, on a rising tide, will spontaneously concentrate its attention on such features of reality as exhibit dynamic, progressive processes—for instance, on trade and industry; an upper class will as naturally be on the lookout for static aspects of contemporary reality and may, for instance, make agriculture the hub of its picture of the social world because there repetition and conservation is the rule, rather than change. Or a lower class may search for the dysteleologies in life and the depressing traits of past history, whereas an upper class will be more inclined to look for the teleologies of existing social arrangements and the glories of today and yesterday. Since reality contains both static conditions and progressions, both adjustments and maladjustments, both good and bad traits, both will have plenty of raw material at their disposal, and both can talk quite scientifically about it. Their knowledge will be sound as long as they keep to the facts. Of course, it will be selected, partial, even one-sided—but so is all knowledge, even that of our scientific geologists.

If it be said now that the geologists have no incentive to go beyond the truth, and hence will keep within it, whereas the social classes, or rather the thinkers representing them, will be induced by their political and other practical preoccupations and interests to dress up the picture of the world in such a way as to enable it to serve propaganda purposes, then it is impossible not to agree. What is particularly apt to happen under the influence of wishful urges is an overstepping of the requisite borderlines. A lower class may, and indeed, often will, maintain that *all* contemporary life is riddled with dysteleologies and carried along by an irresistible stream of development; an upper class may, and often will, assert that society as it is, is completely adjusted to its tasks and dominated by laws which admit of no radical reformation. Karl Marx came near to the first point of view; Vilfredo Pareto to the second. The devil of ideology is always abroad. But that is another matter. And that it really is another matter is clear from the fact that the truth—the whole truth—will include *no* ideology and *all* socially determined knowledge. Ideologies, so we may now formulate our conviction, are alternatives to the truth; socially determined knowledge is part and parcel of it, indeed, constitutive of it—only that in complex societies the different aspect-structures that have arisen must be fused together to give the full truth through their complementarity and combination.

It is the characteristic assertion of Marxism that social classes are the only subsocieties which in principle can, and in practice do, determine human thinking; but the claim is, to say the least, a doubtful one. Speaking empirically and historically, churches and sects also seem to have formed their own specific concretions of thought. We have only to think of the fact that for centuries now a Catholic and a Calvinist view of history have run side by side. Marxists are *a limine* committed to a dichotomous picture of social life: those for and those against the established law of property are respectively the sheep and the goats, and there are no other fronts. Catholicism and Calvinism must therefore be interpreted as class ideologies. But the sociologist who defines a subsociety as an enduring configuration of human relationships, as a settled way of life, need not keep to the same constraining categories; and he has no cause to doubt that religious subsocieties may exert a determining influence on thought, just as classes do. Here we can again apply our test—we can again ask whether we find in churches and sects the decisive reality-forming power. The answer must be in the affirmative.

To apply once more our earlier formulation—churches have (or, what comes to the same in this context, have at times had) reality-forming power *in esse* in so far as they mould and control the lives of their members. A Catholic has grown up under the aegis of a pressure-system different from that which has gone to make a typical Calvinist. The very techniques of social control are different, and not merely the direction into which life is led or forced. But the religious communities also have great reality-forming power *in posse* because they tend, and have at times tended with great vigour and some success, to become shapers of the inclusive society, of the whole social universe. One point must be made quite clear here. We are not asserting that this reality-forming power is a power breaking from the spiritual sphere into the social. This is certainly the way in which most ecclesiastics of all denominations have always been inclined to see the matter. Our opinion is somewhat different. We are asserting that this power wells up from below, not that it comes down from above—that it is an influence welling up from the deeper forces and drifts of social life. Just as a society usually contains a satisfied and a dissatisfied social class, so every society embraces tendencies towards community and tendencies towards association (in the terminology of Ferdinand Tönnies), tendencies towards a close integration of social life and tendencies towards individual freedom. Catholicism and Calvinism are representatives of these very real forces. Catholicism is essentially the community-type of religious life and ecclesiastical organization, Calvinism, with its emphasis on the supremacy of private judgment and its congregationalism, the associational type. It would not be too difficult to work out a paradigm for religious communities parallel to Scheler's table for social classes quoted above. Let us mention only a few items that would have to appear in it.

Catholicism	*Calvinism*
1. Tendency towards an organic world-view	Tendency towards an atomistic world-view
2. Realism	Nominalism
3. Society conceived as prior to the individual	Society conceived as posterior to the individual
4. The community the carrier of all truth	The individual the carrier of all truth
5. Symbolism, Artistic creativeness	Realism, Sobriety
6. Emotionalism, Mysticism	Rationalism
7. Cloistered contemplation as the ideal way to truth (Mary before Martha)	Innerworldly observation as the ideal way to truth (Martha before Mary)

Much could be added to this list. But there is no need to pursue the matter further. All we have sought to show is that the claim of religious communities to be regarded as subsocieties with their own specific crystallizations of thought is not inferior to that of social classes, in so far as they too possess reality-forming power.

No doubt, the social classes and religious communities are the most important subsocieties on which the sociology of knowledge will need to keep its eye when it sets out to help the historian of ideas to fulfil his task. Here we are concerned with principle, not with application, and so we must ask what it is that enables these social formations, as well as the inclusive society, to wield such influence over the minds of men. The answer can best be given with the help of the distinctions and the terminology which George Gurvitch has elaborated in his lectures on social class.[1] Social classes and religious communities are bearers of

---

[1] *Le Concept de Classes Sociales de Marx à Nos Jours*, 1954. Cf. esp. 92 *seq.*, 120 *seq.*

their own specific crystallizations of thought because they are supra-functional groupings.

Gurvitch contrasts uni-functional, multi-functional and supra-functional formations. A uni-functional group (of which an orchestra or a bank is an example) has only one well-defined task to fulfil in social life. A multi-functional group, on the other hand, has several assorted tasks to fulfil, for example a corporation or borough, whose jobs range from dust collection to library services, or the family. A supra-functional group resembles neither the one nor the other. As its name suggests, it is above all enumerable concrete tasks, however long a list we may make of them, and constitutes a totality, rather than a tool, of life. Such, Gurvitch rightly tells us, is the global society; such also is the class, and such, we would add, is the religious community as well.[1] 'It is impossible to give in detail all the tasks which a social class might have to fulfil, for, besides the fact that it is preparing to assume power, is in power, or has lost power, it interprets in its own way all the functions exercised by other groupings and thus cuts across them. It is precisely this supra-functional character of the social class which is the essential criterion of its definition' (92).

It is this supra-functional character, too, which makes the subsocieties which possess it competitors one with another, and competitors also with the inclusive whole. And their clash, whether implicit or actual, whether covert or open, occurs not only in the substructure, the realm of social control, but also in the superstructure, the realm of thought and feeling. It is a clash, not between opposed interests so much as between different totalities of life. 'Each social class is a whole world and would like to become the only world by identifying itself either with the existing global society (in which the other classes would be, if not excluded, then at least . . . kept in a subservient position), or with the global society of the future in which there are to be no more classes' (121). The economic factor may loom very large in the life of a sub-society such as a class, but it is never decisive for the constitution of a class because a class is, as we can see for ourselves in contemporary reality, and as Marx himself would have been only too eager to admit, more than a carrier of economic or power interests. 'The antagonism of the classes', Gurvitch writes, 'is a direct reflex of their incompatibility and of their supra-functionality which are more fundamental than the

[1] Gurvitch asserts (120) that social classes are in practice the only particularist groups which possess supra-functionality. This is perhaps true of modern times, but certainly not of the past. The medieval church came very near indeed to being what she claimed to be—a *societas perfecta*. If Gurvitch urges that *one* organization cannot possibly express the whole reality of a supra-functional group, he is right. But the medieval church had under it, or rather within it, innumerable orders, 'third' orders, sodalities, confraternities, guilds, etc. etc. And there was no lack of tension between these groupings, either.

immediate conflict of economic interests and the struggle for power in the narrower sense of the word' (125). It is because this is true, because classes are different systems of social control, different ways of life, different totalities, in a word, genuine sub-*societies*, that they produce not only ideologies but also a specific world-view, a determinate configuration of thought and sentiment.

(*c*) SOCIAL DETERMINATION AND IDEOLOGICAL DISTORTION: THE
CASE OF MUTUAL DISPLACEMENT

We have so far considered the relation between the ideological contamination of thinking and the social determination of thought, which it is the purpose of the present chapter to compare and to contrast, merely from a static point of view; that is to say, we have considered them as competitors, existing side by side, for the control of human thought-processes. We must now try to see them in their dynamic relationship, as successive elements in the flux of time. And as we turn to this aspect, a new light is thrown on the history of ideas: ideologies and socially determined thought still appear antagonistic indeed; right and wrong can never be confounded and confused; but yet we discover that they are often connected by a chain of historical affiliation, by a process of mutual displacement so to speak, which leads the clear dividing lines we have drawn in theory to look far more fleeting and uncertain in practice.

Once again it is best to elucidate this matter with the help of a concrete example. Adam Smith, in his *Wealth of Nations*, has expressed the conviction that, at the moment of birth, all human beings are endowed with more or less the same potentialities and capabilities. 'The difference of natural talents in different men is, in reality, much less than we are aware of; and the very different genius which appears to distinguish men of different professions, when grown up to maturity, is not upon many occasions so much the cause, as the effect of the division of labour. The difference between the most dissimilar characters, between a philosopher and a common street porter, for example, seems to arise not so much from nature, as from habit, custom, and education. When they came into the world, and for the first six or eight years of their existence, they were perhaps very much alike, and neither their parents nor playfellows could perceive any remarkable difference. . . . By nature a philosopher is not in genius and disposition half so different from a street porter, as a mastiff is from a greyhound, or a greyhound from a spaniel, or this last from a shepherd's dog' (Bk. I, ch. II). Here we have a typical is-statement, a proposition which claims, and to a certain extent deserves, scientific status. It will be regarded as absolute truth in any genuinely egalitarian society such as the society of peasants

83

and artisans which Adam Smith thought he saw coming and which is the ideal-typical substructure of all his pronouncements; and it will have to be regarded as at least a partial truth in all societies, even the most hierarchical and caste-like ones, because it can be demonstrated by the most stringently scientific means that some endowments at any rate of *homo sapiens* are common to all members of the species, even if it be only the capacity of physical cross-fertilization. Hence the proposition of Adam Smith that—as we may briefly formulate it— 'all men are born equal' is both an absolute truth (if formulated with the necessary provisos, which are not to the purpose here), and a relative truth, a truth particularly belonging to a certain society, Adam Smith's semi-realized society of peasants and artisans.

It is true that an ideological element remains in Smith's formulation. He was an egalitarian in politics; he wanted men to be equal in rights and that wish was not altogether unconnected with his doctrine that all men were equal in nature; but this trace of ideological contamination is really irrelevant here. His thought would hardly have been different in substance, if his political bias had been absent or completely controlled. For in 1776 the world had so far advanced towards a *de facto* equality that the contrary proposition—'by nature a philosopher is in genius and disposition at least as different from a street porter, as a mastiff is from a greyhound'—would hardly have been put forward by anybody, and if it had been, would have been received with derision by common opinion. The proposition 'all men are born equal' would consequently have seemed a very appropriate statement of fact in Adam Smith's day.

But when this sentence was first formulated, it was ideological in essence, and not merely the effect of a certain constellation of fact and thought. John Ball's famous text for instance, as reported by the *Chronicon Angliae*, has manifestly all the colour and all the challenge of a political slogan: 'Whaune Adam dalf and Eve span, who was thane a gentilman?' Here we have, not a realistic, near-scientific statement, but a statement inspired by underdog-resentments on the one hand, and revolutionary day-dreaming on the other. Of course, the physical facts were the same in 1381 as in 1776: even in the fourteenth century, as in the eighteenth, all human beings were born capable of mutual cross-fertilization; all had the same sensual—as, with the appropriate dichotomy, they also had the same sexual—apparatus; and so on, and so forth. But these physical facts were so overlaid by social arrangements that they failed to register, or were not considered important when they did. In fact, social arrangements had brought it about that the difference between the different classes had, to all intents and purposes, become a physical distinction. In a world where class endogamy is practised, where like habitually mates with like, castle and cottage will breed different types of man. Much of the difference will assuredly still be an effect of the division of labour, as Adam Smith insists, rather than a cause of it: the horny palm of the peasant woman, the delicate hand of the noble lady; the bent back of the ploughman, the upright carriage of the horseman. Yet when full allowance is made for all this, the fact remains that in a caste-society, and even in a society of relatively closed classes, different masses of genetic endowment and equipment are handed down the ladder of heredity and there are 'two nations'. It is a metaphor in any society to speak of 'blue blood' and to contrast it with the ordinary red blood of the common herd; but in a segmented society it is not an altogether unrealistic metaphor. In such circumstances the proposition that 'all men are born equal in nature' is not an operative truth, even if it is still in part and principle the physical and physiological truth; in such circumstances, the whole proposition is a battle-cry, a programme, an ideology.

The same pattern of words, then, has an entirely different meaning in the mouth of John Ball, the rustic insurgent of 1381, and of Adam Smith, the bourgeois professor of 1776. What is to the former hardly more than a wish-inspired slogan, an ideology, is to the latter in substance a fact-inspired statement, a piece of truth conceived under the influence of a certain constellation of fact, a certain crystallization of life and thought. But—and this is what we wish to emphasize at the present juncture—there is an historical affiliation between John Ball and Adam Smith, the insurgent and the professor, the ideology-pedlar and the propagator of truth. Though irreconcilable in principle and mutually exclusive, ideological and socially determined thinking have often, in history, grown out of one another.

At this point it may be useful to resuscitate a concept coined by an able, though now nearly forgotten thinker—Alfred Fouillée: the concept of 'objective possibility'; and to apply it in a double sense—objective possibility *pro tempore* and objective possibility *pro futuro*. A thought, such as the idea that all men are born equal, must, first of all, be objectively possible at the moment of its formulation. This statement may sound like a platitude; it obviously could not and would not be formulated at all unless it were possible; so why make a song about it? But the matter is a little more complicated than appears at first sight. All that is obvious here is *that* it was possible to conceive of human equality in John Ball's day; *how* it was possible and in what terms it could be conceived and formulated is by no means obvious, and is a question which not only poses a concrete problem for the sociology of knowledge but also confirms its general and basic assumptions.

For the whole way in which 'the mad priest of Kent' thought of human relationships was determined by the society in which he found himself. A man of the fourteenth century could hardly conceive of

85

equality in purely secular terms, as equality in intelligence or physical strength or productive capacity, for instance; conditioned as he was by the way of life prevalent in his world, he could only conceive of it in terms of the religious mould in which his mind was cast. 'Whaune Adam dalf and Eve span . . .' The reference is at once to the state of innocence, of sinlessness, of Christian mythology. That this reference is much more than merely a matter of words can be seen from the fact that the first battles in pursuit of equality were also fought on the religious plane. The Utraquists of Bohemia demanded that the Cup should not be reserved to the priest, but that everyone should be allowed to communicate *sub utraque specie*, by bread *and* wine; it was this demand for which men fought and died. Abstruse, even ludicrous to a later age, it was of vital concern to those ages in which, because of the specific social determination of thought and feeling then in vogue, all problems appeared in a religious guise.

But the Utraquists, like John Ball, were no philosophers; the characteristic way in which the fourteenth century formulated the problem of equality is much better seen when we turn to the colourful Master of Balliol, John Wycliff. His ideas are not only tinged with religion; religion is after all a ubiquitous phenomenon; they bear, what is much more decisive, the open imprint of the social order in which they were conceived and formulated. 'He seems to look upon the whole question from a feudal point of view', Father Jarrett writes in his *Mediaeval Socialism* (n.d., 36). 'Sin is treason, involving therefore the forfeiture of all that is held of God. Grace, on the other hand, makes us the liegemen of God, and gives us the only possible right to all His good gifts. But, he would seem to argue, it is incontestable that property and power are from God, for so Scripture plainly assures us. Therefore, he concludes, by grace, and grace alone, are we put in dominion over all things; once we are in loyal subjection to God, we [rightly] own all things, and hold them by the only sure title. "Dominion by grace" is thus made to lead direct to communism. His conclusion is quite clear: *Omnia debent esse communia*.' An instructive example, this, of how even the revolutionary remains committed to the general framework of thought which social determination—historical specification—has established for his society.

But this is somewhat by the way. What interests us here more directly is the fact that the unrealistic, ideological egalitarianism of Ball and Wycliff and the Utraquists bore in itself the objective possibility of realization; and that, as this realization proceeds, the proposition 'all men are born equal in nature' progressively loses its ideological character and becomes increasingly factual and truthful, until, in the fullness of time, the ideological element becomes vestigial, reduced to vanishing point. It must not be thought that we are asserting or implying here that, in the course of history, the 'idea' fashions 'reality' according to its own image. That would be high treason against the fundamental conviction of the sociology of knowledge; and, what is worse, it would be very largely unrealistic. What happens is not that fact comes into line with thought—the two are never completely divorced—but that *all* life, holding in its grip both substructural fact and superstructural thought, moves *in its totality* from a state where the assertion of a *de facto* equality can be no more than wish, demand, and ideology, to a state where it is near-fact, and where our assertion is the truth, an operative truth as we have called it, a statement in virtual accordance with things as they are, not as they ought to be.

The reader will appreciate the grounds for our present caution in speaking, for instance, of near-agreement between theory and reality, thought and fact, rather than complete agreement. The reason is that no historical society has ever fully realized any theoretically formulable principle, however close it may have come to it. Elements of equality remain even in the most segmental and hierarchical society, elements of inequality remain even in the most uniform and democratic order. What we have called extrapolation—the inferential passage from the mixed to the unmixed, from the impure to the pure—remains an inescapable necessity of any truly theoretical thought (as opposed to mere description), simply because in this world of ours nothing is ever perfect. If we may venture a bold simile here, we might say that it is with societies as with water: just as chemically and bacteriologically pure water is not drinkable, so a society without features that must, from a theoretical point of view, be called impurities, is not practical, cannot be realized in actual life. We have explained this already; but the matter must be brought up again in the present context because it has an important bearing on the problem of objective possibility.

It is because even hierarchical societies contain somewhere in their set-up hidden and marginal egalitarian elements, that egalitarian ideas remain possible even under conditions of extreme class division or caste formation. John Ball could think what he thought and teach what he taught because he had before his eyes the village community with its far-reaching equality among the neighbours; and also because the great community of the Church, even though it had outwardly taken on the organizational pattern of the feudal world, still carried within herself an egalitarian principle, such that *every* baptized person, whether lord or serf, could, by the appropriate rite, be invested with all the privileges of priesthood: 'the bishop's hand heals any stain'. Of course, the more firmly established the hierarchical principle is, the less objective possibility there is for egalitarian ideas to spring up. It was probably much easier for a John Ball to achieve a radical outlook than for a similar man in India or China at the time when those countries were in the grip of a strongly-constructed and well-cemented caste order. But it must be insisted that no caste-order is cast-iron; all have cracks and chinks, as it were, through which other principles of social organization can seep in, and this explains why, in spite of all social determination of thought, i.e. the determination of concrete thought-processes through the existing social order, the human mind is never completely tied to one pattern, though naturally enough the pattern in agreement with things as they are will always be the dominant one.

We may perhaps sum up this whole analysis by saying that objective possibility (especially objective possibility *pro futuro*—the possibility of ultimate realization) can make a wish-determined, unrealistic, ideological set of ideas into the embryonic form of a fact-determined, realistic, scientifically sound world-view. But let us hasten to add that this historical connection between some ideologies and some socially determined forms of thought does not by any means obliterate the difference between them. Though the contrast between the two is much more clearly seen in principle than in practice, it exists in practice no less than in principle. The main question that requires to be answered is this: given that an ideology can, in the course of time, be transmuted into a realistic (socially, i.e. fact-determined, not wish-determined) mode of thinking, when exactly does the change-over take place? The answer is easy enough in theory: a proposition such as that all men are born equal is ideological so long as the ideal type of the given society is a hierarchical order; it ceases to be ideological when circumstances have changed to such a degree that the ideal type of the given society is an egalitarian pattern. Or, to put it negatively: the proposition that all men are born equal is ideological so long as *de facto* egalitarian conditions appear, from the point of view of existing society, as impurities, as deviations from the established norm; it ceases to be ideological when changing circumstances have made it appear from the point of view of existing society, that *de facto* inegalitarian conditions are exceptions, deviations, abnormalities. What entitles us to say of, e.g. Adam Smith, that his thought is socially determined and yet not ideological (or only vestigially so) is the fact that in his world the inequalities inherited from the feudal period already appeared as survivals, as dead wood, as not of the essence of the social order, as decayed cells which the body social would soon discard, and discard, not to its detriment, but to its advantage.

What is ideology in one society then, may be (socially determined) truth in another. We have already given an example of this in pointing out that, even in 1381, some near-egalitarian enclosures existed in a hierarchical world: the villages and the towns. Our specimen proposition ('all men are equal') was much more realistic and much less ideological in relation to them than in relation to the inclusive society, namely feudalism. Other examples could be adduced in plenty. In the first half of the nineteenth century, the writings of the Swiss philosopher Karl Ludwig von Haller were in high esteem on the European continent. They reflected the old-world, patriarchal conditions surviving in his own little homeland, the canton of Berne, and, in spite of all their idealization, were still largely realistic (and certainly in substance socially determined). But outside the country of their origin, they were accepted, not because of their realism, but because they offered possible ammunition for the political struggle of the reactionary circles of Europe. Behold—the members of the 'Christian-Germanic circle' around the King of Prussia could say—this is what a good society is like: it is aristocratic, authoritarian, organic, corporative, conservative. Let us model our fatherland on the image von Haller spreads before our eyes! Thus what was largely realistic and only partially ideological on the Aare, was largely ideological and only very partially realistic on the Spree.

This last example may well serve to round off our study of the dynamical relationship between ideological and socially determined thought. Our main instance—'all men are born equal'—has exemplified the transition of an ideology into a realistic structure of thought. The case of Haller, on the other hand, illustrates a movement in the opposite direction—the degeneration of a realistic world-view into an ideology. When Haller wrote, the canton of Berne was as yet little transformed by the political and social revolution of the period 1789–1830; the Rhineland, to which the Junkers wanted to apply his ideas, had changed a great deal. From John Ball to Adam Smith we travel, as it were, on an ascending line; from Haller to Friedrich Wilhelm IV and his friends on a descending one.

The dynamical relationship between ideology and socially determined thought can thus be seen to be potentially a double one. As historical societies wax and wane, as their underlying principles become concrete and realize themselves or fade out and lose grip on reality, so there is an asymptotic approximation of ideologies (e.g. of a concrete class, such as the bourgeoisie) to a realistic world-view and then again a progressive departure from it. This progressive departure can be seen in the later development of egalitarian ideas as well as in the later fate of Karl Ludwig von Haller's doctrines. After reaching, round about 1776 and 1789, maximum proximity to reality, because the doom of feudal inequalities and the rise of a society of peasants and artisans appear alike to be imminent, the statement that 'all men are born equal' again assumes an increasingly ideological tinge as the specific capitalist inequalities of the nineteenth century rear their head, until the state is reached when an Anatole France can say, in the justified conviction that all will understand his irony: 'The law in its magnificent egalitarianism forbids poor and rich alike to beg in the streets, to steal bread, and to sleep under bridges'. Anyone who asserted around the year 1894 when

Le Lys Rouge was written, that all men were *in fact* equal in initial opportunity, was making an ideological, not a realistic statement. Thus the tide of events may turn untruth into truth and truth into untruth as its waters flow first this way and then that.

Speaking generally, the recessional movement has been as important in the history of ideas as the progressive one. A good deal of economic thought in the nineteenth century, for instance, is wish- and even interest-inspired, clinging to assumptions and assertions which are applicable to a near-egalitarian society, but inapplicable to a class-divided one. No candid person can deny the justice of many of Marx's and the Marxists' strictures in this respect.[1] But the matter is perhaps most obvious in the famous American ideology of 'the land of golden opportunities'. Long after the much-vaunted social democracy of American society—a reality in the country's far-off, halcyon days—had, in fact, become a sham, the ideological assertion remained current that there was free advancement for one and all. 'The office-boy-to-president imagery was once in approximate accord with the facts', writes Robert Merton, 'in the loose sense that vertical mobility was probably more common then than now. The ideology persists however . . . The rôle of this doctrine has changed from that of roughly valid theorem to that of an ideology.'[2] This is a process which has happened in history not once, but often; not in one country only, but in all. To discern and describe it, together with its more attractive positive counter-part, is one of the prime duties of the history of ideas.

We have now said enough to be able to sum up the argument of this second chapter. Ideas and beliefs, we have tried to explain, can be related to reality in a double way: either to the *facts* of reality, or to the *strivings* to which this reality, or rather the reaction to this reality, gives rise. Where the former connection exists, we find thought which is, in

---

[1] If our point of view approaches here to the negative Marxist one, it is worthy of note that the Marxists sometimes approach our positive attitude to 'bourgeois' thought in certain of its historical phases, i.e. our assertion that at certain points of time it is realistic, not ideological. The following passage from Lukacs' *Geschichte und Klassenbewusstsein* (1923, 231 *seq.*) offers terminological difficulties since he describes as 'ideological' what we should never call by that name. Yet it will be clear in its import to the reader all the same: 'At the end of the eighteenth century, the bourgeoisie was ideologically strong and unbroken. She was still so at the beginning of the nineteenth century, when her ideology, the idea of bourgeois liberty and democracy, had not yet been . . . hollowed out, when the bourgeoisie still had the hope, and could have it in good faith, that that democratic, bourgeois liberty . . . would one day bring about the salvation of the human race. The splendour and pathos of this belief not only fills the history of the first bourgeois revolution . . . it also gives the great scientific pronouncements of the bourgeois class, e.g. the economics of Smith and Ricardo, an unprejudiced character (*Unbefangenheit*), and the strength to strive for the truth, to say openly what they have seen.'

[2] *Social Theory and Social Structure*, 1949, 380.

principle, truthful; where the latter relation obtains, we are faced with ideas which can be true only by accident, and which are likely to be vitiated by bias, the word taken in the widest possible sense. The former type of thought deserves to be called theoretical; the latter must be characterized as para-theoretical. Perhaps one might also describe the former as rational, the latter as emotionally tinged—the former as purely cognitive, the latter as evaluative. To borrow Theodor Geiger's simile (with the substance of whose argument we are not, however, in sympathy): thought determined by social fact is like a pure stream, crystal-clear, transparent; ideological ideas like a dirty river, muddied and polluted by the impurities that have flooded into it. From the one it is healthy to drink; the other is poison to be avoided.

As we have pointed out, it is possible, and indeed legitimate, to draw a clear line of distinction in this way; but there are important complications. The chief of them stems from the fact that though the truth is one, it may yet present different aspects to those who view it from different angles, and may thus be splintered and refracted, creating in each of its beholders the impression that he is surrounded by error while in reality he and all others are merely seeing aspects of the truth which are all in themselves equally valid. Thus tensions appear between different points of view and world-views which are the sharper (and the more regrettable) in that they are not adjudicable in terms of 'right' and 'wrong'. And these tensions not only obtain between different societies; they also can and often do exist inside the same society if this society is a highly complex one. Certain privileged subsocieties may exist (following Gurvitch we have characterized them as supra-functional formations) which have the power to determine thought and whose specific conceptions of truth are liable, nay bound, to clash with each other. This fact has given rise to the pan-ideological point of view which we have tried to combat. There is no truth in itself, it has been argued; there are only ideologies. This is quite wrong.[1] 'Let us think of the

---

[1] It is wrong even with regard to the world-views of opposing classes. After having presented the table which we have reproduced above on pp. 77-8, Max Scheler (though to be candid he would not have accepted our whole argument) says this: 'These are inclinations of a subconscious kind, conditioned by class position, to conceive the world predominantly in one or the other form. They are not class prejudices, but more than prejudices: namely, formal laws of the formation of prejudices . . . They concern both what reaches the member of the class as material for the perception of the world and the objective forms in which it reaches him (if there is no special deliberate attention and conscious reflective consideration). Hence they are something much stronger, more persistent and commanding than any mere subsequent falsification of memory and judgment in the sense-perception of the world. . . . It is really a different formal contour which the world itself offers to upper and lower classes, and further to both classes in so far as they have become aware of the fact that they are "rising" or "sinking".' *Die Wissensformen und die Gesellschaft*, 1926, 205 *seq.*

well-known example of the landscape which becomes something entirely different according to the way of life of the beholder,' writes Horkheimer, whose ideas on this head are particularly clear. 'Not only the phenomenon, but the essence is different for the farmer who tills the soil, the townsman who is out for recreation, the huntsman who looks for game, the painter who sketches a picture, the airman who is forced to make an emergency landing, the strategist who assesses the lay of the land.' [1] Yet in all these cases it is the same landscape which is being perceived, and perceived realistically. There is no bias to the six resulting impressions it creates, though there is dissimilarity, for this dissimilarity is merely due to contrasting articulations or accentuations. This simple example brings out and sums up our argument in defence of the assertion that the social determination of thought does not entail its contamination by truth-destroying prejudices. It presents a case analogous to that treated by the sociology of knowledge, except that 'in the sociology of knowledge we are not concerned with single things, like a landscape, and with occupational groupings, but with the experience of reality as a whole and the decisive strata of society'. [2]

But, it has been argued (especially by Theodor Geiger—cf. his *Ideologie und Wahrheit* of 1953), a simile such as Horkheimer's can be turned against him and used to destroy the distinction between ideological and socially determined thought which it is meant to establish. Why does the landscape appear so different to the farmer and the townsman and the painter and all the others? Because they approach it with different practical preoccupations, with different interests in their minds. But is this not precisely the case with ideology? Is not an ideology in essence an interest-determined and interest-distorted view of the world? Is not the true distinction to be drawn between thought committed to practice on the one hand, and thought not so committed, *pure* thought, on the other?—between thought influenced by values and thought not so influenced, value-free thinking?

This attitude is based on a very primitive, indeed naïve, idea of the process of cognition, one that really ought not to survive in this post-Kantian age. It assumes that when we want to know the truth, we must sit back passively and allow 'the facts themselves' to impress themselves on our mind. Only so shall we receive them 'as they are'. In fact, however, we can only receive *impressions* in this way, but never achieve *knowledge*. For knowledge properly so called is an ordered and structured picture of reality, one in which everything has its determined place within a determinate framework, and the principles of ordering and construction are not contained in the things perceived but supplied

---

[1] 'Ideologie und Wertgebung', in *Soziologische Forschung in unserer Zeit*, 1951, 222. Cf. also V. G. Childe, *Society and Knowledge*, 1956, 56 *seq.* and 97.
[2] *Ibid.*

by the perceiving mind. (This will be explained in all due detail in the third chapter.) Nowhere is Geiger's error more manifest than in the passage (p. 161 *seq.*) where he contrasts style in art and in thought. In art, he says, there can be various creative styles, for the artist is not bound to factual data; in thinking there can be only one, for the scholar and the scientist are bound by and to them. This attitude overlooks that the thinker, just like the artist, must reduce an overwhelming multiplicity of impressions gathered in the course of his encounter with reality into a unity, that he must organize them into a coherent picture, and that this organization, this comprehension, is essentially a creative act in the one case as well as in the other. It is a creative act which is achieved from a certain point of view, under a determinate perspective, under the guidance of certain values, and these values are different in different societies; as the perspective and the point of view change from age to age, from country to country, from class to class, there result a series of vistas of the one reality which are at variance with each other though they are all the truth.

People like Geiger operate with much too simple an idea of what the truth is. They say, as an unsophisticated person might, that a statement must either be right or wrong, and that there can be no third alternative. Formally, this is quite correct, indeed undeniable. But the truth is complex and has many facets, and most men are incapable of seeing two of them—let alone all of them—at the same time. It is one of the chief tragedies of the human condition that history has been filled with as many struggles of truth against truth, as of absolute truth opposed to absolute error.

As for the argument that there can be no difference between socially determined and ideological thinking because values are basic to both of them, this again is an over-simple attitude which, to say the least, fails to make the necessary distinctions. For by the presence of values at the root of a thought-process we can mean either *valuations*, in the sense of value-judgments, or *value-facts* which guide us in our apprehension of reality, in our ordering of experience. By following, as we spontaneously do, the value-facts embodied in our social world and its way of life, we arrive, not at a world-view corrupted by value-judgments, but at a world-view which constitutes one possible construct of reality or vista of the truth—the one which is in agreement with our whole social universe, not only with its overall categories of thought, but also with its overall categories of action, in a word, with the constitutive principles which make it, in its totality, what it happens to be.

In one interesting passage, Geiger himself comes face to face with the truth without, however, being able to recognize it. 'The categories within which we collect, order and connect our experiences,' he writes

(143 *seq.*), 'are by no means final . . . But the categories transmitted in scientific education or inculcated by the use of everyday language become habits of thinking. They form a kind of schematic blueprint for the systematization of what we perceive. As long as one moves within the given form of concepts which is familiar through use and wont and authorized by general convention, one feels safe. In this way the traditional concepts may become the object of a vital attachment.' There is nothing in these sentences to which exception need be taken, but Geiger himself misses the significance of what he is saying. His merit consists in singling out 'the categories within which we collect, order and connect our experiences' for special consideration; his failure, in not giving them that special consideration. There are a number of points which he misses or misunderstands.

Firstly, the habits of thought of which he is speaking are connected with—indeed, inhere in—the habits of action, especially social action or interaction, characteristic of the society concerned; secondly, they are not so much ideas which can be described as either right or wrong and tested accordingly, but rather the forms in which truth is apprehended by and in the society concerned; in any case, they have nothing whatsoever to do with the ideological habit, 'the habit of presenting logical imperatives as grammatical indicatives' as Myrdal calls it (p. 10), and thirdly, attachment to them is not the error-inducing, ideology-generating preoccupation which we feel when we follow our pet wishes or day-dreams—the sentiment which Geiger usually stigmatizes as a 'vital attachment'—but adherence to a way of life which happens to be ours, which has shaped our conduct and our mind—in a word, integratedness, not infatuation; fact, not pursuit.

How thoroughly Geiger misses the chance of grasping the truth becomes manifest in the very next sentence. 'The more independent a thinker', he says, 'the more fearlessly, though only after careful consideration, will he throw the old conceptual lumber overboard and without prejudice draw the conceptual consequences from new factual observations.' Here we again have his over-simplified and unrealistic idea of truth and the apprehension of truth. The intellectual history of our kind has consisted not merely in a closer approach to the facts (of which there has indeed been all too little), as if men always beheld the facts from the same angle and only needed to open their eyes wider to get a clearer and clearer impression; [1] what has happened in essence has been an ever renewed approach to the facts, an ever different approach, an approach from varying angles, which was bound to lead to different

---

[1] We shall see later on (in ch. 4) that there is an area of observation in which this does indeed apply. Geiger's error is explicable as an (illicit) generalization from the circumstances obtaining in this restricted area (the area of scientific thought in the narrower sense of the word).

pictures of the world. The difference between these pictures is due not, as Geiger assumes, to the difference between the one truth and countless errors, between ideology-free and ideology-tainted inquiry and research, but to the difference between differing aspects of the one truth all societies have desired and which has come to them all, though in varied guises and manifold forms.

This is not the point at which to enter more deeply into all this, but a brief illustration may be of use. In the modern West, domination of the lower creation has been the prime value; hence a rational technology has developed with an appropriate rational science, which has given us many truths (truths which Geiger would certainly not belittle or question). In ancient India, it was not domination of the lower creation that constituted the prime value, but rather escape from it, release; hence no rational technology developed, and no appropriate rational science made its appearance. In consequence, important truths were missed. But instead, others were found. The specific Indian way to truth was not practical experiment but passive contemplation, a way which was also pursued by the great sages of classical Greece. (It is Geiger's regrettable limitation that he does not notice facts of this kind.) Who would presume to maintain that the path of contemplation is in itself less likely to lead to true insights than the path of active experiment? Both have equal promise, though they will not lead to equal, or even comparable, results. In his primitive way, Geiger appreciates only the achievements of his own society, and fails to appreciate—or even to recognize—those of others. Our submission is that both kinds of society have seen and grasped the truth, though different departments of it, as it were. And in both societies ideologies could spring up to mar those truths. Indian society was no more prone to them than our own. Did it not have its own scholarly discipline, the mortification of the flesh—of that flesh which disturbs the peace and quiet which is essential to a successful pursuit of the ways of contemplation?—a discipline parallel to, though in its content different from, the discipline to which our own scientists must submit in the interests of their work. Ideologies are in either case merely incidental, adventitious, unnecessary, conquerable disturbances of the search for truth. If we think them away, there still remain different habits of thinking which arise from different value-facts (i.e. differing in respect of their social determination) and lead to different mental universes which are none the less equally justified.

That the social determination of thought is *toto coelo* different from the ideology-forming process can also be demonstrated (in a manner which is perhaps less recondite and more practical) by a negative thought-experiment. If we ascend towards the sources of our thinking and encounter a resentment or a wish which has influenced and distorted it, we can expel it from our mind, correct our ideas and modify our picture of reality. There is no difficulty about this, given only the necessary moral and psychological qualities, candour, willingness to submit to self-criticism, respect for the truth, etc. But if we penetrate still further towards the ultimate foundations of our world-view in terms of which all our thoughts are couched, and come face to face with the socially-determined value-facts which are its essential elements, then we can carry out no such operation. If we tried to expel them from our mind, our picture of reality would simply disintegrate: it would fall to pieces, and there would be nothing left of it. This is the reason why the fundamental habits of thinking have proved so strong in history, so resistant to attack, even where they were connected with errors due to the unwarranted generalization of the truth contained in them, even where they were pernicious in their effects, as for instance in the under- lying principles of primitive thinking which Lévy-Bruhl has called 'impervious to experience'. The primitive, when he stubbornly sticks, for instance, to his own pan-animistic world-view, in spite of the practical superiority of the European who wishes to press his own view on him, is defending the very foundations of his mental universe, the understanding of reality that he has achieved—nay, more, his convic- tion of its intelligibility. He fights, not against another thought-structure (which is as yet closed to him), but against mental anarchy. We would all react like that if we were in the same situation. That does not mean that we are for ever enslaved to our original perspective, that we cannot rise superior to it. We can, though it will be excruciatingly difficult, as difficult as any change-over from one commanding habit-system to another—mental or bodily, intellectual or practical—is always bound to be. A man may look at a mountain from two or three or any number of vantage-points. But he cannot look at it from no point at all. If he abandons his own point of view, without successfully substituting any other, partial or total, he removes the possibility of seeing the peak at all: indeed, it is only a slight exaggeration to say that he then removes the whole mountain itself.

Geiger would like to replace our essential and sharp distinction between ideology and social determination by a merely relative and loose distinction between surface-ideologies and depth-ideologies.[1] Some ideologies, he points out, are easy to detect: the wish that is father to the thought looms large behind it; others are far more difficult to unmask, for behind the thought there stretches an impenetrable jungle. But the point is that *all* ideology-inducing forces operate on the psy- chological level, whereas the social determination of thought takes place on the much deeper noological plane. Ideologies may sometimes be

[1] *Ideologie und Wahrheit*, 1953, 94 *seq.*, 174 *seq.* Our own point of view is shared, and most ably upheld, by H. J. Lieber, *Wissen und Gesellschaft*, 1952, esp. 23 *seq.*, 51 *seq.*, 140 *seq.*

difficult to unmask, but in principle they are all detectable, even though they may be heavily overlaid and deep in the subconscious. 'The name of ideology', says Horkheimer, 'should be reserved for that [pseudo-] knowledge which is not aware of its dependence [on extra-theoretical, error-generating factors] but is historically already recognizable for what it is, namely for opinions which, in the face of the most perfect knowledge, have already been reduced to shams, and stand in contrast to the truth.' [1] The sociology of knowledge is not concerned with them at all. It is concerned with one of the conditions of true knowing, namely the social element in the complex of conditions on which all knowledge is dependent.

In a way, this whole discussion of ideology has led us to the same final insight or result as our former investigation of what we called the microsociology of knowledge. Ideologies arise, and can only arise, within a framework of knowing which is already established, within a world-view which is already constituted, just as microsociological influences on thinking can only come into play inside such a frame. The matter is, most happily, capable of demonstration by inductive methods, on the basis of a direct observation and description of reality. Very often when we take two sharply contrasting contemporary theories and investigate their clash, we find that the disagreement is wholly due to the ideological elements present in them, while underneath the layer of ideology there is a yet deeper stratum of conceptions and assumptions which they hold in common, and which they share because it reflects the common reality underlying them both.

Gunnar Myrdal has noted a typical case of this kind: the case of liberal economics and Thorstein Veblen. Mortal enemies on the surface, they belong, at bottom, to the same mental universe. 'According to the liberal theory, entrepreneurs earn profits because they combine productive factors in the most "economic" manner. By seeking profits for themselves, they also increase the efficiency of the productive system. According to Veblen, however, entrepreneurs may also earn profit by thwarting production. They can do this in virtue of certain institutional devices. In a sense, Veblen's theory is, of course, diametrically opposed to liberal theory. Yet, his premises are the same: he, too, thinks of an ideal economy which would maximize production if there were no interventions . . . Veblen's criticism is of the kind which can easily be understood by a liberal economist. It is merely a question of deciding what is an "intervention" and what is "free" or "natural". His criticism does not reject the general presupposition of liberal theory. A liberal can remain inside the boundaries of his theory when he tries to refute Veblen.' Such a statement in regard to this left-wing adversary of liberal economics can also be made of its right-wing adversaries, 'the

[1] *Loc. cit.*, 227.

conservative interventionists'.[1] What all the parties to this discussion shared, in spite of their wide practical divergencies, or differing conclusions, was the fundamental conception of economic society as an interaction of independent entrepreneurs, in other words a certain ideal-typical image of contemporary reality, and this image constituted the non-ideological, realistic presupposition of all their further speculations; these speculations tended in opposite directions because of different social and human ideals, different ideas concerning the Ought, whereas their ideas concerning the Is were very largely, not to say exclusively, the same.

But perhaps we can recognize the same fact more quickly and more easily with the help of the simple example with which this chapter opened. Ideologically, those who wanted to solve the economic crisis of 1931 by cutting down wages and those who wanted to cure it by the opposite method of increasing the purchasing power of the masses, were irreconcilable adversaries, at opposite poles indeed; but their thought-patterns were related, not to say identical in character. For both diagnosed the economic illness of the day as essentially the disturbance of an equilibrium—a disturbance which, under the guidance of certain wishes and valuations, they merely desired to see righted in a different way. Both thought, in other words, of the economic system as an equilibrium system, and this basic conception reflected, not only the prevailing economic theory of the day, but, beyond it, the prevailing economic reality of the epoch of which that theory was a (very largely appropriate) mirroring. It is these ultimate common fundamentals of thought with which the sociology of knowledge is concerned, which form, so to speak, its central problem—not the ideologies which have so far loomed much too large in the deliberations and discussions of those who have searched for the social elements in the origination of human ideas. The next chapter will be devoted exclusively to them.

[1] *The Political Element in the Development of Economic Theory*, Engl. ed., 1953, 104 *seq.*

CHAPTER THREE

THE ESSENCE OF THE SOCIOLOGY OF KNOWLEDGE

(a) OUTLINES OF A SOCIAL THEORY OF KNOWLEDGE

THE detailed and perhaps wearisome investigation of the concept of ideology which has gone before was necessary, not only because the matter is important in itself, but also because it will enable the reader to discern and to appreciate the specific character of the theory concerning the social determination of thought and feeling which will now be systematically developed. The fact is that in the past the whole discussion around the problem of the sociology of knowledge has been so heavily overlaid and bedevilled by the problem of ideology which was hopelessly mixed up with it, that it has been impossible even to focus it clearly, let alone to clear it up. The greatest, or at least most prominent, names in the history of the subject so far are those of Marx and Mannheim: neither of them succeeded in separating the two disciplines which it was the object of our second chapter neatly to distinguish, though both of them seem at times to have moved in the direction of this essential distinction. In the opinion of the present writer, it is an absolutely indispensable precondition of any successful approach to the study of the social element in human thinking.

The whole ambivalence of Marxism in this respect can be seen in the Marxist attitude to the phenomenon of religion. In one of his most pungent formulae, Marx, as is well known, called religion 'the opium of the people',[1] and this phrase, if it means anything, must mean that religion is essentially ideological, either in the sense that religious conceptions provide a wish-inspired dream-land into which the poor of this world can escape out of the miseries of their real existence, or in the sense that they are a tissue of falsehoods which the rich have imposed on their less fortunate brethren to keep them in meekness and subjection. In other words, religion is either a pleasant phantasmagoria indulged in by Lazarus, or a clever trick on the part of Dives, or, indeed, both things at the same time. But whatever it is, it is a mental construct which need not and should not exist, which can and should be discarded

---

[1] Cf. his *Kritik der Hegelschen Rechtsphilosophie*, Introduction.

and overcome. Yet there are other passages in Marxist literature which take up an essentially different attitude. In the introduction to the English version of *Socialism: Utopian and Scientific*, for instance, Engels asserts that in the early days 'every struggle against feudalism . . . had to take on a religious disguise'.[1] The word 'disguise' still smacks of ideology, but the salient point is that the religious world-view is depicted, in this passage, as an inclusive frame of mind in which all thought-processes did, and indeed had to, take place, even the most progressive and revolutionary ones. Here we are much nearer to the sociology of knowledge in the proper sense of the word than to the doctrine of ideology.

It would be interesting to test Marx's whole work for its relative commitment to one or the other type of explanation. Speaking generally, the probable result to be expected of such an investigation is that in all polemical contexts the ideological theory will be found to prevail: the adversary is a deceiver; or he is himself the victim of deception. But in the more theoretical passages,—for instance, in the famous Introduction to the *Critique of Political Economy*—there is a definite and far reaching identification with the point of view of the sociology of knowledge.[2] Does he not maintain, in this classical statement, that it is 'men's social *existence* that determines their consciousness', rather than the *interests* to which this existence (among other tendencies) gives rise?

Of course, in Marx's thought the whole dichotomy is ingeniously covered up by the assumption that there is a class whose special interests do not lead to a distorted but to a truthful picture of reality, in whose case, in other words, ideological vision coincides with realistic vision, wish-determination with fact-determination.[3] Those who do not share the Marxian metaphysic will not accept this conviction which, in its ascription to the proletariat of a messianic mission of world salvation, is itself deeply tinged with religious sentiment. The matter need not be further pursued in this context. For the historian of ideas it is more apposite to remark that Marxism is an attempt—largely successful, though not, it would appear, completely so—to fuse two contradictory philosophical traditions, rationalism and romanticism, the Encyclopaedists and Hegel.[4]

The Encyclopaedists had developed a rather crude doctrine of ideology. Man, being endowed with reason, is in principle always and everywhere in a position to discover the truth. But in the king- and priest-ridden societies of the present and the past, men's heads have been so crammed with falsehoods and superstitions that they were no

[1] 1892, XX.
[2] Cf. Gurvitch, *Le Concept de Classes Sociales de Marx à Nos Jours*, 1954, 28 *seq.*
[3] Gurvitch, *loc. cit.*, 30; Lieber, *Wissen und Gesellschaft*, 1952, 50 *seq.*
[4] Many good things are said on this subject by Hans Barth in his important book, *Wahrheit und Ideologie*, 1945.

longer capable of thinking straight. It was the interest of those who lorded it over the masses to keep them intellectually infantile, to stimulate their sentimentality and dull their intelligence, and this interest (whether clearly recognized by the kings and priests themselves, or more naïvely felt and instinctively pursued) has accounted for all the clouds which have hidden the sun of Truth from men's eyes. When Marx said that religion was the opium of the people, he echoed Helvétius and Diderot and their latter-day disciple Feuerbach—a doctrine which did not allow for a sociology of knowledge since it asserted that once the fog had been cleared, things would be seen 'as they are', and seen by all men alike.

Hegel's approach was radically different. His main conviction is that every historical society has its own appropriate 'spirit of the age' which informs all the mental acts going on inside it, and that consequently whatever is said and thought at any one time is 'reasonable' at that time, however unreasonable it may appear at others. Religion in any form is not to him superstition; it is, while it prevails, a necessary language in which all ideas, without exception, will be couched and cast. Marx broke away from the Hegelian tradition in so far as he replaced the 'spirit of the age' which to Hegel had been the unifying agency underlying social and mental life, by the concept of civil society, the system of economic co-operation on which social life is built. But what Marx retained was the conception that every concrete society has its own appropriate stock of ideas, its own specific mode of thinking and mood of feeling, out of which it cannot stir, and when he (or rather Engels) said that at the end of the Middle Ages the lower classes could not but formulate their ideas and ideals in a religious terminology, he was echoing Hegel rather than the Encyclopaedists, romantic organicism rather than materialistic rationalism. Influences derived from this second tradition pushed him in the direction of a genuine sociology of knowledge rather than towards pan-ideologism. But he never followed them consistently to the end. Instead, he tried to mix fire and water, and though we may admit that as a clever magician he succeeded to some extent, yet his experiment generated a lot of steam into which all his doctrines on this head must ultimately dissolve.

Mannheim was not unaware of all this. Where Marx had joined together, he was inclined to set asunder. Three distinctions which he introduced are of decisive importance. The first is that between a 'special' and a 'general' conception of ideology. In the political and economic struggle, the opposing parties have often tried to undermine each other's positions by showing that the other fellow's assertions were not the truth, but falsehoods, originating either in a desire to deceive the public or in self-deception. In these cases, the assertion usually is that only the opponent is in error as to the facts; the objector's own position is naïvely assumed, or brazenly asserted, to be 'based on the realities of the situation'. Anyone who acts thus, pointing to the ideological mote in his neighbour's eye while disregarding the ideological beam in his own, is operating with the 'special' conception of ideology. But a person who realizes that *all* thinking, including his own, is tied to certain preoccupations and volitions, has advanced to the 'general' conception. He has made a very big step forward, from a political towards a philosophical point of view. It is the same with the second dichotomy which Mannheim introduces, that between the 'particular' and the 'total' conception of ideology. Those who operate with the 'particular' conception see only that certain statements of certain people can or must be understood in the light of their strivings or life-situation, for instance statements in an election campaign; but the other beliefs of the people observed are regarded as unconditioned or unconditionally true. That is where the adherents of the 'total' conception differ, for they have come to understand that substructural conditioning applies, not to disjointed or occasional thoughts and sayings only, but to *total* thought-*structures*, to men's all-important and all-inclusive categories of thinking rather than to individual ideas. Here again the result is a deeper philosophical penetration than any operation of the 'particular' conception can possibly give. Finally, there is the contrast between the 'evaluative' and the 'non-evaluative' conception of ideology. A man may desire to 'unmask ideologies' in order to deflate them; or he may seek for their hidden determinants only because he wishes to understand them, to discover through a study of their origin what their true meaning and bearing is. If so, he is applying the 'non-evaluative' conception of ideology, and he is acting as a scholar should; if not, if his intention is primarily polemical, he is operating with the 'evaluative' conception, and is a politician rather than a philosopher, a man of action rather than a man of understanding.

With these distinctions, Mannheim comes fairly close to the point of view developed in the preceding chapter. What he calls 'the special-particular-evaluative conception of ideology' obviously deals with phenomena which we have described as ideological *tout court*; what he calls the 'general-total-non-evaluative conception of ideology' refers to thought that is 'situationally determined' rather than 'ideological'. Indeed, Mannheim acknowledges that here the word 'ideology' no longer really fits. 'In the realm of the sociology of knowledge', he writes, distinguishing it at least implicitly from the realm of ideology, 'we shall, as far as possible, avoid the use of the term "ideology" because of its moral connotation, and shall instead speak of the "perspective" of a thinker. By this term we mean the subject's whole mode of conceiving things as determined by his historical and social setting'.[1] And in another

[1] *Ideology and Utopia*, Eng. ed., 1952, 239.

context he makes this virtual distinction between the doctrine of ideology and the sociology of knowledge quite explicit. 'With the emergence of the general formulation of the total conception of ideology', he says, 'the simple theory of ideology develops into the sociology of knowledge. What was once the intellectual armament of a party is transformed into a method of research . . .'[1]

So far so good. But Mannheim has still not wholly overcome the confusion between the ideological and the social determination of thinking. The world still appears to him, as it did to Marx, as essentially an arena of struggling social and political forces, and he sees the thought-processes taking place in the human mind as far too closely involved in these struggles. It is characteristic that the social entities which he considers decisive for the constitution of coherent world-views and concrete categorizations of thinking, are above all the social classes and political parties. It is no accident that one of the universes of thought, or 'total ideologies', which he considers most carefully, is the world-image of political conservativism. This preoccupation with, and concentration on, the continuing struggle for economic and political power again imparts to his sociology of knowledge a definite bias towards interpreting ideas partly or even wholly as ideologies in the narrower sense of the word. What he gains in theory, he loses when it comes to practice.

How true this is can be seen from the very title of his main work: *Ideology and Utopia*. These two key-concepts, a perceptive critic has written, 'play an all-important rôle in his conception of sociology of knowledge. . . . Both the ideologist, panegyrist of the past, and the utopian, harbinger of things to come, are primarily anti-intellectualistic [i.e. not concerned with the truth]. They are concerned with emotions, motivations, with the upholding and tearing down of standards, not with knowledge *quâ* knowledge. Rather than a theory, both propound a rationale, a philosophy of life, an inseparable admixture of factionary bias and cognitive fact. The dénouement, the inevitable conclusion to be drawn should be patent indeed. . . . The character of the object of his study has led him into serious confusions, the chief of which is the failure to distinguish between the scientific, the cognitive use, and the evocative, the motivational use of language. . . . Mannheim's confusion in trying to develop an epistemological sociology of knowledge lies . . . in his . . . failure both to distinguish cognitive from non-cognitive aspects of "knowledge" as well as to realize the vitiating influence of just this evaluation component in the "knowledge" of any period.' This latter half of the last sentence is decidedly less than fair. Yet Hinshaw's main criticism can stand: 'If sociology of knowledge, as he claims, traces its heritage directly and immediately to the general theory of total ideology, then it is bound to be inextricably tinged with non-scientific,

[1] *Ibid.*, 69.

103

emotive elements.'[1] Mannheim has often been called 'a bourgeois Marx-ist', and this label, though a trifle malicious, is not altogether unfair as a summing-up of his mental habitus.[2] He came much too close to the pan-ideological conception of the human mind, despite the consciously 'non-evaluative' character of his approach. He reminds one of that great figure of the Old Testament who led his people towards the promised land but was condemned never to enter it, and died on its threshold.

Pan-ideologism, then, must be far more decisively rejected than it has been either by Marx or Mannheim. The doctrine of ideology deals with an aspect of human thinking which borders upon indeed, but certainly does not merge with, the area of social determination. In what is to follow we exclude it resolutely from our considerations, though without forgetting, of course, that in the history of ideas ideologies have played, and continue to play, a highly important part.

The radically non-ideological theory of social determination which we are now about to put forward is remotely indebted to Kantian inspiration,[3] though Kant himself, whose epistemology knows only the isolated individual, man in his relation to nature, and whose ethics, even, are exclusively concerned with inter-individual conduct rather than with social life properly so called, had no inkling of the possibilities opened up by his 'Copernican revolution' for a specifically sociological study of human thought-processes. In the neo-Kantian school, especi-ally in the 'Baden' subdivision of it, these possibilities were later recognized and to some extent developed. Heinrich Rickert is of im-portance in this context,[4] and so too is Max Weber, his disciple.[5] But

[1] V. G. Hinshaw, 'The Epistemological Relevance of Mannheim's Sociology of Knowledge', *The Journal of Philosophy*, 1943, 69 *seq.* Cf. also A. von Schelting, *Max Webers Wissenschaftslehre*, 1934, esp. 98, 168, and part III, *passim*.

[2] For a fair comparison between Marx and Mannheim, cf. T. B. Bottomore, 'Some Reflections on the Sociology of Knowledge', in *The British Journal of Sociology*, March, 1956, 52 *seq.*, esp. 55.

[3] The theory has been suggested, as it were, by Kant, but it is by no means neces-sary to be a Kantian in order to appreciate or accept it. In fact, some of its most distinguished protagonists, for instance Max Scheler, were not Kantians. In *Prinzipien der Geschichts- und Kultursoziologie*, Alfred Weber asserts that it was Kant's disciple Friedrich Schiller who first adumbrated the sociology of knowledge later developed, among others, by Max Scheler and himself (cf. ed. 1951, 11 *seq.*).

[4] Cf. also Dilthey's views as summarized by H. A. Hodges in his book *Wilhelm Dilthey: An Introduction* (1944): 'All thinking in the human studies is axiological. . . . No one can study the whole of history or society, we have to select. No one can tell all that he knows about the thing which he has studied. He has to select and edit . . . we select what we consider to be important . . . and in the last analysis our standard of importance is our standard of value' whereby 'the realm of value includes evil as well as good'—what we flee as well as what we pursue (8 *seq.*). Cf. also Ernst Grünwald, *Das Problem der Soziologie des Wissens*, 1934, 83 *seq.*; Hans-Joachim Lieber, *Wissen und Gesellschaft*, 1952, esp. 9 and 56.

[5] For a brief, but instructive discussion of Weber's connection with Rickert, cf. Raymond Aron, *Die deutsche Soziologie der Gegenwart*, ed. 1953, 94 *seq.*

so far, it appears, the theory has not been systematically set forth. In Rickert's and Max Weber's works it is present only in solution, so to speak: it lies behind their texts rather than in and on the surface of them, and this is not surprising in view of the fact that their prime concern was with other matters. It takes on shape and comes nearer to formulation in Alexander von Schelting's admirable treatise entitled *Max Webers Wissenschaftslehre*. This work contains an incisive criticism of Karl Mannheim's *Wissenssoziologie*, and the position from which von Schelting surveys and exposes its weaknesses is the very same Kantian-Rickertian-Weberian conception of the relationship between social life and human thought whose implications we shall try to bring out here. But von Schelting was content to destroy error; he did not stop to deploy and define the truth. We shall endeavour to provide a positive counterpart to his negative argument, to show what sort of sociology of knowledge is right if Mannheim's pan-ideologism is wrong.

The Kantian theory of knowledge, as everyone knows, is concerned with the origin and nature of man's mental image of the physical world. This image is not simply due, as naïve dogmatism assumes, to the impressions which we receive through our senses. This applies possibly, not to say probably, to the lower animals' picture of their environment, which seems to be a succession of disconnected sensations, freely coming and going and leaving behind them no firm and lasting mind-content. Our view of the world is different—and superior—because we are able to *organize* our sensual perceptions into a coherent and transparent whole, because we achieve an ordered and structured mental picture of the material universe which underlies our whole existence as thinking and acting beings, and makes it possible for us to think clearly and act purposefully. What lifts us to that high intellectual level is not the superiority of our sensory apparatus; indeed, our equipment in this respect is far inferior to that of many beasts. It is the fact that, in addition to our senses, we are also endowed with reason, which all the lower creation lacks, and that reason contains '*a priori*'—from the very beginning, before any encounter with concrete factual impressions—principles of order which make out of the (in itself chaotic) intake of information through the sensory channels that systematic body of intelligent knowledge which we all have and hold. Of things as they are 'in themselves' we know nothing. How could we? It is illogical to assume that *we* could ever know the world as it is *apart from ourselves*. What we know, we know only by and through the categories of our understanding. Yet, for a limited creature such as man is, that is enough. To the question: how is true knowledge possible, we must answer: through the *a priori* apparatus of our mind. Take that away, and knowledge becomes simple awareness, the light of reason the dimness of instinct, the clear-cut contour of reality a dream-like, floating, unmanageable fog.

This, then, is Kant's account of the way in which the individual apprehensions of our eyes and ears and touch and taste—in themselves no more than the raw materials of knowing—become transformed, in the mighty manufactory of the human mind, into that perfectly co-ordinated and connected end-product of the process of cognition, the scheme of knowledge in and by which we humans operate. The intellect is not the passive receiver of truth, but rather its active creator. As Robert Merton has expressed it: 'Despite the etymology of the term, *data* are not "given" but are "contrived" with the inevitable help of concepts.' [1] It is as if innumerable disjointed snapshots were fed into a magic lantern, to emerge at the other end as clear and coherent projections on the mental screen. Kant himself, of course, speaks only of our mind's relation to the physical world. But is it not more than likely that our understanding of the cultural and social, that is to say, the human world, is accomplished in the very same way? We think it is, and we hope to prove it by arguments both unsophisticated and sophisticated.

First a supremely simple example, merely to illustrate the matter. At a certain moment of June 28, 1914, the Austrian Archduke Francis Ferdinand was shot in the streets of the little township of Sarajevo. In the same split second, however, myriads of other events were taking place—events so numerous that all the paper and all the ink in the world would not be sufficient to put them down. Now, *all* these events, including that at the street corner of Sarajevo, were 'in themselves' equally important, or rather equally unimportant. If we take away the historian's observing and enregistering mind, they all shrink equally into mere physical happenings, into shifts of masses of matter, great and small discharges or accumulations of energy, chemical reactions, and what not. But there is no special significance attached to any of them. We can compare them to an open plain that stretches on all sides into infinity. But the moment we bring the historian on to the scene the picture is altered. He will at once single out the shot fired by Gavrilo Princip as an occurrence of historical importance. He will see it and study it—but the rest of the landscape he will not study, nor indeed will he even notice or consciously see it.

Now, what is it that enables him to select, from the infinite number of potential items of cognitive material, the one he is to make into an object of knowledge? What makes it possible for him to stop his eye roaming and roving over the measureless wastes of reality and to focus and fix upon one definite point as if it were an eminence in the plain, a

---

[1] *Social Theory and Social Structure*, 1949, 370. Another good formulation of the same point, though more from the semantic point of view, is to be found in an article by C. Wright Mills in the *American Journal of Sociology*, 1940/41, esp. 322.

mountain towering above the universal flatness? It is an *a priori* content of his mind, a deeply engrained axiom to the effect that 'political events are important'. Without this pre-judgment, without this prior evaluation, his view of the factual scene would never shape and order itself, would never become historical *knowledge*. Take away the basic axiom which we have indicated, and the image disintegrates, dissolves into fog. Just as the physicist's formal *a priori* enables him to distinguish high and low, near and far, hill and dale, and to comprehend the landscape as a whole according to the dimensions provided by the *a priori* category of space, so the historian's social *a priori* puts him in a position to contrast large and small, eminent and not eminent, important and unimportant, and to present an integrated description of historical reality according to the dimensions provided by his own axiological system, the axiological system established *a priori* in his mind—i.e. before the cognizance of concrete facts.

It is the prime contention of the sociologist of knowledge—and with it he goes decisively beyond the orbit of Kantianism properly so called—that this social *a priori* or axiological system is the value-system of the society in which the historian, the seeker after human knowledge, lives. The pre-judgments or prior evaluations with which he works, and which enable him to do his work, are not prejudices or value-judgments in the current sense of the word. The latter unfortunately creep in from time to time, but they are as illegitimate as they are avoidable. His pre-judgments, however, are the value-*facts* at the basis of the contemporary social set-up which encloses him and has shaped his mind—shaped it, *uno actu*, for practical conduct *and* for theoretical contemplation. It is because political happenings are important for our lives that we regard them as important in our thought.

The unphilosophical practitioner may at this point remonstrate and assert that 'of course' political events such as the assassination of a crown-prince are of prime importance, and that consequently there is no need to talk at length about it, let alone to have a theory on the subject. But apart from the fact that it is the mission of philosophy to investigate, carefully and critically, precisely what is taken for granted—'as a matter of course'—by the generality of men, the matter is not as simple as it looks even from a fairly practical point of view. The example we have chosen was (and was meant to be) obvious, trite, commonplace. But we need only shift a short step in the direction of sophistication to show that there is a very real problem involved. The historian of 1650, when he speaks of the causes of a war, is apt to concentrate on feudal titles, marriage contracts, family trees and other things of that order; the historian of 1950, confronted with the same theme, is more likely to talk at length about raw materials, outlets to the sea, the control of markets, and similar factors.

The preoccupations of the older historians will be almost [1] as far below the limits of his own consciousness as they were above those of his predecessors—just as his main preoccupations would have been as far below the limits of their consciousness as they are now above his. Obviously, since 1650, some hills have become dales in the historical landscape, some dales hills. Or, to revert to our earlier metaphor: the images that today appear on the mental screen are significantly, not to say totally, different, because the facts—the self-same facts!—are now seen through a different selecting grid, through a different *a priori* pattern or axiological system; and this grid, pattern or system is different today from what it was three hundred years ago, not so much because our thinking has changed—this is only a partial strand in an inclusive development for the sociologist of knowledge—but because life has changed in its totality, because social reality has passed through a series of evolutions and revolutions since the end of the Thirty Years' War. For the structure of the mind always accommodates itself to the structure of the society within which it has to function.

After these more concrete examples, we can perhaps boldly climb to a higher level of abstraction. Our discussion will be easier if we bear in mind the following scheme or paradigm of the elements involved in the process of cognition:

The subject and his approach	{ *The Categorial Layer of the Mind*	
	The Physical Apparatus of Perception	The concern of
	The Axiological Layer of the Mind	the sociology
The objective world	{ *The Objects of Knowledge*	of knowledge
	The Materials of Knowledge	

In this paradigm, the word 'category' is used in a very restricted, strictly Kantian, sense. What is meant is simply time, space and causality—the *a priori* forms of cognition which enable us to apprehend things in a temporal and spatial order and in mutual connectedness. For radical empiricism, this layer of the mind does not exist, and if this conviction should be correct, our paradigm would have to start one storey lower, with the physical apparatus of perception. The philosophical problem involved—idealism versus materialism—is tremendous. Nevertheless, we need not bother with it here, since for us, who are mainly interested in specifically social knowledge, the physical apprehension of things is a mere background process, however absolutely essential it may be to all other mental processes. We may calmly take the existence of a mental picture of the material universe for

[1] Almost, but not wholly, for he may have read his predecessors' books. Nevertheless, their main interests will always appear to him as 'unreal preoccupations'.

granted, leaving the solution of the difficulties which it raises to the professional philosophers, and concentrate on the rest of the scheme which is of closer concern to us.

If, in this way, nothing need be said in the present context about the formal categories of our intellect and the physical receptors of our body, nothing *can* be said, in this place *or* in any other, about the materials of knowledge—the materials of knowledge as such,—for these are, by definition, outside our mind. All that we are able to say about them is *that* they are; but as yet we have no knowledge of them. They represent, in and by themselves, that which is potentially knowable, in contrast to that part of them which is actually known. They stretch, far beyond the comparatively restricted circle of reality lit up by the arc-lamps of our reason, out into an exterior darkness so wide in extent and so rich in content that it is unimaginable that the limited mind of man will ever be able to know them fully. Max Scheler describes them as the *ens reale* (what is in being) and contrasts them to the *ens intentionale*, that sector of being on which our mind is, so to speak, intent, which it has consciously apprehended and come to know. Strictly speaking, we ought not even to affirm that the knowable behind and beyond the actually known is a collection of facts, for the word fact already means a concrete something that has been cut out of the texture of the materials of knowledge and established, by a mental operation performed by ourselves, the operation of definition, as an individual entity. 'If one understands by a fact something that is simply given without any intervention on our part,' Scheler writes, 'then *definite* facts of any kind whatsoever do not exist at all. A fact would then be that totally undefined, fluctuating and insubstantial sum of chaotic impressions in which as yet no unity or structure or delimitation is to be found. Yet with this chaos our ideas are so little designed to correspond, that it can never be more than the raw material for the form-giving operations carried on by ourselves. A "fact", in both the common and the scientific meaning of the term, is always something already in some way shaped and made concrete by our mental activity. Facts only stand out from the chaos and come, as it were, to be separated out of it, when we put some question to reality; reality's answer or reaction is then the "fact" concerned.' [1] Thus all that we can rightly say of the materials of knowledge is that they comprise everything that is factual, or all that exists; as soon as we focus on any concrete entity, and say that that *is*, we have already created an object of knowledge.

It is a highly gratifying point which must be stated and even emphasized in the interests of a future unified sociology of knowledge, that both Mannheim and the Marxians sometimes operate with conceptions akin to our 'materials of knowledge'. Stanislaw Warynski, for instance,

[1] *Die Wissensformen und die Gesellschaft*, 1926, 270. Cf. also 271 *seq.*

one of the most percipient among modern Marxists, distinguishes, in his *Wissenschaft von der Gesellschaft*, the 'undifferentiated mental unity which is prior to conceptual thinking' and conceptual thinking as such, and though this distinction is on a different level than the one we have drawn (in so far as Warynski's distinction is between two layers of mental life, and not between intra-mental and extra-mental reality), it is none the less a distinction which aims in the same direction and has similar possibilities and implications. 'Scientific thought', he says in another passage, can 'only be the logical and rational systematization of experience.' Here again, we have a line drawn between experience, which is something merely lived, and hence mentally unfocused, and logico-rational thought, which is something clearly known and hence moulded by the mind. Of course, Warynski is a prisoner of that naïve dogmatism or realism which slipped into Marxism from eighteenth century rationalism and has become all too basic a part of it. But there is no mistaking his approach to a quasi-Kantian position.

Other passages show him on the same path. For instance: 'We encounter the world as a conglomerate of facts and as a process. . . . Usually, one understands by thinking the ordering and penetration of experience. In this definition, one factor is not included: the capacity, observed in thinking, . . . to work up the material of experience according to its own wish and will, to make it into its object. . . .' Or, even better: 'Certainly, rational thinking is always also a psychological process, but it is beyond that a principle of ordering the world itself, provided by the structure of the human mind. . . . The so-called purely psychological, instinctual "knowing" is in truth no knowing at all, but an experiencing which precedes the causal-logical working up of the experience. . . .' And, finally: 'The collection of details and the recording of what is externally describable do not yet constitute the whole of reality; on the contrary, they produce a kind of estrangement from it . . . The mere amassing of empirical data, for instance the collection and arrangement of documents, provides . . . meaningless material [only], that is to say material which is not yet material in the proper sense of the word, being at best a technical, but not yet a logical starting-point for science. . . . This [so-called] material must, by the productive scientist, be comprehended in its meaning and given form. . . . It must be produced a second time, this time as true material. . . . For this reason the [factual] raw materials are indeed a precondition for the understanding of reality, but at the same time also its result. . . .' [1]

With all this, Warynski manifestly remains imprisoned in naïve realism. He admits the intervention of the intellect at too late a stage, the point where knowledge-providing experience is transformed into

[1] *Loc. cit.*, ed. 1944, 95, 239, 96 *seq.*, 236 *seq.*, 261 *seq.*

conceptual knowledge, and not where he ought to locate it, at the very inception, nay prior to, any and every concrete experience. Yet the dichotomy which he elaborates has all the same a distant family relationship to our own Kant-inspired distinction between the materials of knowledge and the objects of knowledge, the historical thing-in-itself and the historical phenomenon.

Karl Mannheim, as might be expected, is even nearer to our way of thinking than Stanislaw Warynski. Deeply concerned about the problem of historical relativity, i.e. the fact that different societies have different ideas about the self-same factual phenomena, he draws in effect a distinction between the intra-mental mirrorings of reality (which change from age to age) and the extra-mental reality itself (which, of course, is always the same). It is clear that, in speaking of this extramental reality, he is speaking of what we are calling 'the materials of knowledge'. Here are a few apposite quotations: 'The historical subject-matter (the historical content, so to speak, of an epoch) remains identical "in itself", but it belongs to the essential conditions of its cognizability that it can be grasped only from differing intellectual-historical standpoints. . . .' 'The essence and the actual existence of Hellenism do not dissolve themselves into the various "perspectives" opened up by successive generations of historical scholarship. It is, in fact, "given" as a "thing in itself", approached from various sides, as it were, by different interpretations. We are justified in positing this real being of the object *in se*, for even though no single perspective can do it full justice, it is still given as a control we may use in ruling out arbitrary characterizations.' [1] The very last words of the second passage are perhaps somewhat problematic (for how can the merely knowable control the actually known?), but the rest is a sound approach to the realization that behind the objects of knowledge already constituted as such there lies the sphere of the materials of knowledge, from which these objects are selected by ourselves.

It is good to see in all this an advance from three different angles towards the same working concept. But this concept is a merely negative one and helps at best to set out the terms of the problem which the sociology of knowledge has to solve. Using the terminology of our paradigm, this problem itself can be formulated in the following words: how is it that some of the materials of knowledge, which are outside our mind, come to be transmuted into objects of knowledge which are both outside and inside our mind? Some may think that this formulation is made clearer, others perhaps that it is made obscurer, by adding to it a certain crucial passage from Max Scheler; we should like to quote it in any case leaving it to the enemies of metaphysics to close their eyes to its content. 'Knowledge is an existential relationship, and one which

---

[1] *Essays on the Sociology of Knowledge*, 1952, 105, 171 *seq.*

presupposes the existential forms whole and part. It is the relation of participation of an existing being in the attributes (*Sosein*) of another existent entity by which no change is brought about in the latter. What is "known" becomes a "part" of the "knower", but without moving in any way from its place or being otherwise transformed. This ontological relationship is not a spatial, temporal or causal relationship. "Mens" or "mind" we call the X or the sum and substance of the acts in the "knowing" being by dint of which such a participation is possible; by which a thing, or rather the attributes—and only the attributes—of an existing thing become an "*ens intentionale*" in contradistinction to a mere reality ("*ens reale*") which always and necessarily remains outside and beyond the relationship of knowing. The root of this X, the direction-giving moment for the realization of acts which lead to some form of participation, can only be that self-transcending . . . interest in it [1] which, in its most formal sense, we call "love". Knowledge is there, and only there, where the attributes are, in strict identity, both *extra mentem*, i.e. *in re*, and at the same time also *in mente*—as *ens intentionale* or as "object".' [2]

These words not only indicate the problem, they also point the way to its solution. We select, and thereby focus upon, those elements in the materials of knowledge which we 'love' (or hate) in some way, in which we are 'interested', whether that interest be material or non-material, positive or negative—in short, which correspond to, and are determined by, our order of values. As Alexander von Schelting puts it in a particularly felicitous passage: 'In the materials themselves there are no "indications" of any kind which would enable us "objectively" to separate the essential from the unessential and thus to isolate the historically important individual elements in what happens. Only the axiological view-points (*Wertgesichtspunkte*) bring it about that what is all equally real, from a logical point of view, divides into the individually "significant" and the "not significant".' Or, in Max Weber's words, quoted by von Schelting: ' "Culture" is a finite sector cut out of the meaningless infinity of universal happening, which has been endowed, from the human point of view, with meaning and importance.' 'Empirical reality is "culture" for us because, and in so far as, we bring it into relation with concepts of value.' [3]

---

[1] '. . . *die sich selbst und sein eigenes Sein transzendierende Teilnahme.*' The German play of words between *Teilhabe* (participation) and *Teilnahme* (interest) is not reproducible in English.

[2] *Die Wissensformen und die Gesellschaft*, 1926, 247 *seq.*

[3] *Max Webers Wissenschaftslehre*, 1934, 226. We may notice, merely in passing, that it would be possible, on the basis of these ideas, to formulate a theory of intuition. What happens in intuition is that the mind frees itself momentarily from the constriction of the objects of knowledge and dives down into the boundless sea

If we may be pardoned for descending without ceremony from the august to the trivial, we may illustrate this truth by a homely observation. When a man and a woman see a lady passing in the street, they will (unless the man happens to be a fashion-designer!) receive different impressions and images of her. The man's mind is likely to register her features and bodily form rather than her frock, the woman's her frock rather than her features and bodily form. 'I noticed her clothes more than her face', Agatha Christie makes one of her heroines say— 'women do!' [1] They do, because they are more interested in this aspect than in the other—because their order of values is in all typical cases different from that of the majority of males.

Our chosen example is an a-typical one in so far as the 'societies' concerned—men on the one hand, women on the other—are constituted by nature, not by social forces, and the eye-opening interest or value is rooted in the instinctual rather than the social life (though it certainly is not purely instinctual, as our reference to the dress-designer is sufficient to demonstrate). As this matter, the relationship of the physical and the socio-cultural in the sociology of knowledge, will be touched upon in chapter 4, we shall not allow it to create a diversion at this point. But we may emphasize, in passing, that our instance is not so a-typical as might appear at first sight. For in all societies physical urges coexist with, co-operate with, and express themselves through, culture and the values and conations engendered by society.

Here we must try, to the best of our ability, to characterize the *ordo amoris* of which Scheler speaks and which we have called the axiological layer of the mind—this *a priori* system of social valuations or pre-judgments which enables us to form, out of the infinitude of the knowable, the finite and hence comprehensible universe of the known. Merton has spoken well of the 'cognitive orientations' to which it gives rise,[2] and Sprott equally well of a 'climate of interest' and a 'value climate'[3] as one of the social preconditions of knowing, and preconditions of social knowing. Lieber aims in the same direction when he refers to a 'metatheoretical, activistic directedness of the soul' which precedes and makes possible its taking cognizance of concrete fact.[4] Even Geiger pays his respects to it before passing on to other, and in our opinion less enlightened, considerations; and even he sees it at the back of, and prior to, the very putting of questions to reality: 'At the back of all efforts towards theoretical knowledge, a-theoretical incentives are at work. There is no instance of perception into whose origin the will, an

of the materials of knowledge, bringing back—lifting into the light—insights which had not been achieved before, and more especially, revealing interconnections between elements of the real not yet discovered.

[1] *Murder on the Orient Express*, 1953, 172.
[2] *Social Theory and Social Structure*, 1949, 247.
[3] *Science and Social Action*, 1954, 52, 85.   [4] *Wissen und Gesellschaft*, 1952, 87.

interest, a vital striving, do not enter somewhere, even if it be only the curiosity of the man concerned. . . . How is it, for instance, that the research worker turns to some one definite problem among the thousands possible to him in his science? It must somehow have stimulated his interest to a higher degree than other questions. The choice of problem is at least partially dependent on extra-theoretical considerations. . . . Knowledge [itself] cannot provide the striving for knowledge. . . . Thus it would seem as if the evaluative will were somehow involved in every conceivable statement. . . .' [1] And Geiger rightly adds that this basic fact does not in itself bring our thinking under the global suspicion of being ideological.

All these formulations indicate what the axiological layer of the mind is, and what it does. But the most classical expression and applications of the theory we owe to the genius of Max Scheler. His prime example is the origin of the modern world-view—that inclusive thought-structure which has been the basis of all realistic thinking since the Renaissance, and which, as Scheler has shown, has sprung from an underlying, *a priori* will- and value-structure centred upon the desire to dominate the material world. 'A sociological law of knowledge which comes to the surface in the origin of modern science,' he writes, 'is . . . the way in which the amateur comes before the expert, dilettantism before scientific bureaucracy, love before knowledge. Each new objective realm which science has conquered in her history, has had first to be seized in an access of affection: only then could there supervene an age of sober and intellectually more objective research. A new natural science presupposes for this reason a new feeling for nature—a new valuation of nature. This emotional break-through takes place in the European renaissances beginning with the renaissance of the Franciscan movement (which is still wholly tied to the terms of Christianity) and its successors, but becoming more and more secularized (Telesio, Campanella, Leonardo, Petrarch, Giordano Bruno, Spinoza, Shaftesbury, Fénélon up to Rousseau). . . . The Hohenstaufen Emperor Frederick II and his half occidental, half oriental Moorish circle in Sicily—he was the founder of Naples University—is a point from which this emotionalism radiates out with great force. . . . New emotional relations to animal and plant, that is to say to all which in nature, as something animate, is akin to man, are the bridges to a novel intoxication with nature. The extent and nature of the process of sympathetic empathy into, and identification with, nature are vastly different in the different epochs of human history. At the height of the Middle Ages they reach a minimum in extent and intensity. In the Renaissance this inherent potentiality of man's mind and soul breaks forth with hurricane force. . . . Emotional outbreaks of this kind occur throughout the history of western science.

[1] *Ideologie und Wahrheit*, 1953, 112 *seq.*

. . . It would be an erroneous interpretation of the forces which have overcome the anthropomorphism of the medieval world-view to regard them only, or even primarily, so far as time-order is concerned, as the outcome of rational thinking. To think—that is precisely what the Schoolmen could do more acutely and sharply, more artfully and methodically than the bulk of all the modern generations of scientists. Initially, it was rather an orgiastic and ecstatic, emotional surrender to nature and a new experiential attitude which brought an opening-up of the mind towards the world . . . which led beyond bookish knowledge and narrow anthropomorphism. . . .' [1]

This new love of nature which, in contradiction of the well-known adage, made men attentive to her true character, rather than blind to it, was not like the Christian *agape* which demands the passive surrender of the lover to the loved one, but resembled rather the heathen *eros* with its active desire to appropriate, to have and to hold her. For this reason domination became the decisive axiological element, the central value-attitude, from which the study of reality was undertaken, and which, in the fullness of time, was to lead to the integral modern world-view. 'It is undoubtedly the new conception of power, manifesting itself at the same time theologically in Calvinism and politically in Bodin's doctrine of sovereignty, in Thomas Hobbes and in Machiavelli, which also inspires the age of the new inventions and discoveries in its scientific work, makes a new selection of the objects of knowledge and newly determines its aims. Francis Bacon wants only to "see, in order to foresee", and he wanted to "foresee" only because, and in so far as, this promotes man's power over nature; G. B. Vico declares in the eighteenth century that we can know objects of any kind only to the extent that we are able to produce them ourselves.'

'The theory of knowledge can show convincingly,' Scheler goes on to say, taking his argument a good deal further and making a point we have also tried to make—'that the pure desire for knowledge, the use of logic, mathematics and observation, would never lead us to a mechanistic explanation of the phenomena of nature and the soul (not even of inanimate nature, let alone of animate and spiritual reality); and history confirms it in the most striking manner; and does so the more clearly, the more closely we study the origin of the modern view of nature and reality. The forms of thought and perception from whose active functioning this world-view arose, are by no means constitutionally inherent in the "human mind" as such. The principles of speculation and reasoning, as Kant assembled them in his *Kritik der reinen Vernunft*, are only one possible mode of thinking for our reason, and by no means reason itself; one mode of thinking which . . . the . . . new "will to power" over nature carved out of all "possible" modes of

[1] *Die Wissensformen und die Gesellschaft*, 1926, 115 *seq.*, 124.

experiencing the world . . . In as much as a specific direction of interest and value-system and the rules of preference contained in it precede all possible perception and observation of the world as well as all thinking directed to the grasping of meaning . . . mechanism becomes the anticipatory scheme in which the new bourgeois society apprehends the possible picture of reality. . . . It was not "pure reason", not "the spirit in itself" which at the inception of the modern age sketched out the tremendous programme of a comprehensive mechanistic explanation of nature and man, long before its implementation in physics, chemistry, biology, psychology, sociology etc., but the new will to power over nature, and creative work within her, on the part of a rising society. It ousted, by degrees, on the one hand the high valuation of the dominion of man over man and over the organic realm which had been predominant in the feudal age and feudal society, and on the other the contemplative quest for knowledge of a priestly and monkish society which desired to perceive, and mentally to mirror, the "essences and forms" of reality.'

There was something new, then, about the apprehension of things as it developed from the age of the Renaissance onward; but what was new was only the human perspective, not the 'things in themselves'—only the 'objects of knowledge' discerned in and selected from the permanently given 'materials of knowledge' which are the same at all times. 'No relativism and historism', Scheler goes on to explain, 'follows from all this. If reality did not possess, *ontologically*, a formal and mechanistic aspect, no . . . will to power would be able to separate it out from the experience of that reality. Only the special *selection*, made at a given time, of the modes of thinking, is determined by social and historical factors—not these modes themselves. Each of the mental schemata is ushered in by a specific ethos, by a living system of the positive and negative ranking of values—an *ordo amoris*; and each of these value-systems is carried by a dominant stratum in society which becomes the model of all others. Nothing can better illustrate these laws than the social and historical origin of the modern world-view.' [1]

It is essential to understand that Scheler does not aim to preach any kind of economic conception of the history of ideas: 'The will to dominate is by no means the same thing as the will to utilize. Bacon not only misunderstood the nature of science, but also the nature of technology. Utilitarianism misses not only the specific significance and rank of the "spiritual goods" and values but also the incentive which sets modern technology in motion. The aim and basic value which directs the new technology is not that of devising machines which are economically or in other ways useful and whose utility can be discerned and estimated beforehand. Something much higher is at stake! The aim is,

[1] *Loc. cit.*, 239 *seq*. Cf. also 320 *seq*.

so to speak, to construct *all possible* machines, in the first place only in the mind and with the object of making sure that nature could be harnessed and directed . . . if so desired. . . . Hence also the many playful and impossible technical experiments with the aim of "making" everything out of everything which precede the maturity of the technological age (alchemy, automata, etc.) . . . It is the idea and value of human power and human freedom vis-à-vis nature which inspires the great centuries of discoveries and inventions, not merely the idea of utility. . . . We are confronted with a change of direction in the will to power, away from God and men towards things. . . .' [1]

The main argument which Scheler's explanations are likely to encounter, and which can be brought to bear not only against this splendid example of the sociology of knowledge, but against the subject as a whole, is the assertion, so characteristic of the naïve mind, that there was no need for our modern way of thinking to be evoked by any specious value-experience or value-attitude since it is simply the 'natural' mode of thinking, the mode of thinking which either all men have had, even in the past, or which at any rate all men should and would have had if only they had been 'reasonable'. This argument is all the more dangerous to truth for being based on a half-truth which Scheler, for his part, was so far from denying that he actually emphasized it.

Certainly when and in so far as medieval or primitive man devoted himself to the ideal of 'world-domination', he arrived, or would rationally have been obliged to arrive, at a more or less pan-mechanistic philosophy of life, such as was later developed by the modern West, for it is only when he learns to think of nature as a quasi-machine that man can also learn to dominate it. But the point is that pre-modern man did not devote himself primarily to that value but to other values, and for that reason he saw the universe in very different terms. Scheler distinguishes three types of knowledge which he calls *Herrschaftswissen*, *Bildungswissen* and *Erlösungswissen*—knowledge born of a desire to achieve control over nature; knowledge born of a desire to cultivate and refine the personality; and knowledge born of a desire to achieve salvation. The share of the latter two, and particularly of the last, in the modern mental life is small—as small as the first was in Antiquity and the Middle Ages. 'Of these three ideals of knowledge', Scheler says, 'the more recent history of the West and its independently developing cultural annexes (America etc.) exhibits a systematic, increasingly one-sided and almost exclusive propensity to cultivate the knowledge which aims at a possible practical transformation of the world. Cultural and religious knowledge has been pushed more and more into the background. Yet even of this knowledge directed at controlling and manipulating nature only one possible half has been fostered: that which is

[1] *Loc. cit.*, 173 *seq.*

destined to serve for the domination and direction of *external* (above all inorganic) nature. Internal life- and soul-technique, that is to say the task of extending the power and dominion of the will . . . over the processes of the psycho-physical organism . . . has undergone a far-reaching involution. In the cultivation of cultural and redemptive knowledge, and of that technological knowledge which is concerned with the sphere of vital processes, the Asiatic cultures possess as great an advantage over the rest of the world as Europe has in the field of knowledge which serves the domination of external nature. Positivism and pragmatism are merely the honest, very one-sided philosophical expressions of this real state of modern Western culture. Both make operational science into the "only possible science", without always being clearly aware of it.' [1]

The final statement in this quotation must not perhaps be taken too literally. Our modern axiological system is no simple affair, but highly complex, and has stimulated all manner of researches and in consequence produced all kinds of knowledge. Yet who would gainsay the over-all truth of Scheler's assertion? Surely, in the Western order of values the desire to understand (and control) Nature has in the last three hundred years predominated mightily over the desire to understand God and Man, and the result has been a world-view, a working philosophy, no less fundamentally determined by scientific conceptions (and prejudices!) than was the *imago mundi* of the Middle Ages, for instance, by religion.

Scheler's whole theory, which seems to us the most satisfactory approach to the basic problem of the sociology of knowledge that has yet been tried, is summed up in one crowning concept—the concept of the 'relatively natural [i.e. normal] world-view'. Epistemology has always operated with the concept of a 'natural world-view', meaning thereby the view of the world, of reality, held by the man in the street, the world-view of man simply *quâ* man. Now, this view has almost always been conceived as an 'absolutely natural view', a view which we must expect to find wherever we find man, in all ages and countries. Scheler opposes this conception.[2] If we study what a Kant, for instance, regarded as 'absolutely natural', we are apt to find merely a hypostasation of what was regarded as 'natural' in his age and country. Philosophers have ever tended to absolutize the relative. For modern man it is as 'natural' not to see ghosts and spirits lurking in nature as it is to see them for primitive man. Notwithstanding the possibility that there may be a constant factor running through all social systems and invariably present in man's picture of reality, what concrete men see of the world and in the world, and how they see what they do see, depends—according to Scheler, and also to the sociology of knowledge—on a socio-

---

[1] *Loc. cit.*, 252.   [2] Perhaps he opposes it too much. Cf. our fourth chapter.

historical principle of specification, of crystallization, of ordered selection and co-ordinating construction, and that principle is inherent in the axiological or value-structure prevailing at the time. The world of the absolute cannot be grasped by us humans. How can the finite mind hope to lay hold on the infinite? By our whole constitution we are forced to live in a universe of restricted awareness. Our world-view will always be relative, however 'natural' we who live within it may feel it to be. And in every society the governing relation will be to the axiomata or guiding values in and by which the society concerned has organized its existence, its activities, and consequently also its mental conceptions and procedures. For life, action and thought must always form a working partnership, an inclusive whole.

With this analysis of Scheler's we are obviously far removed from all forms of pan-ideologism and from the whole doctrine of ideology. Yet there are elements both in Marxist literature and in Mannheim which manifestly point in the same direction. In his all-important *Theses on Feuerbach* Marx criticizes and condemns traditional materialism because it regards reality (the reality of which our thought attempts to take cognizance) as something ready-made, an object or assemblage of objects, whereas it is actually something made by us, a product of our practice. In so far as the 'productive' activity of the subject is the starting-point of idealism, idealism is more in the right than materialism. But traditional or classical idealism conceives the 'productivity' of the mind to be alone constitutive of reality, and it deals with nothing but the isolated individual, whereas it is the social process of material production which ought to occupy—even in epistemology—the centre of the stage. For Marx theory and practice cannot be divorced, because in man the knower and the worker are one: he is convinced that the world-view which a society makes for itself is a product of its process of production, just as are the material products to which this process leads. This opinion, which credits man with the power of moulding reality, and that not only on the material, but also on the mental plane, is manifestly akin to the conviction underlying the Rickert-Weber-Scheler tradition which we have just surveyed.

If it was smothered, in the later development of Marxian and Marxist thinking, by cruder, more technically materialistic ideas, it has more recently again come into its own. Commenting on certain passages in Marx's *Zur Kritik der politischen Ökonomie*, Warynski points out that 'in looking at human history, we are originally confronted with the historical process in its chaotic, formless shape'. It is reality in the concrete, from which ordinary thinking then advances towards the abstract. But scholarly thinking travels in the opposite direction. Starting with certain concepts (state, democracy, capital, capitalism, etc.) first acquired in naïve social experience, it lays hold upon the concrete, or rather appropriate parts of it, which, on the mental plane, become the truly concrete only by being thus caught in the clutches, as it were, of the abstract, of abstract definitions. 'The whole as it appears in the head as a mental totality, is the product of the thinking head which appropriates the world in the only way which is open to it,' Marx says. And Warynski echoes: 'Only because man thinks from the very beginning in concepts . . . can there arise the vision of a [mentally] reproducible reality of history.'[1] These passages are perhaps not altogether clear, but, surely, the salient proposition they contain is that there are conceptual frameworks—'anticipatory schemes' as Scheler calls them—in and through which concrete pictures of history arise in different minds according to their social circumstances and class situation, and if this is the correct interpretation of the sentences concerned, then they are not too far removed from the doctrine of Scheler and of this book.

Even more interesting in this respect than Warynski is an earlier writer, Max Adler, who tried to find a quasi-Marxist element in Kant, and a quasi-Kantian element in Marx.[2] Neither Kantians nor Marxists gave him any thanks for his endeavour, but Adler was a well-informed and penetrating thinker whose work commands respect and deserves more credit than it has received. Kant indeed, if we go by his own words, seems to have been interested only in the individual consciousness; so much so that it has been said that his system must logically lead to an absurd solipsistic position. But Adler denies this. Kant seeks, he says, not the laws of knowing, willing and feeling as such, but rather the laws of true knowing, right willing and generally acceptable feeling: hence the social element is by no means overlooked. Behind Kant's apparently individualistic question: 'How is true knowledge possible?' there hides the further, genuinely sociological question: 'How is it possible that in the thought of an individual there arises for this individual an experience which is not only *his* experience, but an experience for *everyone* who undergoes this experience under the same circumstances? How is it that the world is one and the same for all human beings . . .?'[3] If one presses for an answer to this question which is conceived in the authentic Kantian spirit, then one must be led, so Adler argues, to a characteristically Marxian concept: the concept of social consciousness, of socialized consciousness. Though found only in the individual, the human consciousness is yet essentially social; it is 'always related to a

[1] *Die Wissenschaft von der Gesellschaft*, 1944, 79 *seq*. For a very different development of the Marxist position—in the direction of naïve dogmatism—cf. the articles by Paul Szende summarized in Arthur Child's meritorious article 'The Theoretical Possibility of the Sociology of Knowledge' in *Ethics*, 1940/1, 411 *seq*.

[2] Cf. e.g. 'Marxismus und Kantischer Kritizismus', in *Archiv für die Geschichte des Sozialismus*, 1925.   [3] *Loc. cit.*, 345.

system of social conceptions and values'.[1] Only through this fact is social life at all possible. The *a priori* of the human mind comprises not only time, space and the categories, but also the social factor, which is thus as basic to the process of cognition as they are. This may be no more than one man's idea of how Marxism may be changed from a practical-political doctrine of ideology into a fundamental sociology of knowledge in the philosophical sense of the word; but it is a most interesting idea all the same.

Adler and Scheler had many discussions in their day, some of them characterized by considerable acerbity.[2] Now, in retrospect, it appears that, so far at any rate as the sociology of knowledge as a positive study is concerned, in contradistinction to its wider philosophical and political implications, their positions were not so far apart from, or irreconcilable with, each other as they themselves believed. And exactly the same can be said of the relationship between Scheler and Mannheim.[3] At the very root of Mannheim's sociology of knowledge there is the conviction that active man and thinking man are one and the same, and he stresses this unity of theory and practice so much that he often comes very near to the pragmatist position, however much he may think of action in social and political terms, rather than economic and technological ones. 'Even . . . contemplation', he says, characteristically, in one passage, 'is a kind of activity.' But human action, which is thus made a key to the understanding of human thought-processes, is essentially a pursuit of values, and hence there is a natural bridge between Mannheim's domain and Scheler's. Indeed, the span between the two shores seems sometimes very small. In the passage to which we have just referred, Mannheim expresses the opinion that the sociologist of knowledge is 'concerned with the significance for knowledge of man's pragmatic, extra-theoretical aspirations', or with the 'inner link between aspirations and knowledge'; and in another context he writes: 'The discovery of certain facts is connected with certain systematic and social commitments. . . . Certain commitments, as it were, render us sensitive to certain realities of the past, present or future.' [4] Furthermore, Mannheim emphasizes all the time that no sight of reality is possible or even conceivable which is determined only 'by the things themselves'; that every vista of the world presupposes, both logically and practically, a definite point of view—a *location* (Standort) as he habitually calls it, a location within the field of social reality which can and will give us no more than one possible aspect of the real at a time. These are elements—and altogether fundamental elements—in his

[1] *Ibid.*, 347.
[2] Cf. Scheler's *Die Wissensformen und die Gesellschaft*, 1926, 167 *seq.* and the reference there to the proceedings of the *Soziologentag* at Heidelberg, 1924.
[3] Cf. esp. Mannheim's *Essays on the Sociology of Knowledge*, Engl. ed., 1952, 154 *seq.*   [4] *Essays*, 103, 148.

theory which he shares with Max Scheler, and their main disagreements are much more concerned with the comparatively peripheral problem of the permanence of truth than with the central problem of its perception.

In view of all this, Merton has judged that 'Mannheim's conception of "perspectivism" is substantially the same as the Rickert-Weber conception of "*Wertbeziehung*" (which holds that values are relevant to formulation of the scientific problem and choice of materials. . . .)'. Both views start 'from the premises of an inexhaustible multitude of phenomena, the inevitability of selection from these in terms of a conceptual scheme and the relevance of values and social structure to this scheme and the formulation of the problem'.[1] In view of Mannheim's pragmatist-positivist-political bias, this quotation seems somewhat to oversimplify and overstate the case; yet the case in itself is sound enough. Mannheim, like Scheler, and like Adler, believed the process of cognition to be essentially the forming of selected materials of knowledge into a coherent and comprehensible object of knowledge, a feat accomplished under the guidance of a concrete order of values which, forming in and arising out of life, is reflected back on to it when man turns from action to cognition, from practice to theory—a patterned light that will show up those sectors of reality which appear relevant in the given social situation and leave the rest in outer darkness.

Perhaps it is permissible to hope that the foregoing discussion has succeeded in showing what the essential doctrine, the doctrinal content, of the sociology of knowledge is; but even so, it will be helpful to append to our abstract disquisition a more concrete demonstration of how the principle of the social determination of knowledge works in practice, and for that purpose we have chosen as an illustration the transformations which the historians' view of history has undergone in the course of time under the influence of changes in the value-structure of Western society. Yet before we can turn to this subsidiary investigation, it will be well to make explicit a few important points which are implicitly contained in what has gone before, but possibly do not stand out with sufficient clarity.

The first of these points concerns the label which has come to be appended—nobody knows how—to our discipline. Most sociologists and historians have accepted it without much ado, but some have felt it to be a misnomer. 'The sociology of knowledge', writes Alexander von Schelting, 'has no right to its description and should be called the sociology of thinking in general.'[2] This assertion is an unfortunate one;

[1] *Social Theory and Social Structure*, 1949, 261 *seq.*
[2] *Max Webers Wissenschaftslehre*, 1934, 85. Gerard de Gré, whose article 'The Sociology of Knowledge and the Problem of Truth' in the *Journal of the History of Ideas* (1941) is to be warmly commended and recommended, has suggested the term

it seems to miss the whole upshot of our theoretical analysis, which has shown, if it has shown anything, that the social, i.e. the axiological factor is operative in the inception and constitution of a world-view (in our coming-to-know reality) rather than in its further elaboration. Von Schelting would probably be the last to deny this, since he himself takes his stand fairly and squarely in the Rickert-Weber camp. 'Sociology of knowledge' is thus exact; terms such as sociology of thought, of ideas, of culture are much less so. This does not mean that social influences do not pervade the whole of our thinking; assuredly they do; but it is better to call a light after its source than after the spaces which it irradiates.

A second truth which should be emphasized is that our analysis is applicable not only to the origination of the purely intellectual, but also to that of the aesthetico-artistic world-view. The naïve epistemology which was classically expounded by the philosophers of the Enlightenment and which has become the implied metaphysic of the common man of our day, regards art as the absolute antithesis of science in that science is supposedly bound to the facts and art is not; in that science must show the truth of what is, whereas art may explore the beauty of what might be. In scholarship the mind is supposed to be essentially receptive, i.e. passive; in music, for instance, or painting, essentially imaginative, creative, active. This dichotomy is very ill conceived. As we have seen, the human intellect could not possibly come to any determinate knowledge at all if it did not organize its vision of reality: but to organize, to mould impressions, is also the work of the artistic creator. If the scholar and the scientist have in this way something of the artist in them, the artist for his part cannot create, however fertile his imagination may be, without a previous knowledge of reality.[1] Few would deny that all art is a reaction of the artistic consciousness to the experience of life; but that experience is as much a taking cognizance of the factual realm, an assimilation of the inventory of the world that surrounds us, as the parallel activity at the basis of the scholar's and the scientist's work. In a word, the artist, like the pure describer and cataloguer of facts, must make a finite object of knowledge out of the infinite materials of knowledge before he can put pen to paper or brush to canvas or chisel to stone—clearly so, for he is, in the last analysis, a thinker of a kind, indeed, as much a thinker as any chemist or

'gnosio-sociology'. While no objection of principle can be raised against this neologism, it is to be feared that, sounding rather strange, it will fail to gain admission into the canon of language. In any case, it says no more and means no more than 'sociology of knowledge'.

[1] In the message which he sent to Goethe through Bettina Brentano, Beethoven emphasized more than once 'that music is the . . . entry into a higher world of knowledge'. Cf. Turner, *Beethoven: The Search for Reality*, ed. 1945, 123.

physicist. 'A work of art is simply organized experience', a student of music has said,[1] and his statement is not the less true for being so apodictic; but surely, exactly the same can be said of any work of scholarship or science.

Sometimes it becomes quite clear that the two activities are closely akin: there have been painters whose ideal has been altogether scientific —to depict life 'as it is', to give 'the truth' about life. It is obvious that their picture of reality has arisen in exactly the same way as all other realistic world-views and is analysable and explicable in the same terms. But the situation is not so different as it might seem even in the case of abstract art, such as surrealism. Even the surrealist must see before he can paint, the only difference being that his sight will be differently directed from that of the realist. After all, it is not given to man to imagine anything absolutely new; even the most fantastic concoction is merely an unusual combination of things observable by all. Whereas the realist (the respectable painter in the judgment of our philistine society) concentrates on the same features of the materials before him as the man in the street, and does so because he has the same value-system, the same axiological layer in his mind, the surrealist (who is at loggerheads with the prevailing way of life) looks out on to reality through a different value-system, through an eccentric axiological grid, and consequently selects other attributes of the seen and experienced for depiction in his artistic medium, for instance the pure geometric forms thereof. But both the realist and the surrealist define their vision concretely, and must do so if they want to have any artistically malleable vision at all.

There is no formal difference between them in so far as the making of their conception of the world is concerned. The contrast only comes in with the different materials which enter their minds through their differently patterned axiological inlet-systems. Whereas in our society, so largely wedded to scientific preoccupations, the realistic eye lets in a commonplace picture, similar to that of the photographic plate, the surrealist eye lets in a far more reduced and attenuated impression; but

---

[1] Turner, *loc. cit.*, 233. Very significant also are the following passages: 'Musical phenomena consist in the ordered arrangement of sounds which, made in the mind of the composer, have a meaning for the auditor. . . . Such a mind is highly selective and rejects in order to compose. Creation of any sort implies rejection because it imposes a form upon chaos. The greatest minds are those who reject least, those who get most of reality, of the sensation-stuff presented to them, into their framework' (229, 233). If the reader will think out the implications of these statements, he will see that their meaning coincides to an amazing degree with the essential content of the sociology of knowledge developed in this book. The composer's mind is ascribed a double function, that of selection and ordering or form-giving—the very twin-function which in our opinion the mind has to fulfil in the constitution of its *imago mundi*, and which it does fulfil under the guidance of its basic value-conceptions.

it is an impression none the less. Needless to say, it is also the coincidence of the common axiological system with the specific *axiomata visus* of the realistic painter which assures for the latter a favourable reception in the contemporary world. The public 'understand' him, and to understand means, as Sprott has so rightly formulated it, that what is offered 'tallies with what is at any time the common sense'.[1]

However reluctant our rationalists-in-the-street may be to acknowledge the kinship between scientific and artistic thought, the historian of ideas knows very well that it exists in fact and in truth, for he discovers in every age a prevailing common style of thought—the consequence of the common underlying value-structure—which informs all characteristic thinking of the period. No musician can be more abstract than Johann Sebastian Bach, yet it is easy to show the connection even of *his* work with the substructural facts and forces. Born in 1685, he grew up in a world which was trying to make its way towards a system of national and international integration, an integration which, in the given circumstances, could only be achieved through the balancing of independent political forces. How to bring harmony out of diversity—that was the problem of the age, the aim of all endeavour. It is the fundamental theme of scientific speculation such as we see it, above all, in the incomparable Leibniz: nature is based on a pre-established harmony which is yet compatible with an irreducible diversity; all realms of nature must be comprehended as aspects of the pre-established harmony; all human actions must be so contrived as to become elements in that pre-established harmony. Without at all attempting to devalue the invaluable, to make commonplace what is sublime, it is still permissible to say that the same preoccupation is present, the same pursuit predominant, in the music of the great Bach. For he was first and foremost the explorer of the mysterious realm of counterpoint; but counterpoint or polyphony is traditionally defined as 'the combination of simultaneous voice-parts, each independent, but all conducing to a result of uniform coherent texture'.[2] The same wind, as it were, blows through the pages of Bach's *Contrapunctus* [3] as through the pages of Leibniz's *Theodicy*, and both strain forward towards the discovery of the blessed harmonizing forces which are at work in the depths of divine reality. Thus even the most abstract thought of the most abstract musician still stems from the prime value of the age, which shows itself as much in mathematics as in music, in science as in art.

The last of the implications of our theory, and one which deserves particularly strong emphasis, concerns the objectivity and objective

---

[1] *Science and Social Action*, 1954, 126.
[2] *The Oxford Companion to Music*, ed. Scholes, 1950, 233.
[3] *The Art of Fugue*. Cf. *ibid.*, 1151.

validity of socially determined knowledge. If knowledge is indeed, as we have asserted, genetically connected with a pre-existent axiological or value-system, are not its sources hopelessly contaminated in consequence? Must not the presence of any value (or 'ought'-conception) bar the way to truth, prejudice our pursuit of the truth (or our conception of the 'Is')? Is not value-determined knowledge—paradoxically—value-less? Happily, we can answer this question (which has led people like Karl Mannheim into considerable difficulties) with a most emphatic negative. Our sociology of knowledge assumes the necessity of certain pre-judgments with regard to the relative importance or unimportance of the numberless separable and eligible strands of objective reality, pre-judgments without which the constitution of a determinate and manageable object of knowledge out of the indeterminate and immeasurable materials of knowledge would not be possible; but it does not assert the necessity—indeed, it manifestly suggests the non-necessity—of prejudices. Once a picture of the realm of things has been formed in our mind, there is no reason whatsoever why the exploration of the sectors of reality which, on the basis of the decisive values, have been selected for inclusion in it, should not proceed under the guidance of the strictest canons of scholarly and scientific objectivity and lead to results of the greatest reliability and fullest validity. We have said that values precede, and must precede, scholarly work; we have *not* said that valuations must assert themselves in and interfere with it.

There are, it seems, three facets to this matter. Firstly, the values which the sociology of knowledge sees established at the basis of our own, or any other, concrete world-view, are objective values, value-facts, not subjective valuations. They are given in and by the life of the society concerned and exist and are operative before any individual member of that society can ever possibly form or assert any private prejudice of his own. They inhere in and help to constitute the basic pattern of human interaction at the time and place in question, and have for the individual that externality and objectivity which Durkheim rightly claims to be one of the hallmarks of social fact.

Secondly, and more importantly, though the axiological system determines *what* is to be selected from the materials of knowledge for inclusion in the objects or object of knowledge, it does not and cannot determine, *how* this selection is to be carried out. If we want the truth, it must in fact be carried out on the basis of objective tests. Ranke's implied conviction that the understanding of universal history in all its breadth and depth depends upon the adequate understanding and successful study of foreign policy, was indeed a pre-judgment present in his mind before the encounter with the facts (a pre-judgment or axiom that had arisen from his unreflecting experience of contemporary life): but it manifestly did not prejudice his objective treatment of the facts.

What he tried to capture and incorporate into his books was precisely what appeared objectively interesting and important *from the point of view* which he had taken up, or rather which his social situation had marked out for him. To return to the simile which we have used so often before: the vantage point and angle from which a scholar surveys the mountain-range of history will depend on his specific social determination; but not what he will see. A man may look at Mont Blanc or the Matterhorn from the north or the south, or from any number of positions: none of them is in itself superior to any other; none can be singled out by objective criteria as giving the nearest approach to objective truth; they all offer an equal chance of the truth. All depends, so far as truth is concerned, on the man who occupies a given position: if he will open his eyes wide and allow nothing to deflect or dim his perception, he will recognize the mountains as in fact they are. Anybody *in the same place* would have to come to the same results; hence the results are generally valid, and undeniably so. And so it is with all students and all studies of reality. Values manœuvre a man into a certain vantage-point: but valuation need not falsify his vision. He can always speak the truth as he sees it; it will be the *objective* truth *in his situation*. Those who have laid the foundations of the sociology of knowledge which the present book endeavours to develop, Heinrich Rickert and Max Weber, have stressed this over and over again; indeed, Max Weber, as is generally known, was a most fanatical upholder of the strictest canons of scientific objectivity. And he had every right to be, in spite of his insistence on the fundamental part which values play in the constitution of our world-view. Values influence us—and influence us decisively —when we formulate our questions: as for the answers, we are obliged, if we want to be honest, to accept them from reality as reality gives them; we are free to enter into reality by whatever approach-road we choose, but we must always take it as we find it.

Thirdly and lastly, our sociology of knowledge, properly handled, can lead to an objectivity in the treatment of social and historical reality incomparably deeper than any achieved or attainable by those who deny the existence and the influence of a basic axiological layer in the human mind. For the naïve dogmatist, any idea that is at all removed from his own way of thinking is simply 'wrong': it does not 'tally with the facts'. And, indeed, the Encyclopaedists and their disciples, educated and not so educated, have always been most shockingly intolerant. All medieval thought, for instance, has appeared to them a tissue of childishness, idiocy and chicanery. They never thought of asking whether things might not look very differently from another point of view than their own; whether a shift a yard to the right might not force upon everybody a new *visus universalis*. Now this is the very question which our sociology of knowledge raises and answers in the affirmative.

Different value-systems result in different world-views which all 'tally with the facts', however surprising that may be. Discussions across the borderlines of closed social and axiological systems, such as the medieval and the modern, have often, nay regularly, been no more than talk at cross purposes. One party has as a rule missed the whole truth and even the significance of the components of the other's mental universe. This does not mean that *all* ideas ever formulated necessarily partake of the truth, the whole truth, and nothing but the truth. Far from it; a lot of nonsense has been talked at all times. But it does mean that we should not pronounce a statement nonsensical until we have made sure that it is so, not only from our own point of view, but also from that of him who made it. Our sociology of knowledge thus lays on us a duty and teaches us a technique by which to fulfil it. The duty is that we should first put ourselves into the other person's place before we condemn him; the technique, that we can come to understand his peculiar assertions if we try to look out on to the world through the same *axiomata visus* which are hidden in his mind, behind his mind's eye; in other words, our sociology of knowledge supplies an argument for and an education in the virtue of toleration, and it also provides a strict scientific method for the objective testing of the truth-value of concrete thought-contents —an *aqua fortis* for the separation of gold and dross.

(b) SOME APPLICATIONS OF THE SOCIAL THEORY OF KNOWLEDGE

It cannot be shown in a few pages how fruitful an instrument for historical research is the sociology of knowledge inspired by Heinrich Rickert and Max Weber and sketched out in the present book. Perhaps it is not extravagant to hope that its best achievements still lie in the future. But a few solid contributions exist already, and may help us to show what results we are entitled to expect of its more systematic application. Curiously enough, one of the best of them is contained in a work by the very man whose ideas we have repeatedly had to combat in these pages—Theodor Geiger. Though opposed to our whole approach to the problem of the social determination of knowledge, he falls in with it when he comes to handle a concrete aspect of the history of ideas. His book *Aufgaben und Stellung der Intelligenz in der Gesellschaft* (Danish, 1944, German ed., 1949) demonstrates in the most enlightening manner how the contents of a comprehensive culture-complex depend upon the values of the contemporary society and its leading strata.

Speaking of the age of Leo X and Julius II, of Michelangelo and Machiavelli, Geiger writes, almost as if he had made it his conscious task to illustrate our fundamental thesis: 'The mundane culture of the Rinascimento found its basis in aesthetic values. Not research, but fine art and literature determine the cultural profile of the period. The natural sciences are allotted a modest position . . . Among the sciences of the time, philology, rhetoric, philosophy and history take precedence over the rest—the non-operational, meditative disciplines. Even scholarship stands in the service of beauty. The centre of gravity lies in contemplative and cultural, not in pragmatic and utilitarian knowledge. The cult of beauty ranks higher than the need for analytical insight. Mental creativeness is subservient to the sublimation of existence by refined enjoyment.' To Renaissance man, even the state was primarily, in Jacob Burckhardt's classical words, 'a work of art'. If beauty thus became the prime value in terms of which the world was seen and thought expressed, other values were ranked much lower and hence there appeared corresponding deficiencies and *lacunae* in the resulting world-view: 'The unrestrained adoration of the aesthetic values of antiquity smothered the germs of naturalistic thinking. Leonebattista Alberti owed his reputation and his prestige among his contemporaries not to his mathematical, but to his artistic achievements. Leonardo da Vinci's technical genius, it is true, found appreciation because of the services it rendered to the art of war, but it was by far outshone by his renown as an artist. So complete was the aesthetic enchantment of the age that it overlooked the realistic content of ancient literature. No renaissance of the study of nature was stimulated by the elder Pliny. . . . There is much to support the conjecture that physical research, and with it technology, would have blossomed forth somewhat earlier than they actually did if aesthetic interests had not absorbed the best energies of the period' (27 *seq.*, 53).

But it is not enough to show that the character of Renaissance culture was due to the predominance of a certain value-system, and to the relative ranking of the individual values which it contained; the sociology of knowledge, *quâ* sociology, also demands an exposure of the social forces on which these values were based and by which they were carried. Geiger acquits himself of this task in a fashion which leaves little to be desired. 'Rinascimento society is characterized by the petty states of the tyrants and the early adventure capitalism of Italy. Wealth and political power are generally united in the same hand. The banker's son wears the ducal crown, the condottiere amasses a fortune and usurps a throne. Newly acquired wealth and arrogated dominion which are not confirmed by prescription and tradition seek for justification in universally acknowledged values. By the cultivation and protection of the mental culture of his age the political and economic upstart surrounds his position with the aura of a higher dignity. Perhaps the world will thus forget that he has reached the summit of power by way of rapine and deception, violence and murder. In this way the mental culture of the Rinascimento has its political function which it is as well to forget if one wants to enjoy its fruits. But for the sociologist of culture this very function is the decisive thing. The Rinascimento was a lordly culture, created in order to lend splendour and respect to a small circle of select individuals and to raise them high above the common multitude. . . . The luxurious character of this mental life based on the cult of the beautiful corresponds to the social conditions of the age, to the need for prestige on the part of a new master caste' (28 *seq.*).

Geiger advances from these observations to a statement of more general bearing. 'A culture may be the concern of a whole society, even when a mere minority has immediate access to its treasures, provided only that that minority regards itself as the cultural élite of society and is acknowledged as such by the community. It was not so in the Rinascimento. In his cultivation of spiritual values the man of power did not regard himself as an exponent of the people, but stood consciously apart and even underlined in his relation to ancient culture the social distance between himself and the common people. Once upon a time, the priests, as the cultural élite of the Middle Ages, had administered the representative cultural treasures of the age. This representative culture had been the superstructure of a popular culture, a higher, esoteric form of the same spiritual substance. The classical mentality of the Rinascimento was not in the same sense a hypostatization of the popular culture, but its antithesis. . . . The broad masses continued to inhabit the traditional popular culture and had little share in the characteristic cultural goods of the period. . . . Two separate culture-communities stand over against each other without inner connection. Only later is this dualism of cultures overcome by a process of amalgamation, the traces of which we can still detect in the educational ideal of the nineteenth century' (29).

However, the key to the understanding of all the later developments again lies in the shifts which occur within the predominant value-system. Already the northern Renaissance is rooted in a different social stratum from that of the southern Rinascimento: in Germany it is the burgher who propagates a new world of culture, not the princeling—the solid burgher who has risen in the world by the burgher's virtues, not the glittering princeling who has won his position by the condottiere's vices. 'The newly awakened strains of antiquity are transposed in this social atmosphere into a totally different key. . . . Bourgeois earnestness and scholarly thoroughness characterize the German Renaissance whose most important kernel is humanism. . . . The material content of ancient literature found a more receptive soil than its formal beauty. Certainly, even in Germany there was a renewal of the arts, above all of architecture. But deeper still was the revolution in the field of rational thinking, in philosophical and scholarly or scientific thought. . . . The predominance of a rational mentality in the German Renaissance gave the scholar-scientist a better position, from the very beginning, than the artist and poet' (31 *seq.*). In a word, beauty is no longer the central value, but rather sober and solid realistic insight; and with this shift in the axiological system, there comes a total transformation of culture, a new mental universe, such as we find developing from roughly 1600 onward. 'The essential substance and strength of modern spiritual culture does not lie in the sphere of the aesthetic, but in that of reason' (34).

A special field of scholarly endeavour in which every change in the axiological system is soon registered and recognizable is that of historiography. 'Every age writes the history of the past anew with reference to the conditions'—we should say: to the values—'uppermost in its own time', wrote Frederick Jackson Turner,[1] and the same observation has been made by many others. There are, it is true, two reasons for the periodical re-writing of history; one is the discovery of new material and the refinement of historical methods; the other, the one we have mainly in mind at this moment, the change in the vantage-point from which the past is envisaged and surveyed. Sometimes the former factor is very important; a traditional picture of the past may become obsolete simply because a later generation knows more and is better equipped for handling it, and then there is technical progress, as it were, in historiography. Ranke, for instance, the lucky man to whom all the main archives of Europe were first opened, would have had to reconsider and redraft universal history even if he had had no new approach, no new axiological layer to his mind. But the fact is that he *did* have new conceptions of value—a new anticipatory scheme, as Scheler says— within which to capture and arrange the yield of his sources, and in so far as this new value-system induced him to see things differently from his rationalistic predecessors, his work is not merely technically better, but differently *seen*, differently determined from a social point of view, differently accentuated, as it were. 'That universal history must be re-written from time to time', says Goethe in his *Geschichte der Farbenlehre*, 'of this fact there can nowadays be no doubt. But such a necessity does not arise because so much that has happened has been newly discovered, but because new opinions are put forward, because the participant in a progressive age is led to points of view which allow him to survey and judge the past in a new way.'[2]

Thus every generation, almost, has its own historical science, and this is anything but surprising, for how could a historian after 1789, after

---

[1] *Cit.* Merton, *Social Theory and Social Structure*, 1949, 251. For Goethe's parallel opinion, cf. Löwith, *Von Hegel zu Nietzsche*, ed. 1953, 246 *seq.*, and Meinecke, *Die Entstehung des Historismus*, ed. 1946, 552. For a modern illustration of the theme cf. A. Rüstow, *Ortsbestimmung der Gegenwart*, 1951.

[2] *Cit.* Löwith, *Von Hegel zu Nietzsche*, 1953, 249.

1815, after 1848, think as his elders had done before those momentous years? 'Great historiography', an eminent historian has written, 'springs always from the process of history itself, i.e. from life, and receives its first and fundamental direction from the vital struggles and vital aims in the midst of which the teller of the story stands.' [1] Or, as Scheler puts it, in more technical terms, 'the beam of interest which, like the beam of a lighthouse, illumines a section of the past, is . . . always also an effect of the historical present, in the first place of the tasks for the future which are before the mind and will'; it is part and parcel of the 'effort towards a new cultural synthesis' [2] which every new generation has to put forward after the events of its epoch have so shaken the inherited system of life and thought that little is left of what had once satisfied their fathers and forefathers.

What is apt to happen first of all, after the social subsoil has been shaken in a revolutionary period, is that new peaks rise up in the mental landscape and imperatively demand attention. Wilhelm Dilthey has given a good example of this in his *Einleitung in die Geisteswissenschaften*: 'It needed the philanthropic motives of the eighteenth century to bring back into full visibility the everyday things which are common to all in a period, *les mœurs* as Voltaire expresses it, and the changes which take place in respect of these things, along with the extraordinary, the actions of kings and the destinies of States.' [3] Here no new materials had been discovered, no new techniques developed; it was only that a new interest had arisen, that what had been without value for, and hence disdained by, the historiographers of princes, had become valuable and hence worthy of study to the historians of the third estate.

As a rule, of course, axiological evolutions and revolutions result not only in new contours in the historical landscape but also in the levelling down of old ones and in the development of rifts: new mountains rise up at times from the plains, but the plains as often reclaim old mountains. The same bourgeoisie which brought into being the historical study of culture and civilization, progressively forced the description of military and even political matters into the background. [4] M. de Voltaire was as disgusted with the purple passages in which his noble predecessors depicted scenes of battle and carnage, as they would have been with his typically tradesman-like remark that the herring-trade of Amsterdam was a fact of world-historical importance. [5] In this

---

[1] Meinecke, *Die Entstehung des Historismus*, ed. 1946, 220.

[2] *Die Wissensformen und die Gesellschaft*, 1926, 107.

[3] *Cit*. Hodges, *Wilhelm Dilthey: An Introduction*, 1944, 137 *seq*. For similar developments in the nineteenth century, cf. Hashagen in *Versuche zu einer Soziologie des Wissens*, 1924, 247 *seq*. Cf. also Franz Eulenburg, 'Sind historische Gesetze möglich?' in *Erinnerungsgabe für Max Weber*, 1923, I.

[4] Meinecke, *Die Entstehung des Historismus*, ed. 1946, 42.

[5] Meinecke, *loc. cit.*, 109.

way there arise totally dissimilar images of history, all true in their own way, yet all unacceptable beyond the confines of an enclosed circle.

In one of his masterpieces, *Die Entstehung des Historismus*, Friedrich Meinecke has elaborated the contrast between the perception of the past reflected in the works of that prime spokesman of the rising bourgeoisie, Voltaire, and the conservative—Voltaire would have said: obscurantist—conceptions of the contemporary nobility. 'If one asks for the most intimate and naïvely felt interest at the basis of his programme, the answer can only be: he wished to write the universal pre-history of the French bourgeoisie, that civilized, refined, intelligent, industrious and comfortable class of men which was his delight. With their style of life and mentality he compared all historical phenomena and noted what was in accordance with them and what not. The happiness, spirit, morals and customs of the peoples whom he wished to study were laid into this particular pair of scales.' 'To utilize the whole of world history for the service of the enlightenment of the human race, to deduce enlightenment from history,—that became the governing motive of his historiography. . . . Voltaire's undertaking, to support a new universal cultural ideal by a new interpretation of universal history, became the beginning of a new era of occidental thought in general.' 'Often the main . . . merit of Voltaire is seen in his conquest of the masses of so-called cultural materials for the study of history, whereby the history of culture is at times conceived merely as a colourful picture-book of social manners and institutions, memorable technical feats and advances and the material factors of external life, down to eating and drinking. And indeed, what might be called this petty-bourgeois interest in history has in fact been decisively stimulated by Voltaire. He did it as a French *grand-bourgeois* who had become fully conscious of what civil society had achieved, intellectually, economically and technically, since the decay of chivalry and the feudal spirit. He put the deserts of the first French *grand-bourgeois* who had made his mark in history—Jacques Coeur, the financier of the fifteenth century—above those of the Pucelle. . . . In the resignation of Christina of Sweden he celebrated, with gratified approval of royal resignations in general, a victory of urbanity. In his judgment, she gave the greatest example of the true superiority of the arts, of *politesse*, and of refined society over the greatness which is nothing but greatness.'

In all these ideas, Voltaire's basic order of values can easily be seen projected. 'He was concerned in the first place for the quiet enjoyment and free unfolding of bourgeois civilization under the protection of a strong monarchical government. This civilization reached its apex, so he believed, in the two values of the useful and the pleasing. The latter, which comprised all the charms of refined sociability and of the standardized arts, was for him the higher one. But utility, the sum total of economic and technological activity, and the prosperity which it provided, was in his opinion an indispensable presupposition. And so Voltaire directed his attention—not yet in the manner of a social and economic historian in the technical sense of the word, but with the pleased approval of a comfortable bourgeois—towards all those things which, in the nineteenth century, became the objects of the most intense methodical study as the real and material bases of modern culture. Round about him people occupied themselves with these matters for practical reasons; he was the first who had the courage to bring them into the writing of history and to insist that they were the most important aspect of it' (77 *seq.*, 83 *seq.*, 107 *seq.*).

How characteristically different is the picture of the past entertained and propagated by the aristocracy of the age, for instance by Voltaire's contemporary, the Baron de la Brède et de Montesquieu! His loving regard is directed backward, not forward; his interest is attracted by chivalry, not by civilization; his main endeavour is to show the hidden rationality of the institutions of the 'gothic' ages; and nothing is more characteristic of him than his anxiety to give the rhyme and reason of such 'barbarian' phenomena as ordeal by combat, by fire and by water. Such men, Meinecke says, 'still lived in a society which was hierarchical in structure and aristocratic in sentiment. Aristocracies, however, tend to think of conservation and a return to things past, rather than of a constant advancement which may end by progressing beyond themselves. On the contrary, they are apt to contemplate the danger of their own destruction, and this in turn can easily strengthen the belief in the circular movement of all things human.' To the bourgeois or Voltairean devaluation of the past is here opposed an equally scholarly revaluation: equally scholarly because it knows how to seek out and find the facts which support its contentions. 'There appeared already at that time an interest in the bygone poetry of the troubadours which was cultivated —not strongly, but yet appreciably—throughout the whole of the eighteenth century, only to become even more vigorous on the eve of the Revolution, when the French nobility in its growing malaise began to turn more consciously towards its own past. Already in the early part of the century, Boulainvilliers had borne witness to this traditionalistic cult of aristocratic values, and Montesquieu carried it on in his own fashion. Even before his *Esprit des Lois* was published, De la Curne Sainte Palaye, who also collected the poems of the troubadours, had started on his broadly based defence of the honour of medieval chivalry and in November, 1746, laid before the *Académie des Inscriptions et Belles Lettres* the first of his five *Mémoires sur l'Ancienne Chevalerie.* . . . He saw chivalry through the spectacles, so to speak, of an aristocratically-minded nobleman of the Rococo period, magnified with glowing joy its institutions, virtues and achievements, and ended with the regret that in the ignorance and barbarism of those ages, the old knights should have been unable to possess that "culture of the spirit and of reason" by which they could have become ideal men superior to those of Plato' (164 *seq.*, 190 *seq.*). In all this, there is of course a regrettable ideological strain; but there is also a good deal of pure research and solid knowledge, discovered from and related to a definite axiological position, a definite socially determined vantage-point.[1]

A parallel phenomenon to the axiologically determined—socially determined—contrast between Voltaire's conception and writing of history on the one hand and that of Boulainvilliers, Montesquieu and Sainte Palaye on the other, is the conflict, in English history, between the Whig and Tory interpretations of the past. Herbert Butterfield has studied the question in *The Englishman and His History* (1945), and his little book reads almost like a deliberately contrived illustration of the principles of the sociology of knowledge. We cannot hope to exhaust its riches here by any précis, however lengthy, and must clothe our references to it in the all-including word *passim*. The very first paragraph proves that Butterfield talks sociology of knowledge as M. Jourdain talked prose—unconsciously, but altogether naturally. 'Although history may often seem to be, like the natural sciences, an international study,' he writes, 'its interpretation remains more profoundly national. . . . We may imagine that here in England we are free from the prejudices and enthusiasms of other nations. Sometimes we think that our history is the impartial narrative, and we hardly believe that we are performing an act of interpretation at all. But however much we refine and elaborate, it is not clear that we reach—or that without great intellectual endeavour we could hope to reach—more than the English view of Louis XIV. And our best biography of Napoleon is only the supreme expression of what is really the English version of the man's career. We teach and write the kind of history which is appropriate to our organization, congenial to the intellectual climate of our part of the world. We can scarcely help it if this kind of history is at the same time the one most adapted to the preservation of the existing régime' (1). The reader of these pages will be aware that this is not precisely our own view. The penultimate sentence of the quotation, with its reference to the 'intellectual climate' of England, is too vague; the last sentence makes too great a concession to pan-ideologism; but the over-all sentiment professed by Butterfield certainly coincides with the drift and standpoint of the present book.

---

[1] Another instructive and clearly axiological and socially determined contrast in eighteenth century historical thinking is that between Boulainvilliers' and the Abbé Dubos' treatment of Merovingian and Carolingian developments; it would offer another admirable illustration of the truth of the sociology of knowledge. Cf. Meinecke, *loc. cit.*, 170 *seq.*

The cross-roads at which the Whig and Tory interpretations of English history divide, is the reign of John, and especially its main incident, the scene at Runnymede. We describe it without misgivings as 'its main incident'; all contemporary historians would do so, for they have all in substance accepted the Whig version of development which has triumphed in and along with democracy (72, 80). But the curious fact is that to the Tudor historians Magna Carta meant little or nothing. Either they do not even bother to mention it, or they give a summary of its contents which seems today to miss the main stipulation of the document (28). 'Roughly speaking, we may say that only after 1600 do the worship of *Magna Carta* (as the charter of middle-class freedom), the superstition of historic rights, and the Whig interpretation of history, come into effective existence after the curious interval afforded by the Tudor period. All three were born out of the same complex of events and conditions. They are joint products of one live piece of history' (9 *seq.*). Could there be any more convincing application of the principles of the sociology of knowledge, none the worse—indeed, all the better—for being unconscious?

Butterfield shows us how, under the impact of axiological changes, the whole content of the drama changes. To the Tory, John is the hero, predecessor of the great King Hal. Did he not stand up against the 'Italian Priest', against 'The Strumpet's pride that sits upon the Chaire of Babylon'? (19 *seq.*). To the Whig, John becomes the villain of the piece, the enemy of the people, the oppressor, the tyrant. It is his defeat, not his prowess, around which the picture of his reign is arranged. Values have changed, and that is why the facts, unchanged in themselves, appear in changed colours. 'The Tudor age would never have relished the idea that the king should be limited by feudal law—they remembered too well the over-mighty subject, the danger of private rights that menaced the state. The glory of the Tudor age lay in the opposite movement in fact, the victory that the monarch had achieved over feudal limitations and over the whole realm of privilege. Coke, however, interpreted Magna Carta as an affirmation not of feudal law but of the common law. By a subtle elision he aggrandized the common law and demonstrated more plainly its superiority over the monarch himself. He and the opposition lawyers secured the resurrection of the document. ... They envisaged it in terms which the seventeenth century could understand. Thus the Charter once again became a landmark in our history, because thinking made it so' (55)—thinking, so we may add, which itself was made what it was by life, in this case particularly the living forces of budding democracy in their struggle against the decaying absolutism of Stuart times.

It is both amazing and gratifying to see how closely Butterfield sometimes approaches to the theoretical positions developed in this book.

'If we have clung to the past', he says for instance, 'it has been to a nicely chosen past—one which was conveniently and tidily disposed for our purposes' (6). The words 'nicely' and 'conveniently' jar a little, for they suggest that the facts have been 'managed' or 'manipulated', whereas in reality the human mind selects and arranges the objects of knowledge from the point of view of its inherent axiological convictions, spontaneously, naïvely, innocently, so to speak. But Butterfield would hardly deny this. He points out later on that both the Tory and the Whig interpretations had plenty of factual material—plenty of hard and undeniable facts—from which to build their competing structures: 'In the reign of James I some opposition members were taunted in the House of Commons for their industry in the search for ancient precedents. It was suggested then that this was a game which the king could play [too]. . . . Some might even argue [today] that if England had developed into an autocratic monarchy under the Stuarts, she would still have been able to turn back in a similar way and find the seeds of despotism in the same medieval constitution' (80). Butterfield, as can be seen, clearly implies that Whig and Tory history must not be naïvely contrasted as truth and error: both, he gives us to understand, are correct in relation to the strands which they pick out of the tangled web of events as such, and he is correct in this assumption and assertion, however much something in us may cry for a simple division into right and wrong, black and white. And he makes it quite clear that in his opinion (which is ours also) the Whig interpretation of history was not deprived of its initial chances of discovering the truth, and, indeed, of its eventual success in this quest, simply because it started out from certain pre-established axiomatic assumptions: 'The Whig interpretation', he writes, 'began as a step in the direction of a deeper understanding of English history. The Whig historians have not been harmful in what their sympathies enabled them to discern; they have only been harmful at those points where there is an arrest or suspension of sympathy' (71).

What books like Butterfield's illustrate is the contrast between differently directed, axiologically differently determined schools in the handling of individual facts. But the dissimilarities go much deeper and inform the *modes* of thinking as well as the concrete *contents* of historical thought. One of the most outstanding features of historical thought before, say, 1800, is the pragmatic conception of the whole subject, sometimes strongly felt and consciously proclaimed, sometimes merely taken for granted, but always present: history can teach us wisdom, it is a collection of examples and *ad oculos* demonstrations of types of human conduct, good and bad, with their appropriate consequences, also good and bad. In this sense Thucydides wrote in the fifth century B.C. that 'the accurate knowledge of what has happened will be useful because according to human probability similar things will happen again'.[1] In the same sense Leibniz wrote in the eighteenth century A.D. that 'the chief end of history . . . should be to teach prudence and virtue by examples, and then to display vice in such a way as to create aversion to it and to prompt men to avoid it'.[2] Innumerable are the passages in the literature produced in the intervening two thousand-odd years which express the same sentiment. Whence this curious conviction which we can no longer share, which now seems downright absurd to us? The historians, down to such figures as David Hume,[3] selected from the welter of historical materials predominantly those objects which embody and illustrate recurrence, neglecting very largely the individual and unique elements in history, and this was by no means absurd in their own day because the rate of change in human affairs was so slow that stability was not only the prime value, but also the prime impression of historical life.

It took world-shattering events, such as the French Revolution, and that speeding-up of historical processes in general, and of the processes of economic development in particular, which has characterized life since the end of the eighteenth century, to create—in fact as well as in thought—the gap between the present and the past which makes it impossible for us to see them as one reality and forbids us to regard the experiences of yesterday as applicable to the affairs of today or tomorrow. And we are not only aware of the flow of all things; we have also raised it in our hierarchy of values to a higher place than stability. As Geiger has well expressed it: 'Modern society has been called *dynamical*; the intention has been to indicate by this term that changeability is its structural principle. But that does not [merely] mean that it is subject to change. This would apply to any given period for society is a historical phenomenon and history itself is change. But it makes a difference whether society is subject to changes and accepts these changes as a human *fate*, or whether it sets itself to work at every moment for its own transformation and conceives the latter as a human *task*. . . . Modern man does not regard the changeability of his conditions of life, his forms of existence and his ideas as an inevitable destiny; he is not its passive play-thing, but promotes it consciously and deliberately. . . . We depreciate today for the sake of tomorrow.'[4] And because we feel like this, because stability is no longer our prime value, but rather advancement, we pick out of the materials of historical knowledge those facts and strands of development which show progression of some kind, and are inclined to make progress the touchstone

[1] *Cit.* Cowell, *History, Civilization and Culture*, 1952, 2.
[2] *Theodicy*, ed. Farrer, 1951, 217.
[3] Cf. Meinecke, *Die Entstehung des Historismus*, ed. 1946, 202 *seq.*
[4] *Aufgaben und Stellung der Intelligenz*, 1949, 39.

of all our historical thought. Subject to the proper limitations, we are entitled to do this—but no more so than our predecessors were to follow their own line of research; for reality embraces both progress and permanence, recurrence and change.

So deep then is the axiological and social determination of historical thought, even in its most 'objective', scholarly or 'scientific' form, that it extends not only to concretely determined facts but even to abstract modes of determining the facts. Yet it is an influence which goes deeper still. There can be no historical work, however careful, however factual, however technical, which does not rest on certain philosophical foundations, for example on a certain conception of the nature of time, and it is already here, at this deepest of all layers of historical thought, that social determination begins. We cannot dig down to that subsoil here, the operation would detain us much too long.[1] What we have sought to do, and what we hope in fact to have done, is to show that our specific theory of the sociology of knowledge can prove its worth when it comes to be applied to a particular field of scholarship.

It goes without saying that we have not selected historical thinking for close consideration because it is particularly easy in this field to show the operation of the analytical principles of our sociology of knowledge. Any other department of culture would have done just as well—even what Talcott Parsons calls 'imaginative' thought, i.e. thought which is neither concerned with *data*, like 'existential' thought, nor yet with *facienda*, like normative ideas,[2] and which seems in consequence altogether divorced from reality. For such utopian thought is still within the mental framework constituted by the basic crystallization and specification of thinking which we have endeavoured to analyse. Very often, indeed, we find a surprisingly close connection between social life as it is and utopian thought at its most fantastic. Many an Oceana and Erewhon has been no more than a photographic negative of the contemporary social situation. 'Myths, fairy tales, other-worldly promises of religion, humanistic fantasies, travel romances, have been continually changing expressions of that which was lacking in actual life', Mannheim says. 'They were . . . complementary colours in the picture of the reality existing at the time . . .'[3] This is an insight which the sociology of knowledge has possessed from the very beginning. It is often thought that Marx condemned the so-called utopian socialists because they were day-dreamers rather than hard men of action, but this

---

[1] A few references must suffice. For the consequences of the fact that history is at every moment an unfinished, continuing process, see Scheler, *Die Wissensformen und die Gesellschaft*, 1926, 176 *seq.*; for the variation of time-concepts, Mannheim, *Ideology and Utopia*, ed. 1952, esp. 190 *seq.* These analyses of Mannheim, which are among the very best he has produced, are briefly summarized by J. J. Maquet in *Sociologie de la Connaissance*, 1949, 46 *seq.*

[2] *Essays in Sociological Theory*, 1954, 21.   [3] *Ideology and Utopia*, ed. 1952, 184.

is at the very best part of the story. What Marx complained of and criticized was above all the fact that the day-dreams of the Fouriers, Saint-Simons and Cabets were, appearances notwithstanding, far too much like the capitalist reality that surrounded them, except that the shadows had been left out.[1] An idealization, however extravagant in detail, is always an idealization of things existent; and for that reason the sociology of knowledge can deal even with the highest flights of fancy and show their essentially earth-bound nature. This does not mean, of course, that the sociology of knowledge alone can adequately explain the appearance of such phenomena; far from it. It only means that it has a contribution to make and that it can add its measure or its mite to the collective efforts which will always be needed to unravel so complex a texture as the tissue of forces which have conjointly expressed themselves in visions like those of Thomas More, or Harrington, or Bellamy, or Huxley, or any of their kind.

(c) SOCIAL DETERMINATION AND INDIVIDUAL FREEDOM

The sociology of knowledge claims that it is possible to throw light on, and even, within limits, to explain, the origination of ideas, to demonstrate that thought is tied up with, and comprehensible in terms of, life—or, to formulate this assertion somewhat more boldly, to show that each concrete individual thought is genetically connected with an appropriate social life-situation without which it would not have come into being or become what in fact it is. But it is *not* claimed by the sociology of knowledge that ideas are the intra-mental *effects* of extra-mental *causes*. Those of its protagonists who have operated with the cause-and-effect concept, like Max Adler (who believed that all true science is *per causas scire*), have been careful so to define their idea of causation as to make it totally unlike mechanical causation—indeed, the very opposite of it. Whether this is a reasonable procedure; whether it is at all possible to merge the ideas of causation and spontaneity without destroying either or both of them, whether we are not confronted here with an irreducible contradiction in terms, is a problem which we propose to leave severely alone.[2] It does not arise for us

[1] Cf. Korsch, *Karl Marx*, 1938, 53.

[2] Warynski, in *Die Wissenschaft von der Gesellschaft* (1944), distinguishes three varieties of causality: mechanical, biological and mental (149 *seq*.): but is it permissible to class together, be it only verbally, mechanical causality (cause-and-effect) and biological 'causality' (stimulus-and-response)—not to speak here of 'mental causality'—if the most essential characteristic of the cause-and-effect relationship, namely the quantitative equivalence of cause and effect, is absent from the stimulus-and-response nexus? By wrapping the relation of substructure and superstructure in the cloak called 'cause and effect', a quite misleading impression is created, the impression that the two are alike, whereas in reality they are altogether unlike each other.

The Essence of the Sociology of Knowledge

because we refuse, *a limine*, to give ourselves over to a pan-mechanistic view of life, however reduced, attenuated or humanized. The biologist who works with the idea of stimulus and response is in our conviction as much of a scientist as the physicist who works with the idea of cause and effect; indeed, within his field, a better one, since these conceptions are much more appropriate to his sector of reality, namely life, than the pattern of cause and effect can ever be. A flower is not the dead effect of the material factors which are behind it; any analysis of its origin which took account of nothing but the mechanical forces involved in its growth would be unrealistic, not to say ridiculous; for in actual fact it is the living out-working of a whole host of contributory agencies, some of which are characterized by life, spontaneity, creativeness and even freedom. And so it is, *mutatis mutandis*, with the birth of ideas also. The parallel between the cultural sciences and biology may be misleading because the distance between life without thought and conscious life is 'infinitely infinite', as Pascal put it, but it is a much safer and sounder comparison than that between the cultural sciences and rational mechanics which is, after all, only the study of material forces in their interaction with each other in the field of death.

The question, of course, arises: what has the sociology of knowledge to offer if not a causal explanation of the origin of ideas?—and to this query the plain answer is: a method for the *understanding* of human thought both in its origins and in its content. Man may be a free being, but he is at the same time an intelligible one, and nothing can contribute so much to the understanding of him as an examination of the mode of his interaction with other men. When we study the development by which a human being becomes what he is, we find a process curiously similar to that which we have found to be responsible for the formation of any and every *imago mundi*: at the beginning, at birth, there is indefinite, almost infinite potentiality; but nobody can live in pure potentiality; a single concrete actuality must emerge out of the initial indefinite possibilities if an independent and active existence is to become possible; there must, in other words, be crystallization, specification, definition; and this process, which could be called the process of man's realization, is carried on and carried out within the matrix of contemporary social relationships. Man is not wax, nor is society a seal to impress itself on the wax; such mechanistic similes are beside the point. But man is a living creature interacting with others of the same kind, and what he is and what he becomes (positively and negatively) is intelligible in the first place through the clash between his individuality and the social forces in and through which his initial potentialities are transformed into his emergent actuality or personality. If man is to function as a member of his society—and that is manifestly the destiny of us all—he must accept, at any rate in its essentials, the norms

141

(including the world-view) which that society has made for itself under the guidance of its basic values; he must internalize this normative system and this world-view, though he may ring many changes on it; the only alternative to socialization of the individual mind and character is its alienation. The whole process of adjustment between self and society may be carried out in full freedom, but the salient point is that there *is* such a process, and that it opens up to us an avenue towards the understanding of the reality which we call man.

In what we have just said, we are aware of having overstepped the borderline between sociology and psychology, for to study the internalization of culture is undoubtedly the proper province of the psychologist (and the educator). But our excursion *ultra vires* was no more than momentary. The sociologist is only concerned with what is being internalized, not with the process of internalization—the sociologist, in the general meaning of the term, with the norms of society, its external order, the sociologist of knowledge with its world-view or universe of thought. The whole diversion is only introduced here in order to demonstrate that an acceptance of the sociology of knowledge, as we conceive it, carries with it no committal to any causal or deterministic conception of the human mind.

Perhaps we can sum all this up by saying that the sociology of knowledge, as we see it, is essentially a hermeneutic or explanatory method,[1] not a dogmatic ontology. It does not involve any specious metaphysical assumptions concerning the relationship of substructure and superstructure, thought and being—least of all assumptions of a deterministic kind in the strict or technical sense of the word. All it takes for granted is that in man thought and being—individual thought and social being —form an indissoluble unity. But if he who lives in society and he who thinks in private are essentially one person, if there is no divorce between man's social existence and man's mental processes, then the former may and must be able to throw light on the latter, and consideration of the latter in the light of the former must be a help towards the understanding of human thoughts and feelings. The task of the sociology of knowledge is merely to explore—and explore by way of realistic research, by the accumulation of analytical case-histories as it were—how close the connection between social substructure and mental superstructure in fact is, and consequently how great is the

[1] Paul Landsberg, whose opinions closely coincide with our own, has proposed to call the sociology of knowledge an 'anthropological method' 'because its aim is an understanding knowledge of all the historical manifestations of man's life and mentality in and through the becoming unity of his existence' ('Zur Soziologie der Erkenntnistheorie', in *Schmollers Jahrbuch*, 1931, 791). If the word 'anthropology' had not already been earmarked as the label of a specialism, the phrase suggested would have been well chosen, for the sociology of knowledge is indeed essentially an ingredient in a comprehensive doctrine of man. Cf. below, ch. 4.

contribution which the sociological study of mental phenomena can make to the understanding of culture and its development. It is in concrete exploration, not in abstract speculation, that its future must lie. Nothing could be more illegitimate and nothing more unfortunate on the part of the sociologist of knowledge than to pontificate, before encountering the facts, about the ontological nature of the interrelation between thought and life. That such an interrelation exists is perhaps already a metaphysical assumption of a kind; but, if so, it need not be raised to the dignity of a dogmatic assertion; it need only be proposed as a strategic principle which is called upon to prove itself in action and application, and must remain *sub judice* until it has so proved itself by an accumulation of positive achievements.

It follows from the whole character and complexion of our basic analysis that we do not, and indeed cannot, degrade human thinking to the status of an epiphenomenon. The works of the human spirit we regard as something capable of being understood, not as the necessary reflex of a lower reality. 'What we can aim at with our sociological method', Paul Landsberg has written, 'is a deeper historical understanding of knowledge, an understanding which is neither logical nor causal . . . Our sociology cannot be progressive, like that of Comte or of Marxism, in the sense of aiming at the destruction of past achievements . . . It wishes to understand existence and the modes of knowing, and to widen the human mind by inspiring respect' for what otherwise might appear meaningless and even contemptible.[1]

More soberly, we can adduce four reasons why our sociology of knowledge, even though it assumes a vital dependence of thought-processes on life-processes, cannot, in fairness, be accused of denying, or even of deprecating, the spontaneity of the human spirit. Firstly and fundamentally, the mind, for us, is not a passive but an active something, an agent. It constitutes its own universe; it is truly creative. In this we agree entirely with Immanuel Kant. Our difference is merely that we do not regard the mind, *more mathematico*, as a time-less, eternally self-identical intellect, but rather as time-bound and ever changing in its concrete operations, as cast into a concrete mould by contemporary (social) life. And this 'concretization' of it, this casting of it into a determinate mould, does not take place under the impact of inhuman or subhuman forces; it is brought about by a truly human reality, the reality of interhuman relationships, which is itself characterized by freedom and permeated, as it were, by mentality. Clearly, nothing that is alien to the human mind is introduced at any point into our analysis; the salient distinction is not so much between the intra-mental and the extra-mental as between mind-in-operation (in the social field, in

[1] 'Zur Soziologie der Erkenntnistheorie', in *Schmollers Jahrbuch*, 1931, 772 and 808.

practice) and mind-in-contemplation (in pursuit of knowledge for its own sake, in theory). What we are saying is that he who thinks (in theory) has already learnt to think (in practice)—no less certainly, but also no more.

Secondly, though social life, through its implied value-structure, introduces into our mind an *a priori* axiological layer, a pre-existent principle of selection and ordering, an anticipatory scheme into which to fit the facts of experience, it does not, as if by magic, provide a full and complete world of factual knowledge. This knowledge has to be garnered in fact by fact—indeed, it has to be selected and ordered by us, for the principles of selection and ordering must be applied and utilized before they can constitute a mental universe. A picture is not completed when its outlines have been drawn; its spaces must be filled with vivid colours, and there is as much artistry—as much room for true creativeness—in the filling in of the colours as there is in the drawing of the outlines. As H. J. Lieber has put it: 'It is necessary not to misunderstand the sociologists of knowledge and their contention. They do not relate an isolated statement or an isolated piece of knowledge or an isolated judgment directly to social being. On the contrary, the relation between an individual proposition and its basis in social reality is indirect. All individual statements, insights and judgments in the sphere of the cultural sciences are considered as the expression of a total world-view, and only this special way of interpreting the world appears as socially conditioned in its content and structure. . . . The medium through which social being exerts its influence on the formation of knowledge is man . . . who always lives in a determinate social world and thinks in terms of it.' [1] Man is the medium through which the social forces act upon the objective culture of each age, says Lieber, and he is right, but man is no passive medium. He is himself a force; he prolongs, as it were, in the direction of creativity, the activity and action of the social forces behind him (which, as we have emphasized, are human forces, identical with, not alien to, him) and it is through him that these social forces reach their destination, the creation of a concrete culture.

Thirdly, when we come to the consideration of the individual mind, especially the young mind in the process of formation, we find again that it is in principle free, though it may, and often will, forego its freedom in practice. We have already adverted to this fact. The socially established system of values will confront the individual in two forms: as a system of rules of conduct, of dos and don'ts, and as a system of (let us say with Durkheim) collective representations, as a mental universe. Both will be offered to him; both will be pressed upon him; both he must accept if he wishes to become a well-integrated member of the body social. But neither will bind him hand and foot; variations

[1] *Wissen und Gesellschaft*, 1952, 15 *seq.*

from the mean, from modal behaviour and modal thought, will be possible within certain, often very wide, limits. And it is only because of this elasticity of the social code (of mind as well as of action) that the individual will, as a rule, open his personality to it and allow the socially established principles of life and thought to enter in and fill out the vacant spaces. Well does he know that his freedom remains in spite of the limitations which he has accepted. He is not a captive in a narrow prison-house, but rather the inmate of a generously laid-out mansion with many apartments.

Still, it is true that it is very difficult for the average individual to make use of his remaining freedom, real though it may be, if there is nothing to choose from—the situation in many primitive societies where there is a far-reaching (though never complete) uniformity of thought and conduct, simply because there is only one value-system with one appropriate code of behaviour and one co-ordinated set of collective representations. But in complex societies the situation is as a rule more favourable to freedom. For here there are regularly several systems of value side by side, and hence several styles of life and thought, which compete with each other and bid, so to speak, for the individual's allegiance. And it will not be too difficult for the individual to switch from one to the other. For in a complex society the social determination of thought takes place on two levels, as it were: there is the inclusive global society with its effect; and there are the included subsocieties with theirs. There is common ground, and there are mental enclosures: there is a comprehensive universe, and there are restricted kingdoms within it. If we may maltreat the metaphors we have just used, we may say that the common ground offers a *bridge* over which an individual may travel from one enclosure to the other. Under classical capitalism, for instance, material values are paramount: the upper and lower classes share this over-all conviction, though they disagree on many (comparatively minor) points. Now the prevailing pan-utilitarian mode of thinking makes it relatively easy for anybody to extricate himself from the value-system of one class (and its appropriate mental modes) and to integrate himself with that of another. This explains the familiar figure of the renegade and the frequency of his appearance. It is manifestly much more difficult to change from one social system to another totally unconnected with it: for a European to 'go native', for instance, or for a native to become 'civilized'. And thus it is that complex societies allow even more freedom than simple ones—that their members' mind-contents and mental processes are even less amenable to explanation in terms of cause and effect than any others.

But we are still understating the case: in a complex society, the individual has not only a choice between competing world-views, but also the opportunity to transcend them both and achieve a new and wider mental integration; but to make a new and wider mental synthesis out of the initially given materials is eminently an act of creativeness, indeed, the only kind of creativeness open to the human race.[1]

We are pleading, then, for a non-deterministic, non-materialistic sociology of knowledge—one that would disdain to make use, whether explicitly or implicitly, of the concept of causation. Have other, earlier workers in the field approached the problem in the same spirit? To be honest, it must be admitted straight away that many of them have been unable to withstand the lure of this highly attractive, because typically 'scientific', principle of explanation, in spite of the fact that it is taken from rational mechanics, a sphere whose laws are altogether different from those of life, and particularly of social life. Max Adler was not alone in believing that all *scire* is *per causas scire*, and many who have adhered to this creed have been much less circumspect in their formulation of it than he was. All Marxism has passed through a positivistic phase during which its protagonists have tried to make the master's doctrine as similar to science as they possibly could. But this was really a falling away from the master's teaching, and recently there has been a return to the early Marx's less deterministic position. Stanislaw Warynski is a characteristic example of this, and so too is Georg Lukacs, whose influence in Marxist circles has been great, and deservedly so, for his interpretation of the doctrine is most able and revealing.

The Hegelian ideas against which Marx revolted included *inter alia* Hegel's conviction that individual thought is determined—determined *a tergo* as it were: the ordinary man's thought by the folk spirit, the great man's or 'historical individual's' thought by the world spirit, in other words by the spiritual principle of universal history. 'History does nothing', Marx wrote in *The Holy Family*, protesting against such metaphysical speculations. 'It is rather man, real living man who does everything. . . . It is not history which uses men as a means to carry out its ends as if it were a separate person, for it is nothing else but the activity of man in the pursuit of his ends.' [2]

It is to suchlike conceptions that the Marxists have recently returned, and understandably so, for they fit in much better with an aggressive, revolutionary philosophy than any consistent determinism which must logically lead to passivity. This is not to say that Marxism does not contain a strong dose of determinism: it does: 'socialism must come': Marxism's most excruciating difficulty consists precisely in its enforced attempt to combine an objective determinism with a belief in subjective

[1] This is a point on which Sorokin has laid some emphasis. For a brief summary of his views, cf. J. J. Maquet, *Sociologie de la Connaissance*, 1949, 251 *seq.* Cf. also Gurvitch, *Le Concept de Classes Sociales de Marx à Nos Jours*, 1954, 60 *seq.*

[2] 1845 (facsimile ed., 1953), 139 *seq.*

freedom. We cannot at this moment stay to discuss in any detail the very complex theory which has sprung from this attempt to reconcile what is hardly reconcilable, for the theory which has resulted is as ingenious as it is involved. It will be sufficient for our purpose to emphasize that in communist doctrine, as is reflected in Stanislaw Warynski's *Wissenschaft von der Gesellschaft*, the rights and the realities of free thought and free action are safeguarded. Men, he seems to teach, act in pursuit of aims and hence (subjectively) in freedom; but these aims are suggested to them and defined for them by the (objective) tendencies of development, and hence determined independently of their individual wills. 'Man is not only a willing being, but also a being that is part and parcel of a real process of happening.' Yet—and this is important—'this does not annihilate the property of the will to be "free" within its own orbit, though it gives it a new determination (*Bestimmung*)' (135). 'Men' in this view 'are not merely the objects of circumstances, but themselves change the circumstances' (228). If they wish to act rationally, meaningfully, they must (voluntarily) fall in with the drift of things; but they *need* not act rationally. Indeed, ideological deception and self-deception are quite capable of inducing them to swim against the stream. In any case, the mind of man is not univocally determined in its content. 'If we look closely we see that although the ideological structure of individuals is in general determined by their class-membership, the majority of men unite in their thinking and feeling different elements from opposite ideologies which often stand in crying contrast to each other' (251). 'All men, in point of fact, besides those aims which are due to their class-membership and are similar in tendency, have also their own particular aims which are never completely identical, and accordingly also their own individual modes of behaviour' (154 *seq.*). Moreover, even those who rationally decide to follow the lead of general tendencies and the objective course of evolution, do not find their every step plotted out for them. The way must be chosen, however much the end of it may be fixed. 'The laws of sociology represent merely tendencies, concern only the general form of development and leave a relatively wide radius of action for individual "freedom" ' (251).

Yet even in so far as Marxism—'historical materialism'—is a deterministic philosophy, it does not, like materialism properly so called, see human thought and action as dependent upon non-human factors. For as Warynski emphasizes, the determining agency is a specifically *human* reality. What are the forces which, according to Marx and Engels, operate behind and through men's motives and volitions? 'They are nothing extra-social and nothing extra-psychical . . . and least of all are they to be conceived as something mechanical. . . . These . . . forces which are not changeable at will and compel men to fall in with certain

147

social forms of existence are the relations of production: human relations, whose nature is determined by the mode of production, an activity which is again human. . . . Economic conditions are nothing but a system of human relationships' (137, 155). In these passages, Warynski comes very close to the position which we ourselves have taken up and developed in these pages. And, like ourselves, Warynski unambiguously condemns all mechanistic determinism: 'A one-sided causal and mechanistic approach never achieves a full understanding of man as a creature endowed with consciousness' (258).[1]

If 'proletarian Marxism' is thus forced to admit a far-reaching indeterminism into its social theory and sociology of knowledge, we cannot be surprised to find the same in regard to the 'bourgeois Marxism' of Karl Mannheim. 'It is not Mannheim's intention', Lieber writes, 'in interpreting the mind as a function of social life, to set up the latter as the only reality and then—by way of causal explanation— to uncover the causal dependence of the mental world upon the social sphere. If he were to pursue such an intention, he would only be reviving naïve philosophical materialism in a new form. [But] the materialistic thesis of a real causation of the mind by being lies, in principle, outside the sociology of knowledge as Mannheim upholds it. . . . The technical term "interrelation of thought and social being" is meant only to enable the sociologist of knowledge—in despite of all causal explanations—to achieve a specific *understanding* and a particular *interpretation* of the world of the spirit as something that exists within a meaningful context. . . . The term "being", in Mannheim's discussion, has primarily an epistemological rather than an ontological meaning—a meaning pointing, not to a causal explanation, but rather towards structural interrelations.' [2] In other words, for Mannheim, as for ourselves, the sociology of knowledge is essentially a hermeneutic method, part and parcel of an 'understanding' sociology. Thus we find once again that so far as essentials are concerned, a substantial measure of agreement exists among fellow-workers in the field, even though they start from different philosophical positions and strive towards different political ends.

It goes without saying that the freedom of man's mind on which we are insisting, in other words, the inapplicability of the cause-and-effect pattern to the nexus between substructure and superstructure, makes it very much harder for the sociologist of knowledge to 'understand' any concrete thought or theory or artistic creation. But the difficulties involved in the effort to comprehend free men's ideas are no greater (though, alas, no less) than those involved in the parallel effort

[1] Cf. also on all this, Schumpeter, *History of Economic Analysis*, 1954, 438 note 7 and 440 note 12.

[2] *Wissen und Gesellschaft*, 1952, 99. Cf. also Kecskemeti in the introduction to Mannheim's *Essays on the Sociology of Knowledge*, 1952, 19 *seq.*

to understand their actions. Here and there we must, in honesty, distinguish degrees of intelligibility and acknowledge the existence of an outer perimeter beyond which it is no longer possible. That which is completely comprehensible in terms of the sociology of knowledge might be described as 'modal thought'. There are certain forms and contents of thought which express perfectly the 'spirit' of, say, classical capitalism, which represent the unfolding and implementation on the intellectual plane of the social order (of the substructure) which goes by this name. Capitalism is a dynamical society, and so the typical entrepreneur, as Schumpeter for instance has described him, is dynamical too—not only in his actions, but also in his mental modes; capitalism is a rational society, and so the typical *homo modernus* strives to achieve a worldview of the rationalistic variety, presenting a maximum of clarity, comprehensibility, calculability, and a minimum of vagueness, mystery and sentiment; and so on, and so forth. So great can our understanding of the modal mentality become, that we may even venture predictions. When our typical capitalist is faced with any business problem which needs thinking out, we can be sure that he will set about his task in the most systematic fashion, first get his facts right, then consider their implications, then estimate their likely future course, not neglecting to calculate comparative probabilities, and so on, and so forth; and we can also be sure that he will do all this without first having prayed or made a pilgrimage to Walsingham.

Less easily understood than modal thought is what might be called 'non-modal but meaningful' thought. By this we mean thought which is not typical of the established pattern of life, but still intelligible in terms of it. Capitalist society, as it appears in reality, in contradistinction to its pure ideal type, contains large areas into which such principles of rationality, calculation etc. have not penetrated, for instance family relationships. If somebody presses these principles beyond their generally accepted limitations, if he is, so to speak, more capitalist-minded than the modal capitalist, we get a non-modal attitude, though one which is in agreement with, and has obviously grown out of, the prevailing social substructure; an attitude, in other words, which still reflects the established order of being though with some exaggeration and distortion. The super-utilitarian types whom Dickens brings before us in *Hard Times* are of this category.

Even less intelligible in terms of the sociology of knowledge is 'a-typical thought'—thought born of an opposition to the given pattern of life and characteristic of the truant mind, so to speak. By this we do not mean oppositional or revolutionary thought in the usual acceptance of the word, for instance, adherence to the proletarian world-view in a capitalist society, for such thought will more often than not be fully modal or near-modal—being the modal world-view of a subsociety, the proletarian class, and hence representative of, and comprehensible as the outgrowth of, a certain substructural reality. We mean rather the mentality of the man who wishes to loosen, to liquefy, the given concrete pattern of thought, to modify it here and there, or possibly all along the line. In a way this third type of tendency is the opposite of the second. In the second case we had a mental mode central to a social system being pressed outwards towards regions which are not, in general, closely controlled by it: in our instance, the introduction of a calculating attitude into the family circle. Here we have mental modes that are only marginal to a social system being pressed inwards towards the core of that system, into which they are not, as a rule, allowed to penetrate. If, for instance, an entrepreneur allows sentimentality a share in his business considerations, he is in this sense a-typical in his thought. Certainly, his mind is still intelligible, in fact eminently so, but not from the point of view of the social order called classical capitalism. It is understandable—as we may put it, perhaps, in accordance with our general terminology—in the light of general human values or qualities, but not in the light of the specific concrete pattern of thought and feeling characteristic of the surrounding society.

Lastly, there is also thought which is neither modal nor an exaggeration of prevailing modes, nor yet a result of their modification by extraneous human values—thought whose moorings in life are not detectable. One hesitates to describe all such thought as irrational or deranged, but deranged thinking certainly falls into this category. Its hallmark is that it is not sociologically understandable at all.

It follows from all that has gone before that the sociology of knowledge cannot and must not set up as the only indispensable helpmate of the history of ideas. Not only does it not exclude other hermeneutic methods; it positively demands them for its supplementation. This applies above all to the biographical approach. The case of Friedrich Nietzsche offers an instructive example. In many ways his philosophy —more particularly his super-individualism—is a reflection of contemporary social developments. Never before had society been so 'atomistic', never before so favourable to the strong and so unfriendly to the weak as it was in his age. *Laisser-faire* had reached its acme, and it was 'every man for himself'. Do or die was the slogan of the day. Quarter was neither asked nor given. No wonder that such a man should extol the rule and regimen of jungle law: he saw it around him on all sides. But though this explains some of Nietzsche, it does not explain all of him. To comprehend him completely we must also observe his characteristic path through life: his slow loss of social integration, his progressive withdrawal from society and social discipline, his growing loneliness and final restless wandering from place to place.[1]

[1] Cf. Landsberg in *Schmollers Jahrbuch*, 1931, 805 *seq.*

And to grasp why he became uprooted in this manner, why from a man like other men he turned into a man like no other man, a man without friend or family or lasting abode, we must know his whole case-history; or must know at least that, early in life, he was the victim of severe overmothering to which he reacted violently, and, later in life, the victim of syphilis which, as it destroyed the tissues of his body, also affected the texture of his social and mental life. It was this disease which, together with other things, gave his (*a radice* socially determined) individualism an element of extravagance, megalomania and insanity which it is more for the psychiatrist to investigate and explain than the sociologist or even the psychologist.[1] And thus it is always: every theory, every thought owes its origin to a host of contributory factors, and their multiplicity demands for their comprehension a multiplicity of hermeneutic methods—methods in co-operation, not in competition. One alone will never—*never*—do.

Since we have here reached one of the limits of the subject, it may be as well to call a halt to our considerations. But, looking outward, it may be permissible to add in conclusion what we regard as the ultimate aim towards which all the hermeneutic methods, sociological, psychological and other, that may be jointly concerned with the study of the origins of human ideas, should strive in their co-operation. In addition to the satisfactory conclusion of the concrete piece of work they may have in hand, they should always bear in mind the necessity of building up a common canon of research, the elaboration of an integrated strategy. Such a strategy, needless to say, will have to be highly adaptable: not every fortress will fall to the same *coup de main*. Here the psychological techniques will be more effective, there the sociological, in a third case perhaps the psychiatric or even the psycho-somatic or purely physiological. The ideal to be achieved would be an inclusive yet elastic method of systematic attack on all sides, which would first feel for the angle of approach from which it seems easiest to advance towards an understanding of the phenomena concerned, would then exploit the possibilities of this particular approach to the utmost, and afterwards explore the less promising avenues as well, until at last the problem concerned has either yielded up its secret—until we can really see *why* this or that idea appeared at this or that moment, and why this man or that conceived it or gave it a place in his mind—or until we stand before an irreducible residue of incomprehensibility, before an ultimate riddle which the scholar must humbly accept in deference to that overwhelming complexity and mysteriousness of life which will always refuse to be reduced altogether to the puny measure of the human intellect.

[1] Cf. Brinton, *Nietzsche*, 1941, 6 *seq.*, 15.

151

CHAPTER FOUR

THE CONSEQUENCES OF THE SOCIOLOGY OF KNOWLEDGE

(a) THE SO-CALLED HISTORICAL RELATIVITY OF TRUTH

THE sociology of knowledge is concerned in the first place with the origin of ideas, and not with their validity. It tries to understand why people have thought as they have, not to test whether what they have thought was the truth. As De Gré has well expressed it, it 'is relating ideas to persons, and not . . . to the objects to which they may refer'. 'The type of reality about which the ideas attempt to enlighten us does not concern the gnosio-sociologist on an epistemological or ontological level of analysis. It may be real or illusory, material or spiritual, sacred or profane, empirical or transcendental; with regard to these distinctions gnosio-sociology strives to be non-evaluative, and makes every effort to avoid passing value judgments . . . "Knowledge" in the context of gnosio-sociology is a non-evaluative term and carries with it no implications as to the truth or falsity of that knowledge.' [1] The sociology of knowledge investigates neither the coincidence of mind-contents with the appropriate facts, nor yet the co-ordination of the various ideas among themselves: neither the material truth of individual statements, nor the formal truth of inclusive systems of ideas. In other words, it is a positive-descriptive-historical discipline rather than a philosophical and epistemological one.

Yet though the sociology of knowledge *as such* is not concerned with the problem of truth, it has consequences which bear upon that very problem and imperatively demand attention. Indeed, its whole origin as an interesting and independent study was connected with, and occasioned by, a situation in which the truth had become deeply problematic. So long as a society is well integrated, fairly uniform within itself and relatively closed to outside influences, whatever happens to pass for the truth will be willingly accepted as such by the community concerned.

---

[1] 'The Sociology of Knowledge and the Problem of Truth', in the *Journal of the History of Ideas*, 1941, 114.

It is only when class contrasts develop within it which involve different world-views between which it is difficult to adjudicate, or when out-groups are encountered and to some extent lived with, whose ideas are different without it being possible to condemn them out of hand as patently absurd, that a question-mark is set against the traditional assumptions and convictions and an epistemological stock-taking becomes necessary.[1] But it is precisely such a constellation which will also suggest the possibility of, and provide an interest in, some such line of investigation as the sociology of knowledge. If different classes and different societies appear to have different sets of ideas, may these not be related to the social differences with which they are manifestly co-ordinated? It is easy to see why the desire to understand human thought in terms of its social subsoil in life is apt to run in harness with a desire to separate what is right from what is wrong in human thinking. We are confronted with a case of twin-birth. The two lines of investigation are parallel, not identical; but they have come out of the same parent situation.

The sociologists of knowledge themselves have always been conscious of this fact, Karl Mannheim perhaps more than any other. 'It is one of the fundamental insights of the sociology of knowledge', he writes in *Ideology and Utopia*, 'that the process by which collective-unconscious motives become conscious cannot operate in every epoch, but only in a quite specific situation. This situation is sociologically determinable. One can point out with relative precision the factors which are inevitably forcing more and more persons to reflect not merely about the things of the world, but about thinking itself, and even here not so much about truth in itself, as about the alarming fact that the same world can appear differently to different observers. It is clear that such problems can become general only in an age in which disagreement is more con-spicuous than agreement.' Only when the flow of history has been so speeded up that different generations are seen to view things differently; only when horizontal mobility from country to country, or from town to country, has so far developed that different societies are seen to have each their own appropriate world-view; only when vertical mobility, mobility from class to class, has become so common that many indi-viduals are led to recognize that different social strata, even within the same society, have differently articulated and differently accentuated pictures of reality, is the stage set for the appearance of the sociology of knowledge as a conscious pursuit and sustained topic of research. 'It is with this clashing of modes of thought, each of which has the same claims to representational validity, that for the first time there is

[1] Cf. *re* Dilthey's view of the origins of philosophy, Hodges, *Wilhelm Dilthey: An Introduction*, 1944, 91. Cf. also *re* Freyer, Grünwald, *Das Problem der Soziologie des Wissens*, 1934, 220 *seq.*

rendered possible the emergence of the question . . . how it is possible that identical human thought-processes concerned with the same world produce divergent conceptions of that world. . . . Today, there are too many points of view of equal value and prestige, each showing the relativity of the other, to permit us to take one position and to regard it as impregnable and absolute. Only this socially disorganized intellectual situation makes possible the insight, hidden until now by a generally stable social structure and the practicability of certain traditional norms, that every point of view is particular to a social situation' (ed. 1952, 5, 8, 75).[1]

But this 'socially disorganized intellectual situation' not only opens our eyes to a fact, the fact of the social determination of the mental life, it also, *pari actu*, forces on us, whether we like it or not, a question—the question of Pontius Pilate, as excruciating in our own circumstances as it was in his : what is truth? In other words, it not only stimulates us to develop a new branch of historico-hermeneutic learning, it also compels us to reconsider the epistemological reliability of much, perhaps all, that we have so far taken for granted. So long as the 'conceptual apparatus is the same for all the members of the group', says Mannheim, 'the presuppositions (i.e. the . . . social and intellectual values) which underlie the individual concepts never become perceptible'. 'The somnambulistic certainty that has existed with reference to the problem of truth during stable periods of history thus becomes intelligible. However, once the unanimity is broken, the fixed categories which used to give experience its reliable and coherent character undergo an inevitable disintegration' (91). The fair face of truth becomes clouded, its features fleeting and vague, and men must try to regain what they have lost, for it is difficult for them to live without the truth.

Yet it is anything but easy to recover the truth. For the very same situation—the situation of social disunity—which has made the truth problematic, has also created incentives for its continued and progressive destruction. The different societies and subsocieties, while naïvely continuing to regard their own convictions as 'the truth', get busy 'unmasking'—'debunking'—the convictions of the others as error—as ideologies.[2] Collective philosophies become like banners in a battle: to carry their own aloft, but to tread those of the enemy into the dust, is one of the dearest aims of the contestants. As Merton observes: 'Not only do there develop different universes of discourse, but the existence of any one universe challenges the validity and legitimacy of the others. The coexistence of these conflicting perspectives and interpretations within the same society leads to an active and reciprocal *distrust*

[1] Cf. also *Ideology and Utopia*, 252 *seq.*

[2] Cf. Mannheim, *Ideology and Utopia*, ed. 1952, 34 *seq.*, 56 *seq.*, 61 *seq.* Cf. also Hans Barth's valuable book, *Wahrheit und Ideologie*, 1945, *passim.*

between groups. . . . Alien statements are "explained by" or "imputed to" special interests, unwitting motives, distorted perspectives, social position etc. . . . The professional iconoclast, the trained debunker, the ideological analyst and their respective systems of thought thrive in a society where large groups of people have already become alienated from common values.' [1] As we have seen in our second chapter, even the sociology of knowledge, though its whole design and mission is that of a scholarly discipline, becomes involved in this political turmoil by being conceived as, or rather confused with, the doctrine of ideology and pan-ideologism. It is an unfortunate fact that Merton, looking at the older literature, can justifiably say: 'Whatever the intention of the analysts, their analyses tend to have an acrid quality: they tend to indict, secularize, ironicize, satirize, alienate, devalue the intrinsic content of the avowed belief or point of view. . . . Throughout runs . . . the emphasis on the distinction between the real and the illusory, between reality and appearance in the sphere of human thought, belief and conduct.' [2]

The present book, having resolutely, consistently, and systematically divided sociology of knowledge from doctrine of ideology—fact-determination from wish-determination—has taken the whole discussion out of this unhealthy atmosphere. For the desire to unmask error it has substituted the attempt to understand the origins of truth. We are far from anxious to 'indict, secularize, ironicize, satirize, alienate, devalue': these pastimes are for the market-place, not for the study, for the propagandist, not for the scholar. Following Scheler above all, we hold, as has been seen, that every society, and every other supra-functional subsociety as well, can lay claim to truth, the substance of truth, though only one aspect of it—that aspect of reality which offers itself to the beholding eye from the given vantage-point and angle of vision. But, unfortunately, this does not mean that there is *no* problem of truth for us. Obviously and unavoidably there arises the question as to the implications and consequences of the fact that every society has its *own* particular view of reality, its own universe of thought—indeed, its own universe of truth.

The problem of truth—the properly epistemological problem—raised by the sociology of knowledge as we understand it, springs from the fact that every society sees, possesses and holds only one aspect of objective reality, in other words, one part of the truth, but is inclined to regard it as the whole truth, beside which all other world-views must needs appear erroneous. All human perception is limited; but all human beings are loath to acknowledge their limitation. All concrete thought-structures have arisen through the realization of one limited possibility out of an unlimited potentiality; this is precisely what we have called the process of 'concretization'; without it no concrete thought-structure could so

---

[1] *Social Theory and Social Structure*, 1949, 218 seq.　　[2] *Loc. cit.*, 219.

much as arise; and yet the naïve assumption is almost always that this one possibility which has actually come to fruition is the only one that was antecedently possible. The fallacy with which the sociology of knowledge has to deal, so far as the search for truth is concerned, is thus the fallacy of *pars pro toto*—taking the part for the whole. This fallacy can lead deep into absurdity. If it is true, as Kelsen says (though the statement seems somewhat exaggerated) that 'the fundamental principle which determines primitive man's behaviour towards nature is the same as that which decides his conduct towards the members of his own and other groups—the social principle of retribution',[1] then primitive man cannot achieve a sound physical science because he has absolutized what is only partial; and in the same way modern man cannot build up a sound social science if he treats (as he has often done) human relations as if they obeyed the same law as the lever. In either case the *pars pro toto* fallacy has been at work, with nefarious results. It is a fallacy which men need not and indeed should not fall into; but, alas!, they invariably do. It is not difficult to see why. Living as they do among relativities and uncertainties, they have an altogether natural thirst for absolutes and certainties. Perhaps these absolutes and certainties are for ever denied them in their mortal state; perhaps they can only be found after searching far and wide; perhaps one must be a philosopher or a saint to penetrate to their threshold. For the majority of men nothing will do but a short cut, and that is why they raise what chances to be their own order of values and its attendant world-view to the position of the right-in-itself, true-in-itself and beautiful-in-itself.

For scholarship such an attitude ought to be unacceptable, although only too many scholars have been no more able to free themselves from common human limitations than their less sophisticated contemporaries. An outstanding modern historian of culture has written as follows: 'One of the safest (and most useful) generalizations resulting from a study of the history of ideas is that every age tends to exaggerate the scope and finality of its own discoveries, or re-discoveries, to be so dazzled by them that it fails to discern clearly their limitations and forgets aspects of truth against prior exaggerations of which it has revolted.'[2] Be this as it may, for a sociologist of knowledge brought up on and nourished by the Kant-Rickert-Weber tradition it is impossible to remain locked up in the *hortus clusus* of his own mental universe; impossible not to realize that there are other gardens and parklands beyond, which have their own greenness, their own flowers, and their own specific, and perhaps even unique, beauty.

The habit of raising the part to the dignity of the whole has two main consequences. One shows itself in inter-group relationships; the other in

[1] *Society and Nature*, 1946, 49.

[2] Lovejoy, in the *Journal of the History of Ideas*, 1940, 17.

intra-group conditions. The mental intercourse between societies has always been marred by a good deal of mutual incomprehension. To the modern rationalist, the medieval world-view has always appeared as a tissue of absurdities. For a phenomenon like mysticism he has nothing but contempt. Even those who ought to know better often fail to penetrate to the meaning of those phenomena which do not occur in their own familiar world. The challenge to scholarship, of course, lies precisely in the apparent irrationalities and incomprehensibilities of alien culture-complexes; to understand *them* ought to be the scholar's prime concern. But how few have the greatness of mind to penetrate through the outer shell of appearances to the inner kernel of significance! The undertaking is difficult and always hazardous; it is much easier to talk about things as they look than about things as they are. Besides, by simply expatiating on the surface-aspects of an alien culture—an aspect which is sure to create a predominantly negative reaction since its underlying values are, by definition, not the same as those of the student and his society—a man may be surer of the assent of his fellow-men, and hence of the sweets of success, than by fearlessly pursuing the truth, by trying to comprehend the alien culture in terms of its own values.

But it is not only the meeting of cultures that is hindered by the absolutizing of the partial, by the disregarding of limitations; the understanding of one's own culture is also affected thereby. An example will show why and how. During the nineteenth century, progress was a high-ranking, perhaps indeed the prime value of Western civilization. All action was directed towards it, all life dominated by it, and this fact was bound to have, and did have, appropriate consequences for contemporary thought. Going again, from the new vantage-point, over the old materials, the historians of the age collected together all the facts of the past which proved the reality of progressive development throughout the centuries. Much solid truth was discovered in this way. Now, so long as the evolutionist conception of history remained within its proper limits, the limits prescribed by the guiding value itself, it kept to the straight and narrow path of reason and rectitude. If it, for instance, insisted on the reality of progress in technology or in economic life, it was within its rights, for is not the railway-engine faster than the stage-coach, and a world-economy richer than an isolated local one? But the trouble was that historians, or at any rate many of them, did not restrict themselves as they should have done. From the truth that there is progressive development in some fields of human endeavour, they concluded—illicitly, by the fallacy of *pars pro toto*—that there is progressive development in all. A Comte could assert that later painters, composers and sculptors are invariably nearer to absolute beauty, later philosophers nearer to absolute truth, than earlier ones. It is only necessary to reformulate this assertion (which became part and parcel of the common metaphysic of the age) in a more stringent and concrete way in order to show how foolish it is: the railway engine is faster than the stage-coach, consequently Sir Edwin Landseer is a better painter than Giotto, and John Stuart Mill a wiser philosopher than Leibniz. The mental trick by which this nonsense was given the semblance of plausibility was to argue that Sir Edwin Landseer was more realistic, i.e. more photographic, than Giotto, and John Stuart Mill more realistic, i.e. less metaphysical, than Leibniz. But this is to judge painting and philosophy by standards alien to them; it is breaking facts on the wheel of prejudice. The mistake of the Comteans was not, as the pan-ideologists would assert, that they wished for progress, say, in profits, and hence tried to propagate the delusion that progress was a law of life. No; their mistake was that, once the over-all direction of contemporary life had opened their eyes to a certain aspect of reality, they did not, in soberness, keep to that aspect, but applied its principles all along the line. Their error was not a direct one; it was the indirect one of exaggerating the truth. But this, too, is error, whether we like it or not.

It is not difficult to see that the two regrettable consequences of the habit of mistaking, in the field of truth, the part for the whole, are closely connected with each other. Why do the members of one society find it more or less impossible to understand those of another and to appreciate the truth-value of their ideas? because on either side of the dividing line there prevails a different axiological system which, being in itself partial, is treated as if it were both inclusive and exclusive. In a near-perfect capitalist society, where material values reign supreme, little attention will be paid to religious problems. The heritage of a former culture, which was more inclined to pursue the sacred values and the sacred truths, may survive in such a world, but it is apt to ossify and become an alien body within the body social. If such a near-perfect capitalist society were to remember its limitations; if it were to realize that it has no genius for metaphysical speculation, and has indeed grown out of the methods of thought appropriate to its successful pursuit; if, like the wise cobbler, it were to stick to its last, all would be well. But this is not what happens in practice. What happens is that such a society tends to make its own values, tests and techniques into a Procrustean bed into which it squeezes the unfortunate corpus of religious tradition, chopping it head and foot in the fond delusion that this is to reduce religion to the measure of reason. Much of the discussion current in the nineteenth century on this subject is simply beside the point, running along the wrong track altogether. The knowledge of God can never be the product or byproduct of scientific experiment; if it is to be achieved, other endowments of the human mind must be brought into play than those on which the scientist relies in his work. But these endowments the nineteenth century did not know; indeed, it assumed and asserted that none such exist. It was unable to grasp the figure of Saint Francis in any other terms than those of psychiatry. Yet it was as 'abnormal' from the Poverello's point of view as the Poverello was from its. If Saint Francis's life was too little of this world, Comte's and Spencer's was too much of it. They argued about things outside the frame of nature as if they were inside it. But to treat metaphysical problems as if they were physical ones is illogical, and indeed stupid.[1]

Here as elsewhere, men are always ready to see the mote in their brother's eye while they remain blind to the beam in their own. The materialists of 1870 were not slow to point to the absurdity of the 'natural philosophers' of the thirteenth century who studied nature in libraries by pure speculation and talked about blood and bone without having ever seen either. And, indeed, to consider the concrete in the abstract without having first grasped it in its concreteness is a method which cannot but lead to absurdity in the natural sciences. But was their own procedure any more reasonable, when they assumed and insisted that what the eye cannot see and the ear cannot hear, does not and, indeed, cannot exist? Is blindness of the left eye any less distressing a handicap than blindness in the right? Both the theologians of 1270 and the scientists of 1870 went *supra crepidam*, the former when they talked, not about theology, but about science, the latter when they talked, not about science, but about theology.

It is not the least valuable service which the sociology of knowledge has to render that it can teach all men humility and charity, both of which are not only virtues of the heart, but potentially also virtues of the intellect. It shows up the essential limitations of one's own knowledge and thereby inculcates humility; it shows up the rationality in the apparent irrationality of the next door neighbour's point of view and thereby inculcates charity. In so far as the truth is the truth only in its own proper sphere, the sociology of knowledge contains a precious corrective of that most dangerous and objectionable form of error—error arising from abuse of the truth.

But, alas, the sociology of knowledge has its own pitfalls. If the pan-ideologist is too ready to attack because he sees elements of error on all sides, the sociologist of knowledge is often too ready to defend, because he sees traces of the truth everywhere. The observation has often been made. 'To understand what is', M. Alengry has written, 'is to submit to it with less misgiving, is to be prepared to love it.'[2] And he shows how

---

[1] In saying all this, we do not mean to prejudice the issue of theism versus atheism. All we assert is that the positivists of the nineteenth century, having cramped their style of thought, were in no position to tackle it successfully, or even sensibly.

[2] *Essai Historique et Critique sur la Sociologie chez Auguste Comte*, 1900, 390 *seq.* Cf. also 415 *seq.*

this conservative tendency is at work in both Montesquieu and Comte. Another example of the same mental drift is to be seen in Vico, perhaps the first who worked for a sociology of knowledge of the kind adumbrated in this book. His main contention is that, however unreasonable a piece of legislation may look, there is always reason at the root of it: to show the true wisdom of seeming folly is one of his fondest desires. Such a preoccupation can lead as far astray as its corresponding opposite. Conservatism is no less a vice in a scholar than revolutionary sentiment. Thus, over the entrance gate of the sociology of knowledge, no less than over that of the doctrine of ideology, there should stand the words: *caveat qui introit*.

We are confronted, then, with a difficulty of no mean magnitude, and we must face it.[1] But before we discuss it, we must insist that we do not see it as a problem of relativity, so far as the truth is concerned. The truth is always absolute, otherwise it does not deserve to be called truth at all. We utterly repudiate that anarchical historicism which holds that the terms 'relative' and 'true' are reconcilable. The problem which we pose is essentially a problem of the co-ordination of truths—a problem of synthesis. It is meant to lead to a constructive, not to a destructive result. How far such a positive issue is possible, in view of the limitations of human knowing, remains, however, to be seen.

In the literature, the problem has, of course, often been formulated in terms of relativity. 'It was a distinguished physicist, Niels Bohr,' writes Gordon Childe, 'who pointed out in 1938 that the science of man was faced with the same dilemma of relativity as physics, where an interaction between the objects and the instruments of measurement and observation cannot be ignored. Sociologists . . . want to observe cultures. But the instrument of observation is itself culture. The results of observation must be expressed in the categories which we have inherited from our own society. There is an issue that is at once epistemological and sociological.' [2] Many writers have asserted this relativity of all our knowledge, of all our truths, and tried to illustrate and prove it. They have dug deep into the foundations. Some, for instance, have asserted the historical variability of the categories of our thinking in the Kantian sense of the word, even though these Kantian categories are in themselves purely formal—purely empty. 'Kant's firm belief in a timeless,

---

[1] Several authors have strongly, almost passionately emphasized that the problem of the *origin* of thought-contents is radically different from the problem of their *validity*. Cf. De Gré in the *Journal of the History of Ideas*, 1941, 110 and 115; cf. also von Schelting, *Max Webers Wissenschaftslehre*, 1934, 78 *seq.*, 157 *seq.* We agree with them, as the very first words of this chapter testify. But though we are aware that we are crossing a borderline when we take up the latter problem, we have no hesitation at all in crossing it. It would be absurd to suggest that one man cannot or should not speak *qua* historian in one chapter, and *qua* philosopher in another.

[2] *Social Worlds of Knowledge*, 1949, 5.

totally unchangeable logical structure of our intellect . . . has been proved erroneous,' wrote Wilhelm Jerusalem in 1924, and Max Scheler, about the same time, put it even more pungently: 'Kant's table of categories is merely the table of categories of European thinking.' [1]

Such convictions drew much intellectual nourishment from the works of Lévy-Bruhl who tried to show that the thought of primitive peoples deviates from our own in its very foundations in that it is 'pre-logical', i.e. its underlying formal laws follow principles different from those of our own logic. They also found an arsenal of arguments in the books of Marcel Granet who, sprung, like Lévy-Bruhl, from the Durkheim tradition, made classical Chinese civilization his field of inquiry. Both Lévy-Bruhl and Granet asserted—to pick out just one glaring example of their doctrine—that the operative concept of number is radically different in Western culture from what it is either in classical China or among the primitives. In Western culture, number is essentially a quantitative concept, indeed almost synonymous with quantity. In classical China and among the primitives, it tends, on the contrary, to be qualitative. To say 13, is not to say $12 + 1$ or $11 + 2$, it is to say: ill luck. Hence, Granet concludes, whereas for ourselves a larger number like 13 is always superior to a smaller, such as 12 or 11, it may in other societies be inferior, namely qualitatively inferior, for there the reckoning follows a totally different multiplication table.[2] Such arguments must have the same effect on the structure of truth as a permanent earthquake would, even on the most solidly built houses: collapse would be the inevitable result. No wonder that people like Mannheim were prepared to throw the whole idea of truth to the winds: 'It has become extremely questionable', he writes, 'whether, in the flux of life, it is a genuinely worthwhile intellectual problem to seek to discover fixed and immutable ideas or absolutes.' [3] We must learn as it were to live without solid soil under our feet, in a permanent revolution.

Such a life could never be anything but depressing and frustrating, indeed, supremely so.[4] Luckily, it is not quite so inescapable a fate for the human race as Mannheim, Granet and other relativists have assumed. For the absolute truth of the multiplication table need not be brought into doubt—nor that of more recondite propositions of a mathematical kind. The whole concept of 'bourgeois mathematics', which has sometimes been bandied about by the less enlightened votaries of the Marxist faith, is a monstrous absurdity. It is true that not all societies know how to manipulate figures. Max Weber mentions the

---

[1] Jerusalem in *Versuche zu einer Soziologie des Wissens*, 183; Scheler in *Die Wissensformen und die Gesellschaft*, 1926, 60.

[2] Cf. the summary in J. J. Maquet, *Sociologie de la Connaissance*, 1949, 189 *seq.*

[3] *Ideology and Utopia*, ed. 1952, 77.

[4] Cf. Barth, *Wahrheit und Ideologie*, 1945, 304 *seq.*

amazing fact that in the Middle Ages the bankers of Florence, not having at their disposal, as we do, the commodious Arabic system of numerical notation, often made mistakes in their computations and entries.[1] But that does not mean that the multiplication table did not apply in Tuscany in the thirteenth century. But let us meet Granet on his own ground; let us assume that the ancient Chinese were good at their figures and knew how to handle them, and that they still ranked 12 higher in their order of values than 13. Even this involves no denial of the validity of the multiplication table, not even an implicit one. For when the Chinese said that they preferred 12 to 13, they were not talking of numbers at all: they did not doubt that one mandarin must come and join a group of 12 if there are to be 13; they merely believed that metaphysically a group of 13 is not so propitious as a group of 12. In other words, they were talking metaphysics, not physics, magic, not mathematics, when they placed 12 'above' 13. If we may so express it, their mathematics was like ours, but it was overlaid with magic: the physics underneath their metaphysics was in no wise different from any rational physics. Surely, there can only be one science of numbers, for ever self-identical in its content.

As for Lévy-Bruhl's investigations, which in and for themselves deserve every respect, this is not the place to discuss them in all their detail, nor is it necessary to do so since their essential claim has been invalidated by competent critics.[2] It will be sufficient if we adduce two decisive arguments against his doctrine of the relativity of the formal categories of human thought. Firstly, when primitives make statements which seem to deny a basic law of formal logic, they are not acting otherwise than the most modern logician who is at the same time a good Christian. He, too, asserts that in the Godhead Three and One are identical, but that does not mean that he denies the absolute truth of the law of contradiction. He has merely decided not to carry it from physics into metaphysics, and this is quite legitimate since the metaphysical reality is, by definition, under different laws, material *and* formal, from the physical. That the primitive has reserved a wider area in his mind for metaphysics than the modern rationalist is a difference in degree only, not in kind. He, too, often proceeds quite rationally, for instance, when he splits a log or builds a house. In any case when he says, for instance, that he is identical with his totem, a bull frog or a dingo dog, and seems thereby to defy the law of contradiction, he does not and cannot mean that he is physically identical with the animal

[1] A. von Schelting, *Max Webers Wissenschaftslehre*, 1934, 156.
[2] Cf. e.g. von Schelting, 'Zum Streit um die Wissenssoziologie', *Archiv für Sozialwissenschaft*, 1929, 32 *seq*. Cf. above all the same author's book on *Max Webers Wissenschaftslehre*, 1934, 103 note (3), and the literature there quoted (*re* Emile Meyerson).

concerned, but only that he is metaphysically so, an entirely different proposition. Secondly, when the primitive seems to act, from a material point of view, in contradiction of some such principle as that of cause and effect, in reality he is often, not to say always, acting, at least *formally*, in accordance with it. To smear cow-dung on an abscess will not heal it, to apply camomile-extract will. Materially there is a world of difference; formally, none. The witchdoctor is factually mistaken when he believes that cow-dung is a specific against inflammation; but formally he regards it as the cause whose effect will be a restoration of the patient. Hence the categorial nexus of cause and effect is no less operative in his mind than in that of the modern medical man who has merely substituted another more promising curative cause for the same desired effect. What many writers really mean, or at any rate ought to mean, when they say that the primitive mind has a logic different from our own, is that the primitives habitually associate other things than we do, and that their habitual associations are not rationally chosen. But this has nothing to do with formal logic, which is by definition not concerned with the material contents poured into the logical forms.[1]

So far as purely formal propositions are concerned, there simply is no problem of relativity. An example of such a proposition is the assertion that the whole is greater than the part. In spite of all that the super-relativists have argued, there can be no society in which this sentence would not hold good, because its truth springs immediately from the definition of its terms and hence is absolutely independent of any concrete extra-mental conditioning. And the same goes for the proposition that 13 is more than 12. We are not taking here the extreme or classical rationalistic position; we do not imply that truths of this kind are inborn. They may, in fact they do, depend on experience. A man must have seen a whole before he can know that it is greater than its parts; he must have perceived a set of 13 items before he can know that it is larger than a set of 12 such items. But experiences of this kind occur in every society, and hence give rise to the self-same judgments in every society. The content of the experience does not matter. A group of 13 Chinese mandarins offers as good grounds for the assertion that it is a more numerous group than a group of 12, as a group of 13 American stock jobbers or 13 Italian priests. And, so far as material

[1] When (to jump from the most primitive to the over-refined) Hegel claims to have overcome the old system of formal logic and replaced it by a new, according to which thesis and antithesis can coexist within the same totality, in defiance of the law of non-contradiction, he is in fact making a statement about the content of reality (the factual nature of the process of development), and not about the abstract laws of logic, as is well shown by Sabine in his paper 'Logic and Social Studies'. Cf. *The Philosophical Review*, 1939, 164.

things are concerned, the items counted are, of course, absolutely the same from country to country and from age to age: 13 eggs are recognizable under all conditions as a bigger collection than 12 eggs.

All this is so elementary that one is almost ashamed to put it down in black and white, but it is necessary to combat the threat of mental anarchy. In the spirit of our sociology of knowledge we can perhaps formulate the matter as follows: the social determination of thought reveals to every society only one aspect of reality, hiding the others; but every aspect of reality has the same formal determinants (number for instance, or measure) as any other; hence, so far as formal propositions are concerned, there can be no difference between the thought-contents characteristic of otherwise dissimilar cultures. It is true that some societies are very largely uninterested in the formal properties of things, in numerical proportion and such-like aspects; these may remain below the threshold of explicit consciousness, but formal propositions are none the less absolute for that and everywhere recognizable as such. The conviction, however deeply rooted, that 12 is magically superior to 13, can never keep out the recognition that 13 is numerically superior to 12. Nor can there be many societies, however primitive, in which a man would not rather have 13 head of cattle of the same quality than 12. Mannheim seems to admit all this, though in a curiously oblique fashion. 'Perspective', he writes, meaning the socially determined perspective, 'signifies the manner in which one views an object, what one perceives in it, and how one construes it in his thinking. Perspective, therefore, is something more than a merely formal determination of thinking. It refers also to qualitative elements in the structure of thought, elements which must necessarily be overlooked by a purely formal logic. It is precisely these factors which are responsible for the fact that two persons, even if they apply the same formal-logical rules, e.g. the law of contradiction or the formula of the syllogism, in an identical manner, may judge the same object very differently.'[1] One does not perhaps put a doubtful gloss on these sentences in inferring from them that, even according to so relativistic a thinker as Mannheim, mental differences between different societies are not due to differences in the formal conceptualization of experience.

We come to the real problem of relativity (if we may continue to call it so for convenience sake), when we turn away from purely formal propositions and take up the consideration of factual findings, of material knowledge. And here we cannot take a single step forward without having first established and underlined the absolutely fundamental and all-important distinction between facts of nature on the one hand, and social or historical facts in the widest sense of the word on the other. So far as the problem in hand is concerned, there are two

[1] *Ideology and Utopia*, ed. 1952, 244.

decisive reasons why they must be kept apart, and considered separately. The first is that in spite of all evolution, there is an essential permanence in nature which ensures that the knowledge-seeking mind is always confronted with the same sort of reality. Not so in the social sphere. Certainly, there is permanence in social life as well as change, but human relations do not for long remain in the same state. Not all their shifts create a situation which is new in principle, radically new, but many of them do. Mercurial as man himself, they show every year, every month, every day, a new configuration. Permanence there may be, but it is the unstable permanence of habit only, not the stable permanence of natural law. However often an old pattern may be implemented and re-implemented, there emerges, sooner or later, a new one. Consequently, the chances of reaching insights of lasting significance are, *a limine*, very much higher in the natural sciences than in the social ones. 'Successive approximations to determinate states of affairs, and sentences about approximations are, loosely speaking, true in so far as there is an actual correspondence between the sentence and its referents', a recent inquirer has written, summing up a common opinion.[1] In nature there is a 'determinate state of affairs'; hence there can be progressive approximations of the perceiving mind to it, and even an abiding correspondence with it. In society and history there is no 'determinate state of affairs' in the same sense. It is clear what this must mean. We are face to face here with one of the chief consequences of the tremendous key-truth which Vico was the first to bring into high relief: that the facts of society are made, and ever re-made, by us, whereas the facts of nature are not. They are *data* in a much more stringent meaning of the term.

But this is not all. There is, as we have hinted, a second reason why the natural sciences escape relativity, and this second reason is of much closer concern to the sociology of knowledge than the first. Different over-all pictures of reality emerge in different societies, so we maintain, because different societies, under the guidance of changing values, select different aspects of that reality for inclusion in their mental universe. An egalitarian society is interested in the facts that show up human equality, an hierarchical society in facts that show up human inequalities. But so far as nature is concerned, the main guiding value has ever been the same, namely, to achieve an understanding of and control over her— *savoir pour pouvoir*—and hence in all ages attention has been paid to the same aspects of the realm of nature—those which promise us a

---

[1] Hinshaw in *The Journal of Philosophy*, 1943, 66. Cf. *ibid.*, for the fact that later physical theories (such as Einstein's) do not really 'supersede' earlier ones (like Newton's) in the sense that they completely destroy their validity. The later theory is, in physics, and remains, simply a closer approximation to the facts than the earlier was.

foothold in and a whiphand over her. Free as man is, he is still not free to turn his back upon nature, for all his other freedoms can only be exercised when he has satisfied the necessities of life, when he has provided himself with food and shelter. Whether he likes it or not, he must, under all cultural circumstances, pursue, among others, the economic and technological values, the values of science. Greatly as the axiological layer has changed over the centuries, an interest in the lower creation from the point of view of its manageability, from the point of view of manipulation, has always been part and parcel of it.

In order to realize how true this is, we need only think of our bodily health. The adage 'health is preferable to illness' is a value-judgment accepted in absolutely all human societies, and so a desire to know, and to get the better of, health-destroying agencies has been a mind-directing and knowledge-generating value all through history, social evolutions and social revolutions notwithstanding. But what is true of the knowledge and management of the body, is true of all other material objects. Their domination has always been desired and will for ever remain desirable. To return to our basic simile: whereas man has more than once shifted his vantage-point for the consideration of social facts so that these facts appear to him in ever new, and often surprising, outlines, he has always kept to the same spot for surveying the facts of nature (the other sector of his field of observation) so that these latter facts have always offered to him the self-same surface. He has merely learned to look more closely; he has equipped himself with microscopes and telescopes to help out his feeble sight; he has progressively directed his main energies into this field; and he has systematically cleansed that field from the encroachments of alien mental modes and methods of procedure illegitimately introduced into it under the influence of what we have called the *pars-pro-toto* fallacy; in other words, he has increasingly substituted true science for pseudo-science; but he has never abandoned his prime position and preoccupation: to grasp the facts of the lower creation in order to become lord and master over it. Hence while in the cultural sciences there has been a constant building up and pulling down, in the natural sciences properly so called there has been nought but construction—nought but cumulative progress, as Max Scheler has so graphically described it.[1]

It is to Alfred Weber that we mainly owe the elucidation of these matters.[2] He distinguishes two mental spheres which he calls respec-

[1] *Die Wissensformen und die Gesellschaft*, 1926, 28.
[2] Unfortunately his style is too difficult to allow direct quotation. Cf. his *Prinzipien der Geschichts- und Kultursoziologie*, 1951, and for a concise summary Grünwald, *Das Problem der Soziologie des Wissens*, 1934, 174 *seq.*, and Aron, *Die deutsche Soziologie der Gegenwart*, 1953, 58 *seq.*

tively the cosmos of civilization and the cosmos of culture. The former comprises and centres around positive science and technology, the latter around philosophy, religion and art. Drawing our two points of distinction neatly into one, Weber explains that in the area of civilization man is a discoverer of truths whereas in the area of culture he is a creator of values. There is a world of difference between the astronomer who investigates the secrets of the high heavens, and the philosopher who tries to penetrate the mysteries of being. For the astronomer merely attempts to *grasp* the data, the *pre-existent* data: he is entirely controlled by them. The philosopher, however, in so far as he has any data at all, is concerned with their *meaning*: he must *impute* a meaning to them, he must actively body forth the truth, not passively receive it. The case of the creative artist is perhaps even more characteristic in this respect than that of the metaphysician. In any case, the scientist allows himself to be impressed by the objective truth of reality, the man of culture expresses the values in which he believes.

The main consequence of this is that the pronouncements of the scientists, if they are true at all, have ecumenical truth-value. The Tibetan lama cannot deny that the next eclipse of the moon will be at this or that day and hour. But the *pronunciamentos* of the men of culture cannot claim universal validity (even if their authors, in vanity, regularly but vainly lay claim to it): we cannot be angry with a Guru if he does not like positivism, or with a positivist if he does not like Indian esoteric wisdom. Indeed, positivism will have no meaning to the Guru, Indian esoteric wisdom none to the western positivist. Universal history plainly confirms these observations: as Weber shows, all generations have co-operated in the building up of the cosmos of civilization, and its achievements, whether as insights or techniques, spread to all countries; but cultures have their own time and place: they do not travel—neither down the stream of time, nor hither and thither across the surface of the earth. Hence we are confronted here with a contrast of the universal and the particular. In the sciences, the truth is always the truth; but in the realm of cultural values—where is truth to be found?

The plain upshot of this discussion is that we can exclude all scientific knowledge properly so called from the realm of possible relativity, just as we have excluded formal propositions. If it is nonsense to speak of bourgeois mathematics, it is equally nonsensical to speak of German or Jewish physics, as even reputable physicists have done under the influence of a stultifying creed.[1] And, once again, there is cause for rejoicing, for all the main movements which have arisen historically within the sociology of knowledge have substantially agreed on this point.[2]

[1] Cf. Merton, *Social Theory and Social Structure*, 1949, 396 (note 7), 397 (note 21), 398 *seq.* (note 4a).

[2] Cf. Lieber, *Wissen und Gesellschaft*, 1952, 9, 13 *seq.*, 43, 139, 142.

Alfred Weber's own distinction between culture and civilization is, of course, essentially a contribution to the Rickert-Max Weber tradition since it is akin to, if it does not indeed coincide with, the latter's discrimination between nomothetic and idiographic sciences—sciences which (like physics) pronounce laws, and sciences which (like history) are largely concerned with the individual, unrepeatable and unique.

In the Marxist camp we discover at this point once more the same pattern of development which we have encountered before: Marx himself, especially the young Marx, occupies a position not too far from our own; then there supervenes a period of positivism, of 'scientism', when the frontiers between physical and sociological knowledge are disregarded and obscured; and, finally, especially with Georg Lukacs, a return to the young Marx. As for the young Marx himself, one of his chief complaints against Hegel is this, that Hegel has not really overcome the duality of thought and being, theory and practice, subject and object, and that he has failed in this decisive task because his own thinking is too much occupied with man's knowledge of nature, a realm alien to man, and not enough with man's knowledge of society, of interhuman relationships, where alone subject and object of knowing, theory and practice, thought and being, *can* coincide. 'The dialectics of nature', so Lukacs explains the gravamen of Marx's disagreement with Hegel, 'where the subject . . . cannot possibly have a place in the dialectical process, can never become more than a dialectic of movement for the unconcerned onlooker. . . . Hence there arises the necessity of a methodical distinction between the merely objective dialectic of nature and the social dialectic, in which the subject, too, is included in the dialectical relation of mutuality, in which theory and practice become dialectical with regard to each other.'

It is this 'methodical distinction' drawn by Marx which Engels, to the great detriment of Marxism, discarded, or simply failed to appreciate. 'The misunderstandings which arise from Engels's representation of dialectics', Lukacs writes, 'rest above all on the fact that he extends the dialectical method to the knowledge of nature. And yet the decisive characteristics of dialectic—mutual interaction of subject and object, unity of theory and practice, the historical transformation of the substratum of the categories as the basis of their transformation in thought—are not present in the knowledge of nature.' This, in Marxist jargon, is as clear an acknowledgement as can be wished of the necessity and importance of the distinction which, following Alfred Weber, Max Weber, and Heinrich Rickert, we have made between civilization and culture.

Indeed, Lukacs comes even closer, and decisively so, to the position taken up in this book. He draws a dividing line between the knowledge of nature on the one hand, and such departments of the 'objective spirit' as 'art, religion and philosophy' on the other.[1] He points out that even the knowledge of nature is, in a sense, dependent on society, in so far namely as society must gain it, conquer it, achieve it. Yet the truth-content of such knowledge is independent of society. 'Copernican astronomy was correct even before Copernicus; it was merely not yet known.' Moreover, 'once these realities [i.e. insights] are . . . given, they assert themselves according to their own inherent laws and preserve a much greater independence of the social basis [even in the future] . . . than the formations of the "objective spirit" '. And Lukacs adds a very happy and revealing illustration. There are art-forms which continue to charm even though their social substructure has vanished long ago in the abyss of history—Greek sculpture for instance. But then we are not, in the Venus of Milo, confronted only with a work of culture: we are also, and indeed primarily, confronted with an idealized presentation of nature, and since nature's forms are eternal, there is no reason, the socially determined change of esthetic values notwithstanding, why such works of 'art' should not be relevant and appreciated two millennia after their 'creation'.[2]

No less than to Marxian and neo-Marxian thought, the dichotomy of natural and social knowledge is also basic to Mannheim's whole analysis. 'Mannheim . . . did not apply his theory to "all" science,' writes his editor, Kecskemeti, 'he . . . excepted mathematical and natural science from his verdict of "existential determination".' It is easy to give chapter and verse for this assertion. Here is just one set of passages, in lieu of several which could be quoted: 'Scientific-techno-logical thought differs from philosophical thought in that the former type of thought completes just one and the same system during successive periods, whereas the latter starts from new centres of systematization in every epoch in trying to master the increasing multiplicity of the historical world. Because it is the same system that is being built up in science in the course of the centuries, the phenomenon of change of meaning does not occur in this sphere, and we can picture the process of thought as direct progress towards ultimately "correct" knowledge which can be formulated only in one fashion. . . . As against this, we have in philosophy, as well as in the historio-cultural sciences which are closely related to it, the phenomenon of an intrinsically necessary change of meaning. Every concept in these fields inevitably changes its meaning in the course of time—and this precisely because it continually

[1] For the fact that Marx himself insisted on this division and distinction and ascribed 'ideological character' only to religious conduct and the cultural and social sciences, but not to mathematics and the natural sciences, cf. Barth, *Wahrheit und Ideologie*, 1945, 154 *seq.*, and Lieber, *Wissen und Gesellschaft*, 1952, 43.

[2] *Geschichte und Klassenbewusstsein*, 1923, 29 *seq.*, 226 *seq.*, 17, 243, 240 *seq.* Cf. also 225.

enters into new systems depending on new sets of axioms. . . . If we observe the historical line of evolution in these fields, as well as the mutual relationships of the meanings succeeding each other, then we can observe no "progress" towards a unique system. . . .' [1] 'Even a god', Mannheim writes in a somewhat hyperbolical passage—'even a god could not formulate a proposition on historical subjects like $2 \times 2 = 4$, for what is intelligible in history can be formulated only with reference to problems and conceptual constructions which themselves arise in the flux of historical experience.' [2] Even man, however, so we may conclude, can formulate this proposition in its original formal and scientific meaning and see its absolute validity, for that meaning is independent of the flux of historical experience.

When extreme relativists have argued in defence of the relativity even of scientific truths they have repeatedly fallen back on one convenient example: the Darwinian theory. [3] 'The bourgeois interpretation of nature . . . which bases itself on the Darwinian struggle for survival', one of these writers—Karl Korsch—has asserted, 'has done no more than to transfer *post festum* its antecedently existing social conceptions and tendencies on to its idea of nature.' [4] And just as Social Darwinism was essentially a time-bound and time-serving ideology, so there is an ideological element in biological Darwinism as well, and it cannot rank as the absolute truth.

This argument may have some superficial plausibility about it, especially since it is well known that Darwin, the biologist, drew his inspiration from a 'social scientist', or rather economist, Thomas Malthus, but when it is rightly handled it proves the very opposite of what the pan-relativists want it to prove. The proposition that 'life is an ongoing struggle for survival in which the relatively weak are progressively eliminated and only the relatively strong survive', is, in nature, within possible limitations, either absolutely true or absolutely false. What goes on in a jungle or primeval forest now is not much different from what went on there thousands of years ago and will go on there thousands of years hence (unless man intervenes). Hence there can be no historical relativity about the truth value of the Darwinian hypothesis *qua* biological proposition. But things are manifestly different with regard to Social Darwinism. The formula that 'life is an ongoing struggle in which the relatively weak are progressively eliminated and only the relatively strong survive', cannot be applied to all social systems. It would certainly apply to—would, in other words, be true in

---

[1] *Essays on the Sociology of Knowledge*, 1952, 29, 170; cf. also *Ideology and Utopia*, ed. 1952, esp. 22 *seq.*, 44, 70 *seq.*, 243 *seq.* [2] *Ideology and Utopia*, 71.
[3] Cf. e.g. Korsch in *Grünbergs Archiv für die Geschichte des Sozialismus und der Arbeiterbewegung*, 1929, 217. Engels had already used the same example in the same spirit. Cf. Barth, *Wahrheit und Ideologie*, 1945, 325 (note 192). [4] *Loc. cit.*

—a society of which the characteristic hallmarks were a radical in-dividualism and a merciless competitiveness. Such a society can be imagined as an ideal type, and of that ideal type the statement quoted would be an assertion in full agreement with the facts. It was because society in the middle of the nineteenth century had drawn fairly close to that ideal-typical situation—because, to mention just one fact, there were no effective trade unions to mitigate the workers' desperate inter-necine struggle for jobs—that Social Darwinism as we find it in Gum-plowicz, Ratzenhofer and others arose and could claim to be realistic and true. But it is no longer true of the welfare state of the twentieth century in which the weak are shielded, nor yet was it true in the corporate town of the twelfth century, in which social control was far-reaching and of fair efficiency. That Social Darwinism is not, like biological Darwinism, an absolute truth, is perhaps best proved by the fact that it has completely disappeared from our mental scene; Darwinism properly so called can never disappear whatever the state of society, provided only that it is, or was once, shown to be in agreement with the facts of nature.

The pan-relativists, then, badly overstate their case. Not only the mathematician, the astronomer and the physicist may show them the door, but even the biologist, the botanist and the zoologist. And yet, Korsch's statement contains a grain of truth which we must be anxious not to lose. Social developments do not determine the content of scientific developments, simply because they do not determine natural facts; but they may well open the eyes of the scientists to natural facts which, though pre-existent and always there, had not been discovered before. This is what happened in the case of Darwinism; both Darwinism properly so called and Social Darwinism were inspired by Malthus, and Malthus in turn was 'inspired' by the terrible struggle for the trough which he saw going on in contemporary England before his very eyes. Hence both forms of Darwinism—sociological and scientific—share a common root. But in truth-content they are altogether dissimilar, and that is what matters for the present discussion. What is of ecumenical validity in science, is only of conditional validity in sociology.

That there is a relation *sui generis* between social and scientific developments—that social situations as they come and go in historical relativity may lead to scientific insights which remain because they are absolute—has been well observed by Karl Mannheim [1] and other writers. Assuming, as we must, that scientific facts and insights are permanently valid, because they are controlled by a reality which is essentially lasting, there still remains the question why they are formu-lated at this time or that, and not at any other, and on this problem—

---

[1] Cf. *Ideology and Utopia*, ed. 1952, 263 *seq.* Cf. also Max Scheler, *Die Wissens-formen und die Gesellschaft*, 1926, 189 *seq.*

the problem of the time-progression and time-incidence of scientific discovery—social history can shed a good deal of light. Scientific advances are often, not to say always, provoked by and responses to social needs. The history of those needs is the key, as it were, to the history of these advances. It is no accident, for instance, that every war in the history of mankind has brought into being a whole crop of scientific insights and productive techniques; the atomic bomb, and the whole theory and practice of nuclear fission, is merely the most dramatic prototype of a host of cases distributed, chain-like, through the centuries. A vast literature has grown up around this fact,[1] and rightly, for the matter is both subjectively fascinating and objectively important. If studies of this kind are called 'sociology of science' or even 'sociology of scientific knowledge', nobody has any right to protest. But it should be clear that they are concerned only with the factual genesis (as Mannheim calls it) of the scientific knowledge in question, or rather: with the point of time of its formulation, and *not* with the social determination of its content. For there is no such social determination. Over the facts of nature—need it be said?—man has no control. He can only rise superior to her laws by humbly submitting to them.

Perhaps we can sum up these considerations by saying that social life raises certain questions both for the scientist and the man of culture. But whereas the answers which the former gives are in content and validity independent of social life, the answers given by the latter are essentially dependent on it, and therein consists the central problem of the sociology of knowledge as we understand the term.

Unfortunately, there has existed, and still exists, great confusion in this field. Two entirely different things—the social *origin* of certain scientific insights out of a given need at a particular *time*, and the social *determination* of their *content* by a particular substructural situation— have all too often been confused with each other, whereas they must be carefully kept apart, the former being a historically provable and often proved fact, the latter no more than an illicit inference from facts obtaining exclusively in the sphere of social knowledge.[2] Perhaps it may be true to say that the elaboration of that prime mathematical tool, the differential calculus, was suggested, or stimulated, by certain developments and tendencies within the social subsoil: for instance the incipient dynamization of social life, the relative speeding up of historical pro-

---

[1] For some of the names cf. Merton, *Social Theory and Social Structure*, 1949, 393, note 14. Cf. also *ibid.*, 245 and notes 93–6.

[2] Cf. von Schelting, *Max Webers Wissenschaftslehre*, 1934, 131, 237. Cf. also the very interesting discussion of the special case of Max Weber, 207 *seq.* Von Schelting shows how certain insights of Weber's are explicable in the light of his social circumstances and goes on to argue, in our opinion rightly and convincingly, that the claim to validity of these insights is absolutely independent of their (more or less accidental) origination.

cesses, the replacement of repetitiveness in many sectors of the social system by progress, etc.—all seventeenth-century developments which put change on the map and must have raised the problems of change into the light of consciousness with all men, even mathematicians. The fact that the calculus was discovered at nearly the same time by three different thinkers in three different countries—Newton in England, Leibniz in Germany, Pascal in France—seems to point in this direction. But would it not be unreasonable to say that the calculus 'cannot' be a universally applicable tool 'because' it has arisen under the stresses and strains of a specific (possibly unique) social situation? It surely would, because in this case a specific social situation has given birth to a universal scientific achievement—because origin and truth-content have nothing whatsoever to do with each other.

As George H. Sabine has very well expressed it: 'Social theories live a twofold life and play a double rôle. They are beliefs, which arise in the course of human behaviour and reflect the whole nexus of conditions, physical, psychological and sociological, that play upon and affect human behaviour. As such they are themselves existences or events, with psychological and sociological antecedents and consequents, and they may possibly be explained by whatever principles can be adduced to explain human behaviour. But theories also consist of propositions that claim to be true or false, that may be postulated, or proved, or refuted. And the logical operations by which propositions are validated can never, without confusion, be identified with the mental or social conditions that make human beings believe them. . . . And theory no doubt does have psychological antecedents in human purposes, and sociological antecedents in political or economic situations, but these are never its validating grounds. For the truth of a theory depends not upon its antecedents or consequents, but upon what it signifies or what it implies.' [1]

This should be clear. Yet even Robert Merton, whom we have so often quoted with approval in these pages, is uncertain of himself at this point. He says, indeed, on p. 302 of *Social Theory and Social Structure*, 'that, logically, to establish the empirical genesis of beliefs and values is not to deny their validity', a sentence which should *a fortiori* apply to scientific insights. But on p. 289 he expresses himself in a different vein: he speaks of 'the diverse influences of social structure upon the rate of development, the foci of interest, and, perhaps, upon the very content of science'. His hesitation here is most revealing. There is, in his mind, quite obviously the question: *does* the social structure have an influence on the content of science? If he is reluctant to answer it, as in fact he seems to be, we shall answer it for him with a decided negative. And this certainly seems to be the kind of answer indicated by

[1] *The Philosophical Review*, 1939, 174.

his own detailed researches. For throughout his distinguished book, much is said on the social factors which advance and retard scientific achievements, but nothing as to the determination of scientific thought itself by factors of this sort. Indeed, there is a programmatic passage in which he appears to exclude the latter (pseudo-) problem altogether from his scope, and to conceive the sociologist's task in the history of science exclusively in terms of the former—in terms of 'factual genesis' as Mannheim has it: 'The interplay between socio-economic and scientific development is scarcely problematical', we read. 'The sociologist of science is specifically concerned with the types of influence [of society on science] involved (facilitative and obstructive); the extent to which these types prove effective in different social structures; and the processes through which they operate' (347). As can be seen, social forces appear here merely as the locomotives which push or pull the train of science forward, but they are not credited with determining what is carried in the trucks.

If this should prove to be Merton's final opinion, we should heartily agree with him. It was certainly Marx's conviction, as Merton himself points out: 'There was an incipient tendency in Marxism . . . to consider natural science as standing in a relation to the economic base different from that of other spheres of knowledge and belief. In science, the focus of attention may be socially determined, but not . . . its conceptual apparatus' (230). So far, then, as this problem is concerned, Marx's sharp eye seems to have discerned the sober truth.

However, even this is a truth to which certain qualifying provisos must be appended. In speaking of scientific insights throughout the last few pages we have been referring to positive, factual knowledge, of the kind expressed in the proposition that heavy bodies fall at an accelerating speed. But we were not thinking of the half- or three-quarter-philosophical assertions which have crept from all sides under the mantle of science and are much more numerous than the scientists themselves are apt to realize. If, for instance, Aristotle suggests that stones fall at an accelerating speed because they seek to be at home with their mother, the earth, then he is retailing a certain brand of metaphysics and not expounding a positive scientific truth; here we are in the realm of relatives, not absolutes; here we are indeed in the sphere of social determination, for Aristotle's pan-animism is very largely a product of (Greek) community life, just as the pan-mechanism of more modern thinkers can be shown to be at least in part a reflection of the atomistic society of their time, of 'association' in Ferdinand Tönnies' sense of the term. Very often when even well-informed writers argue in favour of a supposed relativity of scientific findings, they do not mean the scientific findings themselves but rather the philosophical assertions coupled with them; they mean the metaphysics of physics, not physics itself. This is clearly the case with Sorokin; [1] it also applies to C. Wright Mills who, in his paper 'Methodological Consequences of the Sociology of Knowledge', [2] takes up a somewhat extreme relativist position. For when his article is read with attention, it becomes clear that he does not in fact assail the absolute character of scientific truths but only asserts that a historical change has taken place in the methods of their verification. In other words, it is not validity he is talking of, but only validation. He says as much himself: 'It is true', he admits, 'that the current "scientific" thought-model . . . distinguishes between the truth of the results and the motives and social conditions of an inquiry. For this paradigm demands that assertions be verified by certain operations which do not depend upon the motives or social position of the assertor. *Social position does not directly affect the truthfulness of propositions tested by this verificatory model.* [3] But social positions may well affect whether or not it or some other model is used by types of thinkers today and in other periods.' [4]

Mills is manifestly concerned with methodology, not with truth as such; he is looking at the philosophical fringes of science, not at its central structure of positive knowledge. Of course, these outer fringes or outworks are important, because science cannot do without certain philosophical assumptions, for instance with regard to the nature of space (and the other categorial concepts—a problem which will come up for closer inspection in chapter 7). [5] But if, for instance, the Babylonians in fact had 'a conception of space as different from the Euclidian as the latter is from the Riemannian', [6] we must not infer that, because of their conceptual apparatus, they would have been *a limine* incapable of seeing the truth of the Euclidian theorems. Nobody can permanently close his mind to their validity—nobody anywhere. All that can be said is that the Babylonian philosophy of nature was different from the Greek, no more. In general, it is not too difficult to separate positive science from its metaphysical accompaniments. For science always asks: *what* is, while in the questions raised by metaphysics there always occurs the further, and disparate, question of *why*.

Secondly (and this is only saying explicitly what has already been said by implication), though society has no influence on the content of scientific knowledge, it is responsible for its limitations. Scientific truths

---

[1] Cf. the summary of his discussions in Cowell, *History, Civilization and Culture*, 1952, 136 *seq.* Cf. also *re* Needham and Cornforth, Sprott, *Science and Social Action*, 1954, 145 *seq.*

[2] *The American Journal of Sociology*, 1940/1, 316 *seq.*

[3] Our italics.   [4] *Loc. cit.*, 320 *seq.*

[5] Cf. Merton, *Social Theory and Social Structure*, 1949, 337, and the literature quoted there. Cf. also Alfred Weber, *Prinzipien der Geschichts- und Kultursoziologie*, 1951, 64 *seq.*

[6] V. Gordon Childe, *Social Worlds of Knowledge*, 1949, 15.

must be conquered, piece by piece, and will be conquered in a society only if that society has the right aggressive spirit, if it puts enough energy and enthusiasm into its scientific research. But whether this happens or not will depend upon the society's order of values. An interest in nature and the technological opportunities it offers is, as we have seen, present in any and every society; in that essential respect there is no difference between different social systems. But there *is* a difference in the relative position of this interest vis-à-vis other interests in the axiological layer, a difference in degree which, in its way, is important enough.[1] In the Middle Ages men had some solid knowledge of the laws of mechanics; otherwise they could not have built the cathedrals of Chartres, or Naumburg, or Canterbury; but that knowledge was limited because interest in such-like matters was limited, and the limitations only begin to dissolve at the end of the eighteenth century when the order of values of the Western world is radically rearranged. The Marxists, in their anxiety to extend the range of social determination as far as is reasonably possible, have strongly underlined this aspect. 'What, on a certain level of social development, is understood by nature, the relation of that nature to man, and the manner of his transactions with her, that is to say, the meaning of nature in respect of form and content, scope and subject-matter, is always socially determined', Lukacs says. 'Nature is a social category.'[2] This may be an unduly emphatic way of putting a minor point, but it is the truth none the less. Geiger, who agrees with Lukacs (and with us) on this point, has stressed that limitation may mean lopsidedness in the system or synthesis of knowledge achieved by a society, and lopsidedness in turn may mean error.[3] Perhaps so; but error is here only secondary. It resides, not in the individual insights which compose the science of the society concerned, and each of which if true at all is absolutely true, but only in the range to which it has restricted its scientific knowledge.

Thirdly, it is possible, though historians of ideas have not yet sufficiently elucidated the matter, that social conditions have some remote influence on scientific thought through the fashions to which they give rise. That fashions do occur in science has often been observed. Sometimes it is fashionable to cure diseases preferably by pills, at other times by the knife; sometimes surgeons first use the knife in one way, then again in another, and later there is often a return to earlier techniques. Such phenomena play only upon the surface, or at any rate should not be allowed to penetrate into the body of science. Here they are mentioned only for the sake of completeness, in order to round off the picture.

[1] Cf. the illustrations in Alfred Weber, *Prinzipien der Geschichts- und Kultursoziologie*, 1951, 63 *seq.*

[2] *Geschichte und Klassenbewusstsein*, 1923, 240; cf. also 144.

[3] *Ideologie und Wahrheit*, 1953, 115 *seq.*, 137 *seq.*

One final remark. In speaking, in this chapter, of the 'absolute' truth or validity of scientific insights properly so called, we have meant only to imply that they are true and valid in every human society, that if correct at all, they are perpetually and universally correct for the human race. We have not raised the further metaphysical question whether they would also be correct for beings radically different from ourselves, with a different sensory equipment for instance. That scientific findings are, in a sense, relative to our apparatus of perception, can hardly be denied, at least not at the start of a philosophical argument about the matter. Even the most refined scientific instruments are still extensions of our eye and ear, just as the most complex machines are still essentially extensions of our arms, hands and fingers. All this raises questions which demand answers; [1] but the answers are not for the sociologist of knowledge or the historian of ideas to give. He has no business to take even a single step beyond the confines of the human world, narrow and oppressive though they may be.

(b) EARLIER DISCUSSIONS OF THE PROBLEM OF RELATIVITY

From all that has gone before it will be clear that what we have called the problem of the co-existence of truths, and others have labelled the problem of relativity, is in essence a problem of the cultural sciences. It is they which are essentially value-bound and bound to changing values; it is they which show the unfortunate consequences of the fact, the only too undeniable fact, that there is no one order of values which all human societies have accepted—the fact which Pascal has treated under the heading 'Misère de l'Homme' and which caused him to break into this *cri de cœur*: 'On what shall man base the economy of the world which he would like to control? Shall it be on the sweet will of the individual? Then all is anarchy. Shall it be on justice? He does not know what it is. Surely, if he knew what it was, he would not have established the maxim which is the most general of all current among men that every one should follow the mores of his country; the splendour of true rectitude would have brought all nations under its sway . . . We should have seen it firmly established in all states of the world and in all ages of history, whereas we see in fact nothing that is either "just" or "unjust" which would not change its quality with a change of climate. Three degrees of latitude upset all jurisprudence; a meridian decides about the truth; after having held the field for a few years, the most fundamental laws undergo a change; right has its epochs. . . . What a

---

[1] A *locus classicus* for their discussion is the works of Max Scheler. Cf. e.g. *Die Wissensformen und die Gesellschaft*, 1926, 92, 299 *seq.*, 352 *seq.*, and *Erkenntnis und Arbeit*, in the same volume, *passim*.

funny justice it is which a river can limit! Truth on this side of the Pyrenees, error on that.' [1]

There can be few serious and thoughtful researchers in the social sciences who have not at times felt like Pascal—felt the cold breath of relativity, the icy hand of instability. The deeply ingrained feeling of inferiority of the social 'scientist' vis-à-vis the scientist proper can be attributed to the recognition, semi-conscious, resisted and resented though it may be, that the findings of the social sciences are not as absolute as those of astronomy or rational mechanics. Yet it will not do to approach this problem in a spirit of undue defeatism. It may yet be possible to show that the greatest difficulty of the social sciences marks also at the same time their greatest excellence.

Let us note, first of all, that just as the natural sciences have a certain, though secondary, sociological element in them, so the cultural sciences embody a certain, though secondary, element of science and technology. What Napoléon in fact said at the Pyramids is a question not so very different from that as to whether gold deposits in fact occur in Tibet or in Timbuctoo. In either case the job to be done by the investigator is a fact-finding job, and the same canons of maximum exactitude and reliability must apply. And this similar scientific task also demands similar techniques: to get the proofs, to compare and evaluate indications, to work from hypotheses towards assured theses, etc. To secure the best sources of information, to collate and edit them, etc. is a task in the field of historical research which can be described as technological without doing violence to the term, indeed, without widening its scope. Even the greatest relativists have admitted as much. [2] And there has been a tendency among historians—though it has been restricted to the narrower and more pedestrian ones among them—to claim that the historian's work is nothing but this, nothing but a specific form of technological, scientific, exact endeavour. But this is no more than naïve dogmatism. Research techniques are ways and means towards the answering of questions; but questions must be asked before they can be answered, and the asking of them—in other words, the seeing them as relevant—is determined, in the social sciences particularly, by the axiological layer of the mind, by the value-structure of the society in which the questioner lives. That Napoléon's words at the Pyramids are important is not a fact of the same nature as the fact that he spoke them; it is not an objective fact like the latter which can be scientifically investigated, and which will be so investigated if there is an interest in it, but rather an imputed valuational fact, necessarily based on a pre-

---

[1] *Pensées de Pascal sur la Vérité de la Religion Chrétienne*, ed. Chevalier, 1949, 125 *seq.*

[2] Cf. Ernst Troeltsch, *Der Historismus und seine Probleme*, 1922, beginning.

existent axiological system which can claim no absolute validity, and is here today and gone tomorrow.

But of all this we have said enough in chapter 3, and there is no need to reopen the matter. The truth is that research techniques can only come into play at all when a meaningful picture of historico-social reality has already been mentally constructed; but the constructing of it is subject to social determination, and inescapably so, whether we like it or not. 'The scholarly canons of textual precision and of respect for historical fact were an outgrowth of the same intellectual principles that were responsible for the ideal of accurate observation in science', writes George H. Sabine. 'Respect for fact and faithfulness to sources are indispensable parts of the social scientist's intellectual equipment, but'—and this is a decisive proviso—'*but* they do not do away with the truth that observation in these subjects is shot through with human interest, from the interest of the actor himself, through that of the reporting sources, and down to the interest of the scholar who makes the last selection and draws the last inference.' [1]

If the natural scientist is a man in a comfortable seat, contemplating a static landscape from a stable vantage-point, the social scientist is, by comparison, a less favourably circumstanced observer looking at a moving picture from a running train. [2] No wonder that he does not grasp the outlines of the reality entrusted to his care quite so clearly and closely; no wonder, above all, that after a while everything seems altered; no wonder also that no sensible conversation is possible across the gulfs of change and time. A round-table discussion on universal history between Otto of Freising, Bossuet, Voltaire, Comte, Marx, Pareto and Toynbee, unless it were and remained small talk about the bare bones of the facts as such, would soon die of mutual incomprehension, if it did not indeed break up in mutual recrimination and hostility. In view of this situation the question has been asked by certain fearless theoreticians whether the whole concept of true knowledge must not be boldly abandoned in the cultural field, and another concept substituted for it, the concept of genuine knowledge—*Ausdruckswahrheit* as Alfred Weber has it, i.e. whether the ideal should not be knowledge which correctly expresses the specific vista and view-point of a given beholder rather than any universally binding impressions made by reality. 'Though no *Weltanschauung* is true in a sense which would make the others untrue,' so this point of view has been well summed up, 'each one of them, while false as a theory, is true as a record of

---

[1] *The Philosophical Review*, 1939, 158, 169.

[2] We cannot, in this book, discuss the contrast between the natural and the social sciences in all its breadth and depth. Cf. however, Warynski, *Die Wissenschaft von der Gesellschaft*, 1944, 31 *seq.*, 121 *seq.*, 143 *seq.*, 158 *seq.*, 163 *seq.*; Lieber, *Wissen und Gesellschaft*, 1952, 116 *seq.* and the literature quoted there (esp. Litt).

vision.'[1] This approach is nothing if not revolutionary. It would substitute for the age-old *adequatio intellectus et rei*, the correspondence between thought and thing, a new *adequatio intellectus et situs*, a correspondence between thought and thinker, or rather, thought and location in social space and time.

The direction in which such a treatment of the history of ideas would lead becomes clear from the following declaration: 'As a response to the decisive experiences of our time, all variants of positivism were basically genuine: from our point of view, they represent a straightforward reflection of the fact that the centre of our experience has shifted from the spiritual and religious sphere to the social-economic one. It was capitalism . . . that was responsible for this shift of the experiential centre to these fields, as well as for the fact that technological and scientific thought became the only recognized prototype of all thinking. It is by no means surprising that a philosophy which sought to provide a world interpretation with this type of experience and thought as its basic frame of reference based its epistemology exclusively on natural science and in its ontology attributed reality only to those spheres which it experienced as real—withholding full theoretical recognition from those spheres which in its practical experience appeared only at the periphery.'[2]

To us it seems clear that positivism, as an integral world view, cannot provide a true representation of the facts in their entirety because it presses the methods appropriate only to the study of one sector of reality (nature) beyond their proper sphere, and we should always unambiguously condemn it for its lack of balance. But such tests would not be applied, nor such judgments pronounced, by a conception of the history of ideas founded upon the idea of 'genuine' rather than of true knowledge. From this point of view, thought would be 'correct' if it were true to a given axiomatic standpoint, and not to a given totality of fact; if it were in harmony with him who sees, not with that which is seen. The term truth would then be used in the sense in which one speaks of 'artistic', as distinct from 'scientific', truth: it would mean honesty, absence of sham, rather than control by objective fact or the ability to command universal acceptance. Indeed, objective fact would be pushed out of the focus of attention altogether and relegated to the outer perimeter of consideration; worse still: the whole concept of objective fact as a touchstone for the truth of the scholar's assertions would be to all intents and purposes abandoned, and we should be pushed towards the position of a man like Fritz Medicus, according to whom historical knowledge is 'a knowing in which there is no object independent of the subject'.[3]

[1] Hodges, *Wilhelm Dilthey*, 1944, 104.
[2] Mannheim, *Essays on the Sociology of Knowledge*, 1952, 150 *seq*.
[3] *Cit.* Sabine in *The Philosophical Review*, 1939, 169.

This mode of thinking has eaten deep into the literature of the socio-logy of knowledge. And yet it does not necessarily belong to the essence of the sociology of knowledge itself, but has seeped into it from a disparate, if kindred, stream of thought, namely historicism. Father of the conviction that truths are irreducible to truth, that truth is in its inmost nature relative, was Dilthey,[1] and men like Mannheim were his disciples, nay, his captives. Mannheim believed, like Dilthey, that there is only *one* absolute truth—namely, that *all* truth is relative. 'The historical standpoint', he writes, 'which starts with relativism, achieves eventually an absoluteness of view, because in its final form it posits history itself as the Absolute; this alone makes it possible that the various standpoints, which at first appear anarchic, can be ordered as component parts of a meaningful overall process.'[2] With such senti-ments Mannheim reaches, and identifies himself with, the famous paradox of Heinrich Heine: 'Change is the only thing eternal, nought is lasting, only death'—the paradox which Marx, too, made his own when he wrote in *The Poverty of Philosophy*: 'The only immutable thing is the abstraction of movement—*mors immortalis*' (Engl. ed. 1935, 93).

This, of course, is an opinion *prima facie* as legitimate as any other, provided that it is intrinsically sound. But the curious fact is that men have never been able to live with it. 'The more people fancy that they can do without eternity,' wrote a thinker of outstanding power, 'the more, in truth, do they need it.'[3] Dilthey, great psychologist that he was, was aware of this: 'Every mental attitude', he says in *What is Philosophy*, 'seeks for a fixed point exempt from relativity.'[4] Indeed, this seeking is as a rule characterized by a certain feverishness: it is as if the Diltheyesque counsel of despair—'there is no absolute truth which we can know'—were bound to give rise to an equally desperate desire to get back to assurance: 'there must be some absolute truth to which we can cling'. This is easy to understand for we are not confronted here with a theoretical problem only: we are also face to face with a horrifying practical danger. When the truth goes out at one door, cynicism comes in at the other. But cynicism will not remain locked up in a library: it will sooner or later affect life, and affect it deeply. Whether men sink into the mire of complete negativism or whether, in revulsion, they throw themselves into the arms of some intoxicating pseudo-religion, will make little difference: the upshot will in either

---

[1] We cannot here follow this historical side of the matter further. Cf. Grünwald, *Das Problem der Soziologie des Wissens*, 1934, 43 *seq.*

[2] *Essays on the Sociology of Knowledge*, 1952, 172. For Alfred Weber, cf. von Schelting, 'Zum Streit um die Wissenssoziologie', *Archiv für Sozialwissenschaft*, 1929, 61 *seq.*   [3] Kierkegaard, *cit.* Löwith, *Von Hegel zu Nietzsche*, ed. 1953, 225.

[4] *Cit.* Hodges, *Wilhelm Dilthey: An Introduction*, 1944, 151.

case be contempt for man, with the ultimate result of cruelty and sadism.[1]

Men will try then, by all means, to wriggle out of the pan-relativistic position. (Even Dilthey and Mannheim did, as we shall see later on, in our last chapter.) One of the escape routes which they have tried has been in the direction of formalism. A most promising avenue to explore, this, at least in appearance, for if this destination can in fact be reached, if the material insights of a science can be transmuted into mathematical propositions, no doubt of the absolute character of its findings can remain. It is characteristic of Dilthey, who would have no generalizing sociology at all because in the social field the concrete and unique is (as he claims) alone meaningful, that he willingly accepted the sociology of Georg Simmel because in Simmel's system all content is drained out of reality and only the remaining 'pure form' is considered.[2]

We see the flight into formalism on the grandest scale when we study the history of economics between, say, 1840 and 1940. At first, there is naïve confidence in the absolute character of the laws enunciated by the classical writers. Nassau Senior's Oxford Inaugural Lecture of 1826 maintained that all political economy can be logically deduced from four simple and self-evident, or at least completely provable, propositions: man is a hedonistic animal; the population tends to outstrip the food supply; industry has a tendency towards increasing returns; agriculture is under a law of decreasing returns. Then comes the violent assault of the historical school against this 'universalism' and 'perpetualism'. Senior's four basic premises are shown to be neither everywhere nor at all times correct. In pre-capitalist society, for instance, man is not hedonistic but tradition-bound: far from trying to maximize his income, 'to better his condition', as Adam Smith had called it, he is content to remain in his old rut, even if this means that his income never goes up, that his condition never gets any better. What was the reaction of the orthodox to this opposition movement? Under a barrage of abusive sneers, they started a retreat towards the formalistic redoubt. The assertion that all men try to achieve the highest possible income or material standard of living became the assertion that all men try to secure the highest possible amount of pleasure. If it was then said that pre-capitalist man was after the maximization of peace and quiet, not the maximization of material enjoyments, the relativistic onslaught could be warded off by saying: certainly; pre-capitalist man wanted to maximize his happiness by moving economically in a circle, capitalist man wants to maximize his happiness by going forward—but both want to maximize happiness, and so both are under the same formal law. Once this line of argument is reached, the position has become

---

[1] Cf. the characteristic case of Ernst Jünger, studied by von Martin in his *Geist und Gesellschaft*, 1948, 159 *seq.*   [2] Cf. Hodges, *loc. cit.*, 60 *seq.*

impregnable. The hedonistic axiom, formalistically redefined, *must* be correct because it is a tautology: all men want to maximize pleasure; pleasure is what men want to maximize.

The seal was set on this thorough-going formalization in the replacement, by Pareto, of the word *utilité* by the term *ophelimité* (desiredness). Instead of saying, as in Bentham's day, that people pursue, to the best of their ability, what is useful to them, it was now said that they pursue to the utmost what they happen to desire. But this shift, basic though it is, was by no means the only one of its kind. For a Léon Walras, or a Gustav Cassel, an economic system is a system of quantitative, quasi-mechanical forces (such as offer and demand) in search of an equilibrium. Setting aside one commodity (gold) as the unit of computation, there are $n-1$ offers and $n-1$ demands which must be brought together on the market, and the problem of economic theory is to find the $n-1$ prices at which this is achieved. But the $n-1$ prices are really given *ab initio*, i.e. they are given implicitly and can be made known explicitly by calculation. For if, after the haggling of the day, after the *tâtonnements*, as Walras calls them, of trial and error, there are $n-1$ offers and demands in equilibrium, there are $n-1$ equations at our disposal, and as we have $n-1$ unknowns the system is mathematically determinate. What more elegant—and what more absolutely true? Wherever there is *any* market, the Walrasian, Paretian, Casselian equations must be correct: there is, there can be, no relativity about such a 'theory'. The trumpets of the relativists can be blown as hard as they like under the ramparts of such an entrenched position, the walls of this Jericho will never come down.

The truth of the matter is, of course, that though a mathematical economics *à la* Walras tells us everything about all markets in the abstract, it tells us nothing about any market in the concrete. Locked up as it is in its tautologies, it can find no contact with the hard facts of reality, and so we have here a science without factual content—in other words, a contradiction in terms. The flight into formalism has proved unavailing,[1] and economists themselves have turned away from it—turned towards the reality, and the relativity, of the world as it is. They have learnt to understand that it is impossible in any and every social science to divide the qualitative aspect of the real from the quantitative, and that it is nothing short of monstrous to believe that a thought-model from which the whole qualitative aspect of reality is *a limine* excluded, can pass for an adequate and representative model of that reality, a model about which one can talk realistically, or even merely reasonably. They are deeply disappointed by the whole formalistic experiment. And the same disappointment must always follow

---

[1] Incidentally, it has proved as unavailing in art as it has in economics. Cf. Turner's *Beethoven*, ed. 1945, 307 *seq.*

formalism outside its proper field such as logic, mathematics and rational mechanics. What is left of Simmel's sociology today? If anything remains, it is not the pure forms themselves, but these forms filled with content, brought near to—in fact swamped by—the wealth of detail which life has spread out before our eyes and from which we cannot for any length of time avert our gaze.

Some of the greatest social philosophers have been permanently preoccupied with the formal problems of the social sciences and they have been so preoccupied because they have felt the lash of relativity and of nihilism on their backs. Max Weber was one of them. 'Again and again,' writes Alexander von Schelting in *Max Webers Wissenschafts-lehre*, 'Max Weber turns towards the formal "how" of knowing as if he could find here, in the fixity and universality of logical form, a "compensation" for the never-to-be-overcome particularity and fragmentariness of all empirical knowledge' (6). But Max Weber was not a man like Walras or Simmel. He was an honest merchant who wanted to sell tangible goods that can be weighed in the scales of history, not a tautology-monger with a shop full of the moonshine of 'pure forms'. 'He who desires to reach the maximum of rational univocality and transparency in knowledge', says von Schelting, 'can follow two paths: he can either try to satisfy that wish on the model of mathematical evidence or of those disciplines which abstract from real happening all that is qualitative and hence only relative, and seek to reduce it to merely quantitative relationships, *or* he can attempt to do it by logic. For Max Weber, the first alternative [—the alternative of Walras and Simmel—] was out of the question. He chose the second' (6 *seq.*).

Now, what is meant by this second alternative? Roughly this: that though the materials on which the scholarly mind sets to work can never be the same in all societies, his methods of working and especially his tests of the truth can, and indeed should be so. 'The logical form', so von Schelting sums up Max Weber's position, 'on which the validity of a concrete scientific statement, and also the revision of that statement and the formulation of a new one rests or should rest, must be conceived as identical [in all circumstances], if [the term] scientific knowledge is to have any sense at all' (8). In other words: according to Max Weber, no social science can be built up that is not caught in the coils of the concrete—but at the same time there can be no social science either that is not also caught in the coils of logic. In the acquisition of knowledge the formal is an ever-present accompaniment of the material, an accompaniment which is self-identical in the face of the most disparate, most rapidly changing, most irreconcilable contents, and it is this absolute feature of our dealings with the relative to which we must cling if we wish to rise superior to the problem of relativity. Perhaps we may characterize the contrast between the pan-formalists

184

and Weber by saying, in our terminology, that whereas they pressed formalism beyond its proper limits, whereas they fell for the *pars-pro-toto* fallacy, Weber was aware of the limitations of the possibilities contained in the formalistic approach but wished to make use of them as far as possible, so far as they are usable at all. Thereby he provided one of the elements out of which can be fashioned a convincing and final answer to the challenge of relativity in the social sciences.

The second way out of the impasse of relativism leads in an entirely different direction—not towards the general and the abstract but towards the specific and the concrete, not towards reason but rather towards a kind of religion. The device it employs is to raise, by an act of faith, *one* particular point of view out of the depths of relativity and to proclaim it, by a bold fiat, as the absolute. The supreme example here, though by no means the only one, is the case of Marxism.

Unlike the pan-formalists, and unlike his master Hegel, Marx does not claim that he can give us the absolute truth here and now *in terminis*. Great sociologist of knowledge that he was, he preached that only an undistorted community can reach the undistorted truth in its entirety, that only a classless society can achieve a vision of the absolute or rather the universally human. But though we are still in the grip of relativity, there are some of us who are much less so than others. These privileged ones are the revolutionary class, and within it particularly the revolutionary élite. Unbefuddled by interest-born delusion, it sees more realistically than do the conservative and reactionary classes, who like to deceive themselves no less than they like to deceive others. To the sublime mission which universal history has reserved for the proletariat, there belongs also, as a natural and necessary concomitant, a privileged position with regard to knowledge. 'Only he who is called and willing to usher in the future', says Georg Lukacs, 'can see the concrete truth of the present.' And in another context, where the intellectual bases of this opinion become a good deal clearer: 'Capitalism pulls down all barriers between the different countries in space and time, as well as the legal dividing walls which separate the estates. In its world of the formal equality of all human beings . . . man becomes, in the true sense of the word, a social creature. Society is *the* reality for man. And so a knowledge of society in its reality is possible only on the soil of capitalism, of bourgeois society. But the class which appears as the historical agent of this transformation, the bourgeoisie, still fulfils its function unseeingly [*unbewusst*]; the social forces which it has set free, those forces which have carried it to victory, confront it like a second nature, but one less transparent than that of feudalism had been. Only with the appearance of the proletariat does the knowledge of social reality reach perfection. And it reaches perfection by virtue of the fact that in the point of view of the proletarian class a position has been found from which the whole of society becomes visible. Only because it is for the proletariat a vital need, a question of life and death, to achieve the fullest clarity about its own class situation; because its class situation becomes intelligible only through a knowledge of the social order in its entirety; because its actions have that knowledge for their indispensable presupposition, has there arisen, in historical materialism, both a doctrine "of the conditions of the liberation of the proletariat", and a knowledge of the reality of the total process of social development.' [1]

In other words, to translate this last sentence into plain English, historical materialism, as the philosophy of the proletarian class, is at the same time both a practical, political weapon in the struggle for social aims, and a social science, an entirely realistic social science, and in fact the only realistic social science that is possible. And it functions as the latter, not in spite of its connection—its identity—with an ideology, but rather because of it. This is a dialectical consummation indeed—out of the same situation which, in all other classes, has produced nothing but error, namely imprisonment in its own interests and prejudices, there will yet, by a total inversion, spring nothing but truth for the proletariat, the class to which Lukacs ascribes the 'mission to lead the evolution of humanity' [2]—to lead social development to its final dénouement, the promised jump from necessity into freedom.

This is essentially a messianic and millenarian doctrine, the claims of which are, in the nature of things, incapable of purely rational discussion and decision. There is no authority which could adjudicate upon them with final validity; if there were such an authority, the problem of relativity would not arise in the first place. The claims of historical materialism to be the incarnation of the truth will appear as convincing to the believer as they appear unconvincing to the unbeliever. The whole doctrine reminds one forcibly of the many dogmatic sectarianisms which have punctuated the history of religion. Each dogma has claimed to be the revealed truth, by comparison with which all other dogmas were but human error, if not indeed diabolical deception. And, like the Sectarians, the Marxists have always subjected all other doctrinal systems to annihilating criticism, but have never turned the critical probe inward, upon themselves. Now, this is precisely what uncommitted scholarship cannot and must not allow. It must put all ideologies alike on the dissecting table and under the microscope. As Max Weber expresses it in a striking simile which he used in his lecture *Politik als Beruf*: the materialistic conception of history is not like a taxi-cab (we are paraphrasing) which the user can stop and leave at will, but rather like a long-distance bus where, once aboard, you have to remain on it and go with it to the terminus. If ideological distortion is asserted of bourgeois thought, then it must be asked, without of

[1] *Geschichte und Klassenbewusstsein*, 1923, 223, 33 *seq.*   [2] 34.

186

course pre-judging the issue, whether proletarian thought is not distorted in a similar way. And a strictly impartial investigation of this question must needs lead to the (totally un-Marxist) conviction that it is.

If the property-owner overcompensates, in his ideologies, his fears of losing his property and thereby deviates from truth in his thought, the property-less proletarian, for his part, overcompensates, in his own ideologies, the inferiority-complex to which his propertyless-ness, and his consequent social humiliation, has given rise in his soul, and this can drive him as far from sober fact as the ideologist on the other side of the fence.[1] The whole messianism and millenarianism of the proletariat is nothing but the semi-conscious overcompensation of a sub-conscious inferiority-complex, typically wish-determined thinking, typical ideology in the pejorative sense of the word. Before the tribunal of scholarship the claim of proletarian 'ideologies' to be acknowledged as essentially non-ideological, as essentially true, has no chance whatever of acceptance, however clever the special pleading of their advocates, from Karl Marx to Georg Lukacs and Stanislaw Warynski.

This argument seems quite sufficient to show up the shallowness of the Marxist attempt to solve the problem of relativity by absolutizing one particular vista or point of view. However, Lukacs has discussed all this, not only on the political, but also on the philosophical level, and it is instructive to follow him for a while into the realm of ontology. His approach is characteristic, not only of the Marxist creed for which he stands, but of a much wider mental movement, the movement called historism or historicism in recent years, and what can be urged against him can be urged also, and with equal force, against writers such as Dilthey, Mannheim and many others.

Briefly, the main submission of Lukacs is that movement is the *ens realissimum*, and not fact as commonly understood. His text sometimes suggests Henri Bergson as much as it does Karl Marx. To quote but one passage out of many by way of illustration: 'If becoming appears as the truth of being, process as the truth of things, then this means that the developmental tendencies of history possess a higher reality than the "facts" of mere experience.' [2] With statements such as this Lukacs has placed himself on an inclined plane where there is no stopping his descent. The facts 'of mere experience' are depreciated more and more, until in the end he sees no point in asking whether our perception of them is correct or not. He puts the obnoxious word 'facts' into inverted commas because he wants to intimate that there are really no such things at all. For facts are pieces cut out of a process, and if they are so cut out, if they are envisaged in isolation, apart from the

---

[1] Cf. my paper 'La Interpretacion Marxista de la Religion y la Interpretacion Religiosa del Marxismo', in *Revista Internacional de Sociologia*, 1954.

[2] *Loc. cit.*, 198. Cf. also 200 *seq.*

stream to which they belong in life, if they are artificially transmuted from ingredients in a flowing totality into independent fixed magnitudes, they become mere dead 'fetishes' [1] and are no longer living realities in the proper meaning of the term. There is no sense, then, in speaking about 'hard facts' and asking whether any man, or every man, sees them as they are: what has been regarded, since Plato, as the root problem of truth, is a pseudo-problem only. It is only a slight exaggeration to say that for Lukacs it is the facts that are likely to be wrong rather than the ideas which people form of them, and given such an opinion a fruitful epistemological discussion is rendered totally impossible.

But we have not yet reached the lowest point. Not only does Lukacs conjure away the whole concept of individual objective fact, but he also removes the very possibility of a meaningful theoretical consideration of such facts—and, indeed, of movement itself though he praises it up as the *ens realissimum*. Just as the isolation of a fact from its matrix in movement kills it and thereby destroys it, so the objectification of movement kills its meaning and thereby precludes the making of any intelligent or truthful statements about it. Truth is revealed in action, not in contemplation, in practice, not in theory. Reality is known to those who function inside it, not to those who detach themselves from it. In so far as the theoretician tries to see it from the outside, he has *a limine* ruled himself out of court. (We are again reminded here of Henri Bergson.) When we see a stream flowing by, we cannot hope to say anything relevant about it, until we have jumped into it and immersed ourselves in its waters, until we are carried away by its living force in the direction of its flow. Clearly, what Lukacs does, or rather attempts to do, is to 'solve' a theoretical problem by the removal of the theoretician. This will never do. A problem is not solved, a question is not answered, by suppressing the possibility of raising it.

All this amounts to a sidestepping of the problem of truth and truths, and not to a solution. The theoretical question of the correspondence between thought and thing must not be raised for it is insoluble; we must be content (so Lukacs implies) with that feeling of accordance with reality which arises from a participation in it. 'Every attempt dialectically to overcome the duality [of thinking and being] in thought that has been made free of every concrete relation to being, in logic, is foredoomed to failure. For every pure logic is Platonist: it is thought isolated from being and ossified in that isolation. . . . Every attitude of pure perception remains marked with the stigma of immediacy; i.e. it stands in the end vis-à-vis a series of hard and fast objects irreducible to terms of process.' In other words: every attitude of pure perception, every properly theoretical attitude is, *a limine* and of necessity, no good.

[1] *Loc. cit.*, 202.

Good alone is 'the solution which Marx adduces in his "Theses on Feuerbach" . . . the transformation of philosophy into practice'. Now, practice is, by definition, focused on one instant, the instant of action, and so only that instant can yield the truth. It is fascinating to see how Lukacs narrows the comprehensive problem of truth down until it comprises, not the whole length and depth and breadth of reality, but a mere split second—that second in which—paradoxically—it cannot possibly be so much as envisaged, because all energies are absorbed in action, in the doing of the deed. 'So long as man', he writes, 'directs his interest contemplatively, towards the past *or* the future, both freeze into an alien being [being alien and incomprehensible to him], and there is posited between subject and object the "noxious space" of the present. Only when man is capable of grasping the present as a becoming, when he recognizes in it those tendencies out of whose dialetical contrast he is able to *create* the future, does the present, the present as a becoming, become *his* present [i.e. does he gain an adequate conception of it]. The concrete Here and Now in which it dissolves itself into a process is no longer a transitory, elusive instant, immediacy in its flight, but the moment of the deepest and most comprehensive decision, the moment of the birth of the new.' [1]

Those who have read their Kierkegaard as well as their Marx will know how to appreciate this passage. It recalls not only the great Danish genius's style of speculation, it recalls his very speech and wording. If the 'instant' of 'decision' is for the religious prophet the moment, and the only one, when man can make contact with the *ens realissimum*, namely God, it is no less so for the secular messianist who has merely substituted his own this-worldly *ens realissimum* for the other-worldly one of his brother—namely history, the flow of events, the ongoing revolution.

Much could be said on all this, but we shall restrict ourselves to the problem in hand—the problem of relativity, the problem of truth. Surely, Lukacs has not solved it—he has merely thrown it out of the window. For, as we have said already, if truth is only to be had in the moment of action, then it is not to be had at all, for in the moment of action the question of the reliability of our knowledge cannot possibly be raised. It is the grim logic of the philosophy of Lukacs and of those who share his creed that practical success becomes in the end, almost *faute de mieux*, the ultimate test of theoretical truth. (It is indeed a logic of a kind, for if history is made the ultimate reality, in other words, is deified, it is only consistent to assign to it all the other rights of the deity, and among them the right to decide, and with finality, about the value and validity of ideas.) A theory is not true if it is in accordance with the facts, but rather if it contrives to shape the facts in its own

[1] 222 *seq.*

189

image; a political theory, in particular, is true not if it can account for the developments which are taking place, but rather if it is able to initiate such developments and see them through. Philosophy is here indeed transformed into practice! Those who are in the saddle are— according to this way of thinking—always right. This is not only Lukacs's opinion, though he might not care to see it thus bluntly formulated, it is also the opinion of his master Hegel, as Karl Löwith has shown in his deeply penetrating study *Von Hegel zu Nietzsche* (cf. 238, ed. 1953). Adriano Tilgher has castigated it in his splendid satires.[1] We need not stay to discuss it any longer, for to bring out its implications is, for all who are not completely obsessed by it, a damning *reductio ad absurdum*.

If the Marxist theory is tested, then, it becomes perfectly obvious that it provides no solution to the problem of truth: neither a solution on the lower political level, for the proletarian world-view can be shown to be a mere ideology, just as the bourgeois world-view is; nor a solution on the higher ontological level, for its ontology absolutizes what is in its inmost essence not absolute, not for ever self-identical, but constantly changing, namely history, and shifts the test of validity from the sphere of theory to that of practice, where no reasonable person will ever expect to find it. Nevertheless, even the Hegel-Marx-Mannheim tradition contains a valuable element which can make a positive contribution to a satisfactory solution of the problem of the coexistence of truths. One of Hegel's most interesting conceptions is the conviction that his own philosophy is not an alternative to the philosophical systems that have preceded it, so much as their synthesis, a summing-up of them all. Earlier philosophies are *aufgehoben*, as he puts it, in the later ones, and particularly in the last of all which he himself has fashioned. Now, the German word *aufgehoben* has, by a curious freak of language, a double meaning: it means both cancelled and preserved. The English word 'suspended' comes near in this respect to the German *aufgehoben*: what is suspended in law is no longer valid; but what is suspended on a nail is still there. So it is with ideas according to the dialectical philosophy: they are suspended in validity but they are incorporated in the new that has replaced them—they are cancelled and they are preserved. If this book has formulated what used to be called the problem of relativity more correctly as the problem of the coexistence of truths, then it is clear that this problem can only be solved by showing how the coexisting truths are to be reconciled, how they can be fitted into each other, how a synthesis can be formed out of them in which the apparent antitheses each find their own place, and all are at peace with one another. Thus the Hegelian and Marxist dialectic points in a direction in which all who seek to overcome the impasse of the appar-

[1] *Lo Spaccio del Bestione Trionfante*, 1925.

ently irreducible multiplicity of aspectual views and truths must attempt to travel if they wish to arrive at their destination. Of course, in pushing forward, they will have to shed the *impedimentum* so basic and so dear to both Marx and Hegel, the naïve dogma that *one* particular configuration of thought (one's own) is privileged over all others, and that all others are merely a preparation for it. They will have to get rid of this self-flattering prejudice and remember the words of Ranke—contemporary and antagonist of both Hegel and Marx—that before God all generations appear with equal rights and that this is also the spirit in which the man of scholarship must approach his subject.

Apart from formalism, which ends in the emptiness of tautology, and from historicism, which leads to the very dissolution of the concept of truth, there is yet a third possible way that has been tried out of the impasse of relativism—flight in the direction of science. If social knowledge can all be made scientific, if a social science can be built up which is as truly scientific as science properly so called, then the problem of truth is solved for, as we have seen, the physical sciences are not in the grip of relativity. Of the many who have experimented with this escape route, Pareto was the greatest. Nearly all thought, he ruthlessly asserted, is a tissue of 'derivations', i.e. of ideologies, rationalizations, myths, stupidities, verbiage, nonsense; only scientific thought is meaningful and correct. A strictly logico-experimental sociology, if such could be developed, would be rid of the irrationalities of common thinking and partake of the rationality of the sciences in the narrower sense of the word. It would be the truth, and nothing but the truth. Its findings would be as little bound to time, place or class as the Boyle-Charles law in chemistry.

How strong the lure of this line of speculation is can be seen from the fascination which it exerted on one of the most outstanding leaders of European historicism, Ernst Troeltsch. Troeltsch was deeply concerned about the anarchy of values which historicism had brought in its train, and cast about for a sheet-anchor which could steady the storm-tossed ship of humanity. Would it be possible, he asked, to extract from the facts of history, despite their relativity, a table of absolute values, values of a wider validity than that of the passing day? In his desperation he believed that only an individual act of decision, an act of faith, such as Luther's *'fides'* or Schleiermacher's 'feeling', an act giving personal —subjective—'certainty' could lift man out of the relative into the absolute. For himself it was to be trust in the Maker, the Creator-God, and His creature, Man. But it is significant that he does not remain in this fideist position and creeps out of it towards the scientific camp. Faith in God, he teaches, progresses the more in effectiveness and purity, the more man succeeds in freeing himself from the influence of nature, the more he succeeds in liberating himself from his original enslavement to natural forces.[1] Here a progress in inner certainty is envisaged which is manifestly parallel to the outer progress in control over the lower creation which the physical scientists have procured us in the course of the centuries. Troeltsch tries to link his faith to science: to gain his absolute with the aid, distant it is true, but yet effective, of the triumphs of scientific research and technology. If this is the method applied by a historicist and theologian, it is not to be wondered at that a rationalist and bridge-builder such as Pareto saw in it the shibboleth that would bring salvation from the curse of universal relativity.

To the name of Ernst Troeltsch we may, indeed we must, in this context add that of his friend Max Weber. Weber, in whose spirit the present book is conceived, who openly proclaimed the relevance of values between which no scientific and universally valid choice is possible to the very constitution of any and every world-view, was none the less anxious to extend the application of scientific methods in the social disciplines so far as was humanly possible, because he was convinced that such certainty as was possible of achievement lay in that direction and no other. But with Max Weber we see already that this particular road is blocked, too, that pan-scientism proves as disappointing in the end as pan-formalism and pan-historicism. For what kind of a picture is it that he builds up, under the influence of such tendencies, of the historical world? History is a progress in rationality, merely interrupted from time to time by that upsurge of irrationality which is brought about by 'charismatic personalities' who, meteor-like, flash across the firmament, only to be extinguished after a dazzling display of evanescent fireworks. Now, this interpretation of history is unfortunately not as scholarly—not as scientific in the best sense of the word—as might be desired. For it manifestly discriminates against the irrational element in life, which is demoted to the position of a secondary phenomenon, a mere interruption of the trend, whereas the rational element is promoted to the position of primary content of history, and magnified, indeed, into the trend itself.[2] But this means, in effect, that it discriminates against the relative, for it is the irrational which is here today and gone tomorrow, whereas the rational, like its perfection, mathematics, is for ever self-identical. Surely, this undue discrimination is wish-determined, not fact-determined; it is ideological; it is the effect of a desire to find in reality more rationality than there is, a desire that has many subconscious urges behind it, but among others also the wish to escape the anxiety-generating fact of relativity and to reach the security-giving haven of the absolute—some absolute, even if it be only an absolute in the making and so poor a one as rationality. What

[1] Cf. Antoni, *Vom Historismus zur Soziologie*, 1952, 73 *seq.*
[2] Cf. Alfred Weber, *Prinzipien der Geschichts- und Kultursoziologie*, 1951, 107 *seq.*, esp. 109.

Weber does is to look for the absolute in reality after he has reduced—not to say drained out—the relative in it. But this is not permissible. Indeed, it is not even logical.

Pareto's case is very similar. With characteristic boldness he splits social reality into two parts—the residues (or springs of action) and the derivations (the modes of thinking or rather talking) and pontifically pronounces the residues to be the key and core of social life, whereas the derivations are only a surface phenomenon, the insubstantial froth that forms over the substance of social life. That substance is the same at all times and places, just as the laws of physics and chemistry are. No problem of relativity arises because there are no variations in human behaviour from age to age and from land to land. Human behaviour is determined by the residues, and the residues are physical attributes of man, drives, something like quasi-instincts. Wherever there are human bodies, there is the same complex of residues (albeit in different combinations); wherever there are human bodies, there is the same kind of conduct; wherever there are human bodies, there is the same social reality. If it looks as if there were change, as if there was such a thing as relativity, this is due to the derivations—those verbal cloaks with which men are wont to cover up the nakedness of their drive-determined (near-animal) actions. Derivations change indeed; age and place seem to influence and diversify them: but, then, the derivations are unimportant. As their name indicates, they are merely derived from the residues, the all-important residues: they are merely the accompaniments of action, the prattle as it were that follows the deed when it is done, the *post festum* rationalizations of human conduct which, in itself, is anything but rational.

If Pareto's account of social life were fair and true, then, it must be admitted, no ink would need to be spilled over the problem of relativity, or the problem of truth, for such a problem would not in fact exist. All pronouncements about matters social would apply to all societies without distinction and would have absolute validity. But, plainly, it is not. It is a caricature of society, not a photograph of it. Human conduct is not one hundred per cent drive-determined; it is very largely, though certainly not entirely, fashioned by cultural factors; in consequence it differs in different cultures and societies; in further and final consequence, what is true at one time or place need not be true at every or any other, and the problem of relativity undeniably exists. Like Weber, Pareto devalues, and indeed abolishes, the relative in reality; but that means that he does violence to reality, that he operates with a thought-model which is unrealistic, at variance with things as they really are.

Pareto's strategy is in the last analysis a simple one: he reduces the complex being man to the animal, the beast, the body of man; he wipes away the whole of culture as if it were only a tissue of cobwebs around social reality and not that reality itself. He is guilty, and to the highest degree, of the fallacy of *pars pro toto*, of applying his scientific (one might almost say: zoological) method beyond its proper sphere. It is clear that he need not, and indeed cannot, find relativity anywhere, for he refuses to take seriously the realm in which that relativity resides, the realm of culture. The cynicism of Pareto and the earnestness of Max Weber both come to nothing because both, by dint of a trick, by turning a blind eye, fail to face the problem of the coexistence of truths.

Pars pro toto will do as little here as it will anywhere else. As we have conceded, formal propositions and physical observations are not reducible to social and cultural phenomena and hence are free from relativity; it is nonsense to speak of historical relativity in mathematics and mechanics. But it is just as nonsensical to say that all cultures are the same and as identical in content as numerical equations or scientific laws. Every society has its own culture which certainly arises upon a natural—physical, biological, zoological, genetic—substructure and is is some degree dependent on it, but which is nevertheless essentially unique, an historical *individuum*, a law unto itself. The Chinese of 1850 were to all intents and purposes the same in body, in flesh and blood, as the Chinese of 1950—yet how vast the change of culture that has occurred! In vain will a Pareto seek to argue such changes away: the facts will rise up against him and demand their due. It is simply impossible to reduce *all* knowledge, even historical and sociological, to scientific knowledge. The point cannot be argued here, nor need it be, since, apart from a few diehard rationalists and odd surviving encyclopaedists, it is now generally admitted that there is an essential and irreducible difference between the 'nomothetic' (or scientific properly so called) and the 'idiographic' (or cultural) disciplines. Pareto was really such an eighteenth-century rationalist and encyclopaedist who, by a freak of fate, had blundered into the twentieth century. Such a throw-back can teach us little. It is not by a sleight of hand *à la* Pareto— by the disregarding of human culture, by the denial of man's humanity, by pan-scientism—that we can hope to solve the difficult problem of the coexistence of cultural systems, of the coexistence of truths.

One last attempt to deal—unavailingly—with this problem must be mentioned before we turn from the negative to the positive, from the ways in which it cannot be solved to a way in which, perhaps, it can be. It is most prominently displayed in Ernst Grünwald's book *Das Problem der Soziologie des Wissens* (1934).[1] Reduced to its smallest

[1] Cf. esp. 12 *seq.*, 102 *seq.* and the last chapter. Cf. also Kecskemeti in Mannheim's *Essays on the Sociology of Knowledge*, 1952, 27 *seq.*, and Mannheim *ibid.*, 137 *seq.*, 142 *seq.*, 163 *seq.* (footnote 1). It is to be feared that Mannheim's attempt to break the *circulus vitiosus* has made matters worse for him, not better. For if he says that

The Consequences of the Sociology of Knowledge

compass, Grünwald's argument can be expressed in a simple syllogism: according to the sociology of knowledge, no proposition concerning social reality is true in the absolute sense of the word; but this assertion is itself a proposition concerning social reality; hence it is not true in the absolute sense of the word; hence it destroys its own validity; hence it is false; hence, finally, propositions concerning social reality *are* true in the absolute sense of the word. 'No long investigation is necessary to demonstrate that this variety of sociologism is a form of scepticism and therefore invalidates itself. For the thesis that all thinking is existentially determined and therefore cannot claim to be [unconditionally] true, claims itself to be [unconditionally] true' (229). This argument (in spite of the fact that it is modelled on Plato's refutation of the sceptic Protagoras in the *Theaetetus*) is no more than an example of sophistry, of the abuse of logical forms for illogical ends: it is certainly not an argument that need be taken seriously. Yet it is worth examining for, with all its absurdity, it may yet be made to yield a piece of the truth.

Where is the weak link in Grünwald's syllogism? Manifestly it is in the minor. 'The assertion that no proposition concerning social reality is true in the absolute sense of the word, is itself a proposition concerning social reality.' It is *not* if by 'social reality' we mean—as we must mean, if the whole deduction is to make sense—the essentially limited, the transient, the time- and place-bound, in a word, the relative. The assertion that no proposition concerning social reality is true in the absolute sense of the word may (within definite limits which are not to the purpose here) be shown to be itself an *absolute* truth because it has its roots, not in the shifting configurations of inter-human relationships, which determine, and must determine, the content of propositions concerning social reality,[1] but in an abiding, nay absolute characteristic of man as such, namely the basic fact that—whatever the circumstances —he can only constitute a mental universe for himself by crystallizing his ideas, by narrowing his mind down from the potentially knowable which is far beyond his capacity, to some limited aspect concretely

'absolute certainty' comes in every epoch from life, from vital experience, not from thought, and that consequently an argument such as Grünwald's is unavailing because it deals with a pseudo-problem which appears only where thought is illicitly considered in abstraction from life, and then adds that every epoch finds assurance in another department of life, in another vital experience (one in ecstasy, another in economics, and so on), he only shifts the *locus* of relativity, but does not remove it. Cf. also Lieber, *Wissen und Gesellschaft*, 1952, 20, 114 *seq.*, and von Schelting, *Max Webers Wissenschaftslehre*, 1934, 76 *seq.*, 99 *seq.*

[1] Cf. what von Martin has to say about the 'Sociology of Sociology', *Geist und Gesellschaft*, 1952, 229 *seq.* Some examples of the *pars pro toto* fallacy among sociologists are given by Ziegenfuss, in his *Gesellschaftsphilosophie*, 1954, 13, 22 *seq.*, 26, 66 *seq.*

known, to some specific world-view which is not absolute (i.e. not acceptable at all times and places) because other human groupings have picked out of the knowable other facts and features and shaped their house of learning from other materials than he. In other words, the relativity of social knowledge is a consequence of, and points back to, an absolute trait of man, a trait which belongs to him at all times and places and thus escapes the coils of relativity.

The whole analysis which we have presented in our third chapter is concerned, not so much with a relative ('world-view') as with an absolute ('man'): it belongs, if one cares to express it in this fashion, to what Kant would have called philosophical anthropology rather than to inductive-descriptive or even analytical sociology. Now this insight opens up a more promising way out of the impasse created by the coexistence of apparently irreconcilable truths than any of the others we have studied: pan-formalism, pan-historicism, pan-scientism; it is a way out fully in line with the theoretical position which we have upheld throughout this book. The solution of the problem of relativity must lie in the development of a comprehensive doctrine of man built up from a knowledge of all human phenomena wherever they are found—a doctrine of man which will reduce diversity to unity, as the diversity of the spectral colours is reducible to the unity of a common light.

(c) THE SOLUTION OF THE PROBLEM OF RELATIVITY: A SYNOPTIC DOCTRINE OF MAN

The main difference between the three attitudes which we have tested and found wanting, and the approach we are recommending in their stead, consists in this, that pan-formalism, pan-historicism and pan-scientism, all three propose, in their various ways, an instantaneous and as it were *a priori* 'solution' to the problem of relativity, whereas our own way is bound to be a long and laborious one. 'To the absolute through the relative' is our device, and in our conviction there is no other avenue which will lead to the desired destination. We conceive the philosophical anthropology which will reconcile and so to speak roof over the mutually alien worlds of ideas which the history of our race has engendered to be attainable empirically and inductively from observation and experience, not speculatively and by means of an *a priori* fiat. The absolute is recognizable, so we believe, in, through and under the relative. We see it every time we perceive something that is not absolute. It is the great error of pan-formalism and pan-scientism to assume that experience yields us the absolute unmixed with the relative; it is the corresponding counter-error of pan-historicism to assert that experience shows us the relative unmixed with the absolute. In fact and in truth, observation gives us knowledge that is essentially relative and absolute at the same time, and the main task of scholarship—a scholarship which is not pure fact-finding, but also aware of ultimate philosophical problems—consists precisely in the separation of the absolute from the relative, of the more than phenomenal from the no more than phenomenal. The absolute is for us, in other words, the common factor in the relative. Our procedure must be that of the mathematician in face of a series of expressions in which a common factor occurs: he extracts the common factor and sets it in front of a pair of brackets, within which the elements of irreducible diversity stand collected. This operation (akin to what in philosophy is known as the phenomenological method) seems to us the only one capable of leading beyond the historical manifold without doing violence to it.

We are calling, then, as the proper answer to the challenge of relativism, for a philosophical anthropology which would be a kind of second-order knowledge,[1] knowledge gained by a processing of the first hand knowledge provided by direct inductive research. We are calling for what Schumpeter (though in a very different spirit) refers to as a metasociology:[2] a metasociology which would be, not a metaphysics, in so far as metaphysics is divorced from the empirical, but a study of man as he appears in all societies, of man *as such* as he appears in and through the various concrete manifestations which, under the impact of different inter-human relationships and historical constellations, he has assumed in the course of history. Of all the great social thinkers of this century, Alfred Vierkandt has come nearest to this search for the common human substratum behind the concrete manifold—not surprisingly, because, more than any other, he was deeply influenced by phenomenology.[3]

The body of knowledge concerning man in himself which we should like to see developed would be able to claim quasi-scientific status.[4] And here, straight away, is one important parallel between it and science properly so called: it can and must progress from partial to total knowledge, from first approximations to ever closer and more accurate ones. Many insights which it has gained in the past—for there is already a solid stock of such insights—have indeed been gained in, and by the

[1] We take this felicitous formula from Lieber's *Wissen und Gesellschaft*, 1952, 135, but in substance we are, at this point, deviating widely from him. For Lieber sees the common factor of all systems of ideas merely in a common attitude—respect for, and intentness on, the truth—whereas we go far beyond this and believe that there is a common kernel, not only in the methods of searching, but also in the results of the search, or rather of the searches. We assume the possibility of a substantive science of man *in terminis*.

[2] Cf. *History of Economic Analysis*, 1954, 120.

[3] For a brief summary of his views cf. Raymond Aron, *Die deutsche Soziologie der Gegenwart*, ed. 1953, 24 *seq.*

[4] We hesitate to call it scientific because we should prefer to reserve this term for the study of sub-human reality, of nature.

help of, ephemeral situations, but the respective insights themselves are not ephemeral; as also happens in science, where an interest or effort due to some accidental factual constellation, a war for instance, may and often does stimulate and provoke achievements which remain long after the conjunction that has given rise to them has passed away— indeed, remain for ever.

Alfred Weber's distinction of man in culture and man in civilization is a case in point. Inspired by a preoccupation which can almost be called a problem of the day, it has nevertheless revealed truths which can be found on, and confirmed by, every page of history. 'It has been said', writes Alexander von Schelting, 'that the differentiation between "culture" and "civilization" springs from a definite, time-bound, indeed specifically German value-attitude, and can have no claim to [general] validity because it does not bring out phenomenal or ontic differences in the objects, but only [reflects] a different mode of their subjective evaluation. It may be', he continues in counter-criticism of this argument, pressed by A. Salomon in his review of Weber's *Ideen zur Staats- und Kultursoziologie*,[1] 'that the emergence of the distinction between the two areas is bound up with a view of life which is historically, psychologically and sociologically conditioned. But the objective [and universal] validity of the findings in question is totally independent of the sources of that emergence in valuations and emotions.' [2]

Another instructive example is the distinction first drawn in the late eighteenth century by authors such as Adam Ferguson and John Millar between man as a social being and man as a citizen. The traditional doctrine knew only the state: it had not yet discovered what was to become known as civil society. Now the emergence of this highly important distinction was due to a contemporary and temporary political crisis. It was the opposition of the rising bourgeoisie to the decaying state of the ancien régime which induced certain writers— above all Jean Jacques Rousseau [3]—to lay emphasis, on the one hand on a common humanity of all men transcending the boundaries of totalitarian and closed territorial states, and on the other, on the social sphere within these states, independent of Leviathan, private, and as purely social, i.e. non-political, as the *humanitas* of all the children of Adam was purely human. Without this ephemeral situation, the old pan-*étatisme* would not have been overcome at the time. But the insight gained in and through that situation was anything but ephemeral. It has taught us a universal truth about man, namely that in *no* society does

[1] Cf. the periodical *Die Gesellschaft*, 1928, 367 *seq.*
[2] *Archiv für Sozialwissenschaft*, 1929, 62. Weber himself makes the same point in *Prinzipien der Geschichts-und Kultursoziologie*, 1951, 33 *seq.*
[3] Cf. Löwith, *Von Hegel zu Nietzsche*, ed. 1953, 255.

the *citoyen* (as Rousseau defines him) totally coincide with the *homme*, just as the state never totally coincides anywhere with society as such.

It does not in any way reduce or undermine the absolute validity of this insight that the historical circumstances which evoked it also gave rise to many associated—and indeed kindred—ideas which were clearly time-bound and transitory only, butterflies born to live a summer's day, making sense in the situation as it happened to exist then, but inapplicable to other situations. Such, for instance, was the assertion that state interference with the economic life of civil society will retard economic development, will act as a brake on progress towards a higher standard of living. This was true in 1776, when Adam Smith issued his plea in favour of *laisser faire*, because at that time there existed an active and aggressive entrepreneurial class whose hands were tied, whose wings were clipped, by an antiquated political set-up, by the pre-capitalist nature of government and administration. But there have been many junctures in history at which state interference in economic affairs has spelt advancement, not retardation, propulsion, not inhibition. To recognize how true this is we need only think of the early years of that same Mercantilism whose dying and deadening forms Adam Smith wanted to see swept into the grave. Here, then, we see relative and absolute truths in close embrace, almost indistinguishable in the literature of the age, yet for all that separable and, we think, in need of separation.

It is clear that if we want to get hold of the common human element in the absolute sense of the word, we must discover and extract it from *all* cultures without exception. Only a truly ecumenical knowledge can yield up the truly ecumenical. That such all-inclusive searching and testing presents the very greatest difficulties; that, in particular, it pre-supposes—what is hard to obtain—a purposive co-operative effort of many specialists, need scarcely be emphasized; yet, though difficult to achieve, it is not impossible. Now this is where radical relativism disagrees. Writing of Ernst Troeltsch, Carlo Antoni has reported that 'according to his opinion, historical knowledge must remain restricted to the area of one's own cultural circle, hence, for us, to occidental culture: all else remains outside because we can understand a totality only in so far as we are capable of feeling its value and significance. We can, he says, grasp only what is already contained in us as a constitutive part of our being, and in so far as the Orient, for example, does not enter into our mental composition, we shall never be able to comprehend it.' [1]

This self-restriction represents a quite unnecessary defeatism; it is in fact entirely gratuitous. We are all of us capable of feeling the value and grasping the significance of *any* human phenomenon for the simple and sufficient reason that it is human. It is true, of course, that the positive

[1] *Vom Historismus zur Soziologie*, 1952, 113.

or material content of the eastern cultures does not enter our mind in the same way as that of western culture, perhaps even that it does not enter it at all. But this does not mean that the cultures concerned must for ever remain to us a book with seven seals.

At this point we must observe a very important distinction, which the radical relativists have failed to draw—the distinction between human mentality *in esse* and *in posse*. It follows from our theory of social determination as set forth in the third chapter of this book. By living within a certain concrete society, our mind is attuned to that society's cultural tradition: it is narrowed down from an almost unlimited potentiality to a very definite and limited actuality. Few of us ever stir out of that actuality—there is no call to do so, as far as the average man is concerned. But that we do, as a rule, remain within it, does not signify that we must. It is no prison-house that holds us fast; it is rather a homestead which we do not choose to leave because we feel it to be our very own. Beyond the mentality which, and into which, we have developed, there always remain the wider possibilities which we have discarded, or been made to abandon. Behind the filled mentalities (plural) *in esse*, there remains the unfulfilled mentality (singular) *in posse*. Oriental culture is contained in it as one concrete possibility of actualization, one of the many mental modalities into which *any* human mind *can* be shaped, as much as into any other. Unless we assume,— what we decidedly reject as both unreasonable and unrealistic—that the specific crystallization undergone by our mind in the course of social living totally destroys its initial elasticity, there is no reason why cultures originally alien to us should not be conquered and made to yield their secrets. Surely, it is a common experience of scholars that even totally remote civilizations may come to be as familiar to them as their own: all that is needed is the establishment of a truly vital contact with them, which certainly is not easy to achieve, but about which there is no insuperable or peremptory difficulty either. It is the very impact of those civilizations on us which makes us capable of appreciating them.

Perhaps it is true, as Troeltsch opines, that 'we can grasp only what is already contained in us as a constitutive part of our being'; one violin will only sing in sympathy with another and produce the same tone if it has the self-same strings; but what *becomes* a constitutive part of our being stands on a level with what is already contained in it, and thus proves in the end as potent a mediator of true and sound knowledge.[1]

[1] Cf. my paper 'Towards a Theory of Social Knowledge' in the *Revue Internationale de Philosophie*, 1950. Brief but convincing statements of the case against excessive relativism *à la* Troeltsch occur also in the following works: Sprott, *Science and Social Action*, 1954, 142 *seq.*; Grünwald, *Das Problem der Soziologie des Wissens* 1934, 250 *seq.* (note 61), cf. also 179 *seq.*; Geiger, *Ideologie und Wahrheit*, 1953, 151. All three passages would well deserve quotation *in extenso*.

Great play is made in this context by some of the pan-relativists with the contrast between the fundamental categories of thinking which, they say, are observable in different societies. (Durkheim's *Formes Elémentaires de la Vie Religieuse* spring to mind at once, but so do various passages from Karl Mannheim.) The necessary implication, if not the direct assertion, is often to the effect that we cannot hope to understand the mentality of other societies because even space and time (not to speak of causality, etc.) are different to them from what they are to us; and since these categories are basic to all experience, their whole mental universe must needs be, and remain, mysterious to us. We, rationalists that we are, think of space and time in terms of quantity: in terms of the measuring-rod and the time-piece. The primitives, on the other hand, the pre-logical tribesmen, conceive of space and time in terms of quality. Two places are distinct from each other, not because they are so many miles apart, but because one is sacred and the other is profane; two periods are distinct from each other, not because so many hours lie between them, but because one is filled by religious exaltation, whereas the other holds nothing but everyday drabness.

Far be it from us to deny or even to depreciate the content of truth in these observations. Even in our own society the Catholic thinks of his place of worship as something set apart, essentially unlike other buildings (*domus Dei, porta coeli*), while to the Protestant the chapel or meeting-house has no metaphysical meaning, as distinct from its quality as a physical location. But these differences in the categories of thought do not destroy the unity of the human kind; and in particular, they do not preclude the mutual understanding of even distant cultures. In our largely quantitative categorial system, there is a definite element of the qualitative: world war II does not mean to me only the years 1939–1945, it also means fear, hope, triumph; home does not mean to me only a pin-point on the map, it also means belonging, contentment, and happiness. And in the largely quality-centred categorial system of the primitive there is—we should almost be inclined to say necessarily— a decisive element of the quantitative. Though he may distinguish in his mind between the cultic places and the rest of his spatial world primarily by the fact that they carry a different emotional emphasis, a different metaphysical index as it were, he also knows full well that they lie so many paces distant from the village square, and the same applies, *mutatis mutandis*, to sacred and secular stretches of time. Thus there is no unscalable wall between the primitive and the modern mind; there is only a dividing line which can be overstepped.

But we have even more immediate and convincing proof of the fact that the actualities of a society do not necessarily blot out all alternative possibilities. Indeed, we have sometimes tangible, even physical proof of it. When the axiological system undergoes a radical change, some of the old structures may survive, even though they fail, or refuse, to come to terms with the prevailing new values. An impressive example of this is the Roman Catholic Church. Though modernized to some extent by such individual reformers as St. Ignatius Loyola and such reforming assemblies as the Council of Trent, she has never really become modern. For this reason those who have been the battering rams and the standard bearers of modern values—the Encyclopaedists of all generations—were convinced that both the mental modes and the institutional body of Roman Catholicism would disappear within a few years. And, indeed, if the axiological system of capitalist society, with its rationality, scientism and all the rest at the heart of it, had ever managed completely to dominate the world, this expectation would have come true. In Coketown, as depicted by Charles Dickens in his *Hard Times* (a skit on the world the calculators desired to create)—in the midst of people educated by, and modelled on, Mr. McChoakumchild and Mr. Bitzer —Roman Catholicism could not have existed. But new values, however much they may overshadow the old ones, never kill them, because the old values, being human and answering to *some* aspect of the creature man, are in a sense eternal. That is why the prophecies of the Encyclopaedists with regard to '*l'infame*' did not come true, and why (sociologically speaking) the Church of Rome has proved indestructible.

In order to give concreteness to this argument, let us mention merely one point of detail: the development of Catholic ritual (and its associated ways of thought) in the direction of symbolism, a direct result of the high ranking of aesthetic values in medieval, Renaissance and Counter-Reformation society. As soon as the modern order of values asserts itself, with its emphasis—its over-emphasis—on soberness, exactitude, absolute clarity, etc., this symbolism becomes increasingly something of an alien body in the totality of culture. Characteristically, it is treated with complete incomprehension, if not hate, not only by atheists, but also by Protestants: the Mass becomes hocus-pocus, a theatrical performance, a kind of sacred dance, as if it were impossible to show forth truths with the help of symbols, as if pulpit oratory were the only method by which religious ideas could be imparted, religious sentiments evoked. But symbolism is one of the main avenues along which human thinking and feeling can move; beauty is one of the prime values which no society can give up entirely, however far out towards the margin it may push it. Catholicism could not be dislodged from its position of power in the world because such values, which are central to its axiological system, can never be completely abandoned and abolished. It is interesting to observe how those who, in opposition to their age, have ascribed a high dignity and value to beauty, have fallen under the spell of Rome: John Ruskin and Oscar Wilde are two examples out of many.

All this goes to prove the possibility of a comprehensive science of man which will show that all the diversities of human nature *in esse* are merely divergent manifestations of a common human nature *in posse*, and will thereby lay the ghost of relativism for ever without denying the width and depth of the differences between different societies and cultures. 'Even historicism', so our basic conviction has been well expressed by another writer, 'has to admit one absolute after all, viz., the marvellously adaptable human mind itself.' [1] It is a substantive and synoptic study of it which we need if we are to escape from the cul-de-sac into which relativism has manœuvred us.

We think of this science of man, this inductive and realistic comprehensive anthropology, as a task of the future. But the past has already provided some essential ingredients for it—indeed, perhaps the first outline of it. [2] For such a science must needs start from what can be called the human situation, the human condition, the human predicament, and of this no generation can be totally unaware. Man, as Max Weber has so lucidly explained, finds himself on this globe faced with a glaring discrepancy between his needs and the means of satisfying them; he must fight nature if he is to survive; but he is too weak to do so with any hope of success so long as he is alone; hence the necessity, not only of economic action, but also of social life. But, so we may continue, social life is impossible without norms of coexistence and the means of enforcing them: individual discipline and social control are alike universal necessities. From them, in turn, spring education and law, both fields of far-reaching human, in the sense of universally human, content. However great the divergencies from society to society, the basic compulsion being everywhere substantially the same, so too will be the solutions attempted, experimented with and retained.

These are some of the basic substructural facts present in every society, but there are parallel superstructural elements also. Since man has a mind which craves satisfaction almost as avidly as his body, there is a universal necessity for some philosophy of life. Men cannot exist like cows, they must live in an intelligible universe. Certainly, the concrete forms of their philosophies of life are vastly distant from each other, but since it is the same questions that are asked, the different answers must at least be comparable. Max Weber does well to emphasize that the presence of suffering in all societies constitutes a red thread pervading all of them and providing a common element in all human history. And he also shows, in some of his most splendid

---

[1] Hodges in *Wilhelm Dilthey: An Introduction*, 1944, 33.
[2] One of the first who attempted to move in the direction of an empirical general science of man, as distinct from a merely speculative doctrine of natural law and human rights, was Montesquieu. Cf. Durkheim, *Montesquieu et Rousseau, Précurseurs de la Sociologie*, ed. 1953, 49, 53 *seq.*

passages, that all men without exception are confronted with the self-same excruciatingly difficult choice—the choice between *Gesinnungs -ethik* and *Verantwortungsethik*. Either they can act according to principle, disregarding the consequences—*fiat justitia, pereat mundus* (Kant)—or they can act for the sake of some concrete end or aim, in which case principle will have to be thrown to the winds (Machiavelli, Bentham). This, too, is part and parcel of the common human predicament which, like a huge bracket, holds together thought-contents and thought-processes of amazing variety.

Let us add, what is important for the sociologist of knowledge, that there is also a universally observable link between the substructure and the superstructure. In all societies men's modes of thought have at least a tendency to come into line with their modes of action. Man, wherever he is, seems to have a spontaneous urge towards over-all consistency. In opposition to Grünwald's sophistical argument pilloried above, the basic assertion of the sociology of knowledge is an *absolutum* in the truest sense of the word.

It is from facts such as these that a supra-historical doctrine of man, as such, would have to start. Its results cannot be anticipated. The great Baconian principle of scientific work—let us go and see—must apply here as everywhere else. Once again it must be said that we can only reach the absolute (the universally human) by laboriously working through the relative (the human in its historical specification). But it is hardly extravagant to assert that the barns of our proposed science will not remain altogether empty. Those of us who are inclined to believe that great art also has a message for scholarship will be impressed by the degree to which artistic work has been able, throughout the ages, to embody and show forth what is common to all humanity. Shakespeare, Molière and Cervantes, Mozart and Beethoven, Rembrandt and Daumier, in fact all artists of world-historical importance, have been products of their age and country, but they have also been more than that. Has there ever been a society without a Don Giovanni or a Don Quixote, a Papageno or a Sancho Panza? Are these not universal human types, differently attired only, differently embellished? [1]

Of course, scholarship must work by scholarly methods, not by vision or intuition. It must humbly follow the lead of the facts. It must work with concrete and well-defined hypotheses and either accept or reject, validate or invalidate them, according to the findings of its realistic research. The literature of the social sciences contains many assertions which could fulfil the office of such hypotheses and lead, if tested and confirmed, to insights of far-reaching importance. For instance: communities tend towards an organological, societies of the associational

[1] Cf. Alfred Weber, *Farewell to European History*, Engl. ed., 1947, esp. 17 *seq.*, 28 *seq.*, 75 *seq.*, 86.

type towards an atomistic and mechanistic philosophy (Tönnies); static societies tend to regard science (in the widest sense of the word) as a closed corpus of truths, incapable of addition or subtraction, which can be expounded and explained by the commentator but not materially increased; dynamical societies tend to assume an open frontier for science beyond which the search for new insights can and should go on all the time (Plessner); upper classes and conservative parties tend to assume that man is born bad, with a depraved nature, lower classes and revolutionary parties are inclined to believe that he is born reasonable, sociable, good and noble (Mannheim); conservative societies, classes or parties find it convenient to uphold 'safe multiple-factor views as to historical causation', while 'revolutionary manipulation calls for belief in a monistic cause' (Mills); [1] 'a system of supermundanely sanctified rights and duties' such as is likely to be preached by dominant strata, will evoke 'beefsteak philosophies', i.e. utilitarian or hedonistic tendencies and arguments, on the part of the corresponding subject strata (Schumpeter); [2] urban societies composed of artisans who know from their work what it is to give form to matter, to shape it according to a pre-conceived idea, tend to develop comparatively rational religions, in which the deity is regarded as primarily the maker and moulder of the material world; rural societies composed of peasants are driven, by the uncertainties of agricultural production, towards comparatively irrational religions in which the higher powers are thought of as open to influence by magical or superstitious practices (Max Weber); 'rhythms of cultural creativity (renascences, for instance) follow a law of generation. . . . They are essentially youth movements. They become effective when a new structure of drives is developed, when the individual is released from the existing cultural inhibitions and norms' (Scheler); [3] cultural efflorescences appear whenever and wherever a society succeeds in freeing itself from a natural anxiety, from the fear inspired by the forces of nature, and man assumes a 'Promethean' attitude (Alfred Weber); 'the principle of allegorical interpretation' is 'necessary in a civilization whose intelligence and moral standards are at odds with its sacred writings' (Dilthey); [4] whenever the social bond loosens, the classes, especially the higher ones, tend to create a literature reflecting upon, and seeking to justify, their existence (von Martin); ages of crisis tend to re-interpret the whole of history, ages of stability prefer to work at the detail of historical knowledge (Sorokin); and so on, and so forth. A long list this, but it could easily be further extended. Indeed, a conscientious collection of all the assertions of this kind

---

[1] *The American Journal of Sociology*, 1940/1, 330.
[2] *History of Economic Analysis*, 1954, 131.
[3] Becker and Dahlke, *Philosophy and Phenomenological Research*, 1941/2, 313.
[4] Cf. Hodges, *Wilhelm Dilthey: An Introduction*, 1944, 25 *seq.*

contained in the works of even the classical sociologists would probably fill a whole book. As suggestions born of a momentary impression, they are no more than interesting; as proven facts of universal application, they would be nothing less than invaluable.

A body of knowledge gained by the systematic testing of such hypotheses would establish the relations which tend to exist between certain substructures and certain superstructural forms, ideas and sentiments. It would develop, ideally, into a general typology connecting types of society with associated types of thought and feeling. It would break through the constraining cordon which the relativists have built up, to the absolute, in the sense of the universally human, without for one moment becoming guilty of the crime of 'empty generalization'. Though rising far above historicism, it would none the less lie in the direction which historicist thought has increasingly tended to explore. Has not the thought of the greatest of all historicists, Wilhelm Dilthey, ended in the formulation of three basic types of *Weltanschauung*? [1] And has not even Ernst Troeltsch pressed forward towards the same kind of conceptualization? [2] As Carlo Antoni has shown,[3] typological thought has waxed in recent years, in the measure in which radical relativism has waned, and today it is very strong even in the country where historicism was uppermost as nowhere else, in Germany, as can be illustrated from the work of such recent writers as Jaspers, Spranger, Otto, Worringer, Klages and Wölfflin.

The general typology which we have in mind (and which would be essentially a development of, though at the same time an advance beyond, the final point reached by Max Weber [4]) would acquaint us with the various axiological vantage-points from which the concrete societies encountered in history have looked out upon the realm of facts, the realm of the materials of knowledge. It would tell us why they have made certain aspects of the real their prime concern and bypassed others, why they constituted their object of knowledge in the way they did. But our science of the second order, our metasociology, our suprahistorical doctrine of man would have to deal with the *results* of man's search for knowledge as well as with the different *directions* which it has

[1] Cf. my introduction to Friedrich Meinecke, *Machiavellism*, Engl. ed., 1957. Cf. also Hodges, *loc. cit.*, 99 *seq.*, 152 *seq.*, and Antoni, *Vom Historismus zur Soziologie*, 1952, 20 *seq.*, 26, 31 *seq.*, and especially 43 *seq.*

[2] Cf. Antoni, *loc. cit.*, 76 *seq.*

[3] *Loc. cit.*, 283. Antoni might also have mentioned the tendency evinced by a few recent historians, for instance Breysig and Eduard Meyer, to generalize certain historical concepts, to speak, for instance, of a 'Middle Ages of Antiquity' or of a 'Greek enlightenment'. Cf. Meinecke, *Die Entstehung des Historismus*, ed. 1946, 428, and von Martin, *Geist und Gesellschaft*, 1948, 16 *seq.*

[4] Cf. von Martin, *Geist und Gesellschaft*, 1948, 227, and von Schelting, *Max Webers Wissenschaftslehre*, 1934, 339 *seq.*

taken. It would have to *co-ordinate* these results. It would have to be what the Middle Ages called a *concordantia discordantium canonum*.

It goes without saying that according to our whole theory of the sociology of knowledge such a co-ordination is possible. If we wish to know the full outline of Mont Blanc, we must photograph it from all points of the compass and then co-ordinate the individual pictures so obtained. Of course, if we happen to live, or would like to live, in Chamonix, we shall be inclined to pay more attention to the northern aspects and slopes than if we find ourselves in, or for some reason prefer, the villages on the south side. But this is not at all necessary. It is the natural vice of naïveté to mistake the face which the world turns towards us for the world itself. It is the corresponding opposite virtue of the philosophical mind to realize that human beings can only grasp one facet of reality at a time and that the full knowledge of it is reserved to Almighty God.

The systematic co-ordination of the elements of fact and truth contained in the discordant aspectual world-views will require a method which cannot be laid down beforehand but must be found and perfected as the work proceeds. Yet it is permissible even now to suggest that such a method might find it appropriate to operate in two stages. The first step would be to see whether apparently irreconcilable assertions about the same reality are not in fact assertions about different realities. An example would be that of the conflict between the medieval and modern conceptions of the market price. The nineteenth century economists derided the Schoolmen because they thought that the price was given before supply and demand had so much as established contact, let alone found an equilibrium; the price was 'always', they said, and 'necessarily', the outcome of the higgling of the market, 'never' its pre-existent norm. In a way this is true, and even an absolute truth. But the medieval conception was also within its rights. For in so far as a price manages to assume the character of a piece of custom, to establish itself within the system of customary law by which a community lives, it is in fact relatively independent of supply and demand, which must then fall into line with *it*, rather than *vice versa*. The difference between St. Thomas and Walras was not that the one talked sense and the other nonsense, but that the one was talking of a society of the community type where norm ontologically precedes individual action, and the other of a society of the associational type where individual action precedes the norm and creates it.[1]

Much can be gained by the application of this method of discrimination. For even conflicting statements about the same phenomenon are

[1] Cf. my lecture 'The Contained Economy', published as Aquinas Paper no. 26, 1956. Cf. also my *History of Economics in its Relation to Social Development*, *passim*.

often capable of co-ordination in the manner suggested. Nineteenth century historical scholarship presented, in successive periods, widely different pictures of the same man—Napoleon. Some were seen with the eye of love and lovingly collected all that showed him in a positive light; others with the eye of hate and assiduously brought together all that showed his weaknesses and his vanities; others again envisaged the Corsican from yet other points of view. All, we must assume, were prepared to accept the facts as they found them; hence all had hold of part of the truth; but the truth in its entirety escaped them all because they had each limited themselves to a specific line of vision. The truth—the whole truth, which is the only real truth,—can only be revealed to him who gives no more weight to one partial view than to another, and who knows how to reconcile them on a higher plane—a feat much more difficult to achieve in practice than a purely theoretical formulation would ever lead one to suspect.

For we are all wedded to our own values, which are the values which control our life in all its implications, and we are reluctant, nay loath, to acknowledge other gods by the side of them. But that precisely is the burden of scholarship: to rise superior to human limitations, to see more of being than can be discovered through a key-hole, indeed, to find the Archimedean point from which the world may be viewed in all its manifoldness, in all its wealth of feature and aspect. 'Man, bound and determined by the reality of life, is set free . . . through the understanding of history,' wrote Dilthey.[1] This is a profound saying. But there are few disciplines which can contribute more to that understanding, and hence to the liberation of man's mind and soul from the trammels of the *hic* and *nunc* than the sociology of knowledge. That is why we have claimed that its greatest difficulty—the problem of the coexistence of truths, the problem of relativity—may, rightly handled, be turned into its greatest strength and glory.

The strategy of systematic discrimination and subsequent co-ordination which we have recommended has, of course, like all things human, its specific limitations. It must not be allowed to degenerate into an empty scholasticism which would remove disagreements simply by hair-splitting distinctions and a clever definitional casuistry.[2] The fact has to be faced that there are hard and fast clashes of conviction between different cultures, whether they be inclusive societies or classes or confessional groupings, which cannot be resolved in this manner because they concern the very same aspects of reality. In such cases we are simply up against what is to us, at the time, the frontier of knowability. But this frontier is never final. The probing into the regions beyond can

---

[1] *Cit.* Hodges, *Wilhelm Dilthey: An Introduction*, 1944, 32.

[2] For an example of how even a realistic typology may become set, schematic, lifeless, cf. Antoni, *Vom Historismus zur Soziologie*, 1952, 90 *seq.*

and must go on, and it, too, can be helped by the sociology of knowledge.

Where apparently irreducible disagreements are encountered, there, the sociology of knowledge would suggest, an inter-cultural discrimination and co-ordination of research methods remains possible, even though an inter-cultural discrimination and co-ordination of the results of the search is no longer feasible. For any and every culture suffers as much from a limitation of research methods as it does from that of the field of vision. Indeed, it is here that the besetting sin of arguing *supra crepidam*, which we have exposed in this book, can be seen most clearly. Our modern society has greatly advanced human knowledge by systematically developing and applying the rational methods of science. That is why it has been so successful in some fields. But in other fields the same techniques have proved unavailing. And this is not surprising, for not only is a society indifferent to the observation of what carries no value in its life; it is also unwilling, for the same reason, to develop the necessary and appropriate ways of looking for it. Modern man, panscientist that he is, has often been helpless and hopeless in his half-hearted efforts outside the confines of science. He has tried to investigate by scientific means what is not, in common sense, amenable to scientific investigation. You cannot put the human psyche under the microscope, nor yet can you scan God through the apparatus of radio-astronomy. The last centuries have sadly neglected, for instance, the methods of sympathy and empathy as well as the methods of mystical experience and metaphysical speculation. In these respects modern man can still learn a good deal from other kinds of man, if only he will be great and generous enough to go to school with him, which he should not, of course, be reluctant to do.

This discrimination and co-ordination of research methods should be the second step in the effort to escape the impasse of cultural relativity and limitation, as the discrimination and co-ordination of results should be the first. Man being what he is, it is even more of a counsel of perfection than the other. But even if it should succeed, and succeed splendidly, a last limitation would remain for the cultural sciences. So long as history continues, their material can never be complete. History is the self-revelation of man, and the longer it lasts, the more facets of his essence does he reveal. 'The world is still too young to fix many general truths in politics', Hume has written in his essay 'Of Civil Liberty'.[1] 'We have not as yet had experience of three thousand years; so that . . . we want sufficient materials upon which we can reason. It is not fully known, what degree of refinement, either in virtue or vice, human nature is susceptible of; nor what may be expected of mankind from any great revolution in their education, customs, or principles.'

[1] Beginning.

With every hour that passes, human relationships undergo new evolutions and revolutions, and with them arise new phenomena which clamour for admission into the canon of the comprehensive science of man, into metasociology, and which must be admitted if it is to be complete. We spoke a moment ago of an Archimedean point which scholarship must occupy in order to be able to see the whole. That was, it must be admitted, hyperbolical language. The true Archimedean point would lie beyond the end of history, beyond the last day. It cannot be reached by us, however much we stretch and strain. Thus our knowledge, however greatly we may extend it, will for ever remain fragmentary. This is part and parcel of our fate. Is it a hard fate? Surely not, for to pursue knowledge is even more glorious than to possess it. 'If God held in his right hand all the truth,' writes Lessing,[1] 'and in his left hand the ever-active longing for the truth . . . and said to me: choose, humbly should I grasp his left hand and cry: give me this, O Father! the Truth Itself is only for you alone.'

[1] *Sämtliche Werke*, ed. Lachmann, XIII (1897), 24.

PART TWO
THE PROBLEMS OF THE
SOCIOLOGY OF KNOWLEDGE

CHAPTER FIVE

PROBLEM A: THE BASIS OF SOCIAL DETERMINATION

(a) INTRINSIC AND EXTRINSIC STUDY OF THE HISTORY OF IDEAS

EVERY thought and theory formulated in the past, every phenomenon and phase in the development of the human spirit, can be
studied in a double way: either as an incident in the history of
ideas, or as an element in the wider history of the human kind. In the
former case, the main question to be asked by the historian will concern
the content of the thoughts and theories in question, and his prime task
will be to comprehend and to evaluate these contents. If he goes beyond
them at all, he will either go backwards towards the intellectual antecedents of the ideas he studies, or forward towards their intellectual
consequences: but if he has made this particular mode of approach his
own he will always remain on the same plane of being, on the intellectual
level, the level of ideas. For this reason it has become customary to
characterize this method of writing the history of ideas as its treatment
ab intra, as its intrinsic study (*Innenbetrachtung*, as the Germans have
it). This must be distinguished from the other approach—the writing of
the history of ideas *ab extra*, its extrinsic study (*Aussenbetrachtung*).
Here it is not so much the content of a thought or theory on which the
student concentrates as its relationship to the wider setting within which
it has been conceived and born. An idea is not only considered as such,
in and for itself, but also as the possible manifestation of wider tendencies, forces or facts, as an expression of realities which lie behind it.
In a word, here there is no remaining within the sphere of being called
the intellectual life, but a going beyond and beneath and outside it.
Hence the name this approach has been given, the label it has received.

'There are two mutually exclusive ways of interpreting ideas,' two
well-informed writers have recently explained, 'intrinsically and extrinsi-
cally. An intrinsic interpretation is that in which a given product of
"mind" is handled as though its significance in form and content lies
entirely within itself. Thus, for example, Kant's *Critique of Practical*

213

Reason could be interpreted exclusively in terms of the logical inter-relation of its parts; thus understanding it as the author himself would presumably have it understood. Contrariwise, extrinsic interpretation is that in which a set of ideas is referred beyond itself. Placed in a context it is relativized in such a way that the context exercises deter-minative power. Instance: Kant . . . grew up in Königsberg when kingly absolutism was the order of the day—ergo, the culminating formula of the *Critique of Practical Reason*, viz. the categorical im-perative, is a mere derivative of . . . a sense of duty pounded in by school, community and professional life.' [1] There is no point in staying to inquire whether the particular derivation suggested in this passage is reasonable or realistic: the essential thing to be grasped is that for the second approach to the history of ideas a search for the extra-mental sources is as characteristic as its absence is characteristic of the first.

The authors call these two ways of interpreting ideas 'mutually exclusive', but they rightly emphasize on the same page that they are at the same time mutually complementary. 'Any so-called intrinsic interpretation is framed within a large number of implicitly accepted and unanalysed extrinsic items; any extrinsic interpretation presupposes the understanding of the idea-system as set forth by its originator.' Sometimes, indeed, the two modes of approach have been felt to clash. C. S. Lewis, for instance, has argued that the more we know about a poet, the expression of whose personality a poem is supposed to be, the less shall we be able to achieve a full aesthetic appreciation of the poem as such. The steadily increasing rôle of biography in literary studies is regretted by him for it is irrelevant, if not indeed detrimental, to the enjoyment of literature: 'When we read poetry as poetry should be read, we have before us no representation which claims to be the poet, and frequently no representation of a man, a character, or a personality at all.' [2] This remark is even truer of music than it is of poetry, and one can, to some extent, sympathize with the sentiment expressed in it. Analysis, derivation, explanation have ever had something deflating, even destructive, about them. But scholarship cannot do without them, and a total comprehension of any cultural phenomenon, even of the most abstractly aesthetic kind, demands consideration *ab extra* as well as *ab intra*. It is the privilege of the aesthete to see the rose in all its beauty and to close his eyes to the rest: the botanist must concern him-self with all its conditions of existence, with its coming-to-be as well as with its being, and he has only done his work if he has understood them both.

A total and balanced history of ideas, then, would move at the same

---

[1] Becker and Dahlke in *Philosophy and Phenomenological Research*, 1941/2, 310.
[2] 'The Personal Heresy in Criticism', *Essays and Studies by Members of the English Association*, 1934, 9.

time along both avenues, carefully keeping progress in the one in step with progress in the other. In point of fact, however, the bulk of the work in the field so far has been of the intrinsic variety—descriptive rather than explanatory. There are many reasons for this one-sidedness, but two of them tower above the rest. First of all, pure description is much easier than explanation. The content of a theory or work of art lies open before us, even if it needs *finesse* to bring it out, and we see it in the clear light of day. Not so its sources. To find them we must dig into the darkness of the subsoil, and there it is difficult to operate. Indeed, all interpretation *ab extra* is problematic, doubtful, venturesome. Nobody can deny this, and those who have rushed enthusiastically ahead, adding one facile 'derivation' to another, have had little inkling of the tremendous uncertainties in which they were unavoidably involved. But, of course, scholarship must be adventurous; it will not do for it to stick to the obvious; and difficulties are there to be confronted and conquered, not to be disregarded or by-passed. The second reason why the extrinsic and explanatory treatment of the history of ideas has made so little headway is of a less technical and more psychological nature. There is a subconscious fear that any 'explanation' of the rise of a cultural phenomenon may, indeed must, depreciate it, make it into a 'mere epiphenomenon'. What may be gained in insight, it is felt, will be lost in value. It can, of course, be argued that such inhibitions are unbecoming, indeed absurd in a scholar; that he must take the world as he finds it; that this whole sentiment confuses two levels, that of understanding and that of enjoyment; and that, after all, roses are not the less beautiful for growing well in horse-manure. But we do not need contentions of this kind in order to combat the argument under discussion (if such it can be called) against the extrinsic-explanatory treatment of ideas and their history. For this whole train of thought foolishly presupposes that consideration *ab extra* will always and necessarily make mental products into something secondary, dependent, epiphenomenal, in relation to extra-mental factors. But this is by no means so. Extra-mental factors may throw light on an act of mental creativity without in the least attaining to the spontaneity, mysteriousness and majesty of that act. So long as the approach from without is and remains a hermeneutic method and does not become a causalistic metaphysic, it will not detract one jot or tittle from the value of cultural achievements. On the contrary.

A splendid demonstration of why and how the intrinsic and the extrinsic study of intellectual developments should co-operate, is suggested by Lovejoy's *Reflections on the History of Ideas*.[1] He refers to the relationship between Locke on the one hand, Berkeley and Hume on the other, and explains that the younger philosophers brought to

---

[1] *Journal of the History of Ideas*, 1940, 21 *seq.*

light implications of Locke's premises which Locke himself had not seen. This statement manifestly belongs to the *ab intra* consideration of the history of ideas: we have before us 'a logically motivated and logically instructive sequence', a connection between minds on the purely intellectual level which it is relevant to notice and worth while to study. But, as Lovejoy emphasizes, 'extra-logical motives help to explain *why* later philosophers noticed these implications'.[1] Berkeley was a conservative man, a bishop: his development of the Lockean position 'dished the materialists completely', and thus helped to defend altar and throne. Hume, on the other hand, was a progressive man, an intellectual, none too well established in contemporary society. Where Berkeley had added new pillars to the house that was standing, Hume pulled supports away from under the structure: he took pleasure in 'horripilating the orthodox', an endeavour in which he was not altogether unsuccessful. This is a textbook example of a complete analysis of the case in miniature. There is offered to us an insight both into the facts and into the forces behind the facts, into the concatenation between ideas and into the relationship between ideas and extramental realities.

(b) TYPES OF EXTRINSIC APPROACH

The sociology of knowledge, as every reader of the present book is well aware, is essentially a method for the extrinsic interpretation of ideas. In Marxian language, it is not concerned with the superstructure as such, which it simply takes as it finds it, but with the light which the substructural facts can throw on the superstructural phenomena, with the interpretation and explanation of intellectual developments from the point of view of their concomitant and underlying social conditions. But it is not alone in the field; it has a number of important competitors, and it is necessary to see it in relation to them. We propose therefore to run briefly though systematically through the main theories concerning the extrinsic determination of ideas, and to show what place our own discipline can fairly claim to occupy in their company.

The first of these doctrines—first in our scale because it locates the mind-determining factor farthest away from the mind itself—is known as geographical determinism. What man thinks depends, in the last analysis, on his physical environment. There are not a few books on great thinkers which begin like Barckhausen's on Montesquieu (1907): 'However large and legitimate the consideration that is given to the personality of great men, one must not fail to appreciate the influence exerted upon them by the circumstances in which they are born and grow up . . . such as their native country. . . . There is no district where

[1] Our emphasis.

the climate and the soil inspire moderate sentiments more than the *Pays Bordelais* where our philosopher saw the light. The climate here is generally temperate. . . . As for the soil, it stretches in an undulating plain to the south of Bordeaux and to the west of the Garonne. . . . Nothing here deceives man about the true proportion of things, and nothing evokes in him grandiose dreams. . . . The hills, being very low, allow one to see wide horizons which take nothing, or next to nothing, from the celestial dome. It unfolds in its whole extent above the head of the spectator. . . . When the philosopher here begins to compare our poor globe with the cupola which surrounds him and dominates him from so high above, he cannot but murmur in humility: "One hears people say: Heaven and Earth; it is like saying: Heaven and naught." But if the Earth is nothing, what then can men be? It is impossible to exalt those worms. . . . Let no one look anywhere else for the origin of that irony which shows on so many pages of the *Lettres Persanes* and in certain chapters of the *Esprit des Lois*' (9 *seq.*).

We see that same principle of derivation on a much larger scale in Buckle's attempt to explain the predominance of democratic ideas in the northern parts of Europe. Dwellers in cold climes, he maintains, need a high carbon content in their food; hence they must eat animal flesh; hence they must hunt; hence they become self-reliant men who will not stand for authoritarian methods of government. It is not our task here to criticize and correct such conceptions, difficult though it may be to resist the temptation: our interest at the moment is typological, not dogmatic. In the literature of the social sciences, this geographical determinism (which we propose to call the *ecological* theory) has loomed very large. The school of Frederick Le Play has summed it up in its famous formula 'place-work-folk': place determines work; work determines the form of the family; the family determines individual character, including the character of mind, the mode of thinking; and so all culture is, in the last resort, determined by geographical circumstances. It was the rocky coast-line of Norway which forced its inhabitants to live by fishing; fishing necessitated comparative dispersal, the small family-pattern, the 'particularist' family; that family educated its children for early independence, and for self-reliance; hence it bore and bred the individualist, democratic spirit. It was on the narrow seaward ledges of Scandinavia that a mentality was formed and fostered which gave the world a whole universe of thought and feeling.[1]

A second theory which seeks the mind-determining agency somewhat nearer to man, but still finds it outside him, in his artefacts, is the *technological* doctrine. Man's thought is said to depend upon his work, his work on his techniques and tools. Of this way of seeing things,

[1] Cf. also Hegel's musings concerning Greece in Löwith, *Von Hegel zu Nietzsche*, ed. 1953, 45 *seq.*

Problem A: The Basis of Social Determination

Gordon Childe has given an illustration in his *Social Worlds of Knowledge* (1949): 'I should be prepared to argue', he writes, 'that a conception of celestial mechanics was impossible to a society that did not use and make rotary machines more elaborate and complicated than the bow-drill, the lathe, and the potter's wheel. These were the only revolving mechanisms in familiar use anywhere till after 600 B.C., when the rotary quern, the trapetum, and other devices comprising several rotating parts were invented. Is it an accident that the music of the spheres is first heard after those devices were in current use?' (12). A little later, Childe points out that so long as 'it was still persons who did the physical pushing and pulling or at best guided the almost equally personal oxen and donkeys . . . [the conception of] causality remains personal. . . . By 400 B.C. rotary mills in Athenian bakeries and revolving olive-presses on Attic farms were performing repetitive tasks that had to be done by hand in every Bronze Age household. So causality could be depersonalized . . . From the seventeenth century the leisured philosophers who have been formulating the world-view of European and American societies have been familiar with machines, operated by the impersonal forces of water, wind, steam and electricity rather than mules or human slaves. . . . Their speculation has been directed to producing a model of reality based on the machine as they see it.' Summing up, Childe asserts that the historical 'worlds of knowledge must each have been, and be, conditioned by the whole of the society's culture and particularly its technology' (22 *seq.*).

In these words we have before us a most characteristic formulation of what we have called the technological theory of the genesis of ideas. Like geographical determinism, it has played its part in the history of the social sciences. Two truly great sociologists have allowed it some influence on their thinking concerning so spiritual a sphere of culture as that of music: Lorenz von Stein in his essay 'Musik und Staatswissenschaft' [1] and Max Weber in the appendix to *Wirtschaft und Gesellschaft* entitled 'Die rationalen und soziologischen Grundlagen der Musik.'

A third doctrine concerning the extrinsic determination of mental phenomena (which tends to give the term 'determination' a much stricter definition than the others are wont to do) shifts the determining element into man himself, yet not into his personality, but into his flesh and blood. The texture of our minds is supposed to depend upon the texture of our bodies. The following quotation may well serve as an illustration of this particular approach: 'There is clear evidence of bodily weakness at various points in Kierkegaard's life. He had to work under a self-imposed and strict discipline, lest he overstrain his powers. Diet, in particular, demanded close attention. He was conscious of some maladjustment between body and mind; his intellectual nature

---

[1] Published in the periodical *Nord und Süd*, 1883.

218

threatened to disrupt the frail dwelling in which it had come to lodge. Most significant of all, on the occasion of his engagement, he went the length of seeking medical advice, only to be informed that his affliction, whatever it was, could not be cured. One cannot but think in this whole connection of some form of sexual impotence, so that it would finally be of a lack of virility that he accused himself. May this be a case in which Adler's analysis applies, and a life-long mental conflict can be traced back to some organ inferiority?' [1] Clearly, a key to Kierkegaard's philosophy is sought here in his organism, in his organic make-up. The frailty of the body is made to explain the fierceness of the mind.

This doctrine is known in philosophy as the *materialistic* theory. One classical—or perhaps we should say: extremist—formulation of it is due to Cabanis who called ideas 'a secretion of the brain', a definition which Vogt further elaborated by saying that 'ideas are related to the brain in the same way as bile is to the liver and urine to the kidneys'. [2] From this conviction it is only a short step to the assertion that thought-processes, being essentially brain-processes, are in the last resort determined by the vital processes of nutrition and digestion. For, according to the food we consume, such will be the *physis* of which mind is a manifestation, a dependent variable. One of the classical upholders of this opinion was a great nutrition expert of his day, Moleschott. Feuerbach pressed the whole theory into the terse formula: 'Man is, what he eats'. [3] Technical materialism of this or a similar complexion, sometimes rightly called physiological or even medical materialism, has been endemic in the West for at least two hundred years, though few writers have cared to give it so pungent expression as Cabanis, Feuerbach, Moleschott, or Vogt.

In this century a kindred doctrine achieved a great, if short-lived *succès de scandale* in the racial theory which dominated Germany, at least officially, from 1933 to 1945. Jews were supposed to be unable to think like Nordics, Nordics like Jews, because their respective minds dwelt in bodies of different hereditary extraction and physical quality, the basic conviction being that mental phenomena are no more than reflexes of physical ones. In the social sciences properly so called, such ideas have played a comparatively minor part, and understandably so. For the more man is conceived as a physical entity, the less can he be regarded as an essentially social being; and though there is no absolute incompatibility between medical materialism and sociology, the two are not what one would call natural neighbours or born allies and friends.

---

[1] Allen, *Kierkegaard: His Life and Thought*, 1935, 30.
[2] Cf. Lange, *Geschichte des Materialismus*, II, ed. 1875, 70, 134, 152, 288.
[3] This well-known saying occurs in Feuerbach's review of Moleschott's *Lehre der Nahrungsmittel*. Cf. his *Sämtliche Werke*, ed. Bolin and Jodel, 1903 *seq.*, X, 22.

Problem A: The Basis of Social Determination

Of far more consequence in the field of social studies has been a fourth theory which shifts the *point d'appui* from man's body into man's mind, but remains materialistic in so far as it conceives that mind as essentially a bundle of drives. A drive is not, like an instinct, unconscious; it is a tendency of the will, accompanied by an appropriate consciousness, in a certain determinate direction, and can become decisive, not only for human action, but also—as this school asserts—for human thought. We have no suitable established word to label this particular dogma, and suggest that it should be called the *hormic* theory.[1] For the hormic theory, thoughts are the workings-out of some desire, striving or conation native to man—either directly, or indirectly, resulting from the inhibition, the artificial thwarting, of the master and motor passion. The prime example that springs to mind is that of Friedrich Nietzsche. The key to everything, for him, is the Will to Power. In the strong it shows itself in its natural form, nakedly as it were, and produces the proudest of all human types, the warrior. In the weak, on the other hand, who have no hope of attaining the power which they crave, it appears in a curiously denaturalized, even perverted shape, and embodies itself in such figures as the wily demagogue or the wheedling parson. It is they who captivate the masses—necessarily so, for the many can never be shepherds and must always be sheep. In either case, for rulers and ruled alike, the ideas put forward and the feelings entertained stem from, and are explicable in the light of, the underlying native will.

Nietzsche's prime *objectum demonstrationis* is, of course, Christianity, the Christian ideology. With its insistence on the blessedness of the meek, on the value of suffering, and on the equality of all human beings, it is a typical slave philosophy. And the better part of human philosophizing has flowed from the same muddy source—the unnatural assertion of weakness against the natural claims of strength. Already in his first important work, *Die Geburt der Tragödie aus dem Geiste der Musik* (1872), Nietzsche raises these speculations to the level of an inclusive theory of culture. There is on the one hand the Dionysian culture, a heroic life of lust, conquest, ecstasy, and beauty; on the other, its Apolline counterpart, born of the weakling's longing for peace, harmony, balance and security. In the history of Greece, the abandonment of Homer and Aeschylus for Socrates and Euripides marks the victory of the Apolline over the Dionysian spirit. And behind Socrates, the perverter, there appears Plato, and, in the not too remote distance, Jesus of Nazareth; and so we receive a key to the understanding of the whole history of ideas, down to Nietzsche himself. It explains even

[1] From the Greek ὁρμή, meaning impulse, appetition. We should like to repeat here our apology, already tendered above, for the introduction of neologisms, but without a clear nomenclature, however uncouth, *distinguenda* cannot be distinguished.

220

science. Fear, Nietzsche says, 'ancient fear, at last become subtle, spiritual and intellectual—at present, methinketh, it is called Science'.[1] Is it not characteristic of Darwin to think in terms of survival rather than in terms of conquest? 'Over the whole of Darwinism, there hovers . . . something of the odour of humble people in need and in straits.'[2] Highly individual though all this is, Nietzsche yet shows us a certain type of mind at work. In Vilfredo Pareto it has found another embodiment, for the *Trattato di Sociologia Generale* is a consistent explanation of social life (and human thought) in the spirit of the hormic theory.

The leading principle of a further (fifth) mode of studying and interpreting or explaining mental phenomena can be formulated in the following way: what men think in theory, depends on the interests which are theirs in practice, the word interest here being taken in the sense of selfish interest, especially economic and power interest. A classical example is afforded by Marat's judgment on Montesquieu. Comparing his conservatism with the progressive attitude of Rousseau, Marat exclaims: 'Montesquieu possessed a great fortune in landed property; he came from a family of notables; he had a wife and children. What a lot of ties!' [3] The implication clearly is that the ties shackled the man's mind as much or more than they did his hands and feet. This doctrine, which might be called the *sympherontic* theory,[4] is capable of very wide, not to say universal application. Erich Roll, in the earlier editions of his *History of Economic Thought*, has tried to apply it consistently to his chosen field. A few quotations will show how he sets to work. 'Misselden's immediate motive for theorizing', he writes, 'was to provide a background for policies designed to foster the interests of the class he represented.' 'It has often been said that Adam Smith represented the interests of a single class. This is undoubtedly true not only in an historical sense, but even subjectively.' 'Ricardo . . . was forced by the same social purpose which was inherent in the *Wealth of Nations* to imply the productivity of capital, he was also determined far more than Smith to represent the claims of landed property as economically unjustified. The resulting theory of rent reflects these two aims.' 'Malthus was a reactionary' characterized by 'advocacy of pre-capitalist interests' in an already capitalist society. And so on, and so forth (2nd ed., 1950, 76, 152, 185, 213). In general, Roll is inclined to find an apologetic strain in all orthodox economics, both classical and

---

[1] *Also sprach Zarathustra*, ch. LXXV. Cf. also his attack on Kant in *Jenseits von Gut und Böse*.

[2] *Die Fröhliche Wissenschaft*, V, § 349. For a deeper study of Nietzsche cf. Hans Barth's *Wahrheit und Ideologie*, 1945, 205 *seq.* Cf. esp. 246 *seq.*, 259 *seq.*

[3] *Cit.* Dedieu, *Montesquieu*, 1913, 323.

[4] From the Greek τὸ συμφέρον meaning profit, advantage.

modern. He operates, as does all sympherontic theory, with a specific psychology, the psychology of self-interest.

This decidedly psychological character of the sympherontic theory helps to distinguish it from the next two items on our list, both of which are sociological in nature. In order to keep within the nomenclature here adopted, we propose to call them *coenonic* theories.[1] As already indicated, there are two varieties to this doctrine. Both maintain that it is social life which determines and explains human thought, but whereas the one singles out some specific social factor or factors as the decisive element, the other believes that society as a totality, social relationships in general, are the mind-shaping agency. The former theory could, for the sake of clear distinction, be called the coenonic-monogenetic theory, the latter, laying the emphasis on the character of society as an inclusive whole, the coenonic-holistic theory.

Since many different strands in the texture of social interaction can be singled out and raised to the dignity of mind-determining influence *par excellence*, many different *coenonic-monogenetic* theories are in principle equally possible, and a number of them have in fact been formulated and advanced. W. H. Auden has presented one of them in a playful vein. His jingle has already been quoted by Robert Merton,[2] but, amusing as it is, it will bear quoting again. It is occupation that is dressed up as the thought-controlling factor in social life.

> Who when looking over
> Faces in the subway,
> Each with its uniqueness,
>   Would not, did he dare . . .
>
> Would not like to know what
> Influence occupation
> Has on human vision
>   Of the human fate:
>
> Do all the clerks for instance
> Pigeon-hole creation,
> Brokers see the Ding-an-
>   sich as Real Estate? [3]

What seems to Auden to be hardly more than a joke, appeared to Max Weber as a promising possibility worthy of serious exploration. We have already touched upon this side of his work, though only lightly. He ascribed to occupation some real influence on the 'human vision of the human fate', for it is precisely in connection with the discussion of

[1] From the Greek κοινωνία meaning society.
[2] *Social Theory and Social Structure*, 1949, 120.
[3] 'Heavy Date', in *Collected Shorter Poems, 1930–44*, Engl. ed., 1950, 116.

religious conceptions that he introduces the occupational factor and gives it prominence.[1] Artisans, peasants and proletarians, he thought, if we look upon their modal conduct rather than upon individual peculiarities, tend to develop in different directions when they come to speculate about the last things. The archetype of an artisan is the potter, in whose hands matter is proverbially as clay. If he wants to make a vessel, he first of all conceives a shape for it in his mind, and then fashions that shape by forcing his will upon the inert, recalcitrant, resistant material. Thus he undergoes, in his daily work, an experience which can become the inspiration of a religious philosophy. The human demiurge can become the model of a divine demiurge. A conception of the deity along these lines will naturally recommend itself, Weber felt, to communities of artificers, for it will fit in with their whole life and experience.

Very different is the life-experience of peasant populations, and for this reason their religious thinking will also show a different face. Unlike the craftsman, who is master of the process of production, the agriculturalist is the slave of uncontrollable forces. When he has placed the seed in the ground, what can he do to make it grow? What can he do to ward off hail and storm and flood and blight? or to procure gentle rains in the spring-time and life-giving sunshine in July and August? Things never turn out for him exactly as they should, and so he thinks of the deity, not as a rational, or even perhaps as a personal, creator, but rather as a collection of mysterious, possibly disjointed, but in any case capricious powers who can at best be cajoled, propitiated and appeased. Here, then, is the source of a second type of religious outlook, with an inherent tendency towards superstition.

An industrial proletariat will feel differently again about the religious problem. The modern factory-worker will not be an obscurantist like the old-time peasant because he is part and parcel of a rational organization; but nor, on the other hand, will he conceive of the deity as a personal creator-god, as the typical craftsman does, because he has no experience of personal creativeness. Thus there will be little in his life to stimulate the development of religious ideas. In the waste-lands of the industrial cities, atheism is likely to flourish, unless the occupational tendency in this direction is cancelled out or overborne by tendencies springing from different quarters. This is a typical coenonic-monogenetic theory. Adam Smith had already anticipated the gist of it

---

[1] We hasten to add that several other approaches are also to be met with in Weber's works. His celebrated derivation of the 'spirit of capitalism' from the 'Protestant ethic' points in the direction of what we shall presently call an idealistic theory. Yet in his darker moods he could also draw near to the sympherontic position, as for instance when he expressed the opinion that the enthusiasm of the knights for the crusades was due to a desire on their part for additional fiefs.

when he wrote: 'The understandings of the greater part of men are necessarily formed by their ordinary employments.' [1] Of course, other factors than occupation may be pushed into the centre of the picture, for instance the political. As for Marxism, with its insistence that one particular set of human relations, namely the production-relations, constitutes the social substructure of the cultural superstructure, we shall speak about it separately in a moment.

Unlike the coenonic-monogenetic theories, the *coenonic-holistic* variety fixes its attention on social interaction as a total system. Many leading sociologists have adopted this point of view, among others Emile Durkheim and Max Scheler. As for Durkheim, Merton has so well characterized his whole approach that we can hardly do better than quote the relevant passage from his pen: 'In an early study with Mauss of primitive forms of classification, he maintained that the genesis of the categories of thought is to be found in the group structure and relations and that they vary with changes in the social organization. In seeking to account for the social origins of the categories, Durkheim postulates that individuals are more directly and inclusively oriented toward the groups in which they live than they are toward nature. The primarily significant experiences are mediated through social relationships, which leave their impress on the character of thought and knowledge. Thus, in his study of primitive forms of thought, he deals with the periodic recurrence of social activities (ceremonies, feasts, rites), the clan structure and the spatial configurations of group meetings as among the existential bases of thought. And, applying Durkheim's formulations to ancient Chinese thought, Granet attributes their typical conceptions of time and space to such bases as the feudal organization and the rhythmic alternation of concentrated and dispersed group life.' [2]

It would be fascinating to follow these convictions back to their theoretical bases, to discuss, for instance, Durkheim's concepts of 'social substratum' and of 'dynamical density', but this is a pleasure we must forego for the present, lest we should burst the frame of this book. For similar reasons, we cannot enter as deeply into Scheler's doctrine as we would and perhaps should. A brief hint must suffice here where our task is merely to establish the dominant types of the extrinsic study of human thought and its history. Scheler thinks in terms of an ontology which distinguishes different spheres of being or reality, some of which are prior to, and fundamental to, others—in a word, in terms of an hierarchical ontology. Now, the most fundamental of all spheres, for Scheler, is that of the *we*. It precedes even that of nature, in so far as only those aspects of nature become 'real' to us which we select—which 'the we' selects. Needless to say, the we also precedes the I, both objectively

---

[1] *Wealth of Nations*, ed. Cannan, 1904, II, 267.
[2] *Social Theory and Social Structure*, 1949, 226.

(or ontologically) and subjectively, as a matter of experience. Scheler speaks of a '*law* of the primacy in existence (*Primatgegebenheit*) of the social structure over all other structures of being, of the "Thou" over the "It" '.[1] It is clear that such a philosophy must see the substructure of all thought in the basic social reality, in the inclusive system of social interaction.[2] It is no accident that Scheler, in a decisive passage of his *Die Wissensformen und die Gesellschaft*, expressly joins forces with Emile Durkheim (cf. 477).

While the coenonic-monogenetic theories occupy the sixth and the coenonic-holistic the seventh place on our list, the eighth is reserved for a doctrine which can best be described by the traditional and well-established term *idealistic*. It has inspired some of the most imposing systems of culture-analysis and culture-interpretation, for instance those of Hegel and Comte, Spengler and Spann, and, more recently, Sorokin in America and Alfred Weber in Germany. Perhaps one can best characterize this particular outlook by saying that it regards all concrete cultural phenomena, whether they be works of the discerning mind or works of artistic creativity, as emanations of some basic mental attitude or philosophy of life, or, more metaphysically, of some indwelling 'culture-soul' (Spengler's *Kulturseele*). For Alfred Weber, for instance, each culture has its own 'physiognomy' which reflects and expresses a 'spiritual entelechy' (*seelische Entelechie* [3]), as the face of a man reflects and expresses his inmost being, his spirit and his soul. Sorokin is convinced that what differentiates different universes of mind and meaning from each other is not only ostensibly, but even fundamentally, i.e. in the last analysis, the difference in the answer given to the 'last questions' —the twin questions: what is the nature of ultimate reality, and what is the supreme value? Three replies are possible in his opinion: either the real is identified with the world of our sense-experience, with the material universe; or this material universe is decried as something ephemeral, delusive, insubstantial, and true reality is considered as lying outside or beyond it; or, lastly, both the sensual and the suprasensual realms of being are acknowledged as equally real in the ontological sense of the word. In the first case, there arises a culture which Sorokin calls sensate; in the second, one which he describes as ideational; and in the third case, if true balance is reached between the physical and the metaphysical, one which deserves to be called idealistic.

[1] *Die Wissensformen und die Gesellschaft*, 1926, 134. Our emphasis.

[2] For a particularly terse formulation cf. *Die Wissensformen und die Gesellschaft*, 1926, 475 *seq*. Cf. also my introduction to the English translation of Scheler's *Nature of Sympathy* (1954).

[3] Both terms occur in Weber's *Prinzipien der Geschichts- und Kultursoziologie*, 1951, 28. A more detailed discussion of Alfred Weber's world of ideas is yet another pleasure which we must deny ourselves.

Problem A: The Basis of Social Determination

The nineteenth century, which tended to equate truth with what is scientifically provable and life with the pursuit of material gratifications, is a good example of a predominantly sensate culture; the ascetics of India and the hermits of the Thebaid who regarded, and rejected, the testimony of our senses as so much delusion and attempted to escape from the world of materiality and materialism, show us the type of an ideational culture; and, lastly, the age of St. Thomas Aquinas and of the great Cathedrals strove hard, and half succeeded, in creating a balanced idealistic culture which gave its due value both to time and to eternity. As Sorokin's chosen interpreter or rather popularizer has expressed it: 'The dominant type of culture moulds the type of mentality of the human beings who are born and live in it. Other conditions being equal, a person's mentality will be ideational if he has had no contacts except with those of a pure ideational culture. If his contacts are with the sensate culture, he will have a sensate mentality. A person in contact with different types of culture will have a mixed cultural mentality. Close association with nothing but an unintegrated culture, or with a multitude of cultures of contradictory character, will produce unintegrated personalities, unless by happy, though unlikely chance, the perfect balance between an ideational and sensate culture is struck to produce the integrated unity of the mixed idealistic culture.' [1]

It is essential for the understanding of the whole theory to realize that it considers the ontological convictions prevailing at a given time, not so much as culture-contents, but rather as culture-premises, from which the culture concerned proceeds and emanates as a whole. In other words, the basic philosophy of a period is, to some extent, granted a higher ontological status than that of all other contemporary ideas; it is in some degree hypostatized, perhaps even reified—though to what extent is uncertain and cannot be discussed here.

We have mentioned, as representatives of this 'idealistic' theory, both Hegel and Comte. [2] Yet there is one important difference between them

[1] Cowell, *History, Civilization and Culture*, 1952, 207. Cf. the whole of Cowell's text, and also Maquet, *Sociologie de la Connaissance*, 1949, esp. 160 *seq.*, 179 *seq.*, and the whole of Part II. On p. 255, Maquet writes: 'The sum and substance of Sorokin's dynamical sociology is an explanation of the fluctuations of socio-cultural phenomena by the changes occurring in the philosophical attitudes. This is an idealistic way of thinking . . . Sorokin tries to give precision to, and to extend as far as possible, the conditioning of social phenomena by philosophical ideas.'

[2] It is no valid objection to the bracketing together of Comte and Hegel, to the ranking of Comte among the idealists, that there is a strong element of physiological materialism in his over-all doctrine, and in particular that he accepted most of the phrenological teaching of Gall, for he was a disciple of romantic idealism as well. What is decisive for us here is that he distinguishes the three stages of world history, the theological, metaphysical, and positive, by dint of their inherent and informing culture-mentalities.

226

and a thinker such as Sorokin. Sorokin sees his three culture-mentalities as systematic alternatives which can and do displace each other in history; indeed, he is inclined to regard history as a cyclical alternation, leading from one position to the others and possibly back again. Not so Hegel and Comte, with their belief in a unilinear evolution. For them the world-spirit is essentially in flux, in a progressive movement, proceeding from a determinate starting-point to a determinate dénouement. So great is their emphasis on the developmental aspects of thinking, that one might be tempted to class them, not with the 'idealistic' writers, but separately, in a ninth category entitled *'evolutionary* doctrines'. What a man's mind is like depends for them very largely, not to say exclusively, upon the point of time at which he lives. This puts a different complexion upon their whole approach to the history of ideas. And yet one hesitates to establish this ninth category. For what develops is after all the Central Mind (as Hobhouse called it), the mind of, or behind, society. Furthermore, to fill up the ranks of this category, deep inroads would have to be made into all the categories we have already distinguished, not only into the idealistic group, but also, for instance, into the coenonic-monogenetic class. Marx, for one, and Mannheim, would belong to our ninth grouping as well as to our sixth. Thus it will perhaps be best, after all, to close the canon with the eighth type, merely appending the proviso that evolutionist convictions may modify, and that deeply, other affiliations.

What is the value of the classification which we have thus elaborated? Lest any one should be inclined to believe that it is no more than an empty essay in taxonomy, a specious effort at bureaucratic pigeon-holing, let us show with the aid of an instructive example how it can help in the handling of the problem with which the history of ideas and the sociology of knowledge are concerned. The now century-old discussion among scholars at large about the true meaning of Marxism, and the hardly less acrimonious debate among Marxists themselves about what Marx, the master, really meant, has always proceeded on the assumption that the Marxian doctrine is a unitary and univocal system. But that is not so, and that is the reason why this whole battle of ideas has not led to a more decisive issue. What commonly goes by the name of Marxism is in fact a bundle of theories, only loosely connected with each other and each moving in a different direction, and those who have expatiated on and quarrelled about 'it' have very often been talking at cross purposes.

The present writer has no doubt whatsoever that Marx belongs in his sixth class, in other words, that Marx's was a coenonic-monogenetic theory. Ideas spring from social relationships, but not from social relationships in general. There is a special set of such relations which are ultimately responsible for the organization of the human mind as

227

well as for the organization of the human economy—the production-relations which are also, at the same time, property-relations.[1] If there could ever have been any doubt that this is the correct interpretation of the doctrine, it must surely have been removed by the resuscitation, in recent years, of Marx's early but important book, *Die deutsche Ideologie* (1845/6). But students of Marx, both hostile and friendly, have not been content with this construction, fully borne out though it is by all the decisive texts. They have dragged him this way and that, until his features have become utterly indistinct. Plekhanov, for instance, tried to link 'historical materialism' with geographical determinism. 'The development of the forces of production', he writes, 'which in the last resort determines the development of all social circumstances, is itself determined by the nature of the physical conditions of geography.' [2] K. A. Wittfogel has since attempted to present a consistently ecological version of the Marxist doctrine, an effort which was bound to lead him far away from Marxian sociologism, and did in fact do so.[3]

Other writers have endeavoured to push Marx into the camp of the technological doctrine. 'There is', Barth has asserted, 'according to Marx the following causal series: a determined state of technique—determined industrial forms—determined property system . . . —determined political superstructure—determined social forms of consciousness which are characterized as religious, artistic, or philosophical.' [4] Robbins has expressed himself in the same vein: 'The so-called "Economic" Interpretation of History is not only labelled "Materialist", it is in substance through and through materialistic. It holds that all the events of history, or at any rate all the major events in history, are attributable to "material" changes, not in the philosophical sense that these events are part of the material world, nor in the psychological sense that psychic dispositions are the mere epiphenomena of physiological changes—though, of course, Marx would have accepted these positions—but in the sense that the material technique of production conditions the form of all social institutions, and all changes in social institutions are the result of changes in the technique of production. History is the epiphenomenon of technical change. The history of tools is the history of mankind.'[5] Those who have read Marx himself may

---

[1] I have developed this contention somewhat more broadly in the lectures on Marx which I delivered in the years 1941 and 1942 in the University of Cambridge.

[2] *Cit.* Adler, *Lehrbuch der Materialistischen Geschichtsauffassung*, II, 1932, 103.

[3] 'Die natürlichen Ursachen der Wirtschaftsgeschichte', published in the *Archiv für Sozialwissenschaft*, vol. LXVII, (1932), and 'Geopolitik, geographischer Materialismus und Marxismus', published in *Unter dem Banner des Marxismus*, vol. III (1929). Cf. for a brief discussion Warynski, *Die Wissenschaft von der Gesellschaft*, 1944, 62 *seq.*   [4] *Philosophie der Geschichte als Soziologie*, ed. 1922, 673 *seq.*

[5] *An Essay on the Nature and Significance of Economic Science*, 1932, 41 *seq.*

find it difficult to accept this interpretation, but if it does not apply to
the master, it certainly applies to some of the disciples, notably Labriola
and Bogdanov.[1]

As for the materialistic theory, we have just found Robbins asserting
that Marx would 'of course' have accepted its basic positions. In point
of fact, however, Marx returned so decided a negative to physiological
materialism, which he despised, that no important book incorporating
this order of ideas has come from the Marxist school itself, and the same
applies to the hormic variant which is apt to stand condemned along
with the materialistic doctrine to which it is akin. Admittedly, many of
the nineteenth century disciples of Marx, from Engels to Lenin, and
most clearly of all perhaps Dietzgen, were strongly attracted by the
materialistic dogmatism of the day and tried, to the best of their ability,
to reconcile the two streams of thought. But although they brought them
near to each other, the waters have never really mingled.

Much more pronounced has been the development of a sympherontic
off-shoot of the Marxist school. Bukharin is the best instance of this.
Speaking of Heraclitus and Anaxagoras, he explains their contrasting
philosophical views by reference to their contrasting interests. Heraclitus
was the offspring of an aristocratic family. He was a supporter of a
monarchical state and a feudal economy. But in his time the government
of Ephesus was in the hands of the popular party, the party advocating
a democratic state and a commercial economy. It was therefore in his
interest to weaken the existing régime as much as possible, and he did
so by developing the doctrine that nothing lasts for ever, that everything
is in flux, implying above all, as Bukharin thinks, that even the power
of the hated faction would one day come to an end. The Athenian
Anaxagoras, on the other hand, was the intimate friend of Pericles, the
master of Athens. It was to his interest to stress the constancy of things,
and he therefore preached a doctrine which admitted no revolutionary
change but only a gradual development without major cataclysms.[2]

As we have already ranked Marx with the coenonic-monogenetic
theorists, nothing more need be said here about his correct affiliation.
But there is a noticeable tendency among certain writers to widen
Marxism into a coenonic-holistic doctrine, and this is not surprising,
since the narrow class point of view implied in the monogenetic creed,
which some would call the one-factor fallacy, must at times be rather
restricting. Even Lukacs in one passage identifies 'the material substructure of the economy' with the 'relationship of men to each other'
tout court.[3] Similarly Warynski, when he comes to interpret the

[1] *Re* Labriola cf. Scheler, *Die Wissensformen und die Gesellschaft*, 1926, 103, 200
seq. Re Bogdanov, cf. Aron, *Die deutsche Soziologie der Gegenwart*, ed. 1953, 74.
[2] *Theorie des historischen Materialismus*, 1922, 208 *seq.*
[3] *Geschichte und Klassenbewusstsein*, 1923, 32.

all-important term production-relations, has this to say: 'They are social [not physical] relationships. . . . The individual members of society are dependent upon each other and production is not thinkable any otherwise than as social production.' 'With this insight', we also read, 'a new aspect of the dialectical method is revealed: every concept referring to the social world, without exception, is defined as a social relationship or as the indirect expression of such a relationship.' [1] Such passages betray an inclination to resolve all conceptually objectified elements into on-going processes taking place between human beings, and this, despite all the emphasis on the objectivity of 'class', constitutes a definite move in the direction of a sociology of interaction, and so also in the direction of the coenonic-holistic position. In general, Lukacs and Warynski lay so much emphasis on process, practice, and activity, that the general habitus of their thought reminds one not infrequently of parallel movements outside the Marxist fold whose whole logic points more towards a coenonic-holistic than towards any other sociology of knowledge.

Finally, what about the idealistic doctrine? Surprisingly—or is it all that surprising?—even this type of view has appeared among the Marxians, and it was no mean member of the school who developed it, none other than the man who, after Engels's death, was by many regarded as the most authoritative interpreter of the message—Karl Kautsky. Kautsky's decisive speculation can be briefly summarized as follows: production-relations depend on production-techniques; but production-technique in turn depends on human know-how; hence, in the last analysis, the determinant of determinants is after all, even according to Marxism, in the human mind. As he himself candidly expressed it: 'The development of the "material forces of production" is in the last analysis only the development of the knowledge of nature under another name. Hence it appears that the deepest foundation of the "real basis", of the "material substructure" of human ideology is a spiritual process, that of the perceptive penetration of nature.' [2]

From all this it becomes plain, how much the discussion of 'historical materialism' would have gained if the participants had only made clear to themselves what they really meant, and what their opponents might have meant. But such clarification is not so easy to achieve as might be assumed. When Karl Mannheim was still in Germany (before 1933), his theory was substantially monogenetic in type, ascribing the power of mind-determination mainly to political and power-relationships. When, later on, he settled in England, he changed over to a more holistic

---

[1] *Die Wissenschaft von der Gesellschaft*, 147, 107.
[2] *Die materialistische Geschichtsauffassung*, 1929, I, 864. Kautsky's version obviously escapes the strictures levelled by Talcott Parsons against Marxism in general. Cf. his *Essays in Sociological Theory*, revised ed., 1954, 23.

standpoint, seeing the life of the intellect as essentially a mental mirroring of social life in its entirety. It is doubtful if he was ever fully aware of his shift of position. He would have been if he had had before his eyes the classification of approaches set out on the preceding pages. Our eight- or ninefold paradigm would have helped him to a fuller self-knowledge, and it can perform the same service for Marxists and indeed for all who are interested in, and indulge in, the extrinsic interpretation and study of the history of ideas.

The typology which we have developed is meant to be, or to become, an aid to further progress, and not, of course, its master. What we mean is that it should be used to provide a better characterization of the various theories concerning the origins of ideas put forward in the past, not that it should be made into a Procrustean bed on which to stretch or squeeze them. Perhaps we can best explain what our eight categories mean and what they can achieve by saying that they are ideal types, in Max Weber's sense of the term. Such ideal types are not to be found in all their purity in real life, though there are frequently close approximations to them. But what is actually to be found in real life cannot be better recognized for what it is than by comparing it with such a set of ideal types—a collection of mentally constructed models representing possible attitudes elevated into full, onesided, artificial consistency and exclusiveness. Just as there has never anywhere been such a thing as typical or textbook capitalism, though we can only talk sensibly about the various near-capitalisms of reality if we know what a typically pure capitalism would be like, so too it is unlikely that we shall ever encounter in the literature a typically pure materialistic or sympherontic theory of the genesis of ideas. But it will greatly assist us in assessing the content and drift of such a doctrine if we have before us the ideal types elaborated here. They are, to borrow a phrase sometimes used by Tönnies, like tongs with which to grip chunks of reality.

Most theories evolved by those who study human thought and its products *ab extra* will, then, inevitably appear 'mixed' from the point of view of our paradigm. This is altogether natural, just as natural as that even a fully developed capitalist society should still have many non-capitalist elements in its make-up. But here and there, there arises the question of consistency. How do the various discordant features fit together? If they do not, we are apt to get a somewhat disorganized whole, and this is far worse in theory than in practice. One great service which our typology can offer is to place before the theorist the claims of logic. If he wants a complex sociology of knowledge, well and good; but he must take care that the dissimilar methods of interpretation which he tries to conjoin do not cut across and countermand one another. Very often different theories have been superficially linked without being organically merged. Taine's formula, for instance, much quoted

231

in the nineteenth century, was: *race, milieu, moment.* It is legitimate, to say the least, to call these factors (which are themselves complex, especially the second) co-determinants of human thought. But *how* do they co-determine thinking? What degree of influence do they respectively wield? Without an answer to this question, the formula is well-nigh useless.

An example of a much more satisfying co-ordination of discordant elements is offered by Taine's contemporary Herbert Spencer. He distinguishes societies according to their total mode of life into war-like and peace-loving ones, and asserts that thought under the one dispensation will be entirely different from thought under the other. To give but one illustration, military societies, accustomed to command and obedience, will tend to develop dogmatisms, particularly dogmatic religions, whereas pacific societies, deciding their public questions by discussion among equals, will tend to be undogmatic, even in theology. This is what we have called a coenonic-holistic explanation. But with it Spencer combines a typically materialistic theory. Men who habitually go to war, will develop warlike bodies, including war-like (especially quick-reacting) brains; these bodies and brains they will then hand on, by heredity, to their offspring, and so there will emerge a wholly militant type of man who will think appropriate thoughts and develop corresponding tastes, not only because his way of life leads him to adopt them, but also because his cerebral constitution determines him towards them. So, too, *mutatis mutandis*, in the case of pacific eras and areas. The second theory is useless because biologists since Weismann no longer accept the thesis, so dear to Spencer, that acquired characteristics are inheritable. But this is beside the point here. Our contention is merely that Spencer knew how to co-ordinate and merge two essentially contrasting modes of explanation.

Spencer really co-ordinates, i.e. joins the two theories on a basis of equality. Others proceed more by systematic super- or subordination, on a basis of inequality. An example of this latter alternative is the work of the Le Play school. Their formula, somewhat extended, reads: place-work-family-folk-thought. Both 'place' and 'family' appear here as determinants of culture, but whereas the family-form is only a proximate determinant, place is the ultimate. In other words, a coenonic-mono-genetic theory is combined with an ecological one. Some of us may not like this particular kind of combination which ascribes more influence over the human mind to rocks and rains than to education, but such as it is, it is formally in full accordance with the demands of clarity and logic.

A rather neat distinction can be drawn between those doctrines which assert that the same factor determines thought in all societies, and, *a fortiori*, in all historical phases of the same society, and those which assume that in different societies and in succeeding ages different influences come to the fore. Of the former type—Merton calls them 'general analytical theories' [1]—Pareto is a prime example. He knows of no development; men are always pushed and pulled by the same 'residues', and though there is apparent change, it is not real, since all the elements are given from the beginning and can at best, like pieces on a chess-board, change their mutual position. Pareto is convinced—to express it in our own terminology—that a hormic theory applies to all societies: thought is always and everywhere the mental counterpart of the drives basic to human nature, a nature which is unalterable and unaltered by time and place.

Very different is the attitude of those theories which Merton has, for distinction's sake, labelled 'historicist'. One principle of interpretation and explanation will not do, according to them, for all societies, nor indeed for succeeding stages in the history of the same society. Sorel was not only a contemporary of Pareto's but even in many ways a kindred spirit. Yet in this matter he took a different road. 'In the history of the primitive peoples', he writes, 'religion plays an extraordinary part. . . . Next to religion, public [i.e. political] life can be regarded as a second factor of social psychology [which rises into prominence later on] . . . In the last phase, the economic sphere moves into the centre of the stage. . . . When we go over from one state to the next, we always find an increase in intellectual freedom. If religion, with its fantastic conceptions . . . imparts to the human mind a certain content, the economy only indicates a direction for the activities of the spirit.' [2] In other words, in our terminology, in primitive society an idealistic theory is indicated: certain metaphysical convictions determine thought; later on, a coenonic-monogenetic explanation is more to the point; politics govern ideas; in modern times it is again a coenonic-monogenetic theory that is most realistic, but now a different subvariety of the type, for politics have yielded pride of place to economics. Very similar is Max Scheler's theory, save only that he sees tribal life as dominated by blood rather than religion, i.e. amenable to treatment in terms of a materialistic doctrine rather than an idealistic one. Social reality is indeed always the ontologically basic reality, and to that extent Scheler stands for an overall coenonic-holistic explanation; but what the social reality itself will be like, depends on the factors predominant at the time, so that further co-determining elements creep in and are fairly well tied into the holistic theory by Scheler's ingenuity. [3]

---

[1] *Social Theory and Social Structure*, 1949, 222.

[2] *Sozialistische Monatshefte*, 1898, 430 *seq.*

[3] Cf. *Die Wissensformen und die Gesellschaft*, 1926, 34 *seq.*, 45 *seq.* For a brief summary, cf. Becker and Dahlke in *Philosophy and Phenomenological Research*, 1941/2, 317.

Problem A: The Basis of Social Determination

An even better example of a 'historicist' sociology of knowledge (in the sense defined by Merton for the special purpose here in hand) is that of Thorstein Veblen. Unspoilt primitive communities, Veblen imagines, are dominated by the 'instinct of workmanship'. This so-called instinct [1] will express itself in certain mental modes appropriate to it: men, for instance, will experience as beautiful what is purposive or adapted to its end. They will find a cow or a cart-horse more beautiful (because more useful) than a war-horse or a race-horse, a natural, flower-studded meadow more satisfactory to look at than an artificial, weeded lawn, a woman with large hands made for work and wide hips good for child-birth more comely than one with long, pale, anaemic fingers and a wasp-waist. But as soon as society alters its character, when property develops and, with it, 'predaciousness', aesthetic conceptions are turned inside out. The race-horse is ranked higher in the scale of beauty than the cart-horse because all that has to do with work is despised, all that has to do with leisure exalted. Meadows are transformed into lawns, women locked up in crippling corsets, their hands made to end in long brittle fingernails painted red which prove beyond the shadow of a doubt that their owners need not, and do not, descend to the degrading level of domestic drudgery, and so on, and so forth. Even religion is transformed from an adoration of the creative forces of nature, from an agricultural rite, into the adulation of an authoritarian personal god modelled on the warrior-noble, the man of power. All these changes of culture come about because the course of history replaces one mind-determining factor by another: first it is a spontaneous drive, the instinct of workmanship; later it is a factitious arrangement of human relationships, the emergence and existence of a leisured master class, and its associated 'pecuniary' canons of thought and taste. In other words, Veblen applies to one stage of social development what we have called a hormic sociology of knowledge, and to another stage a coenonic-monogenetic one, the truly decisive element being, once equality is gone and inequality established, a special feature of social life, the contrast between the creative strata and the parasitical predacious groups which batten on them. [2]

It is interesting at this point to note a definite rift in the Marxist lute. A reviewer of Marx's *Critique of Political Economy* voiced the

[1] It is not a true instinct, but what we have labelled a drive, i.e. not a tendency rooting in the body but rather an attribute of the whole personality. Veblen was quite clear about this, in spite of his use of the term 'instinct' which he probably preferred for reasons of euphony. Cf. Dorfman, *Thorstein Veblen and His America*, 1934, 324.

[2] Yet another instance of a 'historicist' attitude is Alfred Weber. Cf. *Prinzipien der Geschichts- und Kultursoziologie*, 1951, 28 *seq.*, Aron, *Die deutsche Soziologie der Gegenwart*, ed. 1953, 63 *seq.*, and von Schelting, *Archiv für Sozialwissenschaft*, 1929, 65.

opinion that the economic conception of history was indeed applicable to the contemporary world, but not to earlier societies. In the Middle Ages Catholicism has been the paramount influence in control of culture, in antiquity politics. In our terminology, this reviewer was expressing himself in favour of a 'historicist' approach and seeking to explain the medieval system of ideas on the basis of an 'idealistic' theory, and the ancient and modern on the basis of (two different) coenonic-monogenetic theories. Marx would have none of that. Vigorously he rejects the historicist approach and asserts that all societies are under exactly the same mind-determining influence. 'This much, at any rate, is certain,' he writes in *Capital*, 'that the Middle Ages could not live upon Catholicism, nor yet classical antiquity upon politics. On the contrary,' he goes on to say, 'the way in which, during classical antiquity and the Middle Ages respectively, people gained a livelihood explained why, in the former case politics, and in the latter case Catholicism, played the leading rôle' (Everyman ed., I, 56 *seq.*, footnote). In other words, the same principle of explanation, the one suggested by 'historical materialism', holds good in *all* societies.

This was not quite the opinion of Marx's most able modern disciple, Georg Lukacs. He was inclined to think, going some way, though certainly not all the way, with Marx's unknown critic, that historical materialism comes fully into its own only in capitalist society. 'It was not wrong', he writes in *Geschichte und Klassenbewusstsein*, 'to apply historical materialism in its classical form stringently and unconditionally to the history of the nineteenth century. For in the history of that century all the forces acting upon society, have in fact operated purely as incarnations of the 'objective spirit'. In the precapitalistic societies this is not altogether so. In the precapitalistic societies that independence, that setting-itself-up-as-the-aim, that self-centredness and sovereignty, that immanence of economic life which has been realized in capitalist society did not yet exist. Hence it follows that historical materialism cannot be applied to the precapitalist social formations in quite the same way as to capitalist development. . . . Vulgar Marxism has totally neglected this difference. Its application of historical materialism has fallen into the same error with which Marx has charged vulgar economics: it has mistaken merely historical categories . . . for eternal categories' (244 *seq.*; cf. also 238 *seq.*). Lukacs would no doubt deny that he was materially deviating from Marx's opinion as stated in the footnote to *Capital* quoted above; but some difference, in emphasis at least, between him and his master seems undeniable, especially as he is doubtful whether 'purely' economic forces can be so much as identified under pre-capitalist conditions.

Problem A: The Basis of Social Determination

(c) THE COMPETING CLAIMS AND THE CASE FOR THE SOCIOLOGY OF KNOWLEDGE

We have so far proceeded on the assumption that a combination, or at any rate a partial combination, of the eight or nine fundamentally different theories concerning the extrinsic interpretation of ideas and their origin is both possible and desirable. To some extent, this assumption is undoubtedly justified. No two doctrines can, *prima facie*, be thought more irreconcilable than the materialistic and the coenonic (in either of its two varieties): the materialist claims that the character and content of all thought is due to the state of the individual's body, the coenonic that it depends on factors having little to do with the body, namely the individual's inter-individual relationships. It might seem that we are here confronted with a simple choice, with a clear-cut either-or. And yet, life is apt at times to force the two contradictory approaches together into one common endeavour. Von Martin's book *Geist und Gesellschaft* (1948) provides an illustration. It analyses the essentially negative, nay nihilistic world-view of certain groupings of German youths which appeared after the political catastrophe of 1918 and pointed forward to the even more cataclysmic development of fifteen years later, the mortal storm of 1933. To understand a figure like Ernst Jünger, von Martin points out (159 *seq.*), we must first of all realize what it means to be young. It means to prefer action to passivity; it means to give the emotions precedence, indeed primacy, over rational deliberation. Rationality presupposes a coolness, a detachment from things, which, in all typical cases, comes only with increasing age. This, as no doubt even the greatest adversary of physiological materialism will admit, is at least partially due to the physical properties of the youthful personality. Bodily reactions are quicker and more vigorous, energies more free-flowing and abundant, muscles tenser and more taut, inner secretions more potent and powerful. And yet, this body-born tendency of youth towards aggressiveness, towards radicalism, does not in all societies mature into such philosophies as that of Ernst Jünger. According to social circumstances, the whole relationship of youth to age may be one of respect as well as rebelliousness, love as well as hate: it all depends. Even if it is one of respect and love, however, something of the 'natural' youthfulness of youth will remain: even if social forces have managed to produce in youth sentiments of a positive kind, even if they have evoked attachment rather than alienation, the young men will have more sentiment, more romanticism, in their mental make-up than the rest of their community: it is just in their 'blood'. We see by this example how in life different mind-controlling agencies are conjointly at work, and it is plain that their co-operation in practice demands in principle a parallel co-ordination

236

of the respective theories, in this case of the materialistic and the coenonic.[1]

Nevertheless, it is only very rarely that the lion and the lamb will lie down so peacefully together as they do in this particular analytical effort. One of the oldest spectres of human speculation obviously raises its ugly head at this point: the nature *versus* nurture controversy. For however much we may assume that each of the eight or nine archetypal theories has a measure of truth, we cannot shirk the question, which measure of truth is the larger one. However much we may see them as complementary, we cannot close our eyes to the fact that at the same time they are in competition with each other. Most authors, instead of seeking a synthesis of the several possible modes of *ab extra* interpretation, have, on the contrary, embraced one of them and tried to stretch it, in imperialistic fashion, over the whole field. Indeed, they have generally been quite unprepared for any act of toleration, let alone conciliation, and this is not unnatural for if they are properly thought out the different doctrines imply different, not to say irreconcilable, concepts of man.

For the first three—the ecological, technological and materialistic schools—man is essentially a passive creature whose mind gets its impetus and direction from outside: according to the ecologists, from his natural environment; according to the materialists, from his physical apparatus. The case of the technological approach seems to fall into a different category, for the tools and techniques to which it ascribes the key-position in the process of culture-formation are, after all, creatures and achievements of man himself. Yet here, too—if the doctrine is consistently followed to its logical conclusion—the accent lies outside the human beings who do the thinking. If the ecologists see man as in the grip of his physical setting, the technological school sees him at grips with it. It sees him as one who, because he must struggle against nature, must so arrange his life (including his mental life) that it fits in with the conditions and demands of the warfare in which he is engaged. The tools he has fashioned are certainly his triumphs in this everlasting campaign, but they are a little like the broomstick of the sorcerer's apprentice which certainly fetches him water from the well, but is otherwise his master rather than his slave; and the mastery of the tool over the tool-maker is, according to the theory, above all a mastery over the tool-maker's mind. All three doctrines, then, locate the mind-determining factor outside the human sphere, and for that reason they cannot be classed as sociologies of knowledge at all. That man is a

[1] In his *Sociologie de la Connaissance* (1949, 326 *seq.*) Maquet attempts to show how Sorokin's doctrine (an idealistic one) and Mannheim's (essentially a coenonic-monogenetic theory giving the primacy of influence to the power-political factor) can be made to fit together.

specifically social being is to them an incidental rather than essential fact, a secondary feature rather than a primary one. Anybody who regards man as necessarily, centrally, ontologically a *zoon politikon* will feel inclined, nay, bound to reject these three modes of thought, or at the very least to demote them to a subsidiary position.

It is, in fact, the five (or six) other theories which between them constitute what is traditionally called the sociology of knowledge. Now, it can justly be asked why the two flanking ones—number four, the hormic theory, and number eight, the idealistic one—should be counted in here, since they, too, see mental life as the expression of realities, or supposed realities, other than social relations, the one of the drive-structure of man which is inherent in his body and as such precedes human interaction, the other of a culture-soul which is somehow behind culture and thus also outside and prior (ontologically at least) to the community and its processes. But to this question, a convincing answer can be given. A typical hormic theory such as that of Pareto is based on the conviction that the drives (the 'residues') constitute and dominate all social life, including its mental modes; it is a sociology, and because it is a sociology it also carries with it a sociology of knowledge, or rather of ideas. A naturalistic element is there, just as in materialism; indeed, philosophically it is a kind of materialism. But it is not the kind of materialism we find in Vogt and Moleschott, for to these men the flesh and blood alone was decisive, and the quality of man as a social being, interacting with others of his kind, was only a remote and unimportant facet of his nature. This is the very reason why we have drawn a boundary between the materialistic and the hormic camps, and why we have every right to call the latter a sociological theory and the former not. Pareto, whatever else he does, does see man in the circle of his fellows; and the drives with which he operates, such as the residue of combinations and the residue of sociality, have an essential reference to human action and interaction, are filled with social content. As for the idealistic theory, it is in a very similar case. The culture-mentality constitutes society, forms and informs social life. This is strongly borne in upon us when we turn the pages of Sorokin's great works. Much as he has to say about the human mind and its changing forms and contents, he is still essentially an all-round sociologist. His doctrine concerning the genesis of ideas is an aspect of a global sociology, and so it is only right and logical to regard him and his like as true sociologists of knowledge.

Nevertheless, it is clear that it is the two coenonic theories which represent the core and kernel of the sociology of knowledge. They, and they alone, base themselves squarely on the fact that man is a social being; they, and they alone, assert that—in Marx's words—it is men's social existence which determines their consciousness. The sympherontic theory is too deeply sunk in the psychology of interest to qualify as truly sociological, if the word is given a more stringent meaning. Logically, it is plain, it cannot yield a sociology of knowledge as defined in this book at all, but only a doctrine of ideology. If interests come first and ideas second, then ideas become the servants of interests, and no explanation whatsoever is offered of sound knowledge and its origin. The case of the hormic theory is not so different from this as might be assumed. It operates with a psychology of drives, not with one of interests, but it, too, is basically a psychology leading on to a doctrine of ideology rather than to a sociology underpinning a sociology of knowledge. (We are, of course, defining the terms 'sociology' and 'sociology of knowledge' much more narrowly here than in the last paragraph.) If drives come first and ideas second—and nobody could insist more strongly, indeed fiercely, than Pareto that the residues alone are real and primary, the 'derivations' only secondary and insubstantial —then ideas become merely the reflections of the basic drives or strivings and again no explanation is offered of true or pure knowledge and its origin. Thus though the sympherontic and hormic theories are commonly regarded as sociologies of knowledge, they have much less claim to this appellation than the coenonic ones. Nor will this description really fit the idealistic doctrine even though, by common consent, it is regularly applied to it. For it makes ideas the explanation of social life rather than the other way round as a true sociology of knowledge surely should. Like the sympherontic and the hormic theories it is merely marginal to the field properly so called.

All this shows us how deep are the differences between the various attitudes which together make up our inclusive eightfold paradigm. Does any one of them deserve preference, absolute or relative, over the others? Ernst Grünwald, in his pioneering book *Das Problem der Soziologie des Wissens* (1934), has asserted that this is a question to which no rational answer can be given (cf. e.g. 77 *seq.*, 99 and 233). We can only decide between the rival claims by an arbitrary fiat. For, he argues in substance, whether I regard man as essentially a body or a bundle of drives or a mind or a social creature, depends on my metaphysical assumptions and convictions; but between systems of metaphysics scholarship cannot adjudicate, and so we must accept the multiplicity of theories about the origin of ideas as an irreducible and irremovable fact. It is best to describe them all equally as hypotheses, to let them go their chosen ways, and to abandon the hope expressed by Max Weber (and basic to the present book) that the various interpretations of history from specific and apparently irreconcilable points of view may yet in time become so many preliminaries to a fully coordinated knowledge and understanding of history and culture (cf. *loc. cit.*, 249, note 54).

Problem A: The Basis of Social Determination

This defeatist attitude, which it is difficult not to condemn in harsh words, abandons the fight before even the first shot has been fired. The general anthropology or doctrine of man we have called for in our fourth chapter, would give us a scholarly, not a speculative view of human nature which would tell us, without the slightest metaphysical arbitrariness, which of the eight derivations of ideas comes nearest to the facts as they are, and how far even the others possess any specific truth-value of their own. It is only because this sector of human self-knowledge has always been left to the speculators, and has not yet been effectively claimed by scholars or scientists, that we are not further forward in this matter. Meanwhile, it is easy to indicate the ways in which the problem can be tackled with an assured hope of ultimate success.

There are two such ways. The first consists in the inductive study of the formation and functioning of the human mind itself. Is it in fact true that the mind, especially the mind in the making, owes more to the physical apparatus which embodies it than to the social experiences which impinge on it? A question of this kind can, to a very large extent, be answered on the basis of straightforward factual observation. A feral man, like the Indian wolf-child discovered not very long ago, has a brain no different from those of any contemporary who has grown up inside the circle of society: yet his mind is invariably found to be sluggish and dull. Is it no more than metaphysics to assert that physical evolution provides only the apparatus of thought, but nothing else, and hence that the materialistic theory can not be driven very far? Without language, there can be awareness of things but no knowledge of them, for all our knowledge is couched in words; but in so far as we owe language, the use of words, to social life, it follows at once, without metaphysical assumptions, that social life has a very deep influence on human thought-processes. Furthermore, it can be shown that even solitary and silent thinking is a kind of conversation. We really argue when we think, though the person with whom we argue is not material. Hence even introverted thought is really extroverted and social. Is it no more than metaphysics to maintain that the very ability to think is due to what an older, but a wise writer (Eugène de Roberty) has called 'intercerebral stimulation', i.e. social stimulation, and to infer that the coenonic, indeed the coenonic-holistic element must be allotted a high place in the hierarchy of thought-determining factors?

In a well-informed and well-reasoned article entitled 'The Theoretical Possibility of the Sociology of Knowledge',[1] Arthur Child has dealt in a highly conclusive fashion with Ernst Grünwald's 'postulational scepticism'. 'The advocate of a social approach [to the study of the origin of mind-contents]', Child writes, 'must show not merely how the mind

[1] *Ethics*, 1940/1, 392 *seq.*

240

might function: he must show also how it actually arises and what it is. For, if it can be established that both in origin and in constitution the mind is ineluctably social, then there will remain no doubt that knowledge is, in some sense and to some degree, expressive of a social determination.' Now, G. H. Mead's social theory of mind provides precisely what is needed—an epistemological basis on which the claims of the sociology of knowledge can be firmly established. 'One need not accept in its entirety Mead's precise theory of the manner in which mind arises; many of the details, indeed, seem confused and contradictory,' Child says. 'But the more general tenets appear quite susceptible of development into a theoretical foundation for the interpretation of thought from a social standpoint. If mind itself has a social origin—if, that is, it arises through the process of communication—and if thinking consists at bottom in the manipulation of generalized attitudes taken over from the social group as a whole, then there can be no question of the social determination, in some sense, of knowledge and thought. And there can be no question, consequently, of the validity of the interpretation of thought from a social standpoint. Furthermore, if thought is indeed a social process, as Mead describes it, then neither can there be any question that, whatever transcendent determinants may exist besides society, they can determine mind only through the intermediation of social reality. Their function in respect of mind is but secondary; it is society which is primary and basic.' [1] Naturally, we cannot enter into all this more deeply here, for we are not concerned with the collection of such building-stones for the construction of a general doctrine of man as may already exist. Our purpose was merely to make it clear that there is a good deal of sober information which, when brought together and duly completed, will help us to rank the different theories as they ought to be ranked according to their power of explaining reality, according to their realism and reliability.

But lest this approach should still be thought too speculative, we have yet another to recommend which is even more purely inductive. For we need not study the mind directly, as it exists, develops and functions in itself; we can also study it indirectly, through its manifestations. We can work through individual analyses, through case-histories, as it were. We can take up the thoughts of any thinker, look at them and ask: would this thinker in fact have formed this idea if he had lived in a different climate, or had a differently constituted body, or belonged to another class or occupation, or been influenced by some other culture-mentality or culture-soul? We can take the case and test it through in this way by a series of imaginary experiments. If we find that the imagined transposition of the thinker under observation into another climate would, in all probability, have made no difference to his thinking,

[1] *Ibid.*, 416.

then we shall be justified in saying that, so far as he is concerned, the ecological theory has failed; if we are forced to the conclusion, on the other hand, that this man would never have conceived this idea if he had lived in a different physical environment, we shall have to acknowledge that, so far as the instance in question goes, the ecological theory has proved its worth. After this imaginary experiment with the ecological factor we can then subject the case to other such experiments involving the technological, or the materialistic-physiological elements, and so on, until we have run through all the theoretical possibilities. We ought to emerge from this whole train of testing with a good idea as to which factors have been decisive, which more influential and which less, which marginally influential and which not at all. We shall then have a leading case, so to speak, a single secure possession. But, of course, one building-stone does not make a house. We must accumulate cases, pile them up as the builder does bricks before he decides to start building— we must provide materials in plenty, and then we can perhaps venture upon some bolder inference. From the sheer weight of evidence there should emerge in the end an over-all impression and ultimately a conviction as to the correct ranking of the mind-determining agencies, and this impression, this conviction, would, of course, have to be compared and harmonized with the results of the direct study of the mind itself, the insights reached through our first method.

Of course, it is more than obvious and must be admitted that even our second mode of procedure is still very largely, indeed essentially speculative, for what it recommends and would rely on is a string of 'thought-experiments'. But a thought-experiment is not only thought, i.e. speculation, but also experiment, i.e. an asking reality to speak for itself. What we are suggesting that the historian should do, in the crucible of his mind, is precisely what the chemist does in the crucibles of his laboratory. If he wants to know whether a certain element is essential to the production of a given substance, he assembles in one retort all the other ingredients *plus* the element in which he happens to be interested, and in another retort all the other ingredients *minus* the element in which he is interested. He then exposes the two retorts to the same treatment, for instance brings them both up to boiling point, and then considers the results of the process. If the two receptacles turn out to contain identical substances after the experiment, nothing is surer than the inference that x is immaterial in this context; if they are found to contain different substances, then it is clear that x is of material influence in this context, and in the latter case it will also be possible to assess how much difference the presence of x in the second retort has made to the end result. It is exactly in this manner that we would have the historian of ideas, the sociologist of knowledge, proceed. He must, in his testing, first count the ecological circumstances in and then leave them out: he will then see their importance, if any, within the complex of causes (if the word be permitted) behind a certain thought or theory, or operative upon a given thinker and his work. Needless to say, in all this the intellectual experimenter must be as unprejudiced as the experimenter in the laboratory: he must inquire of the facts, as we have put it, and must accept the answer they give him.

The quasi-scientific procedure just outlined, which seems to us to promise better than any other in helping to solve the problem as to which agencies do or do not control the human mind, is not a new toy that we are dangling before the historian's or sociologist's eye, but rather an old and trusted tool. For all we are suggesting is that Max Weber's method of 'causal imputation' should be transferred, or rather extended, from the sphere of external historical happenings to the sphere of internal mental developments, to the history of ideas.[1] (The well-informed reader will have noticed this long ago.) If we wish to apply the concept of cause to historical reality (with all due attention to the enormous differences between causation in nature and 'causation' in social life—with all due provisos and qualifications which are not to the purpose here), then, Max Weber explains, we are at first confronted with an unending number of causative elements. Everything that has happened in the course of human history seems to be connected with everything else. Yet we can sort out the important influences from the not so important and from the downright unimportant factors by systematically asking: would things have gone the way they did if x had not been present, or y, or z? It is by such a procedure, and probably by it alone, that we can achieve in the social and historical sciences something like the results which the scientist, luckier in this than we are, can secure through actual experiment.

It would be foolish to call for the use of this necessarily slow-moving machinery and then lightheartedly to anticipate what the upshot of its working might be. But it is permissible to express, *en attendant*, an expectation; we may, indeed must, be allowed to entertain some belief where the facts do not enable us to deal with certainties. We would avail ourselves of this privilege here and openly declare that we believe the coenonic-holistic theory to be nearer the truth than any other, though we would admit at the same time that all the others, and especially the remaining non-naturalistic ones, also come into the picture as secondary and modifying circumstances. What a man thinks seems to us to depend more on the cultural self built up in him by pervading social influences than on either his physical environment, or the tools he works with, or his body, or his drives, or his interests, or some special factor such as occupation, or yet on some mysterious indwelling culture-soul. We

[1] Concerning this method, cf. von Schelting, *Max Webers Wissenschaftslehre*, 1934, 263 *seq.*

believe that the true basis of social determination, so far as human thought is concerned, is the process of social interaction, that all-important process which consists in the meeting and collaboration of man and man, and which is also, and essentially, a meeting and making of mind and mind. Social life, for us, is in the last analysis something that happens, not something that is, a flow, not a substance, a stream of relationships, not a hard and fast thing. But in this living stream or flow or process, there is a twofold tendency of crystallization at work:

On the one hand, institutions form themselves and achieve comparative fixity, on the other hand modal ideas; and both poles thus produced—ideas and institutions—are determined by, and characteristic of, the parent reality which has brought them forth. It is thus, in our opinion, that the social determination of the human mind basically works. Social life as a process is given direction by certain guiding values which emerge as dominant in the living interplay of individual and group volitions and strivings, and it is these same values which constitute the axiological system by which, as shown in our third chapter, the world-view of the society concerned, and also, notwithstanding a large allowance for deviations from the norm, the world-view of its individual members, is made what it happens to be. 'The social as such', a philosopher has recently written, 'is neither subjective nor objective. It realizes itself at the same time correlatively in two directions—mental inwardness and the external world.' [1] This, we would say, is the sober truth. It also provides, *inter alia*, the answer to the question, central both to the history of ideas and to the sociology of knowledge: what is the basis of social determination of culture, of thought and feeling, of scholarship and art?

[1] Ziegenfuss, *Gesellschaftsphilosophie*, 1954, 12. Cf. also 41.

CHAPTER SIX

PROBLEM B: THE NATURE OF SOCIAL DETERMINATION

(a) THE THEORY OF FUNCTIONAL INTEGRATION

ALMOST from the first page of the present book use has been made of a concept which is obviously basic to the sociology of knowledge as a whole—the concept of social determination. We have been satisfied so far with leaving it rather vague, defining it simply —if this can be called a definition at all—as a meaningful connection and coherence between substructure and superstructure, but not specifying what the characteristics of this relationship are: whether it is close or loose, univocal or compatible with wide variations, one-sided or reciprocal, and so on, and so forth. In a way, this is one of the most decisive, perhaps indeed *the* most decisive problem of the sociology of knowledge. For anyone who asserts that one phenomenon depends upon another, for instance that ideas depend upon social interaction, is in duty bound to analyse the mode of dependence that he is asserting. If he does not do so, he leaves his system wide open to destructive criticism. For this reason we must now squarely face the problem of the nature of social determination. But we have no need to shirk it: difficult though it is, it is none the less capable of a convincing and unambiguous solution.

In the literature, little conscious attention has been paid to this aspect of the theory, even though it is manifestly fundamental.[1] Instead, we find a large variety of terms which, in and by themselves, would suggest confusion rather than clarity, vagueness rather than definite understanding. Merton has compiled a list of the principal terms used

[1] The one and only essay of much importance on the subject is Paul Honigsheim's six-page contribution to *Versuche zu einer Soziologie des Wissens* (ed. Scheler, 1924, 256 *seq.*), entitled 'Stileinheiten zwischen Wirtschaft und Geisteskultur'. It contains a number of seminal ideas, but is not remarkable for depth of penetration. The only point which emerges clearly from it is the rather obvious one that the more fully integrated a society is, the closer the 'stylistic unity' of substructure and superstructure.

whenever the question arises 'how are mental productions related to the existential basis?'—a list which is, in all probability, still not long enough: 'determination, cause, correspondence, necessary condition, conditioning, functional interdependence, interaction, dependence, consistency, harmony, coherence, unity, congruence, compatibility, expression, realization, symbolic expression, *Strukturzusammenhang*, structural identities, inner connection, stylistic analogies, logico-meaningful integration, identity of meaning, correspondence, reflection, bound up with, in close connection with, etc.' [1] *Prima facie*, this looks very bad. Is the sociology of knowledge based, then, on such shifting sands as these? Has it no firm ground under its feet? Must it not collapse and dissolve as soon as the concept of social determination is exposed to the cold blast of scrutiny and criticism?

Luckily, things are by no means so bad as they appear. For in this glutinous mass of verbosity three hard kernels are readily discernible which form the points of crystallization, as it were, around which all the different words, verbs and nouns used to describe the relation of substructure and superstructure, tend to assemble and arrange themselves. The solution of the whole problem really reduces itself to a choice between these three alternatives—if, indeed, such a choice eventually turns out to be necessary at all.

The term of the triad which it is convenient to consider first is the theory of causal determination, the *causalistic* alternative. It has all the clarity and unambiguity that can possibly be desired. Ideas are epiphenomena. They spring from the substructure as a physical effect springs from its physical causes. Given x, the determining substructural element, y, the associated ideas and sentiments are given as well. There is no spontaneity, no freedom about thought: it is the mechanical product of its necessary and sufficient conditions, however much the people who conceive and entertain the thoughts may fancy it otherwise.

Our formulation of the doctrine represents, of course, an ideal type (in Weber's sense). It elaborates and one-sidedly exaggerates the essential content of it; needless to say, it cannot be found in so crude a form anywhere in the literature. Yet there are not a few writers who, with varying degrees of boldness, have pushed in this direction, and who would have been only too happy if they could, in good conscience, have presented such a causalistic account of mental life. The old adage, *Scire est per causas scire*, has rung in many ears, and though its prestige has somewhat diminished since the nineteenth century, it is by no means unrealistic to suspect that it is not altogether abandoned even yet.

A passage in which this tendency comes to the fore occurs in Gumplowicz's *Grundriss der Soziologie*: 'The greatest error of individualistic psychology is the assumption', Gumplowicz writes, 'that it is man who

[1] *Social Theory and Social Structure*, 1949, 221 *seq.*

246

thinks. . . . What thinks in man, is not he himself, but his social community. The source of his thinking does not lie in him, but in the social environment in which he lives, in the social atmosphere he breathes, and he cannot think otherwise than in the manner which results by necessity from the influences of the social world around him which concentrate themselves in his brain' (ed. 1905, 268). This is essentially a mechanistic mode of argumentation. The 'social influences' around a man are conceived as so many determining (and maybe measurable) forces which form between them a parallelogram, and whose resultant is the mind of the man in their midst. We are obviously in the intellectual orbit of physics here, and this is characteristic of the whole causalistic approach; ideas for it are, strictly speaking, internal effects of external causes, and this conviction points straight in the direction of sociological and psychological mechanism. Not surprisingly, few writers have come closer to it, and to our own idealized representation of it, than Charles Henry Carey, the man who endeavoured to build up a Newtonian sociology. His is a coenonic-holistic theory developed in a spirit of quasi-mechanical causalism. The human beings who have associated with each other and formed societies, interchange within these societies goods and services and ideas. The brisker the interchange, the more 'heat' will be engendered; but from heat comes motion, and from motion, progress. In agricultural countries, where the population is scattered, the heat-, motion- and progress-producing give-and-take among associated men is comparatively low and sluggish, and the result is a modest level of development; in economically varied communities, on the other hand, where many people live in close proximity, it is comparatively intense, and so we find here a high level of development. We need only compare Ireland and Turkey, so Carey intimates, with London and Paris, to see that this is true.[1] This is, *inter alia*, a theory concerning the origination and evolution of culture; and it is a mechanistic-causal theory, since light comes, in both the physical and metaphorical senses of the word, from the rubbing together of independent substances. It is certainly no more than rudimentary as a sociology of knowledge and ideas, because Carey only tells us what conditions will, in principle, produce a culture, and does not go on to say what the content of that culture will be; but so far as it goes, Carey's doctrine is an instructive example of the causalistic tendency.

We have given two instances of this first way of conceiving of the nature of social determination in regard to culture and its contents, but we should find ourselves in great difficulty if asked to adduce many more. The truth is that though quite a number of writers have tended in the direction of mechanistic determinism, few have cared or ventured to advance very far along this road. And it is not difficult to see why they

---

[1] Cf. *Principles of Social Science*, 1858 *seq.*, I, 60 *seq.*

Problem B: The Nature of Social Determination

have been so reluctant to rush forward, in spite of all the temptation they have felt. There is something basically unrealistic about mechanistic determinism. We just cannot believe that we all think as we absolutely must. Even a great philosopher like Franz Brentano could express the opinion that it would be illogical to claim indeterminacy for man in view of the fact that he belongs to a universe in which everything seems in the grip of determination. But such arguments notoriously fail to convince; our continuous inner experience seems to teach us that our ideas are in no way predetermined *ab extra* (the word 'determined' taken in its more stringent connotation), but are, on the contrary, our very own. And, truly, there is a simple *non sequitur* at the basis of Brentano's conclusion (which is also the decisive consideration for all who would see the history of ideas in terms of univocal determination). For this conclusion cannot unfairly be formulated in the following way: everything outside us, in the material universe, is determined; therefore everything inside us, in the mental world, must be determined too. It really is difficult to see the cogency of such an inference. No, determinism goes against the grain of most of us, indeed, all of us. It is antecedently unlikely to embody the truth, and the determinists themselves have never managed to prove it. The *onus probandi* is on them. Until they have succeeded—and by better arguments than Brentano's—we can set their theory aside. In any case, our fellow-sociologists and fellow-historians are not likely to be angry with us if we leave the causalistic doctrine out of our further considerations. The *communis doctorum opinio* is heavily against it. And against it, in the first place, because it has never given any inductive illustration of its fundamental thesis. There is no available account, demonstrating, with the help of a concrete example, how external causes actually operate mechanically to produce internal mental conditions as their necessary effect. But a theory without even one convincing application to its credit has ruled itself, at least for the time being, out of court.

Thus the first alternative has left only very slight traces in sociological and historical thought, and need not be expected to figure prominently in its future development. Very different is the case of the second theory, which can best be described as the *functionalistic* doctrine. Many have explicitly accepted it; to many more it is at any rate an implicit creed. So far as the understanding of ideas, their origin and their complexion is concerned, it tends to treat them on the analogy of institutions: institutions are what they are because they have a part to play, a duty to perform, a function to fulfil, in the total economy of social life. It is the same with ideas. In an often quoted passage, Radcliffe-Brown has laid bare the fundamental convictions of this second approach: 'Such a view implies', he has written, 'that a social system (the total social structure of a society together with the totality of social usages in which that structure appears and on which it depends for its continued existence) has a certain kind of unity which we may speak of as a functional unity. We may define it as a condition in which all parts of the social system work together with a sufficient degree of harmony or internal consistency, i.e. without producing persistent conflicts which can neither be resolved nor regulated.' According to this way of seeing things, 'the function of a particular social usage is the contribution it makes to the total social life as the functioning of the total social system'.[1] But in this total social life, this functioning of the total social system, ideas have as large a part to play as usages. If the decisive usages of a society are habits of the body, habits of action, the decisive ideas are habits of the mind, habits of thought: the parallel between them is obvious. Both are inculcated in the individual by the community, and both must be so inculcated if the individuals are to form, and continue to form, a community capable of success and survival. In one of his utterances, Radcliffe-Brown draws the comparison between action patterns and mental patterns in so many words. 'I would define', he says, 'the social function of a socially standardized mode of activity, *or mode of thought*, as its relation to the social structure to the existence and continuity of which it makes some contribution.' And he then goes on to make a statement which allows us to discern the philosophical basis of this whole approach. 'Analogously', he points out, 'in a living organism, the physiological function of the beating of the heart, or the secretion of gastric juices, is its relation to the organic structure [of the whole].' [2] We are here as deep in the organological and biological tradition of sociology as we were previously in the mechanistic mode and mood.[3] The two great hostile schools of thought which, throughout the ages, have confronted each other in the history of social philosophy, have here found appropriate expression even in the narrower field of the theory of thought-determination and regard each other there with as much hostility as they do everywhere else.

As this second theory, the theory of the functional coherence of substructure and superstructure, is a kind of orthodoxy, though not a clearly conceived and consciously defended one, it is not difficult to furnish illustrations of it; on the contrary, a detailed search would land one in an *embarras de choix*. Radcliffe-Brown was deeply influenced by Emile Durkheim, and the latter provides an obvious example of functionalism. If a society is to function, i.e. if there is to be effective

[1] *Structure and Function in Primitive Society*, 1952, 181. Cf. also Nadel as quoted by Sprott, *Science and Social Action*, 1954, 59 *seq.*

[2] *Loc. cit.*, 200 *seq.* The emphasis is ours.

[3] For a lucid and penetrating discussion of the problems which the application of biological modes of thought must needs raise in the social sciences, cf. D. M. Emmet, *Function, Purpose and Powers*, 1957.

communication and co-operation between its members, certain common categories of thought are obviously an absolute necessity. Men cannot go hunting or fishing or feasting together unless they know when and where, in other words, unless there is a set of ideas concerning space and time common to the associated human beings—a set of collective representations, as the Durkheim school are wont to call them. There is a social need, then, for certain common ideas, and this need is supplied by social life itself. Out of its more external facts and processes—the fact that the camp is circular, that rites are performed at the full moon, and so on—there emerge, by a kind of mental mirroring, appropriate internal conceptions, corresponding intuitions concerning the nature, order and dimensions of spatial and temporal reality. The origin and content of these conceptions must, and can best, be understood from the total functioning of the social life which has thrown them up, and from the specific function which they themselves fulfil in their total functioning within that social life. This is, in our terminology, a coenonic-holistic theory connected with a functionalist view of social determination.

Different in detail, but similar in general drift and character, is the doctrine of William Graham Sumner as developed in his *Folkways*. The basic social process is that of mutual adjustment. In their desire to get along with each other, or, even more primitively, to avoid pain, men hit upon certain ways of doing things which guarantee a relatively smooth coexistence and co-operation with their fellow-men. These 'folkways' form a pattern which, as Marx would have expressed it, constitutes a substructure above which a mental superstructure of ideas is in time evolved and erected. 'Men begin with acts, not with thoughts', Sumner writes, but in the end 'sentiments are produced to correspond' (2, 12 *seq.*). Out of the basic folkways which make a society what it is, come *mores*, out of concrete *mores* a general ethos, and out of this ethos a matching culture. The whole is held together in that it is a going concern, a co-operative and integrated life, in a word, a quasi-organic unity. The parts of that unity receive their existence and meaning from the vital forces which sustain and carry along the whole. Ideas are inseparable aspects of the social totality, not separable entities. Here again we have a theory which is as characteristically functionalist in its view of the nature of social determination, as it is coenonic-holistic in its assumptions concerning the basis of that determination.

Most of the terms commonly and currently used to describe the coherence between the superstructure and the substructure, as brought together by Merton in the list reproduced above, are capable of a much more definite and exact meaning than they would otherwise have if interpreted in the spirit of the functionalist theory. Not, of course, the word cause, for that is reserved for the rival doctrine, causalism, but certainly correspondence, conditioning, consistency, coherence, harmony, unity, congruity, compatibility, stylistic analogy, reflection etc. In a well-ordered organism all its integral parts correspond to, are conditioned by and consistent with each other, are in coherence, harmony or unison, are congruous, compatible or analogous and reflect the common underlying style of life. Also capable of a meaningful organological interpretation are two other sets of phrases, often employed in characterizing the relationship between the intra- and extra-mental: the assertion that ideas are 'symbolic' or 'representational', and the assertion that they imply 'a becoming conscious' of their existential bases. With regard to the latter expression, we need only think of the human personality to see that it has a hidden organological reference. The well-balanced, well-integrated person has an inner life which stands in unbroken agreement with its outer comportment. His outer conduct is a manifestation of his inner mentality, his inner attitude a reflection, in the mirror of consciousness, of his outer behaviour. So also with society. The ideas involved here are perhaps a little primitive, but so far as they go they clearly stem from an organological mode of thinking. The matter is not quite so obvious with regard to the interpretation in terms of symbolism. But here, too, the words used make the best sense if given a functionalistic definition. Ideas and concepts are supposed to function together on the mental level in the same way as the extra-mental entities they stand for, symbolize or represent, function together in life, on the level of action. Hence they repeat or re-duplicate a quasi-organic coherence and interaction. And their relation to the realities signified is also a functional one, for, surely, a good symbol is not an arbitrarily chosen *quid pro quo*, but rather an essentially appropriate— a happily matched or harmoniously adjusted one. In all these cases, whatever the verbal cloak, the hard core of meaning is functionalistic, organismic.

All this goes to show how widely accepted the functionalist thesis is, notwithstanding the fact that it is rarely openly stated or consistently elaborated. The truth is that many if not most writers on the subject who seem to have no definite ideas with regard to the nature of social determination, would tend, or be obliged, to develop a functionalist doctrine if pressed to say exactly what they mean and what working concepts they employ. Here we are concerned less with the spread of the theory than with its import. And there two implications stand out at once: the functionalist position is compatible neither with the idea of a unilateral, nor with that of a univocal determination of human thought. In both these essential respects it is in clear contrast to causalism and mechanism. In stating this, we are not, of course, thinking of any such half-hearted or indistinct incarnations as either principle may have received in this book or that; we are thinking of these theories again in their perfection as ideal types, in that pure form, as it were, in which their distinctive theses are uncompromisingly carried to their logical conclusion.

The functionalistic, organismic doctrine, we are saying, cannot consistently claim that ideas are unilaterally determined by their existential conditions. For ideally an organic system is one of interrelationships, and not of one-sided dependences; it is a system in which everything depends on everything else, and consequently the substructure must, in principle, be as much a function of the superstructure as the latter is of the former. Of course, it is not necessary to conceive such a system as a completely symmetrical or synallagmatic order, an order, that is, in which every element depends as much on every other as that other depends upon it. It is quite possible to think of lopsided organisms in which more determinative influence is exerted from one point than from another. Friedrich Engels, for instance, had such a conception of the interplay of the social forces. 'It is not', he says in an important letter to H. Starkenburg, 'that the economic condition is the *cause* and *alone active*, while everything else only has a passive effect. There is, rather, interaction (*Wechselwirkung*).' Still, this interaction is 'on the basis of economic necessity, which *ultimately* always asserts itself',[1] i.e. proves itself stronger. But lopsidedness in an organism means imperfection: it is of the essence of organic totalities to be in principle symmetrical. The human body is in this respect the prototype of an organism, as it is in every other. In any case, every step away from the assumption of mutual interdependence is a step away from the functionalist theory and a concession to its causalist rival. There can be easy stages of transition from the one to the other, the counter-determination of the substructure by the superstructure being conceived as weaker and weaker until at last, in the limiting case, it becomes nil and we arrive at the mechanist-causalist position, with its assumption of a one-sided determination of ideas by extra-mental reality. If then, as we must do in dealing with ideal types, we consider the notion of a perfect organic whole, we shall have to ascribe to its inner life a two-way, not a one-way traffic of form-giving forces, a mutual determination rather than a unilateral domination of a 'higher' by a 'lower' part of the system.

However that may be—if the position be accepted which was developed in the last chapter and is symbolically expressed in the little drawing on page 244, then complete mutuality of influence as between the substructural and the superstructural forces must needs be assumed; in other words, it must be assumed that though ideas depend on social life, social life in its turn also depends on ideas. For in our scheme

---

[1] *Cit.* Adler, *Lehrbuch der materialistischen Geschichtsauffassung*, I, 1930, 191. Cf. Karl Marx and Frederick Engels, *Selected Works*, 1950, II, 457, for an English translation of the whole letter.

everything is traced back to the on-going process of social interaction as to its ultimate source. But that basic substructural process is itself shot through with thought. The human beings who move towards or away from each other in the course of social interaction, who meet in co-operation or hostility, who befriend or antagonize each other, do so as beings with certain mental intentions—intentions without which human interaction would not be possible at all. All human action, and consequently all human interaction, is, as Max Weber has so lucidly shown, intentional, meaningful, directed. But such intentions can only be conceived within a mental universe already constituted and in operation. Hence social life presupposes concrete forms of thought just as these forms of thought themselves presuppose social life. There is no contradiction or circular reasoning here—only mutuality, a moving in step, a functional interdependence. The organizing principle behind all social reality, a totality which includes action-patterns and thought-patterns at the same time, is to be found in the guiding values: it is they which organize action and thought and hold them together in an organic unity. With every move that men make in the direction of building-up a social system, they posit a rudimentary unit of action and thought, thought and action. It is only by a subsequent elaboration or crystallization, as we have called it, that forms of thought and forms of action gain comparative independence. In the living stream from which they emerge, grow concrete and crystallize themselves they are still one—in solution, as it were. And that original one-ness is never wholly lost. For the stream flows on and continues to send eddies and deposits in both directions, changing the crystallizations on either side in the same manner, and never allowing them to break away completely from each other.

All this is implied in the basic conception of society as a quasi-organic unity such as the vast majority of social scientists have always held it to be. But this unity, like all organic patterns, is a multiplicity as well, and the elements which it brings together and holds in its embrace are human beings and their actions, both of which (as we assume until convinced of the opposite) are essentially free. For that reason, social determination cannot be regarded as univocal, any more than it can be conceived as unilateral. Certainly, the modes of thought characteristic of a society must fit in with, and be organically adjusted to, the modes of action characteristic of that society, otherwise it would soon cease to be an operative unit. We cannot imagine a capitalist society with pre-capitalist modes of thought, nor yet a pre-capitalist society with capitalist modes of thought. But though the two halves of the social whole, the substructure and the superstructure, must for ever maintain a minimum of harmony with each other, there are more ways than one in which such harmony can be achieved. When we are hungry, we must eat, and

253

we must not eat poisonous things if we want to survive; but within the limits thus laid down, we are free to nourish ourselves as we see fit. It is the same with the survival of a social order. The modes of action must not be such as to kill the associated modes of thought; the modes of thought must not be such as to destroy the associated modes of action; if they do, the existing society will perish and another, more organically integrated, will take its place. But the conditions of survival thus formulated are only negative, and within them there is full freedom of movement. We may say that a feudal society cannot survive as such if a capitalist spirit develops within it, or a feudal spirit survive if a capitalist society develops around it. We may say that a feudal society must have a feudal spirit and a capitalist society a capitalist spirit. But we cannot say *a priori* what that spirit, that mentality, will be like in detail. For a culture is always freely elaborated by free men. There *is* determination because the mental modes must be capable of organic co-existence and co-function with the contemporary, co-social, modes of action; but there is no *univocal* determination, for many different mental modes may be suitable for association with a given mode of action, and *vice versa*. 'Functional needs', as Merton has rightly said, should be 'taken to be permissive, rather than determinant, of specific social structures. Or, in other words, there is a range of variation in the structures which fulfil the function in question.'[1] A man when he sets out to choose a bride will be determined in his choice by his pre-existing likes and dislikes; yet he will always be able to find more than one girl who might suit him, and with whom he can hope to live in harmony. Or, to change the metaphor completely: a man, when asked a question, can, as a rule, answer it in many different ways; yet if his reaction to the query is to be sensible and meaningful, it must fit both the question asked and the questioner's understanding. Hence there is a situation half-way between full freedom and complete determination.

There may be some who will be inclined to argue that the more indetermination is admitted, the less there is that a discipline like the sociology of knowledge can explain; and that, since we have admitted a lot of indetermination, our sociology of knowledge can explain very little. But in an argument such as this, the word 'explain' is ambiguous. It can mean either to account for the *existence* of a given idea, or to bring out its *meaning*. In other words, it can be used either in an ontological or a hermeneutic sense. But we have already stated our conviction that the sociology of knowledge is a hermeneutic method, not a dogmatic ontology. It does not and cannot undertake to show that what has come to pass was necessarily obliged to do so. That is precisely why we have repudiated the causalist view. It only promises to help us to

[1] *Social Theory and Social Structure*, 1949, 35. Cf. the whole discussion of the 'postulate of indispensability', 34 *seq*.

a fuller understanding of the developments which history has recorded. Now, to a hermeneutic discipline, it does not matter at all whether determination is thought of as unilateral or mutual, univocal or multivocal. Even a free utterance, a spontaneous response, receives illumination from the conditions under which it was made. A statement which does not fit its circumstances, which is out of keeping with the total situation in which it is an element or of which it is a development, is devoid of meaning. It is like a Chinese sentence addressed to Englishmen who know no Chinese, or the blethering of a madman in the midst of the sane. It is the hallmark of meaningful discourse to be attuned to its human setting and hence to be capable of interpretation in terms of it. The sociology of knowledge is there to pursue the possibilities and provide the techniques of such interpretation. It does not need for its success an association with philosophical determinism; indeed, such bad company would only bring it down in the world.

Assuming, then, that the substructure is as much determined by the superstructure as the latter is by the former, in other words, that there is complete mutuality and symmetry between the social forces which interdetermine each other in a social system, what useful insight is it that the sociology of knowledge, as a hermeneutic method, has to offer? It is this: that it is easier to understand the superstructure through the substructure than the other way about; that strategically it is much wiser to go on from a study of a society's institutions to that of its ideas than vice versa. For institutions are a much more tangible reality than ideas are or ever can be. Belonging to the external world, being objectifications of the basic social process in a much more literal sense (of the word object) than the essentially internal thoughts associated with them in a common social flux, they lie, relatively speaking, more openly before our eyes, and submit more readily to our grip, than the spirit, which has ever been likened to the wind—so notoriously difficult to seize and capture. Once we have penetrated to the essence of a society's institutional structure, the conquest of its culture and mentality will be relatively easy. This is, for the historian of ideas and the social anthropologist, a fact of prime importance; the sociology of knowledge fashions for him a tool which he can use with great effectiveness if only he will.[1] The methodological device thus developed can be very neatly distinguished, in respect of its philosophical foundation, from all dogmatic ontology, by saying that it regards the substructure, not as more real than the superstructure, but merely as more readily understood.

The important point, which must not be overlooked in this connection, is that a hermeneutic method only comes into play *post festum*, after life has already provided a phenomenon to be interpreted. Here

[1] Cf. on all this, Stark, 'Towards a Theory of Social Knowledge', *Revue Internationale de Philosophie*, 1950, esp. point 6.

again we perceive a great difference between mechanistic causalism and quasi-organological functionalism, for the crowning ambition of the former will always be to predict developments, not to comment on them after they have taken place. It is a high endeavour and would entitle its votaries to glory in their triumph if it could be made to succeed; but in the nature of things it cannot. Thoughts, like all cultural phenomena, are produced in freedom and spontaneity. Though we may anticipate their general character, we cannot predict their concrete qualities. But this does not matter in the least to an interpretative method. For when the interpreter sets to work, the freedom and spontaneity inherent in all cultural creativity has long ago perished from the earth. When a scholar writes a book or a musician a symphony or a poet a poem, he is under no constraint; he has initially all the liberty he can desire. But as his work takes shape, this liberty drops away from him bit by bit, he consumes it, as it were, as he moves along. Originally confronted by a wide field in which he can roam freely, he progressively traces out a path which then becomes 'his' in a determinate sense of the word: it is the tragedy of all choice in freedom, that the freedom vanishes when the choice is taken. Now all this means much for the sociology of knowledge. It means, to put the matter plainly, that what is not in fact pre-determined may appear pre-determined in retrospect; what is in fact only multivocally determined *ex ante* may appear univocally determined *ex post*. If we take up any thought or theory for historical interpretation, we need not worry about the freedom its author enjoyed when he formulated it; for that freedom has vanished, and what is left for us to deal with can be treated simply as the response to a situation, a product of the circumstances. We can handle it as if it had been the only reasonable response, the only possible product, even though, not being determinists, we know full well that at the moment of its birth it was not.

(b) THE THEORY OF ELECTIVE AFFINITY

The reader who has followed us thus far will no doubt have received the impression that we are making the functionalist theory our own. And he is not far wrong in jumping to this conclusion. Nevertheless, we must ask him to bide with us for a short while yet, for we have still to consider the third alternative approach. Now this third alternative is not to be taken lightly, for among its sponsors figure some of the greatest names in social philosophy—Max Scheler, Max Weber and Alfred Weber, to mention only a few. What such men have believed, deserves the most serious consideration.

The salient characteristic of this third theory is that it ascribes to human thought even more freedom than does the functionalist-organological alternative. Functionalism sees ideas at birth as elements in a totality, and consequently as in some sense and to some degree indebted to that totality for their existence, content and qualities. Here we are face to face with an attitude which tends to see ideas as completely free at their point of inception, we might almost say as strangers descended into this world from some higher sphere. Some protagonists of this way of thinking have indeed been inclined to a Platonic world-view, for example Scheler; others have been extreme individualists, like Max Weber, who found it difficult to believe that our mental processes are ever in any way conditioned *ab extra*. But both have realized that these strangers, once they have entered the sublunary sphere, the social world, must come to terms with it. This is no place for disembodied spirits; even ideas must have bodies if they are to last, and so they will be on the look-out for appropriate human groupings who can take them in and carry them along. But human groupings, of whatever kind, will, for their part, always be on the look-out for appropriate ideas to give expression to their essence and their strivings, for, material as this life is, it nevertheless has a spiritual side to it. Thus there will be a gradual convergence between substructures and superstructures, not coherence *ab initio*. Like will search for, and, when found, link up with, like. Most appropriately, this theory has become known as the theory of *elective affinity*.[1]

We see the doctrine in its relatively simplest form in Max Weber. Weber was much impressed by the fact that the system of ideas which gave itself out as specifically 'proletarian' and was indeed accepted as such by the great majority of the continental proletariat, was not the product of members of that class at all, but rather of two scions of the higher classes—Karl Marx and Vladimir Lenin. He concluded from this that such philosophies are not the simple precipitate of a certain way of life, not the reflection of a given social situation, but rather purely intellectual ventures, creatures of the mind, conceived and born in freedom and independence. But at the time when they were born, there existed in Europe a working class movement which was as yet all body but no mind. It was on the move, but it did not know where to go; it expressed a longing, but it could not have said what for. No wonder that it eagerly embraced the Marxian contention that the working-man was the tool of universal history for the final liberation of mankind from all misery and degradation; and no wonder that the Marxian spirit was only too willing to slip into that giant body with its giant strength, promising as it did to make what was only an intellectual aspiration into a political reality! There took place a process of mutual accommodation between this particular 'superstructure' and that particular 'substructure'; like found, and fitted itself to, like. And thus,

[1] The term is taken from Max Weber. Cf. his *Gesammelte Aufsätze zur Religionssoziologie*, I, 1920, 83, 257 *seq*.

Weber was inclined to suppose, it will always be. Mentalities and movements are not originally one organic system; they are rather the warp and woof which, at first independent strands, are later woven on the loom of time into a coherent texture. Even Weber's central theory—of the affinity between Capitalism and Calvinism—is conceived in the same spirit. Not only is there no causal connection between the two; Weber does not even treat the 'protestant ethic' as a phenomenon of incipient capitalism. One may find it, or religious conceptions like it, in many social settings which contain no more capitalism than exists in any representative society. What Weber really teaches is that modern Western capitalism has been developed by groups of men who made this religious philosophy and moral code their own because they found it convenient, attractive, sympathetic, *sinnverwandt*. It was this slant in Weber's doctrine which prevented many from accepting it as it stood, notably the Marxists whose tendency it has been from the beginning to take it and transform it into a more functionalist explanation.[1]

Max Scheler's theory is very similar to this, save only that it is a good deal more sophisticated, for Scheler connects ideas of this kind with the tenets of the essentially neo-platonic Husserlian school to which he belonged, and whose creed is known as phenomenology. There is a realm of ideas endowed with ontological reality, with true, if metaphysical existence, and when we think, we participate in it. But ideas, though real in another world, are powerless in this, and if they are to gain influence, they must ally themselves with social movements here below, or even with biotic drives. What in fact happens, according to Scheler, is that elements of the absolute world of essences enter into, and become active in, human history when some set of leaders, some élite, accepts them as their own; from thence they spread, by a kind of secondary radiation, to the more passive and imitative masses. Whether the members of the pioneering group accept them in this way and give them power and punch, depends on what these people are like (towards the end of his life, Scheler increasingly concentrated on what their drives were like; he developed progressively towards a hormic explanation). Hence there is, as he thinks, a convergence of thought-forms and life-forms, both of which are at first unconnected, and belong, indeed, to ontological realms of the most diverse type. History is a middle sphere where, owing to the constant intermarriage of spirit and body, new cultural phenomena are continually engendered and born. 'Our method', Scheler writes, 'never explains the meaningful *content* of spiritual culture by the substructural forces (*realsoziologisch*), but only the *selection* of this or that meaningful content out of spiritually equally

---

[1] For further detail cf. von Schelting, *Max Webers Wissenschaftslehre*, 1934, 108 *seq.* (footnote 2), 115 *seq.*, 284, and 375 *seq.* (esp. footnote 2 on 376). Cf. also von Schelting in the *Archiv für Sozialwissenschaft*, 1929, 12 and 64.

possible alternatives.' [1] Obviously, this mode of explanation has its difficulties, in that it tries to link what is essentially unconnected, and perhaps in strict logic incapable of inter-connection. But this need not occupy us here. We have merely sought to give one more example of what is manifestly a theory of elective affinity—of the meeting and mutual adjustment of substructure and superstructure, social life and culture-content.

Alfred Weber, too, entertains opinions analogous to these (though, needless to say, with very wide individual deviations), but we cannot stop to discuss them. [2] Instead, we must hurry forward to meet our main responsibility, namely, to discuss, and if possible to determine, the relation between the functionalist theory and the theory of elective affinity, or, as it might also be called, of the mutual accommodation between superstructure and substructure—a relationship which, *prima facie*, seems to be one of competition, of irreconcilable opposition. But before we take this essential matter up, it may be as well to demonstrate once again what our typological approach can achieve, and what its value is for the clarification of ideas. Not a few thinkers, or schools of thought at least, have attempted simultaneously to move in different directions, so far as the social determination of the human mind is concerned, though apparently quite unaware of the fact that they were doing so. Marxism is once again a good example, but the case of Karl Mannheim is also instructive in this respect.

As for Marxism, there can be little doubt that its implied opinion concerning the nature of social determination is a variant of the functionalist approach. Marx's whole system of ideas cannot be properly understood unless it is seen as a late development of the romantic view of life (which came to him mainly through Hegel, though not through Hegel alone), and romanticism has always shown a tendency to identify itself closely, indeed completely, with the organological tradition in social philosophy. The very basis of 'historical materialism', namely the assertion that men's consciousness is a reflection of their social existence, is manifestly derived from the conviction that consciousness and extra-mental reality form an integrated whole, as they do in the case of any animated creature, for instance man, where the mind is integrated with the extra-mental reality of the body. Indeed, even the most characteristic feature of historical materialism, namely its conviction that processes of production are fundamental and determining processes with which everything else has to come into line, still recall organicism, for is it not a simple fact that food-getting activities are absolutely basic to all living beings, a prime necessity, in

[1] *Die Wissensformen und die Gesellschaft*, 1926, 127. The classical exposition is on pp. 30 *seq.*
[2] Cf. von Schelting in the *Archiv für Sozialwissenschaft*, 1929, 52 *seq.*

comparison with which everything else is secondary only? The basically organological character of Marxian thinking sometimes becomes quite obvious, as for instance in the following passage from the *Critique of Political Economy*: 'The result to which we come is not that production, distribution, exchange, consumption are identical, but that they all constitute members of a totality. . . . There is interaction between the different elements. This is the case with every organic whole.'[1] It is true that in this quotation the mind is not specifically mentioned, but Lukacs rightly says: 'For the dialectical method everything revolves around the same problem, whatever it may happen to deal with: the knowledge of the totality of the historical process. From this standpoint, therefore, "ideological" and "economic" problems lose their mutual rigid strangeness and flow together. . . . The literary, the scholarly formulation of a problem appears as the expression of a social totality.'[2] And Warynski puts it even more clearly: 'Theory . . . is a functional element in a general and necessary totality of interrelations.'[3]

What has kept the recognition of this indebtedness of Marx and his disciples to romanticism out of many books on him is the fact that he defines his *individuum* differently from other organological thinkers. These latter, in spite of all their emphasis on evolution, development, and history, regard the contemporary social system as a unity within which everything has its place, function and meaning. Not so Marx. For him the decisive unity is not that of the contemporary world, but that of world-history. This is a point which Lukacs' admirable book, *Geschichte und Klassenbewusstsein*, has most happily brought out.[4] For Marxism, says Lukacs in a particularly telling phrase, 'the true historical reality is the *totality* of the historical process' (168). It would, of course, be impossible to give detailed proof of the fundamentally organological nature of Marx's thought without writing a whole book about it. Here it must suffice to say that consciousness, for him, is essentially a becoming-conscious of life (with its continuing, all-important struggles)[5]—a conception which we have shown above to be one possible incarnation or expression of the principle of functionalism, of the organological approach.

But though Marx was thus a member of a definite school, namely that which we have ranked as number 2, there are traces at least of numbers 1 and 3 as well in his writings and in those of his followers. Theory number 1, indeed, is not very clearly identifiable in Marx

---

[1] *Grundrisse der Kritik der politischen Ökonomie*, ed. 1953, 20 *seq.*

[2] *Geschichte und Klassenbewusstsein*, 1923, 46 *seq.*

[3] *Die Wissenschaft von der Gesellschaft*, 1944, 189. Cf. also 101 *seq.*, 113 *seq.*

[4] Cf. esp. 25 (comparison of Marx and Spencer), 40, 167 *seq.*, 204.

[5] Cf. Lukacs, *loc. cit.*, 15, 194. Cf. esp. 29: 'The function of theory [is] the self-knowledge of reality.'

himself, and Engels, in various letters, has expressly repudiated the cause-and-effect interpretation of the Marxian doctrine of the origin of ideas.[1] But the hankering after a stricter causalism is there and becomes much more noticeable in later Marxist literature. The closer the Marxists approximated to positivism—the more they felt themselves to be 'scientists'—the greater became their longing for the comforts of a causalistic world-view. Yet they never came wholly to identify themselves with it, the reason being that Marxism is too much of a purely social theory to be able to digest enough mechanism to make a doctrine of the mechanical causation of consciousness and its contents possible within its frame.

As for number 3, the theory of elective affinity, there are quite a few traces of an approach towards its fundamental thesis to be found in Marx's own works. For instance, in his *Kritik der Hegelschen Rechtsphilosophie*: 'It is not sufficient that the idea should press forward towards realization, reality itself must press forward towards the idea'; or, in *Die Heilige Familie*: 'Ideas can never lead beyond an old state of the world, but only beyond the ideas of the old state of the world. Ideas cannot give reality to anything at all. For the realization of ideas men are needed, who provide power.' If it be said that these formulations only reflect the negative aspect of the theory of elective affinity—thought is powerless without 'real' driving-forces—there is also a famous and indeed flamboyant formulation of its positive implication: 'Even theory becomes a material power when it gets hold of the masses.' [2] This sentence might equally well have been written by Max Scheler as by Karl Marx! It was Kautsky who developed these elements of Marx's theory, so much so that a critic could write of him that he ends by arriving at a 'complete replacement of the Marxian dialectical movement of thought by the Machian "adjustment of ideas to the facts" and "adjustment of ideas to each other" '.[3]

Mannheim, writing fifty years after Marx's death, is no more conscious than the latter of the fact that he is operating simultaneously along divergent lines. Basically, we are again confronted with a functionalist doctrine, indeed, with a rather typical one.[4] 'The relationship of

---

[1] Cf. esp. the letter to Starkenburg referred to above p. 252.

[2] *Aus dem literarischen Nachlass von Karl Marx und Friedrich Engels, 1841–1850*, ed. Franz Mehring, 1920, I, 392 *seq.*, II, 225.

[3] Korsch in *Grünbergs Archiv für die Geschichte des Sozialismus und der Arbeiterbewegung*, 1929, 198.

[4] We are prepared to credit Mannheim's thought on this head with more definiteness than Merton allows in *Social Theory and Social Structure*, 1949, 254 *seq.* Cf. also Maquet, *Sociologie de la Connaissance*, 1949, 55 *seq.*, who, after some hesitation, comes in the end to the same interpretation of Mannheim's position as is indicated in the text (cf. 57), and Lieber, *Wissen und Gesellschaft*, 1952, 94 *seq.*, who shares it from the very beginning.

superstructure to substructure and of substructure to superstructure is in truth a mutual one,' he says in a characteristic passage. 'It can truly be said, not only that the spirit which is to be found in the superstructure can only become real if there exists a definite structural configuration of the substructure, but also that a change in the substructure can only come about if the spiritual potentialities in the superstructure have reached a certain state. Capitalism as an economic system could only appear when the right intellectual constellation was ready.'[1] Arguing against Max Scheler's strict dualism and doctrine of elective affinity, Mannheim strongly presses the functionalist point of view: 'For us, too,' he says, 'there is a . . . separation between Being and Meaning; but this . . . duality can no longer be considered as fundamental when we come to examine both terms as parts of a dynamic genetic totality. . . . When we reach "existence" as an ultimate unity in which all phenomenological differences are cancelled, "Being" and "Meaning" appear as hypostatized partial spheres which are ultimately the "emanations" of one and the same Life. For any philosophy or theory of culture or sociology which seeks to transcend the abstract immanence of the various cultural products [i.e. the purely *ab intra* study of them] and to analyse them as part and parcel of an overall life process, the phenomenological duality cannot be more than a provisional device.' And later in the same essay he moves on to a more direct and positive formulation of the functionalist view-point: 'One of the important aspects of the evolution of intellectual standpoints is the contribution they make to the overall evolutionary process within society. It is possible to show in retrospect in what way every single utopia, and also every single image of past history, has helped to mould the epoch in which it emerged.' Consequently, the task of the sociology of knowledge 'consists in working out this *functional* rôle of social, existentially involved thinking . . . To the extent that an epoch is already terminated, to the extent that it presents itself as a completed *Gestalt*, we can specify the functional rôle of thought patterns relative to the goal at which the evolutionary process had been aiming.'[2] This is the very same organicism with the same strong evolutionary slant which we find in Marx, and it is a revealing detail that Mannheim himself italicized the words *totality, functional,* and *Gestalt* in the quotations given above. Indeed, the functionalist view-point is almost ubiquitous in his writings and

---

[1] 'Das Problem einer Soziologie des Wissens', *Archiv für Sozialwissenschaft*, vol. LIII, 1925, 632. We offer our own translation at this point, in lieu of that given in the *Essays on the Sociology of Knowledge*, 1952, 163, which is not in complete verbal agreement with the original.

[2] *Essays on the Sociology of Knowledge*, 1952, 161, 176 *seq.* For a criticism from the point of view of the theory of elective affinity cf. von Schelting, *Max Webers Wissenschaftslehre*, 1934, 109, footnote.

dozens of passages could be adduced in which it is more or less clearly and consciously expressed and propagated.

Nevertheless, Mannheim sometimes falls unwittingly, just as Marx did, into those modes of analysis and argument characteristic of the theory of elective affinity which he continues to condemn so strongly when he meets them in men like Scheler. One of the most important chapters of *Ideology and Utopia*, for instance, begins as follows: 'The decisive turning-point in modern history was . . . the moment in which "Chiliasm" joined forces with the active demands of the oppressed strata of society. The very idea of the dawn of a millennial kingdom on earth always contained a revolutionizing tendency . . . [but it was only] in the Hussites, and then in Thomas Münzer and the Anabaptists, [that] these ideas became transformed into the activistic movements of specific social strata. Longings which up to that time had been either unattached to a specific goal or concentrated upon other-worldly objectives suddenly took on a mundane complexion' (190 *seq.*). Is not this a clear case of the *meeting* in time of ideas and movements, rather than of their functional inter-connection *in genesi*? Speaking more generally, Mannheim observes, a few pages earlier: 'It happens very often that the dominant utopia first arises as the wish-fantasy of a single individual and does not until later become incorporated into the political aims of a more inclusive group.' This thought is really typical of Scheler, rather than of Mannheim himself in his more settled mood. It is true that he soon reverts to the functionalist view. 'What is new in the achievement of the personally unique "charismatic" individual', he says about twenty lines further down, 'can only then be utilized for the collective life when, from the very beginning, it is in contact with some important current problem, and when from the start its meanings are rooted genetically in collective purposes' (185 *seq.*). But this only shows that functionalism predominates in Mannheim's thinking, and does not alter the fact that he can on occasion slip into a very different mode of explanation without noticing that he has gone astray.

(c) A RECONCILIATION OF THE CONFLICTING THEORIES

The time has now come to assess the merits of this third theory, that of elective affinity, and to weigh it against its only serious rival, the theory of functional interrelation, whose high deserts have already been duly acknowledged. One important deficiency in the former stands out at once: it finds, and must find it, very much more difficult than functionalism to account for the influence of ideas on social life, an influence whose reality even Engels was ready to acknowledge. Since the substructure, according to functionalism, or at any rate one brand of it, is the interaction of men in society, and since men, in all their actions and interactions, always and necessarily behave as thinking beings, functionalism encounters no obstacle at this point: ideas can impinge upon the on-going social process of human interaction, and help to shape it, just as it shapes them, for they have emerged from it and remain in uninterrupted vital contact with it all the time. But the theory of elective affinity postulates an initial gap between social reality and ideas, and this basic assumption is bound to create problems. In reading Scheler, one is confronted with the picture of a curiously divided reality. On the one hand are the eternal ideas dwelling above us in the high heavens; on the other there stand the social movements propelled forward by animal drives, initially without thought or ideals—a mere mindless mass uneasily on the move. Clearly, if these notions were to be taken seriously—and we must not forget that, according to Scheler, the gap to be bridged between substructure and superstructure is the whole gulf between physical and metaphysical—a meeting of the two could not be imagined at all; for how could a mindless movement select for itself ideas that would suit it; and how or why, on the other hand, should ideas descend from their heavenly abode, incarnate themselves in this world or mingle with the dross and dirt of these lower spheres? Clearly, for the theory to work at all it is necessary to assume that the substructural bodies have enough *nous* in them from the very beginning to be able to recognize and appropriate ideas which are congenial or useful to them. But if we assume this, as we must, then they alone appear as active; they alone decide upon the realization, and even the elaboration (in human terms) of ideas: they alone work the sluice-gates (to use Scheler's own simile) through which ideas can enter this world of ours as the sunbeams enter a house through the chinks in the curtains. But if so, thought is altogether powerless.

Now, Scheler does not shrink from this conclusion. 'Where ideas find no forces, interests, passions or drives of any kind, or their objective counterpart in institutions,' he writes, 'there they are totally without significance for real history. Nor is there anything that could be called the "cunning of the idea" (Hegel) by which it could, so to speak, slily "make use" of interests and sentiments and so master them . . . The course of real history is to that extent perfectly indifferent to the implied demands of spiritual production.' [1] Surely, such an attitude is altogether unrealistic. We have in recent years been presented with Schumpeter's interesting and convincing analysis of the fate of capitalism. [2] Capitalism, as he rightly explains, is not decaying and dying a lingering death because something is amiss in its organizational substructure; indeed,

---

[1] *Die Wissensformen und die Gesellschaft*, 1926, 31 *seq.*
[2] *Capitalism, Socialism and Democracy*, 1942.

that substructure has, if anything, gained in strength and stability over the last eighty years; it is doomed because a change has taken place in men's attitude to it, and to its values. This is a clear case in which ideas, impinging, as we have put it, upon action, and through them outwards upon institutions, have asserted themselves with decisive success in world history. According to a theory such as Scheler's, this could never have occurred. Or rather he would have to argue, like the cruder Marxists and materialists, that the mental changes that have taken place are not the real causes of what has happened (though Schumpeter demonstrates that they were), but only symptoms, a kind of musical background, as it were. In effect, to cut a long story short, there is a tendency in Scheler, in spite of all his Platonic exaltation of ideas, to reduce them, so far as this life is concerned, to the level of epiphenomena, as Dahlke and Becker have rightly recognized.[1] But in so far as this is the case, the theory of elective affinity is no better than the materialistic doctrine of causalism, and all the reasons we have given for rejecting the latter must also, in fairness, be pressed against it.

Of course, it could be argued in defence of elective affinity, that it is not necessary to go to extremes as Scheler obviously does. It could be said that substructure and superstructure are both active, rather than that the former is active and the latter passive; that they are like the opposite poles of two magnets which mutually attract each other. True; but what are the logical implications of such an argument? The more power is ascribed to ideas, in other words, the more ideas are brought on to a par with the substructural forces, the more we abandon in fact the theory of elective affinity which is a special mode of explanation precisely because it assumes an essential ontological difference between substructure and substructure—the more, in other words, we are on the way back to functionalism, to quasi-organicism. And if we go to the end of the road, if we suppose complete equality in strength as between superstructure and substructure, then we are again thinking in functionalist, quasi-organological terms—with one important difference. This difference is that consistent functionalism sees substructure and superstructure in a *state* of mutual adjustment, whereas the corrected theory of elective affinity tends to see them *in course* of mutual adjustment. Now, this shows us wherein the true value of the doctrine of elective affinity lies. Its claim to dislodge and replace the theory of quasi-organic interaction clearly fails; but it can, and indeed must, be accepted as its complement and corrective. For the functionalist conception of the nature of social determination shares the besetting sin of all functionalism, of all organicism, namely an overemphasis upon the unity of the body social. In a completely organized and internally

[1] *Philosophy and Phenomenological Research*, 1941/2, 322.

harmonious society (if such a thing can be so much as imagined), there would be, by definition, no processes of mutual adjustment; there would, again by definition, exist perfect all-round adjustment, and in such a society nothing would be needed, and nothing could be used, for a total explanation of all phenomena, substructural as well as superstructural, beside the functionalist theory. But in societies as they really are, with loose textures and frayed edges, where much is wanting to internal consistency and where alien influences continually tend to break in from all directions, there is clearly room for some such additional mode of analysis as that of elective affinity; there is room and indeed need for it, as a secondary and subsidiary explanation, reducing the quasi-organic interpretation to its proper dimensions and supplying an elucidation of the processes which tend to lead towards the final (or ideal) state of complete integration which quasi-organicism all too lightly assumes to be the actual (and real) state of affairs.

The positive contribution which the theory of elective affinity (thus chastened, and itself in a chastening rôle) can make to the understanding of the history of ideas, can be seen from Alfred von Martin's essay, *Soziologie der Kultur des Mittelalters*, which is perhaps the best example of its concrete application.[1] At the beginning of the Middle Ages we find, as von Martin explains, on the one hand a tribal world, the world of the Germanic and Romanic tribes, with its own specific social tradition and inherent tendencies, and on the other hand a disparate world of ideas and sentiments represented by the Church, a mental world born in Antiquity and carrying its legacy forward into the future. At first, the two spheres are closed to each other, like circles which perhaps touch but do not intersect; as time goes on, they merge more and more until complete coincidence is well-nigh reached, and this precisely is the making of the Middle Ages. Now the initial situation clearly excludes the application of the theory of functional interconnection: the tribal 'substructure' is north of the Alps, the Christian 'superstructure' south of them; the twain have as yet not even met. Here, if we want to explain what has happened, we need the theory of gradual adjustment, i.e. that of elective affinity, rather than that of mutual adjustedness, i.e. that of quasi-organic coherence. Of course, as the two elements whose interpenetration, as von Martin demonstrates, constitutes the essence of the Middle Ages, come to merge with each other, it becomes less and less applicable, and the rival theory of functional integration more and more so; which goes to show—and this is the point we wish to make—that the two are complementary rather than mutually exclusive, occupants of neighbouring territories rather than contestants for the same.

[1] Reprinted in *Geist und Gesellschaft*, 1948, 15 *seq.*

Problem B: The Nature of Social Determination

It cannot be our task here to follow von Martin's fascinating essay in its detail. We must be satisfied to take from it one or two *aperçus* by way of illustration. One is afforded by the developments in the economic sphere. As the operative unit of medieval economic life was comparatively small and had the character of a face-to-face group, there was strong social pressure on those concerned—buyer and seller, master and man—to treat each other, not as strangers would, but as neighbours ought to do. As one would expect on general grounds, this pressure tended to become institutionalized, and hence there resulted, for instance, the guilds, those characteristic institutions of the medieval town. Their aim was to fix a fair price which would be acceptable all round. But—and this is the point the theory of elective affinity is anxious to make—these substructural, institutional developments led to the reception into the medieval system of life of certain suitable superstructural elements, of certain kindred ideas or collective representations, which cannot be said to have been its products or dependent variables. When St. Paul, for instance, demanded that nobody should overreach his brother in business (I Thessalonians 4), he was speaking from an environment which was not that of a medieval town community. Indeed, he was expressing (if we are to believe von Martin) a purely ideal desideratum; he was stating a piece of abstract moral theology which was pressing forward into life rather than growing out of it. The practical fair-price policy of the medieval town and the philosophical fair-price preaching of the medieval church were simply predestined, by their inherent contents and tendencies, to ultimate fusion, and this fusion, when it came, produced the well-known doctrine and the legislation surrounding the concept of *justum pretium*.

A further example of this mutual accommodation and final harmonization of social substructure and philosophico-theological superstructure can be seen in the phenomenon of chivalry, that very climax and flower of medieval civilization. Chivalry was essentially a synthesis of soldiery and sanctity, that is to say of substructural realities (soldiery) and superstructural aspirations (sanctity). 'The Church had educated the knighthood for its religious ideals and ecclesiastical purposes,' von Martin writes. 'The protection of the weak now became a knightly *point d'honneur*; in relation to the external world, the arms of knighthood were put into the service of the struggle against heathens and heretics. . . . The knightly ethos of self-discipline, which sprang from the spontaneous spiritual dynamism of this estate, met this [ecclesiastical policy] half way: it was ready to acknowledge religious and ethical values, if it saw them in agreement with its *esprit de corps* and was thus able mentally to digest them. *Triuwe* and *staete* are virtues immediately intelligible to the vital feelings of a liege-man', for *triuwe* (faithfulness) and *staete* (steadfastness) were merely the mental

267

concomitants and unavoidable implications of the real (social and economic) relationship of the feudal nexus between lord and vassal. 'By conceiving his relation to God as a personal relation of vassalage and an obligation of honour, belief in God appears to [the knightly] religious and ethical consciousness as faith in God [*triuwe*]—and this accords well with the ecclesiastical concept of *constantia* in the Church's moral philosophy. And in the same way the knightly virtue of *mâze* [moderation], the expression of the predilection, characteristic of this status group, for a noble form of living, for style, harmonizes with the *temperentia* of the ecclesiastical doctrine, and that of *milte* [generosity], the highest lordly virtue of the knight—in the sense of *noblesse oblige* —with the virtue of *liberalitas* taught by the Church. Thus an ethos which is social in origin comes ... into line with the religious ... conduct generally demanded by the Church.' [1]

Not only in these two examples, but throughout his whole exposition, von Martin is consciously trying to implement the theory of elective affinity and to demonstrate its value and validity. Indeed, he openly formulates it, and that more than once. 'The origin of a unitary culture always presupposes the meeting of a spiritual idea with a substructural (*realsoziologischen*) reality,' he says in one context, and in another he affirms even more clearly: 'In order to be able to enter into historical life, the idea always needs the alliance of some tangible interest—only then will it be capable of achieving broader effects, of advancing from the purely private sphere into the social. This does not signify', he cautiously adds, 'that the idea as such is powerless, only that its ideal power stands in need of co-operation with a real force if it is to exert influence on a wider front.' [2] In spite of this last proviso, which merely proves that he is not an extremist, and is not prepared to go so far as Max Scheler does, von Martin shows himself in these and similar passages an upholder of the conviction that the decisive process which we have labelled 'social determination' is essentially a coming-to-terms of the purely ideal with the purely real, of consciousness with social existence—a process in which the ideas get by far the worst of the bargain: 'The alliance of the spirit with life is ... for the "pure" spirit always a *societas leonina*.' [3]

But is this really what he is talking about? Is the development of medieval life—even according to his own description of it—really the entry of a disembodied spirit into a spirit-less, or at most semi-inspirited, body, thus producing the balanced compound of spirit-and-body which is medieval culture? Surely not. What happened in fact was not that a 'spiritual idea' met and merged with a 'substructural reality', but that

---

[1] *Geist und Gesellschaft*, 1948, 38 *seq.*
[2] *Ibid.*, 23, 16. Cf. also 71 *seq.*, 90 *seq.*   [3] *Loc. cit.*, 72.

two ways of life came to meet and mingle. Von Martin's convictions could be illustrated in the following diagram:

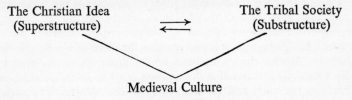

But this is a mistaken view, for what took place was really this:

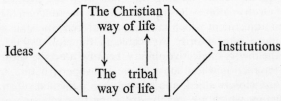

In so far as this latter representation (which is merely an elaboration of our earlier sketch) is correct, the basic conceptions of the theory of elective affinity are wrong. And, indeed, they *are* wrong. For if Christianity had been no more than a spirit without a body, wandering at large, it would never have been able to break into the tribal world and bend it to the image which it contained of what a society should be like. Far from having no body, it had a very strong body—the Church, which, not without good reason, regarded herself as the prolongation, as it were, of the Roman Empire. What von Martin says about her shows how living, how real a society she was—and not just a society, but an institution as well, almost a state. Surely, a concept like *temperantia* was as much the crystallization of an on-going social life with its inherent striving for perfection as was the concept of *mâze*. So long as the two streams of life were as yet separate, *temperantia* did not mean what *mâze* did, or *vice versa*. It was only when the two currents of being had flowed into each other, had become to all intents and purposes one process of interaction, that the different meanings merged as well, or rather became merely overtones and undertones above and beneath a common central layer of meaning. Von Martin himself would hardly be able to impugn this interpretation, which sees the adjustment of discordant elements as a process in the substructure, and not as a process between substructure and superstructure, because he himself sometimes falls into the organological mode of thinking and talking. In the decisive chapter (no. 4) entitled 'Spiritual Ideas and Substructural Reality' he speaks, like a good functionalist, of a 'correspondence of idea and substructural interest' and writes, in so many words: 'Indeed, the idea was to a large extent a reflex of reality, even though it, for its part, influenced reality in return.' [1] This is more than a stylistic lapse: it is a proof that the functionalist theory corresponds more closely to the facts than does the doctrine of elective affinity. We are not detracting here from the acknowledgment of limited truth accorded to this doctrine a few pages ago; it is and remains the merit of the Scheler-Max Weber-von Martin theory to have drawn attention to an aspect of reality which the functionalist explanation is apt to overlook because it exaggerates the unity and the uniformity of the substructural pattern, the process of human interaction; we are merely arguing—and this is the final point we are making for—that even the process which the theory of elective affinity has recognized and the functionalistic not, the process of adjustment which must always precede the state of adjustedness, is more satisfactorily explicable in functionalist terms than in terms of the theory of elective affinity, because it occurs within a context of social interaction where substructure and superstructure, thought and conduct, are closely allied, and not between a divided substructure and superstructure which are merely struggling towards each other.

By choosing von Martin's essay as our *objectum demonstrationis*, we have, in a sense, loaded the dice against ourselves, for nowhere will men in general allow a more palpable meeting of spirit and body than in the case of the encounter of Christianity with Germano-Romanic tribalism. Is Christianity not in fact a set of ideas come down from heaven? The present writer would be the last to deny it. Yet this does not disturb our argument at all. For even the teachings of Jesus were, and were meant by Him to be, the soul in a body social, the Church, and no less an authority than St. Augustine expressly says so. [2] The supernatural origin of Christianity, if such we assume it to be, does not do away with

[1] *Loc., cit.* 24. Cf. also the very large concession to the functionalist view on p. 73.

[2] Cf. Dillistone, *The Structure of the Divine Society*, 1951, 94 *seq*. It is a fact which a book like the present should not fail to emphasize that both Protestants and Catholics have implicitly accepted the necessity and fruitfulness of a hermeneutic method such ast hat of the sociology of knowledge for the due interpretation of the divine message (only Fundamentalism is different in this respect). For though the divine message is a revelation, the revelation of a higher reality, it was none the less presented in a form which fitted the social circumstances of its day and place. We need only think of the parables of our Lord, with their homely use of everyday things for the conveyance of a deeper meaning, to see how true this is. To get at that meaning, we must penetrate the outer crust of socially determined, historically given, ideas to reach beneath it the generically human and ultimately the divine. The difference between Protestantism and Catholicism lies only in a secondary feature. For Protestantism, the revelation is a momentary one, and its explanation can only be helped on by attention to contemporary circumstances; for Catholicism it is a developing revelation, the Church, as the mystical body of Christ, bringing forth ever new truths, wringing collectively ever new aspects, from the original *depositum* of faith. In either case, the social environment in which it worked or is still working appears highly significant for the understanding of the divine message itself.

the fact we are pressing against von Martin, that what interacted with the tribal 'substructure', the Germanic and Romanic tribes, in the so-called Dark Ages, was not a disembodied 'superstructure', Christianity, but the Church, a *societas perfecta* as she is rightly accustomed to call herself, a perfect, i.e. a complete society. And what this complete society met, penetrated and engulfed, was again not a spiritless 'substructure without superstructure', but a *societas perfecta* just like herself, a social order, tribal not only in organization, but also in thought and feeling. It is not two halves that join themselves into a whole in the history of the early Middle Ages, but two wholes that combine and form a wider whole, a wider *societas perfecta*.

Needless to say, many other examples than this might have been taken up for discussion, which would not have aroused the suggestions and sentiments inevitably connected with the very word Christianity. Nevertheless, the case of the so-called Dark Ages is a most instructive one. It brings out one essential point: namely, that the theory of elective affinity can only operate and be applied where a society is internally riven, and composed, in effect, of two or more semi-independent sub-societies. Western society was multiple in this sense in the Merovingian and Carolingian ages when two social systems, one secular, the other sacred, one cisalpine, the other transalpine, one strongly localized, the other strictly international, one as yet barbarian, the other the heir to an ancient civilization, were beginning to adapt themselves to one another. Even the later history of the West did not completely unify and harmonize the two basic elements of the medieval world, as von Martin shows in the subsequent parts of his analysis. This is, as it were, a textbook example of the process of mutual adjustment which the Weber-Scheler-von Martin theory has in mind, but wherever it is to apply, there must be some division, some duality in the substructural process, in social interaction, for otherwise we have adjustedness and hence a situation which is fully and exclusively covered by functionalism.

These considerations have given us all we need for a final summing-up on the issue of the nature of social determination. If we disregard the purely ideal case of an internally perfectly co-ordinated social organism (a thing as impossible to find in history as chemically pure water is in nature), we discover that all societies exhibit both an area of integrated thought and an area of thought which does not seem to stand in organic relationship with the prevailing form of social interaction and organization. So far as the former is concerned, its relationship to the social substructure, to social reality, is clearly amenable to explanation in terms of adjustedness and functional interdependence. With regard to the latter, it might be thought possible to regard it as socially unattached thought, still in search of attachment to and alliance with social forces, but this theory raises very great, indeed, strictly speaking, insoluble difficulties. For if it is consistently carried out, as it is by Max Scheler, we find, confronting one another at the start of the supposed process of mutual adjustment, on the one hand lifeless thought, on the other thoughtless life, and it is impossible to see how the two could ever come to combine. In strict logic, what 'affinity' can there be, what 'election' or 'selection' can take place, between purely physical and purely metaphysical entities, movements in this world and essences in that? No, the case of apparently unintegrated thought-forms and their integration with social life must be understood in a different way. We must see even these from the very beginning as connected with and carried by streamlets of life which tend to flow towards the broader waters of the social process and endeavour to mingle with them. Wherever there is a superstructure, there, in our opinion, is also a rudimentary substructure, at least *in posse*. It is for this reason that ideas are able to exert influence in and on history, an influence which the votaries of the theory of elective affinity are forced by their theoretical position to deny or to play down in the face of proof to the contrary. As against them, we contend that ideas do have such influence, and we are enabled to do so by our assumption that wherever there is a thought-pattern, there must also be an associated action-pattern as well. For the sociologist of knowledge, that is an unavoidable assumption, and it is unavoidable even on the basis of the general sociology of knowledge developed by Scheler and Max Weber themselves—indeed, precisely because of that basis. For both taught that ideas come into existence under the aegis of guiding values, and values, in their very nature, are never 'pure ideas' of the Platonic variety, residing in a metaphysical empyrean without reference to human affairs, but always calls to a definitive mode of action as well as sources of a definite mode of thought, continually giving birth at the same time to subjective beliefs and attitudes and to objective features of life. These considerations have eventually led us to accept the theory of functional integration as the substantial truth in matters of social determination. The alternative theory of elective affinity has only induced us to modify this position to some extent by adding to its study of adjustedness a due attention to the process of adjustment, a dynamic annexe, as it were, to an originally all-too-static mode of explanation.

As for Max Weber's starting-point, the assertion that ideas appropriate to the life-conditions of one society or subsociety are often formulated by members of another, e.g. that what purports to be a proletarian philosophy was worked out by the bourgeois Marx, Engels and Ulyanov Lenin, it does indeed rest on a true observation. Yet it fails to prove the possibility of thinking that is initially without roots in social reality—a seed falling into the human soil from some ethereal region. On the contrary! The very names given as examples show that what came to birth in the minds of these men was a world-view attuned to a basic axiology which was also bound to evoke parallel action. Here, as everywhere else, theory and practice cannot really be divorced. The examples of Lenin, Engels and Marx as renegades from their respective classes prove, not that thought is possible without an underlying value-structure, but merely that nobody is forced to remain in the accidental life-situation, the particular axiological circumstances, into which he happens to have been born. Men cannot fly, but they can move freely from place to place. This fact, however, raises an entirely new problem —that of the closeness of integration, the degree of determination, and to this we must now turn.

CHAPTER SEVEN

PROBLEM C: THE DEGREE OF SOCIAL DETERMINATION

(a) EXTENT AND INTENSITY OF SOCIAL DETERMINATION

THE subject-matter of the present chapter can briefly be described as the problem of human freedom in thinking, in face of the social determination of thought. 'Within human knowledge'—so Northrop has framed the question—'are all ideas conditioned by socio-cultural facts, or only some?' [1] To this must be added a further, though kindred, query: within human societies and subsocieties, are all members conditioned in their ideas by socio-cultural facts, or only some? In other words: to what degree do the substructural forces control ideas, and to what degree do they control thinking men?

By formulating the problem in this way, as a problem of the *degree* of social determination, we may appear to have begged a very large and even decisive question. For is it a foregone conclusion that there should be some degree of substructural control over every thought, however fantastic, and over every life, however deviant the person concerned from the established mode and mean? Should we not rather have spoken of the *range* or limitations of social determination and attempted to draw a borderline, on the one side of which it can be said to obtain and on the other not?

In the literature, the problem has very often been seen in terms of such a dividing line between an area of determined and an area of free thought, and the concrete questions asked have then been concerned with the correct placing of some given set of concepts in relation to this dividing line. For instance: are the categories of thought—time, space, causality—determined or free from determination? Does the determining influence of social forces extend so 'high' as that, or does it stop 'lower down', with social and economic ideas, or lower still, with political pleadings and party slogans? Such an approach is meaningful and even necessary where the basic conception is that the struggle for

---

[1] Preface to Maquet's *Sociologie de la Connaissance*, 1949, 10 *seq.*

power or some such motive is the fundamental social process from which formative and content-fixing influences radiate in all directions. Mannheim's attitude is characteristic in this respect. The sociology of knowledge is in his system conceived as the study of 'total ideologies', and these total ideologies are seen as arising when 'particular ideologies' overflow the banks of the political or economic sphere in which they have their original home and engulf and submerge a world-view as a whole. 'Even abstract categories and principles of [mental] organization, which are seemingly far removed from the political struggle,' he writes in *Ideology and Utopia*, 'have their origin in the meta-theoretical pragmatic nature of the human mind' (246 *seq.*), meaning by 'pragmatic' mainly political and economic. Here indeed it is pertinent to ask whether there is not some Mount Ararat to whose summit the waters will not attain. But from our point of view such speculations are impossible. For if one starts from the Max Weber-Rickert tradition, which ultimately leads back to Kant, one must take one's stand at the very inception of the human mind; one must see the working of social determination at the very root of all thinking, as an *a priori* determination which is (ontologically) far in advance of any 'ideological' conception and, indeed, is the very presupposition of the rise of such conceptions, as of conceptions or ideas in general. As has been explained at length in chapter 3, it is only the socially determined value-pattern of a society which makes rational thinking a practical possibility and constitutes a framework within which thinking can take place at all; ideas being hardly imaginable outside it, if indeed by ideas we mean clear and conscious thoughts, and not merely the vague awarenesses characteristic of the animal consciousness.

Still, the question can sensibly be asked, if only for argument's sake, whether it is not possible for a man, after his mind has been formed and conditioned by passing through that socially determined matrix of thinking which constitutes his culture and society, to cut himself adrift from it and resume the complete freedom which his mind has lost in the process of its social determination. (We are not, of course, referring to that loosening of the ties of social determination which comes about when we acquaint ourselves with the ideas of other cultures and societies and conceive their world-views and value-systems as alternatives to our own; for we are then merely enlarging our outlook without abandoning the firm ground under our feet; we are speaking of *total* liberation.) Without absolutely denying it to be possible for a man to escape by the back door, as it were, from the mill he has been through, we must surely ask what sort of mental baggage he could possibly take with him, if such a thing were to happen. His ideas could surely not be formulable, for in order to formulate them he would again have to use words whose meanings were determined by the social, substructural process; and, *a fortiori*, they would not be communicable or intelligible to others. They would be no more than a private dream-world, a succession of floating images. Such a man, it is to be feared, would be classed as insane by his fellows. He would have estranged himself from his parent society in such a way as to make it unavoidable for them to regard him as anything but a fit object for the alienist.

We believe, then, that the influence of social determination is omni-present and all-pervasive, that it establishes all-inclusive frames of reference, total mental universes, which may indeed be exchanged for others but can never be escaped altogether. A man may live in any number of different societies, but if he is to be and remain a man, he must live in *a* society, for to be human is to be a social being. God (or Nature or Whoever has made us) has made us so. Hence the problem of freedom, *vis-à-vis* social determination, which we aim to discuss in this chapter is for us merely a problem of the degree of intensity to which social determination penetrates the consciousness of individuals, not a problem of its range or extensive limitations. Our minds can be and indeed are free within the socially-established frames of reference, but they are not free to pass beyond them.

It is a strong confirmation of the truth of this opinion that those who have thought and spoken in terms of a range of social determina-tion have practically all been led to conceive it in the end, as we do, as an all-embracing range. Mannheim is again a good example here. Though at variance with his approach, we are in agreement with his conclusion. 'It could be shown in all cases', he states, 'that not only do fundamental orientations, evaluations, and the content of ideas differ but that the manner of stating a problem, the sort of approach made, and even the categories in which experiences are subsumed, collected and ordered vary according to the social position of the observer.' [1] He is also accustomed to speak of styles of thought as characterizing certain subsocieties.[2] But a style is not a mode exhibited only in some phenomena; it is rather a tendency which expresses itself in all that falls under its influence. It is the pressure of the facts which drives Mannheim in this direction, and it is only the particularity of his starting-point which prevents him from reaching the truth more quickly and smoothly. For his analysis is mainly concerned, as we know, with political thought, on the one hand with political parties, and on the other with social classes. Now political parties are not, in our opinion, capable of developing their own social determination of thought; they produce ideological growths rather than perspectives of reality. But it is other-wise with social classes. For a social class is basically a way of life, and

---

[1] *Ideology and Utopia*, ed. 1952, 130. Cf. also 246 where an illustration is given. Cf. furthermore the summary of Mannheim's relevant ideas in Merton, *Social Theory and Social Structure*, 1949, 252 *seq*.   [2] Cf. e.g. *loc. cit.*, 104.

if so, it must have a tendency to define—to crystallize out as it were—the mental modes organically and functionally appropriate to its mode of being. Caught between these two different social formations, but treating them as if they were in the same case, confusing, moreover, socially determined with ideological thinking, Mannheim was, not surprisingly, at first uncertain as to how far social determination would reach.[1] But the more he thought of class rather than party, of the inclusive society rather than the classes included within it, the more he recognized the fact on which we are dwelling, namely that social determination spreads its net over the whole area covered by the social life concerned.

Already, half a century or so before Mannheim, Nietzsche had undergone a similar evolution. Starting from a specific and even personal concept of the social struggle—ascending *versus* descending life, master race *versus* slavish underlings—he had at first seen mainly the ideologies near to the arena of conflict as socially determined, but later had come to realize that all thought-forms are what they are because they have arisen within certain social constellations.[2] Earlier still, Marx, too, had pursued the tendencies arising in and from the 'production-relations' outward towards the all-embracing periphery of human thinking. Once the process of production is mechanized, the worker ceases to be a person and becomes 'pure labour force'—a cog in a machine, as the saying goes—i.e. he ceases to be an entity endowed with qualities and becomes a purely quantitative agency. But this development has effects far beyond the confines of the factory. All attention to quality tends to fade out until life, reality as a whole, is seen in quantitative terms. Marx goes so far as to intimate that in the process time (originally, *quâ* flow, essentially qualitative) becomes transmuted into something purely quantitative, a kind of quasi-space—so many empty moments which can be seen side by side, as it were. Here, too, the inclination is to regard the range of social determination as progressively coinciding with contemporary mental life as a whole.[3]

Those sociologists who, unlike Marx, Nietzsche and Mannheim, were not unduly preoccupied with political and class struggles but kept their attention on social interaction in its entirety, have from the very beginning tended to assert, and even to emphasize, the all-pervasiveness of social influences in the intellectual life of men in society. Durkheim and his school were particularly insistent in this regard, and in this particular respect a sociology of knowledge drawn from the Max Weber-Rickert-Kant tradition can only join forces with them and accept their findings. Granet, especially, has made the convincing, if obvious

---

[1] Cf. Merton, *loc. cit.*, 253 *seq.*
[2] Cf. Barth, *Wahrheit und Ideologie*, 1945, 227, 287, 337 (note 71).
[3] Cf. Lukacs, *Geschichte und Klassenbewusstsein*, 1923, 100 *seq.*

point that since all thinking is clothed in words, and since these latter are social formations, born of social intercourse, all thinking must needs be rooted in and coloured by social life in its concreteness, a thesis which he succeeded in developing in a very pleasing and penetrating manner in his book *La Pensée Chinoise* (first published, after many important preliminary studies, in 1934) which made a deep impression on his fellow-sinologists.

By insisting in this way that *all* human thinking is dependent on social reality, because our basic picture of the world is constituted under the guidance of the axiological system under which contemporary society lives and acts, we are not, of course, propagating any kind of determinism in the narrower, quasi-mechanical sense of the word. (We hope that no suspicion to that effect has entered the mind of any of our readers!) We are indeed ascribing to social determination a maximum of extension, but that need not and in fact does not mean, that we also attribute to it a maximum of intensity. If we did so, we should be in glaring contradiction, not only with the central assertions of chapter 6, but with the whole tenor and tendency of this book. We have rejected causalism, and we reject it again. We believe that there is always some degree of determination, but not that it is always of high degree. There are people who are up in arms as soon as they hear the very word 'determination' applied to the human mind, and who see in it nothing but a sly disguise for the brutal theory of determinism. For them it is all a matter of *principiis obsta*; once some degree of determination is admitted, they feel, complete determination will be asserted before long. In point of fact, however, none of the thinkers who have made a significant contribution to the sociology of knowledge in the widest sense of the word has ever pushed very far in this direction.

Not even the Marxists have cast serious doubt upon the true spontaneity of human thought. Among them, Friedrich Engels was as ready as any, and indeed readier than most, to bring the so-called materialistic conception of history as close as possible to crude materialism, in the philosophical meaning of the term. His book on the *Dialectics of Nature* is proof of this, for in it he is much further removed from the idealistic tradition of Hegel and much further advanced towards the materialistic position of, say, Büchner, than Marx ever was. Yet even he thought and said that there is a good deal of specific indeterminacy within the general area of determination in human thinking. A remarkable letter to Conrad Schmidt of October 27, 1890, discusses the relationship of legal ideas to the economic substructure and admits without compunction, and with no sense of making any undue concession, that this relation is not one of complete dominance or determination. Once the division of labour has developed so far, Engels writes, that a stratum of professional lawyers has formed in society, a 'new and independent sphere' is opened up which is indeed in 'general dependence on production and trade', but has also a life of its own. 'In a modern state, law must not only correspond to the general economic position and be its expression, but must also be an expression which is consistent in itself. . . . And in order to achieve this, the faithful reflection of economic conditions is more and more infringed upon.' The same relative freedom is also conceded to religious and philosophical speculation.

In case it should be thought that these are the blundering statements of an old man who had lost his grip on the essentials of the Marxian theory, it is instructive to add the following sentence written by the young Marx in the famous *Introduction to the Critique of Political Economy* which is the pre-eminent *locus classicus* of 'historical materialism': 'Certain periods of highest development of art stand in no direct connection with the general development of society, nor with the material basis . . . of its organization.' Merton, who quotes these passages, adds in conclusion: 'Such terms [in Marx's writings] as "determination" cannot be taken at their face value; they are characteristically used very loosely.' [1] In other words: even Marx and Engels were not determinists.

If it is not, then, the intention of sociologists of knowledge, either open or concealed, to preach or propagate determinism, if they think in terms of partial rather than of total determination of the superstructure by the substructure, the question at once arises: how *far* are ideas determined? what is the exact degree of determination? In other words: how coherent is a society with regard to its mental modes? A remarkable effort was made by Sorokin and his associates to find a statistical answer to these queries. Starting from his basic typology which distinguishes ideational, sensate and idealistic cultures—cultures which attribute ultimate reality to the supra-sensible realm, or to the material realm, or which see both realms as equally real—Sorokin and his colleagues classified the various cultural productions of a period, and more especially its books, accordingly, and thereby arrived at a concrete conclusion as to how far an age or a generation may be said to have been dominated by one or other of the three distinct culture-premisses. This conclusion left little to be desired on the score of apparent exactitude, for it was presented in the form of a figure—a percentage. Thus it was found that —to quote, by way of illustration, a single index-number from a whole welter of statistics—empiricism, an incarnation of the principle which ascribes reality only to what is observable in sense-experience, dominated the eighteenth century to the extent of 37·5 per cent, the nineteenth

---

[1] *Social Theory and Social Structure*, 1949, 228 *seq.*, 387 *seq.* For the original texts, cf. *re* Engels, *Sozialistische Monatshefte*, XX/XXI, 4 Oct. 1920, and *re* Marx, *Grundrisse der Kritik der politischen Oekonomie*, ed. 1953, 30.

century to the extent of 42·6 per cent, and the first two decades of the twentieth century to the extent of 53 per cent.[1] Unfortunately, it is impossible to accept all this as more than a very first and very distant approximation to the facts.[2] The three classes used are far too wide to fit the culture-content of any concrete society. They throw together into the same basket such figures as Epicurus and Bentham, and though Bentham was certainly an Epicurean of a kind, his doctrinal system is in no way elucidated by this vaguest of all vague labels. The very great difference between the ancient and the modern representatives of 'sensate thinking' is due precisely to their having lived in differently circumstanced social systems. On the other hand, Sorokin's method throws into different baskets such figures as Bentham and Kant, and though they may have been worlds apart in some respects, it is also true that they had many features in common. We need only think of the dominant rôle played by the twin concepts of liberty and equality in the philosophical speculations of both thinkers. And this community of preoccupations is due precisely to the fact that they shared a common social background, the age of the French Revolution, which had made liberty and equality its resounding battle-cry. Surely, it is obvious that, from the point of view of a sociology of knowledge, Sorokin divides what should have been united, and unites what should have been kept apart.

But our criticism of Sorokin's experiment is not on matters of detail; it is one of principle. His whole procedure assumes *a radice* the possibility of quantifying what is qualitative, and this is almost like supposing it possible to square the circle. A book, or a work of art, is all quality, because it is all spirit. The unity of a culture consists in the stylistic similarities shown by its ingredients, not in their statistical identity. There is really nothing that can be counted, though there is a good deal that can be compared. It is to be feared that the sociology of knowledge will never be able to get much assistance from statistical techniques. Much though we may regret the fact, it will always have to rely heavily on the more cumbersome monographic and descriptive methods.

Much aid may conceivably be given to the sociology of knowledge at some later date—and even to the theory thereof—by an entirely different kind of inductive investigation, namely the public opinion and mass communications research now vigorously pursued in some countries, notably the United States. Starting from purely pragmatic considerations such as the requirements of commercial, political and war-time propaganda, it has obvious implications, none the less, for the question

---

[1] Cf. Maquet, *Sociologie de la Connaissance*, 1949, 177. Sorokin's whole gigantic effort is sympathetically reviewed both in this book and in Cowell's *History, Civilization and Culture*, 1952, *passim*.

[2] Sorokin himself does not do more. Cf. Merton, *loc. cit.*, 389, note 70.

as to how far a society or class may be said to be a mental unity. At present it is too early to draw any reliable theoretical conclusions from the practical data that have been amassed; but further results from this source may well turn out to be rewarding.[1]

In the meantime, we must make do with more abstract considerations. But these need not be thought of as purely speculative in the bad sense of the word, a mere product of arm-chair cerebration. For the subject under consideration—the degree of integration achieved and achievable in different societies and subsocieties—has been long and carefully studied on the level of action, and the conclusions there reached can, with few adjustments, be analogically applied to the level of ideas. It is clear from the very start that there is a close parallel between the two spheres. We have emphasized that men's thought can be free within the area of social determination but that they are not free to step outside it. So it is also with action. Men's conduct is free within the area of social ordering but they are not free to contract out of society, so to speak. In either case the very word freedom has meaning only with reference to an underlying norm to which it is contrasted. On either level the individual is in the grip of social forces, but in each case the ties which bind him are elastic bands rather than iron shackles.

The following quotation, in which Sprott is referring to the degree of integration achieved in society considered as a system of human interaction, holds good also, *mutatis mutandis*, for society as a system of mental inter-communion: 'The concept of deviance implies the concept of order. We have at the back of our minds the notion of a social system with its normative regulations, and deviance is the departure on the part of the participants from culturally expected rules of conduct. This abstract pattern is a kind of ideal. . . . It is, in fact, never realized. In simple small-scale societies, as Malinowski and . . . Firth . . . have pointed out, the cultural pattern is abstracted by the social anthropologists from the uneven personal conduct of the actors who weave it. We have an abstract notion of the dance, but in the actual dancing each dancer has his or her own style, and the young lady in the back row may want to attract special attention to herself. Although each member of a society becomes a separate human being, recognizing himself as different from the rest through social intercourse, although he acquires the ambitions, specific desires and resentments that he does acquire through contact with other people, he does absorb his experience in his own way. . . . He will be drawn well into the social pattern, or only partly so, according to his experience. . . . He himself has his own specific endowment of potentialities, and he has his own unique version of the culture which has produced him.'[2]

[1] Cf. part III of Merton's *Social Theory and Social Structure*.
[2] *Science and Social Action*, 1954, 104 *seq*.

281

Problem C: The Degree of Social Determination

Different in accent, but similar in substance is the following utterance from Gurvitch, which adheres to the French tradition in laying rather more stress on the unity of the social order than Sprott is inclined to do: 'The collective consciousness is a partial interpenetration of individual consciousnesses, an interpenetration which admits of a scale of gradations. The individual consciousnesses can neither be identified with, nor separated from, the collective consciousnesses: they participate in each other. . . . In the last analysis they are only different directions within the same psychic current, within the total psychic phenomenon: directedness towards the We, the group, global society, for the collective consciousness; directedness towards the I for the individual consciousness; directedness towards the Other and the relationship with him for the consciousness called interpersonal. But these three poles are always there; their tension and their connection constitute one of the essential aspects of all psychic life and especially of all consciousness. From this point of view the collective consciousness has as much right to be regarded as real as the individual consciousness; it even possesses a certain primacy over the interpersonal consciousness because it serves as a basis for the communication between minds.' And Gurvitch adds the important reminder that the elements that have to come to terms with each other and order themselves into an operative and co-operative whole, are not only social norms and the individual versions thereof but also the many intermediate collective consciousnesses, such as that of the class. 'Inside each group there are as many collective consciousnesses as there are differentiated We's.' [1] Social integration as a process consists in the mutual adjustment of all these mental structures; social integration as a state in the degree to which this process has succeeded.

That a high degree of mental conformity is unnecessary to the functioning, and even flourishing, of a social order, can be seen from the fact that some societies—and among them especially our own—positively encourage originality and independence on the part of the individual. To be sure, our school-teachers are expected to introduce their pupils into the arcana of our cultural traditions, to make them 'good Britishers' or 'good Americans', but they are also urged to get them 'to think for themselves'. A brief consideration will make it clear that, however paradoxical it may seem at first sight, the coherence of society is strengthened rather than weakened by such encouragement of deviance from the norm. A society is never at a standstill. The human relations within it are in constant process of re-arrangement, and there

[1] *Le Concept de Classes Sociales de Marx à Nos Jours*, 1954, 130 *seq.* Much that is stimulating in this context may also be found in Ziegenfuss's *Gesellschaftsphilosophie*, 1954, 42 *seq.*, but his mode of expression may be less acceptable to the average Anglo-Saxon reader.

is also at all times the stream of history carrying it forward into the future and thereby occasioning many changes, great and small. Such re-arrangements and changes are much easier to bring about if social control (whether of mind or conduct) is comparatively loose, rather than hard and fast. What is rigid may easily be broken, but cannot with equal ease be re-adjusted and re-formed. Many a war has shown that a liberal country is more elastic than its authoritarian adversaries, more adaptable, more resilient, and better able to absorb and digest shocks.

In this respect, as in so many others, a sound society resembles a sound organism, whereas the enforcement of 'dead' uniformity makes social co-operation cold and automatic as it did in some eighteenth century armies, and imparts to the whole an 'unnatural' stiffness—a kind of *rigor mortis*, as it were. Here as everywhere, life implies spontaneity, the ability to stretch and strain. But we must not go too far. Freedom is never absolute. A person who deviates too widely from the norm becomes incomprehensible to the rest of his society; his activities appear 'meaningless', and he must pay the price of his independence. At worst he may be treated as a madman; in less extreme cases, he may be denied recognition, promotion, or even his daily bread. How many brilliant scholars have been denied academic honours, how many inspired artists public support? The history even of European culture is unhappily full of pertinent examples, from the well-known tragedies of Mozart and Schubert to the private miseries of countless anonymous victims who have remained unsung. Freedom there is, it is even fostered and to some extent rewarded, but it is always freedom *in* society, not out of it. Deviance must remain within the bounds ordained for it or the deviant becomes 'cut off' from the 'body social' to which he belongs and is condemned to wither away like a severed limb.

Perhaps we can best explain the relationship between what Sprott calls 'order' and 'deviance', and what Gurvitch calls 'collective consciousness' and 'individual consciousness'—the relationship between social forces on the one hand and individual freedom on the other—by appealing to the simile of theme and variation which is familiar from the field of music. Anyone listening to Brahms's 'Variations on the St. Anthony Chorale' or to Reger's 'Variations on a Theme of Mozart', is made aware, at the same time, of both the common theme and the individual variations. Sometimes the variations move so far away from the basic theme that it is very difficult still to recognize it; sometimes again the theme is so prominent that one might almost suppose that it is simply being repeated, with little or no attempt to individualize. But there is always both a concord and an opposition of norm and uniqueness, and it is their mutual tension as it unfolds, as it waxes and wanes, which marks the character of the whole. The theme constantly asserts itself, and the variations as constantly ring the changes on it, and even try to escape from it, but cannot do so without passing out of the totality of meaning and so losing their own identity. So it is also with social coherence and individual freedom in matters of the mind. The mental life of a society is not unity *and* diversity; it is unity-in-diversity and diversity-in-unity. As to the scope and limits of possible individual deviation from the central theme, it is impossible to lay down a general law for this, unless it be to say that, generally speaking, the more closely textured a society is, the narrower the limitations will be, and the looser its coherence, the wider the latitude within which the pendulum can swing. Societies will vary greatly in this respect according to their total integration, which is no less decisive for the freedom of the individual mind than it is for the freedom of individual action. Such societies will form a whole gamut or scale, at one end of which we shall find the most closely-integrated community, with the thoughts and beliefs of its members all lying close together, and manifestly so, and at the other the most incoherent types of association in which it will be well-nigh impossible to discover a common theme beneath the discordant variations, although even here such a common theme must exist in the depths if total dissolution of the social bond is to be avoided.

So much for the variations between different societies in respect of the general degree of mind-determination by social forces. In order to proceed with our analysis, we must now turn our attention away from comparisons between societies and fix it on the interior of their respective social or cultural systems. Each culture contains many departments: law, religion, philosophy, and so on. Are all these spheres of mental activity determined to the same degree, or are there significant variations from one to another? If the reader will once again look at the symbolic diagram on p. 244, he will be led to suspect that there are in fact significant variations of this kind. Some cultural phenomena, such as law, lie close to the process of social interaction, i.e. to the substructure; others, such as religion, lie further away, but still fairly close to it; still others, such as philosophy, are, comparatively speaking, far removed from it. It is, on general grounds, difficult to escape the impression that the former will be much more closely controlled by existential influences than the latter, and it is equally difficult to avoid the expectation that empirical investigation will bear this impression out. Law has always kept closer to life than philosophical speculation has done—and had to do so. For legal thought which does not subserve the needs of the existing society and its vital processes is useless; at all events, it ceases to be legal and becomes philosophical instead. It is far more reasonable and realistic to speak of feudal or capitalist law (and even legal theory) than it is to speak of feudal or capitalist epistemology. This is an observation already made by Friedrich Engels. Writing, on January 25, 1894, to Heinz Starkenburg, he expressed himself as follows: 'The further the particular sphere which we are investigating is removed from the economic sphere [we should say: from the basic process of social interaction] and approaches that of pure abstract ideology [better: ideas], the more shall we find it exhibiting . . . deviations from the expected development. . . .' [1] In the present state of our knowledge, one hesitates to say of this statement (or any other) that it adumbrates a law of social determination; but perhaps it is not unduly rash to remark that it looks uncommonly like one, or like becoming one.

A good illustration of it occurs in Scheler's classic work *Die Wissensformen und die Gesellschaft*. What a society thinks about the divine, Scheler explains, flows as a rule from four sources: (1) its traditional lore (popular religion); (2) the visions of its charismatic *homines religiosi*, saints and seers; (3) the experiences gained in the practice of cult and ritual customs; and (4) the conceptions of its metaphysical thinkers on salvation and the deity. Now, 'the sociological conditioning of the content of religious knowledge applies by no means equally to the sources of knowledge just named but always in the first place to the religious family, tribal, town and folk traditions, and also to the professional cult techniques. . . . The religious ideas of the *homines religiosi* and the religious concepts of the metaphysicians . . . are sociologically far less conditioned' (71). If this is a correct observation, and we have no doubt that it is, then it follows that the degree of social determination of a given cultural sphere depends on its closeness or remoteness in relation to the ongoing process of social interaction. Traditions and rituals are closely interwoven with folkways, indeed, *are* folkways: the visions of seers in the desert, the musings of thinkers in their studies are not, though it should not be forgotten that even isolated saints and retiring philosophers are still social creatures whose minds have been formed in the common matrix, under the influence of the prevailing axiological system.

From this point of view it is not so surprising as some authors seem to have thought that 'the very categories of thinking' should show (in their non-formal aspects) the imprint of the environing social system. For such concepts as space and time are deeply involved in human interaction, and necessarily so. Without them no common hunt or feast could be arranged, no act of co-operation whatsoever organized. The categories appear 'remote from practice' only if by 'practice' one means economic or political struggles; it is only to be expected that theorists who confuse the sociology of knowledge with the doctrine of ideology should be somewhat amazed to find that even the abstract conceptions of time and space turn out to be what they call 'ideological'. They are not really ideological because they have no connection with a society's

[1] Karl Marx and Frederick Engels, *Selected Works*, 1950, II, 458.

285

internal and internecine class wars. But they are socially determined because they inhere in, and, on theoretical formulation, arise from, the 'practice' of inter-human relationships and interaction.

The degrees of social determination postulated in the quotations given from Engels and Scheler are most clearly developed in a brief but important paper by Carl Brinkmann entitled 'Der "Überbau" und die Wissenschaften von Staat und Gesellschaft.' [1] Brinkmann distinguishes three spheres lying above each other, three storeys, as it were, in the house of culture. The lowest is that of *mores* and law; above it rises that of science; and above that again the spheres of religion and art which can be bracketed together because both are forms for the symbolic understanding of reality. The closeness of the first two to life, and their comparatively high degree of determination by the substructure, can be seen in the fact that they are as internally divided as social reality itself: in morality and law, there is the rift between Is and Ought, fact and norm; in science, the contrast between science as knowledge and science as power, pure insight and technology. It is only on the highest level, that of symbolic vision, that the antinomies of existence are overcome, that diversity is subdued and unity reigns. It is mainly there that man's mind can show its inherent freedom; and it is mainly from there that man's will can turn back towards reality and assert itself against it.

A very different distinction concerning the degree of social determination has been drawn in some quarters between the content of thought and the forms of thinking. It can be asserted either that *what* is thought depends on social being, or that the *how* of thinking is conditioned in this way. [2] Many would reconcile themselves to the former assertion, but only relatively few to the latter. The *how* of thinking is widely regarded as identical in all societies, even though the *what* may be allowed to differ greatly. We have dealt with this problem in so much detail in our first part, especially in chapter 4, that we need not reopen it here. Our conviction is briefly this, that even the *modes* of thinking, the *how* of thought, must be split up further into a socially determined and a socially undetermined sector. In so far as the concatenation of ideas in the human mind is purely formal, i.e. purely logical, it follows principles which, in their concrete content, are not indebted to social life. But such thinking consists merely in making explicit what is contained in the definitions used; it is a mere elaboration and exposition of necessary implications. But there is also a more material mode of thinking, and this is undoubtedly indebted for its character to social life. What people habitually associate in their minds depends, not on formal

---

[1] First published in *Schmollers Jahrbuch*, LIV, 1930, 437 *seq.*, now reprinted in *Wirtschaftsformen und Lebensformen*, 1950, 9 *seq.*

[2] Grünwald, *Das Problem der Soziologie des Wissens*, 1934, 104. Cf. also Scheler, *Die Wissensformen und die Gesellschaft*, 1926, 203 *seq.*

logic so much as on certain mental habits which dominate them, and these habits are deeply influenced, indeed determined, by the social facts, factors and forces present and operative in the concrete contemporary and local setting.

Cardinal Newman drew the important distinction between 'paper logic' (i.e. formal, abstract logic) and 'the logic of life'.[1] It is untrue to say that the primitives have a 'paper logic' different from our own, as if they would be unable to realize that the square root of 4 is 2. But the logic of their lives is not the same as ours. It is subject to a high degree of social determination, just as the *what* of their thinking is also apt to be. Formal logic is socially determined only in the marginal sense of the word, i.e. only in so far as it presupposes a mind in working order, which has gone through the process of crystallization and has been shaped or made in the process of social living. As for scientific knowledge, it is in still another case. In one sense, as has been explained, it is as socially determined as historico-sociological knowledge, for it depends on the axiological system of society for its possibility: we cannot know all about nature, we must concentrate our attention if we are to be able to know at all, and that concentration of attention is guided by the values developed in social life. If different societies are alike in this respect it is merely because they are alike in value-structure. But in another sense, scientific knowledge is not determined as historical or social knowledge is, for its area of observation, its field of objectivity, is given to us, and its laws cannot be changed as we wish.

One topic that is very often brought up when the area of social determination is discussed, is the question of survivals and anticipations. Ideas no longer in keeping with the realities of life are said to hang on; ideas not yet in keeping with the realities of life are said to appear before their due time.[2] Of the former phenomenon Mannheim gives as an example the bourgeois world-view. Originally, during its fighting days, the bourgeoisie was highly idealistic, in pursuit of a utopia or rather eutopia; later, when it had got into the saddle, it turned conservative, scorning all attempts to improve the world. 'This sceptical attitude [to human betterment]', Mannheim writes, 'corresponds primarily to the social position of a bourgeoisie already in power. . . . Nevertheless,' he adds, something of the old idealism still hangs about the bourgeois mentality: 'the concrete development of their present

---

[1] Cf. my paper 'Towards a Theory of Social Knowledge', in the *Revue Internationale de Philosophie*, 1950, part 7.

[2] It is well known that the concept of survival has played a very great part in social anthropology. To those who accepted the fundamental tenets of functionalism and perhaps tended to push them too far, it explained why there were present in primitive societies institutions (and ideas) of no apparent utility or survival value. We cannot enter into this matter here. Cf. however Lowie, *The History of Ethnological Theory*, 1937, esp. 44 *seq.*

mode of thought is also to some extent sociologically determined by the historical situation in which they had their beginnings.' With regard to anticipation Mannheim ventures a much more radical assertion. 'Every "actually operating" order of life is at the same time enmeshed by conceptions which are to be designated as "transcendent" or "unreal" because their contents can never be realized in the societies in which they exist, and because one could not live and act according to them within the limits of the existing social order.' [1]

We have ourselves already referred to Roman Catholicism as a mentality which has survived all through the modern age, even though its value-system is different from that prevailing in modern, i.e. capitalist society, but we must be careful here not to exaggerate the degree of indeterminacy of human thought and feeling. For although the integrated value-structure of the Church no longer coincides with that of secular life (as it probably did to a large extent during the Middle Ages), it is none the less true that the individual values it comprises have survived in society at large, albeit with different degrees of emphasis and in different combinations. It is this fact which has enabled a religious philosophy formed in another social setting to 'hang on', indeed, to flourish, under capitalism. Hence, we are not really confronted with a survival from the point of view of social determination. We have before us, rather, a variation remote from the central theme. It is significant in this respect that the Catholic theologians have not rated the modern world so much for wanting the wrong things as for putting last things first and first things last: the contrast lies in the *ordo amoris*, not in the *res desideratae*. Moreover, though there has been no full accommodation between medieval church and modern world, it has not been wholly lacking. Adjustedness has not been achieved, but there has been some adjustment. Indeed, there invariably seems to be some degree of adjustment in the case of every so-called survival. Mannheim has acknowledged this himself. 'It appears to be a generally valid law of the structure of intellectual development', he writes, 'that when new groups gain entry into an already established situation they do not take over without further ado the ideologies [i.e. the characteristic modes of thought and feeling] which have already been elaborated for this situation, but rather they adapt the ideas which they bring with them through their tradition to the new situation. Thus liberalism and socialism, as they entered a situation more conducive to conservatism . . . on the whole preferred to adapt the original ideologies that they brought with them to the new situation.' [2]

It is with anticipations as it is with survivals. They are not complete strangers in the land in which they sojourn, they have a foothold somewhere upon the social soil, or even a root in its subsoil, though it may

[1] *Ideology and Utopia*, ed. 1952, 228, 175.   [2] *Loc. cit.*, 224.

only be a marginal and precarious one. The supreme example here is the case of Soviet Russia. Some have argued as if the Bolsheviks had introduced a post-capitalist way of thinking into a pre-capitalist country, a theory of class war into a society without classes, or at any rate without that industrial proletariat which is nevertheless the cornerstone of their theoretical system. Such talk overlooks the fact that Marxism, in so far as it caught on at all in Russia, caught on with the urban proletariat, the workers of the Putilov plant, for instance, and that it was only the unique favour of circumstance, coupled with political genius, which raised the Bolshevik 'ideology' to the level of an official creed. Furthermore, and this too is decisive, it is even now no more than an official creed. As it stands, it has still not conquered the vast masses of the Russian peasantry. Perhaps it will; but not until the whole way of life of those peasants has already been transformed beforehand, and nobody knows that better than the Bolsheviks themselves. No, 'anticipations', like survivals, are never absolute. They are possible only when they lie in the line of some social force, however weak it may yet be. Mannheim again acknowledges this, in spite of his radical pronouncements about 'transcendent or unreal conceptions': 'The possible utopias and wish-images of an epoch as conceptions of the not-yet-real are oriented about what has already been realized in this epoch (and are not therefore chance, undetermined phantasies, or the results of inspiration). . . . In this sense, the relationship between utopia and the existing order turns out to be a 'dialectical' one. By this is meant that every age allows to arise (in differently located social groups) those ideas and values in which are contained in condensed form the unrealized and the unfulfilled tendencies which represent the needs of each age.' [1]

There is no need, then, to suppose that 'survivals' and 'anticipations' are phenomena disclosing serious limitations in the area of social determination. Both are possible only because the culture-complexes concerned have a meaning in contemporary life, the one 'still', the other 'already'. A survival or an anticipation having no social substratum at all is unimaginable because its idea-content would be meaningless to the age. What appears as an anachronism in relation to society as a whole, is invariably not an anachronism in relation to a subsociety contained in that society. Of course, we are speaking here of how people think, not what they say. Sometimes a society or a class that is moving from one position to another may sport a strictly conservative mode of expression and pour its new wine into old bottles; it may then look as if there was more of a spiritual survival than there really is. At other

---

[1] *Loc. cit.*, 262, 179. For Scheler's views on the survival and possible transference of ideas cf. Dahlke and Becker in *Philosophy and Phenomenological Research*, 1941/42, 315 *seq.*

times such a society or subsociety on the move may prefer a more revolutionary language, but then it is very often rather old wine that is simply made to reappear in a new bottle with a gaudy label on it; the superficial observer may then be left with the impression that there is more futuristic thought than in fact there is. For either alternative plenty of examples could be adduced; but the matter is too obvious for any historian of ideas to require such exemplification.[1]

Still, survivals of old and anticipations of new modes of life and thought will, by definition, only be undercurrents in the continuing process of social interaction, and for that reason we may assume that, being less involved in the realities of the existing situation, they will be less under the grip of the 'real' substructural forces of the day than the mental modes that happen to be modern, contemporary and appropriate. We must concede them a comparatively high degree of indeterminacy, just as we did to philosophy and other pursuits remote from the market place. But however high that degree of indeterminacy may be, it will never be so extreme as to make it impossible for an open-eyed hermeneutic method to find a key to the proper understanding of such phenomena somewhere in the social circumstances which formed the conjuncture under which they were born.

(b) THE LATITUDE LEFT TO PERSONAL INDEPENDENCE

We have so far discussed the freedom of ideas, what at one time would have been called the freedom of the objective spirit; we must now consider the freedom of men with regard to their ideas, the freedom of the spirit in its subjective incarnations. Here, too, a generous span of indeterminacy is assumed on all hands. It may be true in general that human beings have a spontaneous tendency to grow into the modes of thinking appropriate to and predominant in their society, class or set, just as they have a tendency to drop into the associated modes of conduct; but there are plenty of exceptions, illustrious and otherwise, to prove the rule. Most scions of the German middle class have indeed become petty bourgeois in mind as well as in standing, but one developed into Karl Marx. Most Russian small town boys have adopted the ideas as well as the professions traditional in their circle, but one has become known to the world as Vladimir Lenin.

However strong the tendency has been in the past to generalize, to think of men as members of a class rather than as individuals, the essential uniqueness of the individual has hardly ever been seriously denied in the literature of the sociology of knowledge. This applies even

[1] Some instructive cases are discussed in the essay entitled *Ausgänge des Mittelalters* in von Martin's *Geist und Gesellschaft* (1948), e.g. those of Joachim of Fiore and Giovanni Villani.

to historical materialism. Perhaps with an eye on the dramatic example of Philippe Égalité, Marx and Engels observe in the *Communist Manifesto* that when a ruling class approaches its discomfiture and dissolution, a small fraction of it will ally itself to the revolutionary class, a development which they expected to repeat itself in the future just as it had already done in the past. 'As ... at an earlier period, a section of the nobility went over to the bourgeoisie, so now a portion of the bourgeoisie goes over to the proletariat, and in particular a portion of the bourgeois ideologists who have raised themselves to the level of a theoretical comprehension of the historical movement as a whole.' This is an unambiguous acknowledgment of personal freedom in matters of thought which is none the less direct for being implied, and similar acknowledgments occur throughout the writings of the two fathers of modern socialism.[1] Marx even coined a word to describe those individual proletarians who were unwilling to accept the rôle and 'ideology' of the proletarian class—the word *Lumpenproletariat*.

If even Marx and Engels allow that individual mentalities need not necessarily coincide with the consciousness proper to their class, though they regularly do or may in most cases be made to do so, it is not surprising that other, less doctrinaire authors should have shown no disposition at all to assert that the individual mind must be regarded as committed to definite, objectively given modes or contents. Sometimes they have ventured very far in the direction of indeterminacy—surprisingly so for sociologists. Thus Mannheim has expressed himself as follows: 'Where the nobility became the bearer of culture it broke through the fixedness of a class-bound mentality in many respects.'[2] Max Scheler's point of view is similar: 'It is not untrue that even very formal kinds of thinking and valuing differ according to class—though only in the great majority of cases, for everybody can, in principle, rise superior to the ties of his class affiliation. . . . The class prejudices, and even the formal laws governing the formation of class prejudices, are in principle "conquerable" and can be "suspended" for every individual of the class. They are merely "mental inclinations and tendencies", "tendencies of a subconscious nature to conceive the world preferably in one form or another".'[3] There is no need to prolong this list of quotations.[4] Let us close it with a particularly lucid passage from von Martin's *Geist und Gesellschaft*: 'For man there is always "the other" possibility as well: to revolt against the influences which impinge upon him; to

---

[1] Cf. for some of them Gurvitch, *Le Concept de Classes Sociales de Marx à Nos Jours*, 1954, 15 *seq.* and 25.

[2] *Ideology and Utopia*, ed. 1952, 139.

[3] *Die Wissensformen und die Gesellschaft*, 1926, 204 *seq.*

[4] For Max Weber's opinion cf. von Schelting, *Max Webers Wissenschaftslehre*, 1934, esp. 384 *seq.*

make necessities out of predispositions is not to judge sociologically, but sociologistically' (209).

Every one of these quotations amounts to a further implicit, if not more or less explicit, rejection of the principle of quasi-mechanical, univocal, causalistic mind-determination. But each of them therefore also raises afresh—though in a new guise—the question which has occupied us before: if there is so much indeterminacy, if the individual can after all think as he likes, if the wind of the spirit bloweth where it listeth, what is the value of a sociology of knowledge, even if it be considered merely as a hermeneutic method? We must take this matter up here once again, turning our discussion towards the specific aspect which confronts us most directly at this particular juncture—the freedom of the individual, of the subjective mind. Our reply to the challenge must again be based on the combination of functionalism and the theory of elective affinity with which we have hitherto operated, though now the latter will probably have to be allotted a more prominent place than before.

Considering, to begin with, the implications of the functionalist point of view, we must note first of all, that a functionally coherent or interfunctioning system does not require for its operation—or even for its successful operation—a close adjustment of organs or parts. To put the matter somewhat crudely: every one needs a nose, but the size of noses is not very material. A man or a woman with too long or too short a nose in proportion to the rest of the face or body may be less pleasant to look at than one whose nose is 'just right', but he or she will be none the less healthy for being disproportionate in this one particular. A proletarian world-view is none the less proletarian or operative as such in a society if it exhibits, in those who represent it, very wide deviations from the abstract or average norm. This, of course, is merely our old argument: variations on a theme do not destroy the theme itself. Arthur Child has stated the point very well: 'Attitudes . . . because of the subjectivity that is of their essence . . . are liable in principle to a modification in accordance with the prior psychological structure of the individual into whose mind they are being incorporated. They must also undergo change in accordance with the changes in that structure after they have already become part of it. In other words, the individual possesses the power of modifying individually the group attitudes that he incorporates into the structure of his mind.' [1]

Secondly, and this is much more important, such is the elasticity of a truly inter-functioning pattern, whether organic or merely quasi-organic, that the influence of the parts on the whole is no less than the influence of the whole on the parts. If a part deviates from the whole, it is not only the part that is out of harmony with things, but the whole

[1] Cf. 'The Existential Determination of Thought', in *Ethics*, 1941/2, 184.

as well, and adjustment may come about as much by a modification of the whole as by a renewed conformity of the part. As soon as we think of the system, or super-system, as dynamic, or merely as elastic, individual non-conformity by no means implies a rupture thereof. Again Child is right when he says: 'The individual is not a mere individual: he is a socialized individual; and it is, indeed, in the very process of socialization that he emerges as the individual he is. But socialization being a reciprocal process, implies both the receptiveness of individualization and the dynamic initiative of individuality. Thus, in so far as the individual is significantly an individuality, he cannot merely accept the influences of the social context in which he functions: he must transform them, and he does transform them . . . In so far as an attitude has meaning within the life of an individual, the individual expresses it; and, if, in the expression, he alters it, he simultaneously proposes it as a modification of the group attitude in general. And this modification of the group attitude in general is possible because of that very subjectivity of attitudes which allow them their modification as incorporated into the psychological structure of the individual.'[1]

Thirdly and lastly, in saying that a system is functionally integrated, and that the understanding of its part-phenomena may be aided by endeavouring to see them in terms of that integration, nothing is asserted as to the degree of that integration. Integration may in fact be very poor, but attention to it will still be helpful. A bad liver is still a liver; a bad egg is still an egg; a non-conforming proletarian is still a proletarian.

But perhaps this last statement goes too far. A non-conforming proletarian, it may be urged, may still be objectively a proletarian, but subjectively he has ceased to be one if his mind is no longer filled with the appropriate modal contents; and we must not forget that we are dealing here with thought and its determination. This is true, and here as elsewhere the functional-organic principle must not be overworked. Let us posit the crucial case, then, of the man who, in his thinking, is not merely a bad specimen of the mental mode appropriate to his social station, but totally at variance with it. In other words, let us posit the case of a Marx or a Lenin, each of whom left his father's house and slammed the door behind him. What has the sociology of knowledge to say to that—the case in which the functionalist formula would seem to have become utterly useless, since there is no longer a mere deviation from the norm but a total rupture with it? No light, it is clear, can be thrown on Marx's or Lenin's thought by the fact that they were born members of a ruling class, for they had become so radically estranged from that class and its characteristic attitudes before ever they put pen to paper as to be altogether incomprehensible from the point of view of

[1] *Loc. cit.*, 184 *seq.*

293

their original social location. Is not the sociology of knowledge, even as a hermeneutic method, here at the end of its tether? It refers us, for the understanding of mental contents and processes, to the social background of the minds concerned; but here that reference seems to be unavailing.

Three defensive moves are possible in reply to such an argument. The first would insist that the defection of a deviant obviously does not destroy the intelligibility of the abandoned position in respect of its social determination. Marx and Lenin ceased to think like members of the upper class, but that does not mean that the characteristic mentality of that class can be any the less successfully analysed and explained by the methods of the sociology of knowledge. To quote Child once again: the possibility of non-conformity, he says, is always there, but 'this possibility does not prejudice the group character of the attitudes, for their origin, at least, was a group origin. . . . Inasmuch as most men think virtually altogether in the forms provided by the attitudes of their groups, it is probable that in the vast majority of cases the group attitudes undergo no significant change in the mind of the individual.' [1] In other words, even if the sociology of knowledge could only explain the norm, it would be able to explain a lot. The functionalist approach in the social sciences has had few critics so stern and severe as Robert Merton; yet even he admits that it is applicable to the basic pattern of a society: 'The mesh of expectancies constituting every social order', he writes, 'is sustained by the modal behaviour of its members representing conformity to the established, though perhaps secularly changing, culture patterns. It is, in fact, only because behaviour is typically oriented toward the basic values of the society that permits us to speak of a human aggregate as comprising a society. Unless there is a deposit of values shared by interacting individuals, there exist social relations, if the disorderly interactions may be so called, but no society.' And, in another context: 'The notion of functional unity is *not* a postulate beyond the reach of empirical test; quite the contrary. . . . That all human societies must have *some* degree of integration is a matter of definition.' [2]

Not only definition is involved here, however, but degree also. Society could not reasonably be defined as an integrated, inter-functioning system, unless deviation were the exception that confirms rather than invalidates the rule. Now, it is not difficult to show that though all men can, in principle, contract out of the mentality of their society or class or set, few of them choose, in practice, to do so. (This is our second defensive argument.) Contracting out presupposes a special mental effort (quite apart from the courage needed to brave the more material pressures that may well be brought to bear on the renegade) which few

---

[1] *Loc. cit.*, 184.   [2] *Social Theory and Social Structure*, 1949, 134, 28.

people are either able or willing to put forth. To live, and consequently to think, means for most human beings to live and think according to the modes into which they have been born and educated. Only those who do more than live and think, namely who reflect upon life and thought, are likely to lift themselves out of the accustomed rut. But to reflect is, as the very etymology of the word indicates, a bending-back, a going against the direction that is normal and natural, and for this reason it will only be the exceptional individual who will, as a rule, venture forth from the home in which he has been reared, turn away from the fountain at which he has drunk or withdraw from the tables at which he has been nourished. This again is very nearly a matter of definition. Unless a man is altogether out of the ordinary he will not stir out of the ordinary routine of existence, either in conduct or in thought.

However, our chief and crowning argument in this matter of individual freedom and the social determination of thought is drawn from a consideration of this very phenomenon—the extraordinary personality who frees himself from his native ties, who breaks through and throws off the original determination of his mind. What, so we must surely ask, will happen to him after he has left his father's house and slammed the door behind him? Will he for ever roam the streets? If he does, he will fall into total alienation from life as it is and end up outside society. He will assuredly not become a Marx or a Lenin. No, if he is a man determined to remain inside life, he will find himself a new abode, join a new family, look at everything from a new angle more congenial to him personally than that of his former associates. He will occupy a new vantage point from which to survey reality; in other words, he will exchange the old determination of his thought for a new one. But he will not be in a position to live without all social determination. His freedom is very real, but it is a freedom to choose, not to refrain from choosing. Indeed, even after he has chosen, he will still remain largely free, for in his new determination he can again adopt a variation very far from the modal theme.[1] But for all that he must take his basic cue from social life, and that is why his new and deviant line of thought can be no less successfully analysed by the hermeneutic method of the sociology of knowledge than his old conformist one. Between the two there certainly lies a moment of crisis, the defection from one axiological system and the assumption of another. But this will be an incident in

---

[1] Needless to say, a man who has withdrawn from one position and entered into another, will often still have elements of his old affiliation about him, both in his value-system and in the world-view derived from it. It is an awareness of this 'imperfection' which has led many converts to become 'more papal than the Pope'. We mention this phenomenon only for completeness' sake; it has no bearing on the argument of the text.

his private life rather than a social occurrence. It will interest his biographer rather than a student of the spirit of the age. It will be matter for the psychologist rather than the sociologist of knowledge.

We can easily reconcile these considerations with the principle of functionalism and may even express them in terms of it. If we take a multiple, internally-divided society in which alone a change of axiological affiliation is likely to become practicable, for instance a capitalist society with two or more distinct classes, we may say, without unduly stretching the term, that some of its members function as capitalists, others as proletarians, and still more so if, in the Marxian manner, we think, not of a more or less abiding social system, but of history as a process of flux. Those who function as capitalists are those who stand for the capitalist order of values; those who function as proletarians are those who stand for the proletarian order of values. By and large those who function as capitalists in this sense, who are, in other words, capitalist-minded, capitalists in the subjective sense of the word, will also be those who are capitalists according to objective criteria, in that they own property, hire and fire labour, &c. &c. But functional and personal, objective and subjective affiliations need not coincide, and therein consists men's freedom of thought. They can come down on whichever side of the fence they please; they may perhaps even refuse to come down on either side of it and so look out onto the world from a vantage point on the borderline where the two hostile territories meet; but they cannot leap into the air and then stay there. For to be a man at all is to stand upon the soil of society, to function somehow in society, and that is the limitation of human freedom—at least of the freedom of those who wish to be men as their fellows are.

In this last paragraph we have taken modern society for our example and spoken of men of bourgeois origin functioning in society or history as proletarians and of native proletarians functioning as members of the bourgeoisie. Actually, similar phenomena are observable all through history. One that springs to mind is that of medieval monasticism. Such orders as the Benedictines and the Praemonstratensians were typical products of a feudal world; very often, indeed, they were regarded as aristocratic, as a retreat for the nobility (German: *Herrenstifter*). Yet they harboured many peasants and not a few townsmen as well, and that not only physically, but spiritually also. When later the mendicant orders appeared, they were typical outgrowths of town life. It is characteristic that they dropped the principle of *stabilitas loci* so typical of the older monachism. Nor were the Franciscans and Dominicans town orders only; they were, as the Catholic historian Schnürer has said, 'altogether focused on the urban proletariat and intelligible only from its point of view'. Yet the two most outstanding of all Dominicans:

296

St. Dominic himself and St. Thomas Aquinas, were of noble parentage. St. Thomas, like Marx, was a case of realignment, and his brothers were as angry with him as some of Marx's social set were with Marx. 'It is of no importance', writes von Martin, 'from which estates the monasteries mainly recruited themselves; the aristocratic character of pre-Franciscan monachism is not disproved by the fact that the majority of the monks did not belong to the aristocracy, any more than is the bourgeois structure of the regular clergy, after the mendicant movement, by the fact of their very largely . . . aristocratic membership.' [1] The Benedictines, we may say, functioned as part and parcel of the higher feudal strata in their world, just as the Dominicans did of the lower urban strata in theirs, personal life-histories notwithstanding.

The theory of men's undeniable freedom of thought and its operation in face of the equally undeniable social determination of thinking—a theory centring on the possible discrepancy between a man's personal and his functional integration—was first developed within the Marxist camp, in Georg Lukacs's book *Geschichte und Klassenbewusstsein* (1923), whose high qualities deserve to be acknowledged by friend and foe alike. Marx had already foreshadowed it, for he invariably ascribes a certain consciousness to the proletariat and not to individual proletarians, to the bourgeoisie and not to the individual bourgeois. For Lukacs, the proletarian class-consciousness is the mentality ideally suited to the objective position of the proletariat in society and history. But what is ideally suited is not always what is actually found. Hence the proletarians must be educated so as to become the true proletariat; the working-class must be educated into its own appropriate 'ideology' —it must, so to speak, be induced to become in reality what ideally it is already—and this educative mission is the task of the Party, characteristically conceived here as an *avant-garde*. As this process of education proceeds, there is an asymptotic approximation of the ideal collective consciousness of the proletariat as a class on the one hand, and the actual personal consciousness of individual proletarians on the other. The consummation of the development is then the Revolution.[2]

---

[1] *Geist und Gesellschaft*, 1948, 42 *seq.*

[2] It is impossible for us to enter more deeply into Lukacs's specific contentions. Those who wish to become further acquainted with them must be referred to the following: Grünwald, *Das Problem der Soziologie des Wissens*, 1934, 129 *seq.*; Child, 'The Problem of Imputation in the Sociology of Knowledge', in *Ethics*, 1940/41, 213 *seq.*; Gurvitch, *Le Concept de Classes Sociales de Marx à Nos Jours*, 1954, 47 *seq.* Deeply influenced by Lukacs are Grünberg, cf. *loc. cit.*, 90 *seq.*, and also Mannheim, cf. *Essays on the Sociology of Knowledge*, 1952, esp. 186 *seq.* In Lukacs's own book, the following passages are perhaps the most remarkable: 52 *seq.*, 57 (motto), 62 *seq.*, 86, 92 *seq.*, 213 *seq.*, 228.—Important and revealing also are Warynski's adumbrations concerning 'self-criticism' (by which an individual can and must bring his subjective mind into line with the objectively indicated mentality) in *Die Wissenschaft von der Gesellschaft*, 1944, esp. 288 *seq.*—It is not at all surprising that Lukacs's

Problem C: The Degree of Social Determination

All these speculations are none the worse for being presented in a guise which must needs be unacceptable to the majority of scholars. It is easy to detach their truth from the political and propagandist trappings in which Lukacs presents it. Using Max Weber's terminology, we may express it by saying that it is only in the limiting or ideal-typical case that subjective and objective spirit fully coincide, that personal and functional alignments are one, that every individual will think the thoughts modal to his society or subsociety, whatever that subsociety may be. But that does not mean that there are mental productions which are inexplicable by the hermeneutic method known as the sociology of knowledge, for the ideas of the man who has uprooted and replanted himself can be imputed to the social reality or grouping in which he has found a new mother-soil. As von Martin convincingly shows, much of the essential kernel of the Thomist world-view is intelligible as a reflection of medieval town life, and fully intelligible only as such, notwithstanding the fact that he who voiced it was born in a castle and not in a city, among nobles and not in a bourgeois home.[1]

All in all we feel more than ever justified, in the light of this discussion, in returning to our previous assertion—namely that the man or mind in revolt does indeed raise a problem for the student of the history of ideas, but that it is more a problem for the individual psychologist than for the sociologist of knowledge. Of course, in dealing with this kind of problem, even the individual psychologist will very often be again led towards social reality as the quarter from which most light can be thrown upon the mysteries to be elucidated. We have assumed all along that Karl Marx started out as a bourgeois and only later developed a revolutionary mentality. But this is not quite true. Marx was never merely a bourgeois; he was by extraction a Jew, and thus a bourgeois with a difference. Far from being firmly established in the upper class, figures such as he are neither in it nor out of it. Not out of it because of their occupation, their wealth, their manners: not in it because of their alien race, their religion, their sheer lack of acceptance by others of their class. Such a situation easily breeds revolt: Marx was at least a semi-revolutionary even as a boy, when he was still dwelling in his father's tents.

Von Martin has emphasized that the spread of Franciscan piety into the upper class was furthered more by women such as St. Elisabeth than by men.[2] Surely, this is not a fortuitous phenomenon! Women, as a relatively underprivileged group within a privileged class, are

exposition should prove so easily assimilable into this book, for before becoming a Marxist, he had been a disciple of Rickert and Max Weber, and much that he had learned at that early stage remained with him for ever after and indeed accounts for a good deal of what is convincing in his book.

[1] *Loc cit.*, 57 *seq.*   [2] *Loc. cit.*, 50.

understandably more receptive to waves of thought and feeling, to movements welling up from below, than are men, who constitute an élite within the master race.

Another psychological, and yet social, source of possible revolt is revealed in the case of St. Francis. He was, to start with, no underling or outsider of any kind, but he belonged to the 'second generation' of the rich Bernardones, and the second generation of *nouveaux riches* has always suffered from feelings of guilt, of bad conscience, where the rougher and tougher first generation has experienced no uneasiness but rather pride and exaltation.[1] This situation, too, (more than once depicted on the stage by Henryk Ibsen) is fraught with tensions which may easily lead to the defection of a young man or woman, to a leap across some social hurdle or dividing wall. In some cases, of course, such as those of St. Thomas Aquinas and Vladimir Ulyanov, the psychological motivations of their break with their original class are not obvious, and it may well be possible, as the present writer would unhesitatingly admit, that even the most searching biographical research and psychological analysis would yield no answer to the question as to why these men should have turned their backs on the traditions in which they were bred and brought up. *Individuum est ineffabile*, as Goethe liked to say. Who but Almighty God can really say why some hear a call and accept it, whereas others do not?

We have conducted this whole discussion in the terminology of the functionalist doctrine, and there is no reason why we should not have done so. But it is important to emphasize that we could just as well have cast it into the language of the doctrine of elective affinity. For what is it that a man does when he frees himself from one system of life and ideas and allies himself to another? Plainly this, that he abandons a set of ties and thoughts that does not suit him and goes in search of one that does: in other words, he follows the principle of elective affinity. We see again that the full truth does not belong to either theory to the exclusion of the other, but rather to a judicious combination of the two, a mixture in which functionalism must on the whole predominate, but in which elective affinity, too, is a necessary ingredient. Indeed, if the substance of our suggested solution of this problem is considered, rather than the form in which we have chosen to present it, it becomes clear that it is very largely inspired by the latter theory. He who wishes to play a part upon the social scene, must select for himself a rôle which is suited to his personality. To function is to function according to one's choice, whether the latter be explicit or implicit, an acceptance of the initial and accidentally attributed function or the assimilation of a new one.

[1] *Loc. cit.*, 43.

Problem C: The Degree of Social Determination

(c) THE INTELLIGENTSIA—A PRIVILEGED GROUP?

There now remains for consideration only one major problem falling under the general heading of 'degree of social determination', and it has been raised in its most dramatic form by Karl Mannheim. His claim, to put it succinctly, is that the intelligentsia is a privileged group so far as the social determination of thought is concerned, for in their case the determination is particularly slight. And because it is so slight, the intelligentsia may achieve what the more deeply committed strata will always fail to acquire, namely a 'total perspective' in which the contradictory and yet complementary one-sidednesses of the various coexisting partial, and particularly party, 'ideologies' are overcome.

The intellectuals, so Mannheim argues, are, in modern democratic society at any rate, recruited from practically all social layers: the University absorbs and reshapes the sons and daughters of bourgeois and proletarians, townspeople and country-folk, Catholics and Protestants, and so on, and so forth. Hence there is, to begin with, great heterogeneity. But heterogeneity wanes and homogeneity waxes in the academic atmosphere: *ex pluribus fit unum*. 'Although they are [in view of their diverse origins] too differentiated to be regarded as a single class', Mannheim writes, 'there is, however, one unifying sociological bond between all groups of intellectuals, namely, education, which binds them together in a striking way. Participation in a common educational heritage progressively tends to suppress differences of birth, status, profession and wealth, and to unite the individual educated people on the basis of the education they have received.' However, this unification does not lead to a dead uniformity but rather to a complex unity in which the original diversity is to some extent preserved. 'With the increase in the number and variety of the classes and strata from which the . . . intellectuals are recruited, there comes greater multiformity and contrast in the tendencies operating on the intellectual level which tie them to one another. The individual, then, more or less takes part in the mass of mutually conflicting tendencies.' All this creates the presuppositions of a free—an 'unattached'—mind. Education loosens the original attachment and onesidedness, interstimulation adds the more positive virtues of toleration, elasticity and universal understanding. The end result is 'a relatively classless stratum' capable of, and predestined for, the elaboration of 'the fullest possible synthesis of the tendencies of an epoch'.[1]

It is clear straight away that these observations and deductions are much more relevant to the doctrine of ideology than to the sociology of knowledge properly so-called, which Mannheim, as we know, failed

[1] *Ideology and Utopia*, ed. 1952, 138, 140, 137, 146.

300

to distinguish with sufficient clarity. It is crude prejudices that an academic education—if successful—will remove, rather than the more subtle propensity to see reality from this side or that, in terms of one implied axiology or another. But an element of truth remains, even for the sociology of knowledge, for a higher education may, and often does, lead also to a widening of values and horizons, provided only that it has not concentrated over-much on the imparting and acquisition of mere techniques. And there is another point on which we can agree with Mannheim, namely when he asserts that the typical intellectual, being a semi-contemplative, is likely to be less under the influence of social determination in his thinking than those who must be classed as men of action, since he is relatively less deeply immersed in the stream of (practical) social interaction. 'The person who is not oriented towards the whole through his education, but rather participates directly in the social process of production, merely tends to absorb the *Weltanschauung* of that particular group and to act exclusively under the influence of the conditions imposed by his immediate social situation,' says Mannheim, and with every show of justification. The intellectual, on the other hand, can be shown 'to be less clearly identified with one class than those who participate more directly in the economic process'.[1] And for this reason his mind may—though one hesitates to say that it must—be freer than that of the man more immediately involved in affairs and the conflicts and struggles which they bring with them.

So far, so good. But freedom is, as we have seen, essentially freedom of choice. If the intellectual does not wish to remain locked up in a private world, if he wishes his voice to be heard outside the narrow circle of his sphere of technical scholarship, he must bind himself somehow and at some point into the ongoing social process, and it is in his account of how this happens that Mannheim lays himself open to serious criticism. There are, he asserts, two courses of action open to the unattached intellectuals: 'first, . . . a largely voluntary affiliation with one or the other of the various antagonistic classes; second, scrutiny of their own social moorings and the quest for the fulfilment of their mission as the predestined advocate of the intellectual interests of the whole.' [2] In other words, the educated man, returning from the *hortus clusus* of scholarship to the hurly-burly of everyday discussion, may either make himself the hackwriter of any class he fancies, or may become the arbiter, the umpire enthroned above them all.

This idea of the intellectual's rôle is decidedly less than realistic. Certainly, the two alternatives outlined by Mannheim are in principle open to the educated man—he may sell himself to a party or he may remain an uncommitted observer. But neither will be chosen by many. Both will be exceptions rather than the rule. It is between two other

[1] *Loc. cit.*, 138 *seq.*   [2] *Loc. cit.*, 140.

alternatives that the choice seems to lie—if the word choice be permitted in this context. For intellectuals, like most other people, tend to slither rather than step into a particular position and point of view. (This is already one reason why it can be said of Mannheim that he has over-dramatized the part they play.) The educated man will either continue to speak with the voice of the class from which he has sprung, and use whatever equipment he has acquired in his higher education for the clearer formulation of the world-view of that class; or he will make himself the mouthpiece of another class—but then it will regularly be his own class, the class of intellectuals, the brainworking élite. What Mannheim failed to see, and herein lies his greatest error, is that the intelligentsia is a class like any other, not unattached, but, like every class, attached to its specific social location, world-view and set of interests. 'Even the intellectuals will arrive at a consciousness of their own general social position and the problems and opportunities it involves,' Mannheim says, '—though not a class consciousness.' [1] It is this last half-sentence which proves that Mannheim did not altogether contrive to see things as they really are. In claiming for the educated man—for University Professors like himself—a privileged position *vis-à-vis* social determination, was he not merely a fond victim of 'ideological self-deception', 'ideological delusion'? It would indeed seem that he was. [2]

Of the first possibility we have indicated—that the intelligentsia should remain attached, both in its theoretical world-view and its political ideologies, to the subsociety which has mothered them—there are many illustrations. [3] Mannheim himself was of Hungarian origin, and he could have found much to support our contention, and little to support his own, in the country of his birth. The intelligentsia of Austria-Hungary before 1918 was (if we exclude the Jewish contingent) predominantly recruited from the lower middle class and later in life stood almost to a man for the values as well as the interests of that stratum. This is not the place for detailed proof; but it could easily be given. Suffice it to say that, politically speaking, doctors, lawyers, teachers and all the rest belonged almost exclusively to the Catholic parties. This alignment is symptomatic. Other ages have shown parallel phenomena. How many medieval bishops thought or felt differently from their noble brothers and cousins, from the feudal aristocracy from which they came, despite the fact that they were the intellectuals of the day, and often highly trained intellectuals at that?

A good deal more interesting is the second possibility—the develop-

---

[1] *Loc. cit.*, 142 *seq.*

[2] Cf. Geiger, *Ideologie und Wahrheit*, 1953, 181, and *Aufgaben und Stellung der Intelligenz in der Gesellschaft*, 1949, 64.

[3] Cf. Geiger, *Aufgaben und Stellung* &c., esp. 99.

ment of the intelligentsia into a fully-fledged social class with its own appropriate determination of thinking.[1] Under what concrete conditions this is likely to happen is another matter into which it is impossible to inquire here: one obvious presupposition is the existence of intellectuals in fairly large numbers, but there are others rather less obvious. The social bases of such a development seem, however, clear. In defining the notion of class one can either follow Marx's more objective or Max Weber's more subjective description: in either case the intelligentsia will appear as potentially a separate class. For Marx, the crucial point in class affiliation is relation to property: the upper classes are the controllers of property, the lower class are the property-less, the proletarians. However close one may wish to keep to this dichotomous scheme, the intellectuals must be allowed, by its own terms, to form a third class. They are not propertied, since they possess no material means of production (factories, houses, mines, etc.)—but they are not property-less either, for their own labour-power is so highly trained and specialized that it represents the full equivalent of a capital item. Hence the intellectuals are a *tertium quid*, a class on their own.[2] From Max Weber's point of view one must needs come to the same conclusion, though perhaps a little more quickly. For Weber a 'status group' is a group that has its own specific 'social estimation of honour': an employer has and receives a different feeling of prestige and 'belonging' from that of a working-man or a peasant. But in this respect the doctor, lawyer or teacher manifestly have their own distinguishing position, i.e. form their own status group, and no realistic person will deny that this is so.

Observation will fully bear out these theoretical assertions. Often, though not always, the intellectuals genuinely are a separate class and acknowledged as such. Many medieval bishops, as we have said, were noblemen rather than clerics, but many medieval clerics were intellectuals rather than peasants or burghers or even aristocrats. (This is true more especially of the clergy regular, the monks; the name of St. Thomas Aquinas again comes to mind.) At all events, they had their

---

[1] In accepting this possibility, we are in serious disagreement with Geiger's book quoted in the immediately preceding footnote. Cf. *ibid.*, esp. 88, 100. When Geiger says that there are circumstances in which an intelligentsia is 'for professional reasons' likely to be '*en bloc*' revolutionary or conservative (cf. 127), he is controverting his own argument. He does so even more when he admits that the intelligentsia is 'an independent social stratum' (37), 'a social type with its own specific place in society' (63), and writes: 'The outlook on society of the individual member of the intelligentsia is just as much moulded by this collective point of view as the social conceptions of the working man, the peasant, the entrepreneur, &c. are determined by their respective class positions.'

[2] Very interesting in this respect are the opinions of the Marxist Karl Kautsky summarized by Gurvitch in his *Concept de Classes Sociales de Marx à Nos Jours*, 1954, 41 *seq.*

own 'standing', and one knows what that meant in the medieval world. In the Renaissance the position of the *literati* was even more unambiguous, and we are again indebted to Alfred von Martin for an illuminating study of it.[1] Once more the details would lure us off the main track, and we must firmly refuse to pursue them. Only one or two brief quotations can be given to clinch the matter: 'The educational élite of the humanists', writes von Martin, 'takes its place by the side of the recently-formed propertied class as a new upper stratum. Both try to separate themselves off from the people whence they come but whom they despise as *vulgus*. The rhetoricians are helped in this by their very language; it is sociologically significant how the humanists avoid, so far as possible, the "vulgar language", i.e. Italian, and reserve for themselves, in the exclusiveness of their Latinity, a special position. At the same time, by the classical purity of that Latin, they set themselves off from the other side, i.e. the clerical representatives of scholastic education. . . . Yet in displacing the clergy there is no desire to seek contact with the social strata "below". No, what these men wanted was to secure a leading position for themselves . . . and thereby a new social cleft was opened up which was added to that which capitalism had created in the economic sphere.' [2] Humanists and merchant-princes, *nouveaux riches* and *nouvelle noblesse de l'esprit*, rose together in the world, as this quotation indicates, but von Martin rightly insists that the two new classes must not be confounded. Their capital was not the same, nor was the basis of their social estimation—wealth in the one case, *virtus* (in the sense of education) in the other.[3] From the very beginning, indeed, there were the makings of a class contrast and a class conflict: 'The inclination of the money-bags to despise the intellect, the inclination of the intellect to despise the money-bags'—a double tendency *always* dividing the two élites, as von Martin rightly emphasizes.[4]

Perhaps this whole excursion into the past is unnecessary in order to prove our point against Mannheim, namely that the intelligentsia, so far from being 'a relatively classless stratum', forms in fact an independent class. For who, living in this world of ours, can be unaware of the bitter resentment so many intellectuals nurse against the monied circles, resentment which explains the well-known fact that capitalist-conservative parties are patronized to a much smaller extent by typical intellectuals than radical parties, Liberal and Labour? [5] Mixed up with all

[1] Cf. *Geist und Gesellschaft*, 1948, esp. 94 *seq*.
[2] *Loc. cit.*, 94 *seq*.; cf. also 100 *seq*.
[3] Cf. *ibid.*, esp. 107 *seq*., 117 *seq*., 120 *seq*., 127 *seq*., 151 *seq*.
[4] 109, 209 *seq*., 230. Cf. also Geiger, *Intelligenz*, 3 *seq*., 7.
[5] The prominence of non-proletarian, intellectual figures in the so-called Labour Party is striking: the names of Attlee and Gaitskell head a list which is very long

the other struggles that are afoot in the contemporary arena, there is also a definite class-struggle going on between the intellectuals, greedy for power, and the captains of industry, loath to lose it. To think of them as standing aside, uncommitted, detached, predestined to act as referees on the field of political manœuvre, is to live in Utopia, not in Britain, France or the United States.

What matters most for our purposes is that the intelligentsia is a true subsociety within the framework of the inclusive global society, and as such constitutes a very real substructure within the contemporary system of social life, to which there corresponds, as its due accompaniment and reflection, an appropriate, identifiable, specific superstructure, contained certainly within the limits of the general mentality of the age and country in question, yet recognizable as an independent variation on the common theme. Without embarking on a digression inside a digression by attempting to define an intellectual,[1] one thing is clear: that he is a man who reflects upon life, rather than acts within it; a man, as Geiger expresses it, who 'measures all material reality with the yard-stick of theory and intellectuality'.[2] But this in itself imposes a limitation on, and imparts a bias to, his mind: he will incline towards rationalism,[3] and at the same time towards radicalism, for he who merely speculates in his study can more easily run to extremes than he who moves among the manifold resistances of the market square. This double tendency towards rationalism and radicalism—towards a radical rationalism—which is inherent in the very nature of the intellectual strata (cf., e.g., the Scholastics!) is particularly prominent in the modern intellectual, for all life and thought since the Renaissance have been pressing forward towards ever greater rationality. The result, among many of the modern intelligentsia, is a super-rationalism which tends to blind them towards many non-rational values, for instance those of tradition, of religion, and even of art.

The truth of this assertion is perhaps easiest to see and most clearly, too, in those countries which still possess an old-style peasantry. Not only are those who have come to be called 'the young scientists'

indeed. These men, however much they may think of themselves as the representatives of the working people, are, in reality, no more than their allies. The Labour Party is in fact a common enterprise shared by the labour interest with a wing of the intelligentsia—the special class called the 'intelligentsia'.

[1] Cf. Geiger, *Intelligenz*, 12 *seq.* and 18 *seq.*, for Geiger's own definition and a summary of Schumpeter's opinions.

[2] *Loc. cit.*, 23. Cf. also 71 *seq.*, 128 *seq.*, 132 *seq.* It is because of this inherent and altogether natural attachment to theory and intellectuality that so many intellectuals become critical of the powers that be (even when they themselves have sprung from the upper classes) and turn against them—a fact which sheds much light on the cases, discussed above, of Marx, Engels, Lenin, Kropotkin &c. Cf. Geiger's very apposite remarks on this subject, *loc. cit.*, 134.

[3] *Loc. cit.*, 37 *seq.*, 46 *seq.*

S.K.—X

absolutely blind, as a rule, to the fact that the villages around them have a genuine culture of their own, though it is not the culture of the towns in which the intellectuals (an exclusively urban group [1]) reside; almost invariably they are positively contemptuous of it, even, and actively hostile towards it. Culture means for them what is rational, not what is real, what is made, not what has grown, what is calculable, not what is spontaneous. It is vain to expect of such people a deeper understanding of alien thoughts and lives. The intellectual mind—meaning the modal mentality of the modern intellectual, formed predominantly by the artefacts of urbanism, science and mechanization—is anything but an open mind. In many of its more characteristic representatives it is almost as closed a mind as can well be imagined.

Of course, it remains true—though this is not what Mannheim is chiefly asserting—that any genuine conquest of social determination, any genuine understanding of more than just one's own circle of life and thought, must come from members of the intellectual class, for it is they alone who have the knowledge and freedom to study, and penetrate into, the essence of cultures other than their own. But to be an intellectual is not enough. To grasp the meaning of what, by one's own standards and those of one's own society, must necessarily appear meaningless, is a task to which many are called but few chosen. Education, unfortunately, is not a sufficient preparation for it: to it must be added certain personal characteristics which are much more rarely found. Max Weber felt that there ought to be a definite moral element in the man who sets out to discover the rationality of the apparently irrational: he must be intent on the truth; he must be ready to follow it whithersoever it may lead him; more than that, he must be able to conquer and control the thousand-and-one influences which would interfere with his intentness on and pursuit of the truth; in a word, he must be an ascetic of a kind. But such asceticism alone will still be unavailing, for self-discipline, even at its highest and best, remains a merely negative qualification. What is ultimately decisive is the presence or absence of a spirit of *caritas*, of *agape*—that loving willingness to meet the other on his own terms, that positive preparedness for self-surrender in the face of realities and values different from one's own, without which nothing human, whether individual or social, will ever yield its secret to him who searches for it.

[1] Cf. Geiger, *Intelligenz*, 89, 118, and esp. 140 *seq.*

CHAPTER EIGHT

PROBLEM D: THE CONQUEST OF SOCIAL DETERMINATION

(a) THE PRAGMATIST APPROACH

IN the literature of the sociology of knowledge, and more especially in the Marxist contribution to it, the concept of 'false consciousness' occupies an important place. Now this catch-phrase can be given two meanings which should be kept apart, even though they are undoubtedly akin. A consciousness can be false either in the subjective or in the objective sense of the word. A state of mind may be out of harmony either with the man who entertains it, or with the reality to which it refers. In the first case, we have false pretences, in the second, factual error. The remedy must always be more realism, but in the one instance it will have to be more realism about oneself, and in the other more realism about the world before one's eyes or under one's feet.

A figure well known in capitalist and other essentially competitive societies is the little man who conducts himself as if he were a big one —the twopenny-halfpenny grocer who talks as if he were a captain of industry, the suburban woman who gives herself the airs of a society lady. Such a person will either mislead nobody, or others, or himself; if nobody at all or only other people, his consciousness will, by definition, not be false; if himself, it will be. Such cases, which correspond to the first or subjective definition of false consciousness, are by no means rare. But they are not the concern of the sociology of knowledge as defined in this book. For these falsified states of mind are wish-determined, not fact-determined. They are ideological; and for that reason they fall into the field of psychology, and possibly of psychopathology, rather than into the area of cognition properly so called. It is precisely the absence of knowledge, of acquaintance with or submission to the facts, which makes the consciousnesses involved unrealistic, delusory and false.

The phenomenon of false consciousness in the first meaning of the word is thus beyond our ken—and so too is the corresponding phenomenon covered by the second possible interpretation of its import, as we are now about to show. But this second case requires a somewhat more careful consideration. Its problem is at least capable of formulation in the language of the sociology of knowledge, and that alone gives it a *prima facie* claim to our attention. There are, so the Marxists tell us, axiological positions which cannot, by their very nature, yield a truthful picture of the objective world, which must, in those who maintain them, lead to a mentality that is at variance with reality. Or, to come down to a more concrete level, the capitalists, simply because they are capitalists, are condemned, so long as they remain what they are, to live enclosed in a delusory or dream world, to carry in and around themselves a false consciousness. It is only the proletariat that occupies a vantage-point from which the world appears as it really is; it is only the proletariat that possesses a value-system which can and does enable men to recognize the truth. Karl Mannheim has described the problem of false consciousness in this, its objective sense, as 'the problem of the totally distorted mind which falsifies everything that comes within its range', and has claimed that it is more than a psychological phenomenon: 'Marxism,' he says in a passage which shows perhaps better than any other that he, too, was a Marxist of a kind, 'was able to go beyond the mere psychological level of analysis and to posit the problem in a more comprehensive, philosophical setting. The notion of a "false consciousness" hereby acquired a new meaning.' [1]

Here again we have a theory which was first sketched out by Karl Marx and later developed more fully, and especially more technically, by his most brilliant twentieth-century disciple, Georg Lukacs. Briefly —and we must be brief, for we see the problem of truth in an entirely different way—the assertion is that the bourgeois mind tends to think in terms of things where it should think in terms of social relationships, and in terms of stability where it should think in terms of movement. In either case there is *Verdinglichung*—a word which can perhaps best be translated as 'reification'. Life freezes, as it were, into cold hard forms while in reality it is both humanly alive and historically in flux. A mentality which can take in neither the human character of the social world nor yet its historical quality is manifestly condemned to miss the true meaning of reality and is in fact a mentality 'every cognition of which is necessarily wrong'. [2]

Marx himself applied this concept of false consciousness mainly to 'bourgeois economics'. There is, first of all, his celebrated doctrine of the 'fetishism' of the commodity. When we buy a thing in a shop, we have the idea that we are really buying *a thing*, and that this is all there is to the transaction. But in point of fact we are not merely buying a thing but rather the congealed labour-power of another human being,

[1] *Ideology and Utopia*, ed. 1952, 62, 66.   [2] Mannheim, *loc. cit.*, 62.

and the handing over of a half-crown piece in return for the wrapped
parcel is not merely an exchange of objects but rather a human relationship, a relationship of inter-human co-operation. As Marx sees things,
we have made a fetish out of the commodity: it is fashioned by us, yet,
like the primitive who adores the piece of clay which he himself has
shaped as if it were really something apart from him, we treat it as
something independent of us, indeed, as a thing valuable, and even
powerful, in itself. When *we* buy and sell dead things, we, or rather the
'bourgeois economists', say that *they* (i.e. the things) exchange. Yet
buying and selling, like all economic activities, are, rightly understood,
moments, elements, in a social process.

Now for the bourgeois, even the bourgeois scholar and scientist,
this essential quality of life is masked. It takes a revolutionary act to
penetrate through the deceptive outer crust to the true inner meaning,
which is social, not economic, human, not *dinglich* (thing-ly). But the
consequences of the initial misunderstanding of what really happens do
not stop there: blindness in one eye is followed by blindness in both,
partial error by total perversion of all thinking. For once economic life,
that is to say social life, is assumed to be essentially a handling of things,
it becomes of necessity a realm of being which stands (as things do)
over against man as something objective, alien to him, controlled by
natural forces, in fact, a kind of second nature. In so far as classical
economics is given over to this way of thinking—and Marx has very
little difficulty in showing that it is—it is all delusory. Far from being
as alien and uncontrollable as the eternal rocks, socio-economic reality
is in fact a reflection of human working and willing. Far from being
a sphere in which man must take everything as he finds it, it is a sphere
in which he can have everything as he wants it; far from being a realm
of universal stability or at best unceasing repetition, it is teleologically
developing towards a grand cataclysm: the realization, on man's part,
that here he is master, not slave; and his consequent assumption of true
mastery over what is his; the leap from necessity into freedom.

As can be seen, the concept of false consciousness lies at the very
heart of the Marxian doctrine. Lukacs gives it a turn which leads far
beyond economic theory into the citadel of all mental activity. Those
who wish to follow him thither should read the fourth essay in his book,
entitled 'Die Verdinglichung und das Bewusstsein des Proletariats'. [1]
Here a few characteristic illustrations may suffice. 'To be radical', says
Marx in *Zur Kritik der Hegelschen Rechtsphilosophie*, in a passage which
Lukacs takes for his motto, 'is to grasp a thing at its root. But for man
the root is man himself.' In other words, a wrong idea of man will

[1] *Geschichte und Klassenbewusstsein*, 1923, 94 *seq*. Other important passages are
the following: 27 *seq*., 33, 43 *seq*., 50, 58 *seq*., 73 *seq*. Cf. also Warynski, *Die Wissenschaft von der Gesellschaft*, 1944, esp. 201 *seq*., 273 *seq*.

spread through the whole tree of knowledge and contaminate it all. The bourgeoisie, we are given to understand, is under such an idea, for it operates with the concept of a stable 'human nature' (the very word 'nature' is taken to be a tell-tale word in this connection), and, like M. Proudhon, does not realize 'that history is nothing but an un-interrupted transformation of human nature'.[1] The result is that 'bourgeois sociology', for instance, falls into formalism; it deals with the forms which endure, not with the contents which change, and hence it grasps at the shadow and misses the substance. 'Bourgeois philosophy' is in a similar case. Starting as it does from the inherently unsound position that true theory must be divorced from practice, that valid philosophical insights can only spring from a contemplative attitude, it sees a gap opening up before it between thinking and being—a gap which does not exist in reality but only in its imagination, being in fact its own invention or rather creation—and finds itself faced with the unpleasant necessity of having to bridge this non-existent gap, to make identity out of duality. Is it any wonder, Lukacs seems to ask, that metaphysical, mythological and phantasmagoric forms of thought should result, that philosophical speculation should degenerate into a sort of shadow-boxing, and prove unable to get the better of besetting difficulties which are ultimately no more than a millstone which it has tied around its own neck? There is no difference in this respect, Lukacs emphasizes, between bourgeois idealism and bourgeois materialism; the latter is merely 'Platonism with a negative sign'.

But perhaps the 'ideological' field in which the falseness of the bourgeois consciousness becomes most blatantly obvious is the study of history. History is by definition that which flows, but the perverted historians make it into a stationary affair. Ranke's famous saying, that all historical epochs are equally near to God, is interpreted by Lukacs in this spirit. 'All are equally near to God' means that all can and should be seen as if on one level; but if they are all on one level, and thus co-ordinated, they cannot be ordered before and after, as successive stretches on the moving belt of time, and hence they appear as what they are not, and the historians' consciousness is false. 'Historiography is a task laid upon bourgeois thought, but it is a task which it cannot fulfil.' We see that no matter in which direction the bourgeois mind seeks to travel, it always runs into a blank wall which it has no means of scaling and cannot hope to conquer.[2]

For the proletariat such a wall does not exist: it enjoys a wide, uninterrupted view of reality in its true forms and colours. We need not follow Lukacs into his discussion of the 'correct consciousness' for, by

[1] Marx, *Das Elend der Philosophie*, ed. 1885, 147 *seq.*
[2] The reference should really be *passim*, but cf. esp. 58 *seq.*, 172 *seq.*, 220 *seq.* The quotation is from p. 59.

definition, it is unproblematic. Instead we must ask: what exactly is it that clouds the eye of the bourgeois? Does he see a phantasmagoric rather than a real world because of what he *is* or because of what he *wishes*—because of the *facts* of his social situation, or because of the *strivings* which it inspires? In the former case, the hapless bourgeois would indeed have no escape from error: in the latter, he would. For all recognition of the truth presupposes a realistic attitude; every human being must conquer his wishes if he does not want to fall victim to wishful thinking. If the doctrine of false consciousness asserted no more than this, it would merely be stating the obvious. But it does assert a great deal more. It asserts that no amount of intentness upon truth, no degree of self-control over delusion-producing desires, no objectivity however consistent, or even heroic, will enable the bourgeois to reach a realistic picture of things, and especially of history. He is enclosed in a house whose windows are all crooked, like distorting mirrors, and make the landscape beyond appear both limited in depth and out of its true shape.

There are many passages in Lukacs's book where this assertion—that the bourgeois world-view is *necessarily* unrealistic, and the bourgeois himself *inevitably* burdened with a false consciousness—is openly made. 'It must be asked in the first place', he writes in a crucial passage, 'how far, within a certain society, the totality of the economic system of that society is visible *at all* from the view-point of a definite position inside the process of production.' (The italics here are Lukacs's, and they give point to his question.) 'It is the task of the most careful historical analysis to make clear, with the help of the category of objective possibility, under what circumstances a true conquest of delusion, a penetration to the real interconnection with totality, lies at all within the realm of possibility.' Now, if this question is raised in regard to the bourgeoisie, the answer is that such a conquest of delusion and penetration to an understanding of the interconnection of things, is beyond the bounds of 'objective possibility', i.e., in plain English, is impossible. 'The [bourgeois] class consciousness is, in an abstract and formal view, at the same time also a distinct *unconsciousness*, due to class position, of their own social and historical position. . . . The "falseness", the "delusion" which is contained in this state of things is therefore nothing accidental, but precisely the expression, on the mental plane, of the objective economic structure.' 'The limitation which makes the class consciousness of the bourgeoisie a "false" consciousness, is objective; it is the situation of the class itself. It is an objective consequence of the economic structure of society, and in no way incidental, subjective or psychological.' [1]

But all this is mere assertion. The main query is: *why* is the bourgeoisie so sunk in error? And if Lukacs's answer to this essential question is

[1] *Loc. cit.*, 63 *seq.*, 65.

investigated, it appears that the falseness of the false consciousness is after all not quite so necessary as it seemed—and was claimed to be—at first sight, and above all not quite so 'objective' and 'unpsychological' as he tries to make out. Only in relatively few passages does Lukacs go into the reasons for the perversion of this perverted mentality, but one or two of them are highly revealing. The following is perhaps the clearest of all: 'Bourgeois thinking must come up against a barrier which it cannot overstep because its starting point and aim is invariably, though not always consciously, an apology for the existing order of things or at least a proof of its unchangeability.' [1] Highly characteristic also is Lukacs's account of the quarter in which the bourgeoisie first comes to a dead stop when it sets out in search of the truth. It is the theory of crises. The bourgeois, including the bourgeois economist, cannot see that economic crises are anything more than temporary indispositions of an otherwise healthy social organism; he cannot grasp that they are necessary symptoms of a mortal endemic and progressive disease. He *cannot* see the facts as they are; we say this because that is the purport of Lukacs's text. But surely, we now hasten to add in criticism, what he ought to have said is that the bourgeois *will* not see the facts in their true light, that he does not *care* to or *wish* to be enlightened about his approaching doom. Obligingly, Lukacs himself states that even the bourgeois *could* be realistic if only he *would*: 'The theoretical solution [of the problem of crises] is scientifically given.' [2] It is merely that those who stand to lose by the truth, do not face it, but turn away and look to the other side. But if this is so, then surely the sources of falsity in this false consciousness are after all subjective and not objective, psychological and not social. In our own terminology—and this formulation brings out the true importance of the present argument—the perverted mind is perverted because it is wish-determined rather than fact-determined, because it is ideological, not because it is shaped or specified historically on the basis of its value-structure. The clear inference is that even the bourgeois can see things exactly as they are if (like other people) he resolutely excludes his practical preoccupations from thought and sight and forces himself to be a disinterested rather than an interested observer.

It is more than likely that Lukacs would accept these deductions. But he would probably go on to argue that a bourgeois who is willing to envisage the end of the bourgeoisie and the end of capitalism, is a bourgeois no longer. It is the hallmark of the true bourgeois to sacrifice everything, including the truth, to the survival of his class. So be it. There is no need to quarrel about definitions. The final point we have been heading towards, and which we now hope to have reached, is this —that the phenomenon of false consciousness, however much it may be

[1] *Geschichte und Klassenbewusstsein,* 59.   [2] 65.

dressed up as a problem of the sociology of knowledge, is in reality a problem of psychology; the bourgeois mind, if there is such a thing, is delusion-ridden, not because it looks out onto reality from a specific axiological, historical, and social vantage-point, but because it allows other interests to enter into the process of perception, of acquiring knowledge,[1] where only one interest should rule—namely, the pursuit of truth. Far from proving that there are some human beings whose consciousness *must* be false, the doctrine of false consciousness, as developed by Lukacs, merely proves in the end that none *need* be. Lukacs comes very near to stating this himself. 'The ideological history of the bourgeoisie', he writes, italicizing the whole passage, 'is nothing but a desperate struggle against the understanding of the true character of the society it has created.' [2] In other words, the truth is beating in upon the bourgeoisie, only it does not wish to accept it. But if it does not *wish*, then it is not by its objective situation disqualified from receiving it, and the whole concept of a mentality 'every cognition of which is *necessarily* wrong' falls to the ground.

This important result can be made doubly or even trebly secure by appending to it two further supplementary considerations. The first concerns the 'correct consciousness', the proletarian consciousness, to which Lukacs ascribes a free and full chance of attaining truth (though not, needless to say, the actual possession of it *a priori*). He calls 'the proletariat . . . the first subject in the course of history which is (objectively) capable of an adequate social consciousness', i.e. a consciousness adequate to, in accordance with, the facts of reality.[3] Surely, even this consciousness is correct only in so far as it restricts itself to the sober and scientific exploration of the area of being visible from its specific axiological vantage-point, and eschews all wish-determination, all wishful thinking. The matter has (unfortunately, perhaps) been put to the test by an arbiter whose verdict is precisely that which Georg Lukacs's standpoint would regard as final, namely, history, practice. When Marx urged, against Proudhon, that history is essentially the continuous transformation of human nature, he made a statement that is in large part true and capable of factual proof. But the truth thus enunciated is after all only a partial truth, and this Marx, and the Marxians, and all the other spokesmen of the revolutionary movement, would have seen if they had not allowed hopes (wish-determination) to creep in and to some extent to overpower judgment (fact-determination)—if they had not allowed the ideological element to overlay knowledge. Instead of testing how far human nature is changeable, and

---

[1] Lukacs himself describes 'interest' in the sense of economic (selfish) interest as the source of the perversion of the bourgeois mind. Cf. e.g. 74 *seq.*, 78. A few pages later he even speaks of the bourgeois ideology as 'a more or less conscious attempt at falsification'! (80).   [2] 78 *seq.*   [3] 217.

how far persistent, they assumed it to be totally transformable. They entertained and spread the facile belief that the tiger of the capitalist jungle could be turned into the lamb of the socialist pasture. Once private property in the means of production was abolished and replaced by common property, the adage 'everyone for himself' would disappear and the maxim 'all for all' take its place. The experiment has been tried and found wanting: in the Soviet sixth of the world, new forms of the 'exploitation of man by man' have sprung up, based, not on the control of private property, but on the possession of political power. In so far as it did not foresee this—and to foresee such developments does not exactly call for supernatural or prophetic endowments—the proletarian consciousness was as 'false' as the bourgeois consciousness when it denied the feasibility of far-reaching social reorganization because 'human nature does not permit it'. On either side of the dividing line of the class struggle, so we must conclude, there are in operation ideological, i.e. distorting influences, in addition to axiological, i.e. truth- and knowledge-giving crystallizations of thinking, and to the extent that the former interfere with the latter, insight and understanding must retreat, error and delusion prevail. All classes, as can be seen, are in precisely the same boat in this respect.

Our second supplementary argument concerns the central concept of Marx and Lukacs, the concept of reification. In and by itself, it rests on a true observation. Men *do* have a tendency to see human relationships in terms of things; they *do* show an inclination to transmute the flowing into the static, the historical and relative into the persistent and absolute. But this double propensity was in evidence long before the capitalist order, and such ancient philosophers as Zeno already exhibit it in operation. And there is every likelihood that, as a source of error, it will long outlive the bourgeois dispensation. The reasons for this have been lucidly explained by Henri Bergson.

Man, as nature has fashioned him, is physically ill-equipped for the struggle for existence. He has no ready-made tools to fight and feed with, as the animals have, nor has he the appropriate instincts. All he initially possesses are the potentialities of his hand and brain. These are certainly vast, but they must be turned into actualities before they can be of any avail. To make them actual, to put them to use, thus became man's inescapable, absorbing, and, for many centuries, exclusive task. But these centuries unavoidably imparted a definite bias to the human mind. Locked in a desperate and deadly battle against his environment, man's intellect became attuned to the facts and forces of that environment; it became an outward-looking intellect. His mind learnt to understand, to deal with, and to dominate the sub-human reality around him, but neglected (because it had to) the exploration of the human reality inside him. In this way it became predominantly mathe-

314

matical, technological and even materialistic. Anything, for instance, that is today presented to it in quantitative terms is easily taken in, for number and extension are properties of the external world; anything, on the other hand, that is laid before it in qualitative terms—of senti- ment, say—causes difficulty, the qualitative being too intangible for its taste, too mysterious, too 'woolly'—or rather, too unaccustomed. No wonder that the intellect, formed as it was in man's victorious war against his initial odds, should attempt to press every idea into the mental modes appropriate to the manipulation of an extended world of materiality, should tend to think of time in terms of space, of mental life and inter-psychic relationships in terms of things, and of history in terms of stability, or at best of a pre-ordained progress towards man's complete world-domination. Reification is thus an inherent pitfall of all thinking where the study of human and historical reality is con- cerned, and must be resisted if we are to avoid the emergence of a false consciousness concerning these sectors of being.

Between these Bergsonian speculations and the Marxian position, there is a much smaller gap than might be assumed at first sight. For though all societies have been absorbed in the struggle for power and control over the outer creation, capitalism has been preoccupied with this task to a much higher degree than any other; and because it has made the domination of nature its central and overwhelming interest, it has also carried to extremes the tendency to reification—what Marx calls 'the self-alienation of man', i.e. the conception of human realities as if they were objects or things alien to him. In so far as this is so, it is easy to build a bridge between Bergson and Marx. But a great difference remains: the tendency towards a false consciousness in matters social and historical is rooted, according to Bergson, not in the class-division of society and the desire of the upper classes to defend it, but rather in the general condition of man, his position in the material universe. If he is right—and the present writer has no doubt whatever on that score [1]—if he has discovered one of the deepest roots of the one- sidedness of all human thinking, then no social revolution will radically change the situation; truth will only be achieved if man learns, in spite of his natural and unavoidable preoccupation with nature, externality, quantity, and so on, not to press the concepts thus formed and the methods so developed beyond their proper limits, and to acknowledge that the phenomena of social life and history demand a treatment different from that appropriate to our dealings with matter, that the live must not be handled as if it were dead.

The problem under discussion—the problem of 'false consciousness' —is one on which Karl Mannheim's ideas are much sounder, at bottom,

[1] Cf. my paper 'Henri Bergson—A Guide for Sociologists' in the *Revue Inter- nationale de Philosophie*, 1949.

than the Marxist theorems to which he is otherwise so deeply indebted. He distinguishes states of mind congruous or incongruous with the state of reality within which they respectively occur [1]—i.e. realistic and unrealistic mentalities, fact-determined and wish-, hope-, fear- or dream-determined thought. Within the latter category he makes a further distinction, into ideologies and utopias. Ideologies have conservative effects; they tend to preserve the *status quo*. Utopias on the other hand are revolutionary in implication; they tend to subvert the existing order of things. To give an obvious example: if people believe in a heaven unrealizable here below, they follow a wish-, hope-, fear- or dream-image; their ideas are 'situationally transcendent' [2]; but this will not undermine the existing social order; on the contrary, it is likely to lend it stability. If, on the other hand, they believe in the possibility of a heaven on earth, realizable under certain conditions within the frame-work of space and time, they are certainly again following a wish-, hope-, fear- or dream-image and have 'situationally transcendent' conceptions, but—and this is the difference—these conceptions will lead to appropriate action and ultimately perhaps produce a social cataclysm. We are not interested here in the further definitional refinements and historical deductions pursued by Mannheim, for we are not concerned with ideologies, whether they be described as ideologies or utopias. We must note only, and to Mannheim's credit, that he recognizes the true facts of the situation: in the centre a kernel of realistic, fact-determined, truthful thought, or rather knowledge; to right and left of it areas of thinking which are less than realistic, which are ideological and utopian. With them a sociology of *knowledge* has no concern.

Its concern is, of course, with ideas that are 'situationally immanent', with the mentality 'congruous with the state of reality within which it occurs', and to this, after this long but not unnecessary détour, we must now turn our attention. The question is: how far does the social determination of thought influence its objective validity? what is the relation of thought sprung from the value-facts of a society, and thus attuned to its very being, to the absolute truth? Three different answers have been attempted to this query. We shall study them in turn, and we shall find that, not surprisingly, they correspond and are akin to the three doctrines encountered in chapters 6 and 7—the causalist theory, the functionalist theory, and the theory of elective affinity. Naturally, the difference between these three basic approaches will appear here in a new light: it will reflect their philosophical rather than their sociological implications. It will turn above all upon differences in the definition of that vital, yet, alas!, so elusive concept of absolute validity, of objective truth, without which no epistemological inquiry can be so much as formulated.

[1] *Ideology and Utopia*, ed. 1952, 173.   [2] *Ibid.*

Problem D: The Conquest of Social Determination

The first of the three alternatives is characterized by its ruthless radicalism. Its thesis is quite simply that no socially determined idea deserves to be described as true, that the very fact of social determination destroys, or is incompatible with, objective validity. The main representatives of this doctrine which, for distinction's sake, we wish to label the *negativist* theory, are Friedrich Nietzsche and Vilfredo Pareto. It is not difficult to see that the conviction underlying it is cousin-german to the fundamental principle of causalism. If ideas are not conceived by us, but caused in us by forces which operate behind us, which push us *a tergo*, then there is no reason why they should be realistic. They will indeed be fact-determined, in the sense that they are determined by the substructural tendencies that work themselves out in our minds; they will indeed be intelligible in their genesis and explicable in the light of it, for they will subserve the vital strivings which give them birth and support them in their operation; they will indeed be congruous with the reality within which they occur, to use Mannheim's mode of expression; they will be taken for the truth, but they will not, as a rule, be true in any higher or absolute sense of the word.

If there is in man an instinct or drive for self-preservation, it is easy to see why he should develop the idea that his soul is immortal, for the latter is a natural reflection, in the mirror of the mind, of the biotic tendencies underlying human existence; or, to change our metaphor, it is a continuation, on the mental plane, of the self-same determinants which dominate our whole being on the lower, submental level, the level of the blind but all-powerful animal cravings in whose grip we remain and whose hold we cannot escape. Beliefs of this kind are manifestly of great help to us in the business of living, for they reconcile our knowledge that we must die one day with our wish to go on for ever. They still our deepest fears; they remove our most agonizing anxiety. But we are just rational enough to be able to recognize that convictions of this sort are delusory rather than factual. There is no scientific way of proving that the soul really does survive the death and dissolution of the body, and consequently all we can say is that thought determined *a tergo* has its uses, but not that it is true. Indeed, we can go further: it is the very falsehood of our beliefs which gives them their utility and at the same time persuades us that they are true. 'The falsity of a judgment is for us not yet an objection against the judgment,' Nietzsche says. 'The question is how far it promotes life, preserves life, preserves the species, perhaps even improves the species; and we are in principle inclined to assert that the falsest judgments . . . are for us the most indispensable ones, that without an acceptance of logical fictions, without a measuring of reality against the purely imaginary world of the unconditional, self-identical, without constant falsification . . . man would not be able to live—that renunciation of false judgments would

317

be tantamount to a renunciation of life, a negation of life.' [1] For the naked truth is always shocking, repulsive, death-dealing, destructive. If we were forced to face it in all its brutality, most of us would despair and commit suicide. But we need not face it, for it is shrouded in a tissue of delusions which keep it from our eyes. These delusions are thus of vital importance to us, and they coincide, more or less, with the area of socially-determined thought. Society is a great romancer: it romances to some purpose, but none the less it romances. It produces myths, rationalizations, derivations, but—apart from the sciences in the narrower sense of the word—it does not produce insights, and understandably so, for it has no interest in and no stomach for the facts as they are. In this way, socially-determined thought is in the last analysis identical, and that necessarily, with untruth. 'Truth', as Nietzsche defines it in a typically fearless paradox, 'is a sort of error without which a certain kind of living beings could not exist.' [2]

This whole mode of argumentation has, as can be seen, a rather aristocratic complexion: truth is not for all but only for some, not for the weak, but only for the strong—according to Nietzsche for the superman, according to Pareto for the super-scientist. The super-man is he who dares to look reality in the face, seeing it as a war of all against all in which no quarter is given, a condition of cruelty, mercilessness, bestiality and death. To him who has once recognized it for what it is, all civilization, including even the traditional idea of truth, becomes a sham, the cacophonous whining of weaklings. 'The truth is terrible: so far falsehood has been called the truth.' [3] It is more terrible even than the Darwinists assume, in so far as there is still a teleological element in their philosophy. Nature is not, as they would have us believe, a grand, and in the last analysis purposive, mechanism for the production of ever more efficient species; it is 'absolutely dominated by chance, that is to say the very opposite of purposiveness'.[4] What can the intellect of man, that queerest of all queer phenomena, do for him in this universal charnel-house? Only one thing: help him to survive; it is 'an aid given to the most unfortunate, most delicate, most perishable of all beings'.[5] But how can it help him? In one way only: by inspiring a facile optimism where all the facts would seem to support the blackest pessimism.

Thus a tendency to falsification is at the very root of all spontaneous, unreflective, unscientific thinking. Its hidden but real aim is not knowledge, but to make a world unfit for habitation appear fit to live in. 'We live only through delusions.' [6] 'Men are deeply immersed in delusions and dream-images.' [7] Art is a collection of 'noble phantasmagorias'; religion is no better (unless it be a collection of phantasmata

---

[1] *Gesammelte Werke*, Musarion ed., 1923 *seq.*, XV, 10.   [2] *Ibid.*, XIX, 19.
[3] XXI, 276.   [4] I, 420.   [5] VI, 76.   [6] VI, 18.   [7] VI, 76.

which are not noble); philosophy, as Theodor Lessing was later to express it, is a *Sinngebung des Sinnlosen*, an ascription of meaning to that which has none, a kind of 'poetizing in abstractions'.[1] Poetizing, of course, may mean two things: exalting the truth, or perverting it. According to Nietzsche, current philosophy, especially of the Platonic variety, involves the latter. The world as it is is a world in flux; but a world of flux is unpleasant to live in; it is like living aboard ship with a heavy swell under the keel. So poetizing transmutes flux into stability, a world of becoming into a world of being, reality into fiction.[2] The result is a falsification of the facts, the substitution of imagined and artificial categories for natural ones. Indeed, this falsification of the facts infects the very language we use. It is metaphorical and anthropomorphic throughout. Every time we form a concept, we are doing violence to the truth, for a concept is reached by equating what is not equal. 'What gives us a concept is the overlooking of what is individual and real.' [3] We have no right to speak of a house in the abstract if there is no such thing—if there are in reality only individual houses in the concrete. Manifestly these speculations of Nietzsche's strike at the root of all thinking. All logic even, for how can logic be true if its most basic tool—the concept—is itself based on fiction? 'Even logic rests on presuppositions to which nothing corresponds in the world as it is.' [4]

Is it said that a society, a system of social co-operation, cannot function without truth, a platitude often heard and uttered? The fact of the matter, according to Nietzsche, is that a society does indeed need common conventions and common concepts for its functioning, but not conventions and concepts that are true (whatever the meaning given to the term). In other words, at the foundation of all collective existence there must lie a delusory conception of truth, but not its reality—a shadow, but not the substance. And that is not surprising, since men are made for life, not for knowledge, for practice, not for theory. The world being what it is, knowledge and theory are no more than luxuries, works of supererogation, marginal phenomena. Indeed, it is doubtful whether true knowledge and true theory are possible at all. Things in themselves, says Nietzsche in a half-turn towards Kantianism, are 'unknowable'.[5] 'The blunder of philosophy', he writes in a passage which may well serve to summarize his convictions, 'consists in this that, instead of seeing in logic and the categories of reason means for the manipulation of the world, for utilitarian purposes, people thought of having in them the criterion of truth, or of reality. In point of fact, the "criterion of

---

[1] Letter to Paul Deussen, printed in Hoppe's edition of Nietzsche's *Briefe*, II, 1938, 192 *seq.*; cf. 194.

[2] XI, 147. Cf. also Barth, *Wahrheit und Ideologie*, 1945, 228 *seq.* As the reader can see, there is a link not only between Nietzsche and Bergson (which will surprise nobody), but even between Nietzsche and Marx (which *is* surprising).

[3] VI, 81.   [4] VIII, 25.   [5] XIV, 273.

truth" was merely the biological utility of such a system of all-pervading falsification.'[1]

Nietzsche, as is well known, was given to a highly imaginative, almost hysterical, mode of expression, but he was at the same time most insistent that his thought was consonant with science at its soberest. And, indeed, there is in him a definite tendency towards a consistently pan-mechanistic view of existence. This becomes particularly clear in his last great work, constituting, as it were, his testament—*The Will to Power* of 1888. Life, he tells us there, is a becoming, the content of which is the never-ceasing internecine struggle for power of quasi-living power, quanta, power-monads, each one urged on by an indwelling will-to-power which is the very secret of the universe. Much though he fancied the mantle of the prophet, he often speaks here in the accents of the scientist, referring to his ideas and postulates as 'naturalistic' and 'physiological' and writing such sentences as these: 'Our holiest convictions, our immovable positions with regard to the supreme values. are [but] judgments of our muscles.' 'Moral values are sham-values compared with physiological ones.' 'An experiment might be made to see whether a scientific order of values could not be built up simply on a numerical and quantitative scale of power. All other values are prejudices.'[2]

It is this tough super-scientism which links Nietzsche with Vilfredo Pareto, a spirit more kindred to his own than any other in the twentieth century. If we study social reality as all reality should be studied, namely 'logico-experimentally', i.e. truly scientifically, we find—so Pareto teaches—that human action is controlled by a set of drives which he calls 'residues' because they remain as the hard core of reality when all delusory wrappings have been stripped off. These residues or drives determine all the comings and goings on the stage of life, as the hand of the puppet-master determines all the antics of his figures in a Punch-and-Judy show. But, oddly enough, the actors in the *comédie humaine* have minds of their own, or at any rate a kind of consciousness, and fancy themselves more than animals or automata. Their minds demand a sop, their consciousness a play-thing, and this is provided by the 'derivations', or thoughts and beliefs which, objectively speaking, derive from the residues, but which subjectively appear to the people who harbour them as 'their ideas', 'their convictions', 'their philosophies'. The scientist alone knows them for what they really are: the insubstantial mental manifestations of substantial physical realities, the unimportant concomitants and accompaniments of drive-determined

---

[1] XIX, 74 *seq*. Cf. on Nietzsche the very thorough essay in Barth's *Wahrheit und Ideologie*, 1945, 205 *seq.*, and the literature quoted in its notes 107, 108, 109 and 121.
[2] XVIII, 223, and XIX, 156. Cf. Alfred Weber, *Farewell to European History*, Engl. ed., 1947, 117 *seq.*, 137.

action, the prattle, as it were, with which men like to surround their deeds. And they are only prattle: truth they have none, indeed, they need none and cannot have any. They are, in the last analysis, rationalizations whereby people give their utterly irrational (because body-born) behaviour *ex post* a pretentious rational appearance.

Thought, to Pareto, is thus not so much a superstructure above a substructure as a work of supererogation. It can change nothing in life, which is in the unbreakable grip of natural necessity; it can only make the reality of life seem less compulsive and repulsive to man, and spread a veil over the animality of the human condition. But this means —and here Pareto agrees with Nietzsche—that human thinking is all delusory. The function and effect of a veil (or mask, or disguise, or vestment, or varnish, or coating [1]) is to hide the facts beneath it and make them imperceptible; the point and purpose of a rationalization is to feign rationality where there is no trace of rhyme or reason. Apart from science, which is a breaking-loose from, a rising above, the natural limitations of man, there is no sound knowledge anywhere. As one turns the pages of the four vast tomes of *The Mind and Society*, and especially those of the third volume, one becomes increasingly depressed. Thought, so far as it is spontaneous and not scientific, appears not only identical with falsehood, but even as man's greatest weakness, his final degradation.

There have been other upholders of this philosophy—Henryk Ibsen's 'vital lie', for instance, is also based on it [2]—but there is no need to study them all. The outline of the doctrine should be clear. What are we to make of it? We have treated it so far as a genuine sociology of knowledge, and that is justified for according to its construction and form it has every right to be acknowledged as such: there is a substructure (of the hormic kind; the will to power, the pattern of residues); there is a superstructure (man's imaginings, the derivations); and there is a bond of determination between the two. As can be seen, all the ingredients of a sociology of knowledge are basically there. But the scene changes when we shift our attention from the form and construction of the doctrine to its content and result. From the latter point of view it is decidedly not a sociology of knowledge, but a pan-ideological theory. Apart from science, which is not socially determined, there is, it claims, no knowledge at all, but only delusion. Certainly, the delusion arises not so much through wishful thinking, a will-o'-the-wisp that runs

---

[1] These terms which sum up Pareto's conception of the derivations in a striking manner, are used by himself. Cf. e.g. *The Mind and Society*, 1935, I, XII, 144, 171, and II, 591, and the whole of ch. III in vol. I.

[2] Cf. Geiger, *Ideologie und Wahrheit*, 1953, 97. *Re* Sorel and Delaisi cf. *ibid.*, 18 *seq.*, re Georg Adler and Valeriu Marcu cf. Warynski, *Die Wissenschaft von der Gesellschaft*, 1944, 222 *seq.*

ahead of men; it arises rather from men's enslavement to the body, from the physical forces which push them from behind. This marks a certain difference from other pan-ideological doctrines, but, when all is said and done, only a minor one. The hard fact of the matter is that for Nietzsche, Pareto and their followers all thought is ideological, and thereby they already fall, by definition, clean outside the area we have described, and which all should describe, as the sociology of knowledge. Thus here again, as in the case of Marx's doctrine of false consciousness, we have something that is a sociology of knowledge in appearance rather than in reality.

Still, it may be urged that little is done by wielding definitions as if they were weapons, and that we must give better reasons for saying that Nietzsche and Pareto have not provided a satisfactory sociology of knowledge. After all, the results of a search into the effects of the social determination of knowing cannot be anticipated. If we are to be honest, we must allow that it may turn out to be negative, showing that sound knowledge is not possible, and that all human thinking is beset with error and bound by delusions. Even such a scholar as Hans Kelsen could remark as follows: 'In view of the hunger for reality of so many sociologists it is perhaps permissible to ask whether it would be at all surprising if one were forced to state that in the sphere of sociality there exists nothing except ideology.' [1] Needless to say, that possibility has, in principle, to be admitted. But both Nietzsche and Pareto have profoundly misunderstood the nature of society. Surely, if there is broad agreement on any point of sociological theory, it is the conviction that the social order rests on, indeed consists in, the *control* of those animal instincts which constitute human nature in the narrower sense of the word. Competition is a *regulated* form of the struggle for existence, not an unregulated one; marriage is a *regulated* form of mating, not an unregulated one; and so on, all along the line. Man may rightly be called a beast; but he resembles more the inmates of a circus than the animals of the jungle or the prairie. Nietzsche and Pareto, all too deep in their physiological and zoological conceptions, do not see this, and thereby they miss the whole point. But someone who knows neither what society is nor what man is nor what culture is, cannot, manifestly, achieve a sound sociology of knowledge.

This argument seems a peremptory one, but perhaps it is not even necessary. For though both Nietzsche and Pareto would like to convince us that they are unprejudiced scientists, no two men could have been less so than they. Nietzsche's case was that of a maniac, a megalomaniac, and though his ravings were ingenious, they were not, and could not be, realistic. Pareto certainly was sober enough, but he was not realistic either, and that for a reason none too different from

[1] *Cit.* Warynski, *Die Wissenschaft von der Gesellschaft*, 1944, 211.

Nietzsche's. For he was filled with contempt for man, and such a sentiment is no less destructive of the truth than is the admiration and deification of man (by the early Liberals for instance) which aroused all Pareto's ire and scorn. Few would deny that man is indeed an earth-bound, body-bound creature; but few would at once infer for that reason that, unless he is super-man or super-scientist, he is hopelessly incapable of truth. The possibility, which nobody can in principle gainsay, that human thinking may all be delusory, was by Nietzsche and Pareto assumed at the very outset as a proven fact. Those who make such an assumption have forfeited, *a limine*, all standing as scholars; prejudice is writ too large across the 2000 pages of *The Mind and Society* for it to rank as a work of any authority.

We are resolved, then, to banish the negativist theory from our further considerations, as we did its causalist cousin. All the larger, then, must loom the second alternative theory concerning the relation of socially determined knowledge to objective truth, which one might have been tempted to call the positivist theory, if this term had not already been earmarked for another use. Certainly, its assertions are highly positive. If the former doctrine forcibly rejects all ideas established in a society and supported by common consent as error, this, in diametrical opposition, is inclined to accept them all as truth. Whatever operates or functions as the truth within a certain social order at a given time, that *is* the truth—such is perhaps the most concise formulation of the decisive definition behind it. No lengthy argument is needed to demonstrate that this conviction fits in exactly with the functionalist conception of social determination: the matter is too obvious to call for explanation.

Some such definition of truth has accompanied sociology all through its history. We find it in Comte, who gave the science its name and its independence. We find it already in those who taught Comte—the rationalist Condorcet and the romantic de Bonald. Condorcet believed, indeed, that many of the earlier convictions of mankind would turn out to be, and be recognized as, erroneous in the coming age of reason when the race would reach intellectual maturity, but he insisted none the less that they were unavoidable, and hence had to be accepted as the truth, at the period when they first became current. As for de Bonald, his claim was simply that men have at no time any workable criterion of validity except common consent, the *consensus omnium*: and so, whatever higher beings may have to say, that which ranks as the truth here below *is* the truth—for nothing else is, or possibly can be.

Ideas of this nature, though, needless to say, of a much more sophisticated cast, have played a prominent part in later sociological literature. Bypassing for the moment the case of Karl Marx, who also belongs

323

Problem D: The Conquest of Social Determination

to this fold,[1] let us turn our attention to their most prominent protagonists in the twentieth century, Emile Durkheim and Karl Mannheim. Both Durkheim and Mannheim maintained, at least by implication, that 'the truth' is that which functions as the truth in a given society, and that there is not much point in trying to rise superior to this limited conception of validity. Durkheim's opinions on this head are surprisingly radical. What is it, he seems to ask, that enables anyone to say that his subjective, personal ideas are right or otherwise? Only the possibility, he answers, of setting them against an objective, impersonal standard. This decisive standard (beyond which we cannot go, as it is the very criterion on which we depend in all our judgments) is the collective experience of the society to which we belong. The *sentiment de la vérité* is, rightly understood, nothing but the apprehension that our individual experience is in conformity with the supraindividual experience of the enveloping group.

Hence the very concept of 'objective' and unchangeable truth is a reflection of the basic reality of social life, the relationship between individual and collective representations, between man and society. Logic is no less a product of social life than, say, ethics; or, to put it even more stringently: logic, even at its most abstract, is no less a product of social life than ethics at its most pragmatic,—*mores*, custom, convention; and all this applies as much to thinking *sub specie aeternitatis* as it does to thinking *sub specie temporis*. 'Logical thought is possible only from the moment when, above the fugitive conceptions which they owe to sensuous experience, men have succeeded in conceiving a whole world of stable ideas, the common ground of all intelligences. . . . Impersonality and stability are the two characteristics of truth. . . . It is under the form of collective thought that impersonal thought is revealed to humanity. . . . Impersonal reason is only another name given to collective thought. . . . Each civilization has its organized system of concepts which characterizes it. Before this scheme of ideas, the individual is in the same situation as the *nous* of Plato before the world of Ideas. He must assimilate them to himself. . . . The collective consciousness . . . being placed outside of and above individual and local contingencies . . . sees things only in their permanent and essential aspects, which it crystallizes into communicable ideas. . . . Hence the individual at least obscurely takes account of the fact that above his private ideas, there is a world of absolute ideas according to which he must shape his own. . . . This is the first intuition of the realm of truth.'

It could be argued, of course, as Durkheim knows full well, that truth is agreement with objective fact, not agreement with collective thought. But he brushes this argument away: 'A collective representation presents guarantees of objectivity by the fact that it is collective: for it is not

[1] Cf. Geiger, *Ideologie und Wahrheit*, 1953, 40 *seq.*

324

without sufficient reason that it has been able to generalize and maintain itself with persistence. If it were out of accord with the nature of things, it would never have been able to acquire an extended and prolonged empire over intellects.' Even scientific truth, with all its tests and techniques, is for Durkheim dependent for its validity on its agreement with collective representations. 'In the last resort, the value which we attribute to science depends upon the idea which we collectively form of its nature and rôle in life; that is as much as to say that it expresses a state of public opinion. In all social life, in fact, science rests upon opinion.' [1] The very last words are perhaps the most instructive of all; they show the whole extent of Durkheim's pragmatist 'sociologism' in the theory of knowledge.

However different the framework within which Karl Mannheim develops his ideas about truth and untruth, and about the relation of socially determined knowledge thereto, these ideas themselves are very similar in type to those put forward by Durkheim. The one major difference (a difference in emphasis) seems to be that for Durkheim an individual's ideas are true if they enable him to think harmoniously with his society, whereas with Mannheim the more relevant question is whether they enable him to act harmoniously in his society. If ideologies and utopias are both unrealistic, the former because they are behind, the latter because they are ahead of the times, then it follows that realistic thought is that which is fully adjusted to the times, and this means, as Mannheim himself explains, that it is thought which works in 'hitchlessly', as the Americans would say, with the established social pattern, the ongoing social process. 'In a word,' Mannheim writes, 'all those ideas which do not fit into the current order are "situationally transcendent" or unreal. Ideas which correspond to the concretely existing and *de facto* order are designated as "adequate" and situationally congruous. . . . Contrasted with situationally congruous and adequate ideas are the two main categories of ideas which transcend the situation—ideologies and utopias. [2] . . . This conception of ideology (and utopia) maintains that beyond the commonly recognized sources of

---

[1] *The Elementary Forms of the Religious Life*, Engl. ed., 1915, 1926 reprint, 435 *seq.*, 444, 446. So far as the substance of the argument is concerned, Durkheim's position is closely approached by Sprott, as can be seen from his *Science and Social Action*, 1954, 160 *seq.*, and by Gordon Childe in his *Society and Knowledge*, 1956, cf. esp. 84 *seq.*

[2] We must at this point disregard the complication which arises from the fact that so-called utopias 'function' in a society in a negative sort of way—by undermining it and preparing its downfall—and are to that extent 'realistic'. Their realism arises from the onward flow of history, from future and as yet contingent developments, not from the functioning of the contemporary order. Perhaps we can express Mannheim's ideas in this respect best by saying that utopian modes of thought have no validity, but may receive validation later (if they turn out to be successful).

error we must also reckon with the effects of a distorted mental structure. . . . In the same historical epoch and in the same society there may be several distorted types of inner mental structure, some because they have not yet grown up to the present, and others because they are already beyond the present. In either case, the reality to be comprehended is distorted and concealed. . . .' In either case we are confronted with untruth.

This is a very terse summary of Mannheim's position, but it brings out the salient point in which we are mainly interested here, namely that for him truth (what he himself, somewhat cumbersomely, calls an undistorted mental structure) means essentially adjustedness to social life, i.e. adjustedness without either revolutionary or reactionary tendencies and implications. This key-conviction is possibly even clearer in the following quotation, in which we take the liberty of italicizing the decisive sentence: 'The attempt to escape ideological and utopian distortions is, in the last analysis, a quest for reality. These two conceptions provide us with a basis for a sound scepticism, and they can be put to positive use in avoiding the pitfalls into which our thinking might lead us. Specifically they can be used to combat the tendency in our intellectual life to separate thought from the world of reality, to conceal reality, or to exceed its limits. *Thought should contain neither less nor more than the reality in whose medium it operates.* Just as the true beauty of a sound literary style consists in expressing precisely that which is intended— in communicating neither too little nor too much—so the valid element in our knowledge is determined by adhering to rather than departing from the actual situation to be comprehended. . . . Accordingly, from our point of view, an ethical attitude is invalid if it is oriented with reference to norms, with which action in a given historical setting, even with the best of intentions, cannot comply. . . . A theory then is wrong if in a given practical situation it uses concepts and categories which, if taken seriously, would prevent man from adjusting himself at that historical stage.' [1] Adherence to what is actual and adjustedness in action to the given constellation of things are obviously the two operative concepts in Mannheim's mind, and they give us his epistemology in a nutshell.

In view of these last remarks, we shall be neither over-bold in interpretation nor over-strict in judgment if we say that for Mannheim the true *is* what will work. His thought manifestly falls in with the homely proverb according to which the proof of the pudding is in the eating. For him, practice is the judge of theory. In this connection, Marx had already written candidly as follows: 'The question whether human thinking possesses objective truth, is no question of theory, but a *practical* question. It is in practice that man must prove the truth, i.e.

[1] *Ideology and Utopia*, ed. 1952, 175, 84 *seq.*

reality, power, this-worldliness of his thought.'[1] Gordon Childe, too, expresses himself in exactly the same spirit in his *Society and Knowledge*: 'The sole criterion of the correspondence with reality of . . . society's world of knowledge . . . is the success of actions based on rules deduced from it' (1956, 59 *seq.*).[2] Such statements lay bare the philosophical foundations of Marx's and Mannheim's attitude, and of that of their associates. Theirs is a form of pragmatism, and for this reason we propose to describe the whole school in the context of this chapter as *pragmatist*, rather than functionalist, in character. This kinship between Mannheim on the one hand, and such writers as Peirce, Schiller, James, and Dewey on the other, has not only been noticed by critical investigators such as Hinshaw,[3] but was known even to Mannheim himself who, theorist though he was, apparently had no objection to being classed with those to whom theory meant little and practice everything.[4]

It is at this point that the critique of the pragmatist theory, of the Comte-Durkheim-Mannheim tradition in the sociology of knowledge, can best begin. The assertion that whatever proves itself workable in practice, must also be true in principle, fairly cries out for criticism; nothing can possibly be more questionable, or more obviously so, than the proposition that external success is a test of intrinsic value.[5] Nietzsche and Pareto, if they have proved nothing else, have certainly demonstrated that this is a facile and fatuous assumption. Furthermore, to mention what is even more generally assumed to be important, the pragmatist doctrine casts doubt upon the unity of truth, its property of being one and indivisible, and upon the existence of a truth binding on all societies. For if truth is no more than the assemblage of those propositions which 'work' in a certain situation, then different situations are likely to have each their own 'truth'. This is a matter which deserves, and must receive, our closest and most urgent attention. It will be expedient, however, to postpone its critical consideration until we have acquainted the reader with the third theory in the field, which is

[1] Second *Thesis on Feuerbach*, cf. Karl Marx and Frederick Engels, *Selected Works*, 1950, II, 365.

[2] Cf. *ibid.*, 107: 'There can be only one *test* of truth . . . That is action', etc. Cf. furthermore 127.

[3] Cf. 'The Epistemological Relevance of Mannheim's Sociology of Knowledge', in *The Journal of Philosophy*, 1943, esp. 68 *seq.* Cf. also Lieber, *Wissen und Gesellschaft*, 1952, 105 *seq.*

[4] The nearness of the pragmatist theory to philosophical pragmatism can also be seen from C. Wright Mills's article 'Methodological Consequences of the Sociology of Knowledge' (*American Journal of Sociology*, 1940/1, 316 *seq.*, esp. 322 *seq.*). Mills is a consistent upholder of the Durkheim-Mannheim definition of truth. Cf. furthermore the whole of chapters VI and VII in Childe's book.

[5] Cf. Znaniecki, *The Social Rôle of the Man of Knowledge*, 1940, 26 *seq.* Mannheim's sharpest critic in this matter is Alexander von Schelting. Cf. his *Max Webers Wissenschaftslehre*, 1934, esp. 117 *seq.*

Problem D: The Conquest of Social Determination

the only serious rival of the pragmatist doctrine—the theory of truth
and untruth which corresponds to the theory of elective affinity in the
social determination of ideas, and which, for reasons which will become
clear before long, can best be described as the *metectic* theory. For we
shall find again, as we did before, that to all intents and purposes the
choice before us lies between it and functionalism, or, as we shall put it
here, where the two competing traditions appear in new guises, between
the metectic and the pragmatist views.

(b) THE PLATONIST APPROACH

If the pragmatist definition of truth goes back to Auguste Comte, the
father of sociology, the metectic has come down to us from the man who
can justly be considered as sociology's first parent—Giambattista Vico.
But its roots reach even further back, right into antiquity, for Vico
received it, like so much else, from the great Plato. According to this
philosophy, truths are not found in and fashioned by human societies,
but subsist, for ever unchangeable, in a supernal realm of their own.
They are, as it were, laid up in heaven, and to lay hold on truth here
below means to participate in the truths that lie above. 'Metexis' is the
Greek word for participation; hence the term we have chosen to
characterize this Platonic tradition in the sociology of knowledge.
Uncommon and uncouth it may be, but it provides a label which will
really indicate what is in the bottle.

Leaving aside a whole host of lesser figures, we can study this third
theory best with the help of Max Scheler's writings, for among sociologists Scheler was the most outstanding Platonist, and among
Platonists the most outstanding sociologist. It is, of course, no accident
that the very same man should appear as a characteristic representative
both of the theory of elective affinity in the field of social determination
and of the metectic theory in the field of epistemology in the narrower
sense of the word, for the two doctrines are clearly contiguous: indeed,
one could almost say that they coincide. For the theory of elective
affinity asserts, as we have seen, that societies and social movements do
not create their own philosophy and philosophical traditions, but select
them from a range of pre-existent and independent 'ideas'. It is only the
shortest of steps from this position to the Platonist theory that the
pre-existent and independent ideas, from which societies and social
movements in fact select the beliefs that suit them, form a self-subsisting
ontological realm of truth outside the frame of space and time; and that
the concrete truths perceived within that frame and formulated in
human language are parts or aspects or reflections or manifestations
of this realm. And this precisely is the characteristic thesis of the
metectic theory.

328

Scheler by no means denies that different conceptions operate as 'the truth' in different societies. Indeed, he emphasizes this fact as much as Mannheim or Durkheim are inclined to do, and possibly even more. 'According to the opinion maintained in this book,' he writes in *Die Wissensformen und die Gesellschaft* (1926), 'it is a fallacy to assume that absolute historical constancy of the forms and principles of "human" reason which the greater part of all theorists of knowledge has hitherto naïvely presupposed as the unchangeable object of their research. . . . To talk of some sort of factual "unity of human nature" as a pre-condition of historiography and sociology is therefore useless, nay pernicious. A common law of style and structure informs only the living cultural elements of *one* group at a time, the religion and art, science and law of *one* concrete culture. We absolutely reject that idol of the age of enlightenment and of Kant—the definite "inborn" functional apparatus of reason supposed to be given to *all* men from the very beginning' (V, 12). Not only are the contents of the mind, and even those contents which carry the index 'true' or 'false', 'absolutely true' or 'absolutely false', different from age to age, from country to country, from society to society, but the very categories and forms under which the contents are ordered, are infinitely diversified. 'The pluralism of groups and forms of culture is the position from which all sociology has to start' (13).

But, and this is decisive, this pluralism does not, in Scheler's view, divide the house of truth against itself, all appearances to the contrary notwithstanding. This division is indeed a fact, but it is not, for the metectic theory, an ultimate fact, and thereby it differentiates itself most decidedly from the pragmatist point of view. If we work back from the many concrete truths which human societies adhere to, truths which one might perhaps for the moment call 'physical' because they have found embodiment, we shall ultimately come upon the metaphysical truth which is one. Scheler undertakes to show how the pluralism of world-views arises in the first place, and thereby reduces it to a secondary phenomenon, whereas for the pragmatist school it is and remains a final, irreducible, absolute fact, perhaps the only absolute they admit.

Scheler has called the process whereby the one truth becomes splintered into many, 'functionalization', but this term, it is to be feared, hardly indicates the essence of his account. Briefly, his opinion is this. Different societies, in their encounter with the objective world, undergo different fundamental experiences. They are struck by different aspects of that world, take in different complexes of facts and connections between them and so on, than other societies do. Thus at first only the mind-*contents* are concrete, specific, limited, distinctive. But the matter does not stop there. The fundamental experience will penetrate deeper and deeper into the mental structure and come in due course to dominate the very functioning of it. This is the 'functionalization' to which Scheler refers.[1] The very *forms* of cognition used in a society, the very concepts, the very apparatus of the mind itself, are specified in the process, and in the end there arise specific, indeed, irreconcilable *a priori* schemas—Scheler calls them 'apriorically subjective apparatuses of thought' (15)—which make nonsense of the rationalistic assumption that in the last analysis all human beings think alike—or ought to. For if we study how they do think—in the concrete and material sense of the word, and not merely in the abstract and formal sense—we are forced to acknowledge that they think in many different ways, though all these ways are fully human, fully justified and indeed fully rational.

The human mind—to summarize Scheler's standpoint—is not only differently filled in different epochs, but differently constituted. In this respect, then, there can be and are many different truths. But 'they all spring from the perception of the *one* ontic realm of ideas and value orderings' (13), and hence, behind all the apparently exclusive universes of validity, there lies the One Real that imparts true validity—and ultimate unity—to them all. 'In spite of our assumption of a multiplicity of organizations of reason,' Scheler writes, 'we escape philosophical relativism. . . . We escape it—in a manner similar to that used by the Einsteinian theory in its own field—by so to speak suspending the absolute realm of ideas and values (which corresponds to the idea of the essentially human) high above all factual, hitherto formed value-systems of history, by for instance regarding all orders of preference, all orders of purposes, all normative orders of human society in ethics, religion, law and art as without exception relative and historically as well as sociologically conditioned, preserving nothing but the idea of an eternal objective *logos*. To penetrate into the transcendent secrets of this *logos* . . . is not given to *one* nation, one cultural circle, one or all former cultural ages, but only to all together, including the future ones, in collective co-operation' (13 *seq.*).[2]

It is this belief in an 'eternal objective *logos*' which decisively separates the metectic thinkers from the pragmatist ones. For the latter, the multiplicity of social formations means also a multiplicity of minds and truths; for the former, the multiplicity of social forms, minds and truths finds an ultimate unity in a meta-social, metaphysical reality—that same 'eternal objective *logos*' whose existence at the very heart of being is asserted by Scheler and his fellow-Platonists. In comparison with his views, Mannheim and Durkheim are indeed not only pragmatists in the technical sense which we have here given to the term, but also positivists

---

[1] Cf. *loc. cit.*, 378. The second paragraph on this page contains what is perhaps Scheler's clearest exposition of his concept of 'functionalization'.

[2] Cf. also Dahlke and Becker in *Philosophy and Phenomenological Research*, 1941/2, 314, and the further references given there.

in the current acceptance of the word. Scheler is well aware of the unbridgeable gulf which separates him from these men. He stigmatizes them as upholders of 'positivistic sociologism', i.e. as men who have ascribed to the social forces a power and influence far beyond what they really possess—the power to determine what is true and what is false *in itself*. He writes: 'We have to reject "sociologism" (a pendant to psychologism) which neither distinguishes the forms of thought and cognition from the "forms of being" nor the subsequent reflective knowledge of both forms from these forms themselves; which (with Kant) traces the forms of being back to the forms of thought and cognition but (in opposition to Kant) derives these subjective forms themselves from the operational and linguistic forms of "society". To this doctrine of origins there corresponds a conventionalism in logic and epistemology such as was first asserted by Thomas Hobbes: "true and false lie only in human language" . . . According to this "sociologistic" doctrine it is not only history that becomes a *fable convenue* but the scientific world-view in its entirety. . . . Such blunders of sociology are avoided if all functional forms of thinking are derived from the functionalization of true insights into the essence of things themselves, and if only the selection which lies behind [a concrete] functionalization is regarded as the effect of society and its perspective in relation to the realm of "pure" meaning' (55).

In the light of these revealing, though difficult, utterances, we can perhaps sum up the contrast between the pragmatist and metectic theories by saying that the former treats the verdict of society as in all things final, whereas the latter allows an appeal beyond it—an appeal to a tribunal which we have just heard described as 'the realm of pure meaning', and which might be more simply described as 'the realm of eternal truths', provided it be understood that these truths refer, not to the phenomenal things in this our world of becoming and contingency, but to things-in-themselves, the *noumena* or essences laid up in the metaphysical world of absolutes where all is rest, permanence and self-identity. We may also say that for the pragmatist doctrine all truth is relative to the circumstances within which it 'works' and proves itself, whereas for the metectic theory everything is both relative and absolute at the same time: relative, because every society grasps only one aspect of 'The Truth', the aspect which is congenial to it and is for this reason selected by it, and absolute, because even an aspect of The Truth *is* The Truth, because the part participates in the whole, and because the quality of the whole is necessarily present in the part.

Arguing more against Marxism than the positivistic relativism of Durkheim and Mannheim, Scheler asserts that the whole contrast between absolute and relative in the definition of truth is apparent rather than real. 'The solution of this seeming contradiction', he says, 'consists in this, that the categorial systems of knowing, thinking and valuing which form and transform themselves in the history of man, through the functionalization of [basic] insights into the essence of things, are (*inter alia*) class-determined in their selection, but not in their validity' (204).[1] Dahlke and Becker sum up the situation as follows: 'The perspective of social interests determines [for Scheler] the selection of the *objects* of knowledge only, not its content, and still less its validity. . . . The structure of society determines in part the forms of the mental processes through which knowledge is reached, though . . . all functional thought-forms are secured by grasping the essence— *Wesenserfassung*, not socially determined—of the objects themselves.'[2] Validity, then, if it is given at all, is absolute; all that is relative is the angle of approach to the absolute, the peculiar perspective or view-point of a society. The reader will assuredly recognize in these Schelerian opinions an approach that is deeply embedded in the foundations of the present book.

In case Scheler's highly personal utterances should have proved difficult to assimilate, we append here a few quotations from the writings of another representative of the metectic school, Alfred Weber: 'It is true', he writes in *Farewell to European History* (Engl. ed., 1947), 'that there are different kinds of value-accentuation and thus various combinations of the values which, as Nietzsche puts it, "can be imposed on humanity". But all of them are only temporal shifts of emphasis and differences in vision, and all refer back to what I have again and again shown to be the existentially decisive, objectively actual, both immanent and transcendental power-world that shapes us. . . . It may very well be and is in fact quite likely that other great cultures of different spiritual and psychic structure apprehend the transcendental nature of man differently from us Westerners, hence arriving at different conclusions. . . . [Nevertheless,] life is at bottom immutable and changes only in its manifest pattern. . . . It can only be shallower or deeper, can only comprehend more of the strata of immediate Transcendence or less. Thus it is always only a new coloration of something unalterably given, a novelty that results from a variation of the historical surface pattern, from the "Becoming", which is indeed nothing but a change of foreground. . . . Becoming in our view is the type, the form, the limit of every possible but in the deepest sense invariable experience of Being, and hence the mode of all its possible novelties. These can only be a recrudescence or a rediscovery of something old, something immemorially experienced, "new" in so far as they acquire their particular physiognomy and their special tone from man's consciousness and

---

[1] A position analogous to Scheler's is that of S. Marck, summarized by Grünwald in *Das Problem der Soziologie des Wissens*, 1934, 149 *seq.*
[2] Cf. *Philosophy and Phenomenological Research*, 1941/2, 319.

experience in a given historical and sociological context, from the constellation of the moment. In other words: all "novelties" must come from the same depth-dimensions as the earlier ones, and the nature of the transcendental zone which touches them, must, even though the mode of expression be different, be self-identical' (139, 166, 154 *seq.*). 'Here is the key', Weber writes in his concluding pages: 'Self-incarnating forces lie beyond the phenomenal world, they come from a sphere that knows nothing of its conditions, and are therefore absolute. . . . These forces, being above time and space, must be unchanging like all the transcendental substrata, and therefore in the human sense of the word, eternal. . . . The[se] absolute powers undergo what we can best call variation by incarnation . . . on their entry into the particular time-stuff wherein they are made manifest. . . . Since they themselves are not simple but extremely complex and not to be seized unequivocally by logic, their appearance presents a widely different physiognomy according to time and place. That is their historical variability which, however, in no wise affects the absoluteness and unconditionalness of the powers lying behind it' (195 *seq.*).

(c) THE ROAD TO TRUTH

These last passages may have made the meaning of the metectic theory clear, in so far as anything in its nature so deeply metaphysical can ever become clear at all. We have now reached the point where we must finally confront the question: which doctrine deserves preference—the pragmatist or the metectic, that of Durkheim and Mannheim, or that of Scheler and Alfred Weber. In facing a parallel problem in chapter 6, when we asked ourselves whether there was more truth in the functionalist conception of social determination or in the doctrine of elective affinity, we had little hesitation in deciding that functionalism was sounder than its rival, and that the latter could only contribute a minor modification to the final solution. Here, where we are, after all, discussing a rather different problem, since it is the validity of our mental conceptions that is at stake and not merely their origins, the difficulties before us are very much greater, even though, as we have seen, we are again forced to choose between two theories, and theories that are in fact akin to those whose competing claims we have already adjudicated. Indeed, the indications are that we are now faced with a question to which it may in the nature of things be quite impossible to give any scholarly or scientific answer at all.

Before we continue, let us note first of all that it seems hardly possible to reconcile or combine the pragmatist and metectic conceptions, and thus to escape the dire necessity of choice. For these two theories, and the negativisitic one as well, have grown out of and represent philosophical traditions which have always existed side by side, and no solid and lasting bridge has ever been erected between them. As Dilthey has shown, there are, in the last analysis, three basic philosophical attitudes. The first he calls 'naturalism' and means thereby the mental outlook traditionally known as materialism. According to this way of thinking, the 'knowledge of reality has its foundation in the study of nature. . . . In the system of knowledge of the world which thus arises, the concept of causality holds sway . . . And since in our view of reality the physical world so predominates in extent and power that the units of mental life appear only as interpolations in the text of the physical world . . . this explanation of the world takes on the form of an interpretation of the world of mind in terms of the physical world.' [1] Here we have the basic philosophy in and behind causalism and negativism. The second type of world-view Dilthey calls 'objective idealism'; one of its most characteristic forms is pantheism or panentheism. The world is seen here as an integral whole in which body and mind, nature and spirit are blended and indissolubly intermixed. Indeed, reality is understood on the analogy of the human being, in whom body and mind are one, being suffused by the same life-principle. 'All reality then appears as the expression of something inward, and so it is conceived as the unfolding of a mental system operating consciously or unconsciously.' [2] Although it may not be obvious at first sight, the pragmatist theory belongs here, and more specifically the theory of Mannheim, a distant disciple of the purest of all objective idealists, Hegel. Surely, his salient conception is that theory and practice (intra-mental and extra-mental reality) are one, and form between them a self-enclosed interlocking whole beyond which there is nothing that could throw light on its life—that life which is the ultimate reality.

It is in this conception of ultimate reality that the third basic form of philosophy—subjective idealism, or, as Dilthey prefers to call it, the 'idealism of freedom'—differs from the objective view. For subjective idealism, the true reality is not (as with naturalism) the physical universe, nor yet (as with objective idealism) the world-organism, i.e. the world-body and world-soul, but rather a reality that lies beyond the world of sense, beyond the physical world as well as beyond the mind-suffused universe. Subjective idealism, stemming from Plato, is a truly metaphysical philosophy, in fact the metaphysical philosophy *par excellence*. Before its inspired eye, there 'arises the schema of mind's independence of nature, or of its transcendence'.[3] It is a dualistic philo-

---

[1] *Cit.* Hodges, *Wilhelm Dilthey: An Introduction*, 1944, 153; cf. also 152 and 99 *seq.*   [2] *Ibid.*, 153. Cf. also 152 and 100 *seq.*
[3] *Ibid.*, 153 *seq.*; cf. also 152 and 100, and Lieber, *Wissen und Gesellschaft*, 1952, 56 *seq.*

sophy, whereas the other two are characteristically monistic. Clearly, it is from this deep well that both Scheler and Alfred Weber, and indeed all metectic thinkers, have drawn sustenance and wisdom. What confronts us, then, in the conflict of the pragmatist and metectic doctrines, is not a simple surface difference of opinion such as could be resolved by discursive reasoning or scientific proof, but a wide cleavage concerning the last things—the eternal enigma itself.

Our painful dilemma, therefore, is that we must choose, and yet cannot. Even without entering into the depths of metaphysical philosophy, it becomes abundantly clear on closer consideration that neither the pragmatist nor the metectic doctrine is satisfactory or convincing, not to say acceptable. The mortal weakness of the former is surely obvious. It is hardly too much to say of it that it has no conception of what truth really is, for this word, if it is to mean anything, must mean more than 'convention', 'wide currency' or 'general acceptance'. Mannheim's test, according to which a belief is valid if it enables its holder to operate smoothly within, and to co-operate smoothly with, his society, is in reality no test at all. In a society of fools, any chosen form of folly would have the highest pragmatic value so far as social co-operation is concerned—but that would not make such folly wisdom, or madness sanity, or error truth.

The very least that can be held against the pragmatist doctrine is that it is all too deeply imbued with the spirit of relativity. 'We cannot insist too much upon the different characteristics which logic presents at different periods in history', says Durkheim, setting as it were the tone. 'It develops like the societies themselves.' [1] Such relativism is a natural and necessary concomitant of pragmatism. If different societies exhibit or represent different systems of action and interaction, and if the truth is whatever happens to fit in with these individual systems, then every society must in strict logic possess a materially different concept of the truth. And this is indeed what the philosophy under discussion implies. 'The Ptolemaic system *was* true as long as it enjoyed unchallenged social endorsement', says Childe, himself italicizing the operative word *was*. It *was* true because 'it did . . . enable men to predict eclipses and occultations with reasonable accuracy and thus enabled mariners to find their way about uncharted seas and helped cartographers to map their coasts. In fact it worked, and its successful applications guaranteed its truth'.[2] The protagonists of pragmatism speak without misgivings of 'relative truths' [3] as if truth—we are almost inclined to say the real truth—could ever be anything but absolute! Their position in this matter can easily be gathered from C. Wright Mills's somewhat too lighthearted

---

[1] *The Elementary Forms*, etc., 439.
[2] *Society and Knowledge*, 1956, 109 *seq.* Cf. the whole of ch. IX.
[3] E.g. Childe, *loc. cit.*, 106.

statement: ' "True" is an adjective applied to propositions that satisfy the forms of an accepted model of verification . . . [but] in research we cannot fruitfully impose "ours" [i.e. our verificatory model] upon past thinkers. There have been several models in Western thought. . . . Truth is always conditional, not absolute.' [1] The word 'always' in this last sentence is particularly difficult to accept. Is the proposition that two and two make four also conditional only—and does anything really deserve to be called true that is not as true as the proposition that two and two make four?

With Mannheim, this truth-destroying relativism appears in the form of a consistent historicism. [2] 'What this doctrine asserts', writes the editor of Mannheim's *Essays on the Sociology of Knowledge* (1952), Paul Kecskemeti, in a passage of his introduction which goes right to the heart of the matter, 'is . . . that the subject talking about history and related topics can achieve only one kind of "truth", that is, a communion with, and participation in, the real trends and forces of history. To be out of touch with the basic trend is to miss the truth; identification with the basic trend will guarantee true knowledge. . . . [For Mannheim] "truth" is first and foremost an attribute of existence, and only secondarily of discourse. One *is* or *is not* in the Truth; and one's possession of Truth depends on being in communion with a reality which "is" or embodies truth' (15). This lucid summary, incidentally, covers not only the case of Mannheim but also, at least in essence, that of Durkheim, for the latter's deepest conviction is clearly that the truth resides or inheres in social life, and that error consists in the individual's being 'out of it'. Assuming now that this is an adequate characterization of Mannheim's and even Durkheim's standpoint—and we have no doubt that it is—two important corollaries follow at once, and both of them are purely negative in character.

Firstly, if history is the truth and to attain to truth is to be in harmony with history, then truth can never partake of the absolute or the eternal. For history is change, and so implies a constant revolution even in truth so-called. 'His sociology of knowledge', Kecskemeti writes of Mannheim, 'in spite of his disclaimers, was certainly a relativistic doctrine. . . . Knowledge will shift its basis as trends change' (*ibid.*). 'We always attribute only partial validity to particular assertions,' Mannheim admits, [3] and in his polemic against Scheler, he explains that the finding of a truth is not for him the grasping of an eternal verity 'but a creative concretization flowing from historically unique constellations'. [4] In other

[1] *The American Journal of Sociology*, 1939/40, 324 *seq.*
[2] Cf. Lieber, *Wissen und Gesellschaft*, 1952, 82 *seq.*, and Aron, *Die deutsche Soziologie der Gegenwart*, 1953, 76 *seq.*
[3] *Ideology and Utopia*, ed. 1952, 257.
[4] *Essays on the Sociology of Knowledge*, 1952, 165 *seq.*

words, truths are in his opinion made and re-made—the word 'creative' is characteristic of this view [1]—and not merely recognized. They are 'constituted' and not merely 'realized'. 'For the historicist,' Mannheim frankly declares, such 'entities do not exist apart from the historic process; they come into being . . . in it.' They are as much our handiwork as history itself, and consequently in no sense of the word above us. Every 'historically unique constellation' breeds and bears its own—but there are none such in the unchanging heavens. This means, in the last resort, that we have to live without a fixed guiding star and are thus in the unbearable position bemoaned by Pascal: 'Truth on this side of the Pyrenees, error on that!'

Just how deep this radical relativism penetrates can be seen from the fact that Mannheim not only regards 'particular assertions' as limited in validity—being valid at some places and times, but not at others—but considers even the very *idea* of truth as subject to historical and geographical variations. In other words, according to his view, not only do different societies entertain different convictions as to what is true and what not, they differ even as to the meaning of the word 'truth' itself. 'The concept of truth', he writes, 'has not remained constant through all time, but has been involved in the process of historical change. . . . The very principles, in the light of which knowledge is to be criticized, are themselves found to be socially and historically conditioned. Hence their application appears to be limited to given historical periods and the particular type of knowledge then prevalent.' There is more in the same vein that need not be repeated here. Suffice it to say that Mannheim's relativism reaches its climax in the assertion that the whole 'conception of truth in general', the whole 'construction of a sphere of "truth as such" ' is 'utopian'.[2]

This is the first implication of Mannheim's position. The second is, if possible, even more inimical to the conceptions of 'right' and 'wrong' with which philosophers, and even plain men, have worked down the centuries. If truth, as he opines, is an attribute of existence rather than of discourse, we can never say with full assurance of any sentence, statement or formula that it is really true. We can indeed *act* truly as it were, and we do so by acting in accord with prevailing customs or the trends of development; but we can hardly be sure that we ever *think* or *speak* truly, for so far as thoughts and words in and by themselves are concerned, the decisive test is missing—successful practical working in conjunction with life and its progressive tendency. Again we find that Mannheim condemns us to move for ever in the dark so far as the

---

[1] It recurs constantly on this page: 'the completely new, creative rôle of the moment', 'the creative centre of the evolutionary process', 'products of the mind . . . the process of their creation'.

[2] *Ideology and Utopia*, ed. 1952, 259 *seq.*

reflective consciousness is concerned. His pragmatism is all too pragmatical. It has no room for such a purely theoretical concept as truth
divorced from action, truth in itself. But this can only mean that his
doctrine, considered as an epistemology, fails at the very point where
success would seem to be most vital, if not downright decisive—the
testing of *knowledge* for its validity, the weighing of *ideas and beliefs*
in the scale of truth.

There are indications that Mannheim himself was not altogether
happy about this super-relativism and pragmatism; his own courage
seems at times to inspire him with fear. I am not preaching relativism,
he says in self-defence, only 'relationism'. By the concept of relationism
he means that if we formulate a truth, we should not do so in abstract
and absolute terms, but must always include in the formula the concrete
conditions to which it is related, i.e. under which it really holds good.
For instance: we should not say: 'x is true', but 'x is true, provided there
are a, b, and c'; not: 'all men want to maximize their money incomes',
but 'all men want to maximize their money incomes if they live in a
society which has private property as its fundamental institution and is
rational, competitive, &c, &c, &c.' This is sound so far as it goes;
indeed, it could lead us out of relativism if Mannheim were in a position
to concede that the same conditions can in principle exist at different
periods, so that the self-same propositions may possibly return to
validity. These propositions would then in fact be of more than limited
validity. But this is precisely what Mannheim cannot admit. For however similar two situations may be otherwise, they are, in the case of
recurrence, by definition separated by a stretch of time. To put it otherwise: however much the other conditions may coincide, the time-
condition can never be the same. This would not matter if time, for
Mannheim, were a neutral medium, as it is for so many other thinkers,
a medium without influence on what happens inside it; there would then,
in effect, be no time-condition, no time-index, that would have to be
taken into account. Nothing, however, could be more diametrically
opposed to his way of thinking. Super-historicist that he is, he regards
the flow of time as an absolute, an absolutely irreducible factor of
differentiation between successive social situations or developmental
stages. History does not and cannot repeat itself according to this
philosophy. But this means, of course, that the same truths cannot, after
all, be valid more than once, and we are back in the depths of relativism.
Mannheim is manifestly the prisoner of his own historicism. In vain does
he try to wriggle out of the manacles he has himself clasped upon his
wrists. Ziegenfuss is by no means too harsh when he says that
Mannheim's whole distinction between relationism and relativism is no
more than 'a play upon words'.[1]

[1] *Gesellschaftsphilosophie*, 1954, 67.

Problem D: The Conquest of Social Determination

That relationism is in fact no more than another name for relativism is abundantly clear from the following quotations which we may set down without further comment: 'Relationism signifies . . . that all of the elements of meaning in a given situation have reference to one another and derive their significance from this reciprocal interrelationship in a given frame of thought. Such a system of meanings is possible and valid only in a given type of historical existence, to which, for a time, it furnishes appropriate expression. . . . A modern theory of knowledge which takes account of the relational as distinct from the merely relative character of all historical knowledge must start with the assumption that there are spheres of thought in which it is impossible to conceive of absolute truth existing independently of the values and position of the subject and unrelated to the social context.' [1] If this is not relativism, then what is? Mannheim's last word, like his first, is pure relativity: 'We must reject the notion that there is a "sphere of truth in itself" as a disruptive and unjustifiable hypothesis.' [2]

However much we test and turn it, then, the fact remains that the pragmatist doctrine is useless as an epistemology; it does not so much as conceive of the possibility of absolute truths where man and his society are concerned. In this respect, the metectic theory is undoubtedly its superior. Scheler, as we have seen, knew full well that what we meet with in this phenomenal world of ours is only concrete man, man in his historical, spatio-temporal specificity, not man as such, the abstract element of common humanity, which is nowhere embodied or discoverable in its pure form. But he also knew—and this gives an entirely different complexion to his philosophy—that behind the phenomenal there lies the noumenal, behind accidental appearance the enduring essence, behind the merely relative the Absolute, and by his concentration on this he shows the way which all exploration must pursue if it is to reach, or at least approach, the Truth in the proper meaning of the term. Man-in-himself, like Kant's thing-in-itself, may be no more than a limiting concept, a boundary-stone, as it were, on the dividing-line between the knowable and the unknowable, but unless, in our philosophical peregrinations, we keep our eyes fixed on it, we shall be wanderers without aim, wayfarers without chance of attaining our destination. For our destination is to push upward and outward as far as we possibly can, to penetrate to the outermost perimeter of the realm of knowability. It is degrading for us to be satisfied with permanent enclosure within the confines of the ephemeral; we must *attempt* at any rate to stretch out our hand towards the eternal, even if it should ultimately prove to be beyond our grasp.

We therefore believe that in its aims and objects at least the metectic doctrine is preferable to the pragmatist one. But, alas, as a substantive

[1] *Ideology and Utopia*, ed. 1952, 76, 70 *seq.*   [2] *Ibid.*, 274.

dogmatic theory it has one great weakness from the point of view of practical scholarship. It speaks to us of a realm of eternal verities, essences, or absolutes, to which we are directed, but it cannot tell us anything concrete about them. This realm—where is it? Its contents—what are they? They lie, if anywhere at all, beyond the horizon which our natural eyes enable us to see. The truth of the matter is that the metectic theory is an altogether metaphysical one, and that we cannot therefore lay upon anybody the duty of accepting its basic idea. As soon as we place ourselves at its point of view, we find ourselves surrounded by an aura of uncertainty, divination, and even dimness. It is no accident that Platonism is a profoundly religious philosophy. It is no accident either that Max Scheler, the modern neo-Platonist *par excellence*, was also the author of one of the profoundest religious books of the century, *Vom Ewigen im Menschen.*[1]

This quasi-religious aspect of the metectic theory is the side from which it lies wide open to attack, and, not surprisingly, Karl Mannheim directs his assault against it. He calls the 'ideal of a realm of truth as such which, so to speak, pre-exists independently of the historical-psychological act of thought, and in which every concrete act of knowing merely participates' an 'extreme spiritualistic metaphysics' and says that it 'originated for the purpose of proving the inadequacy of "this" world'—in other words as an 'ideology' of the religious. 'The positing of a sphere of truth which is valid in itself is intended to do the same for the act of knowing as the notion of the beyond . . . did for dualistic metaphysics in the realm of ontology, namely to postulate a sphere of perfection . . . measured by which all events and processes [in the human sphere] are shown to be finite and incomplete.'[2]

This may be something of a blow beneath the belt, but another argument of Mannheim's is far more telling, and also a great deal more fair. The assumption of a realm of eternal verities and values is itself

[1] Cf. my introduction to the English edition of Scheler's *The Nature of Sympathy*, 1954, esp. part II. If we had had more room at our disposal, we might well have discussed in some detail at this point the opinions of Heinrich Rickert on the potentialities of historical knowledge of absolute validity, but as things are we can only refer the reader to pp. 230 *seq.* of Alexander von Schelting's *Max Webers Wissenschaftslehre*. Briefly, Rickert argues that since the historian's world-view depends upon his axiological system, an axiological system which could claim absolute validity would yield an absolutely valid body of historical knowledge. Now, all the material values accepted in concrete societies, i.e. among some men, point back to formal values which must be acceptable in all societies, by all men. Hence, etc. The present writer is convinced that such reasoning is theoretically sound, but unfortunately it is altogether unhelpful in practice: the Kantian Rickert leads us nearly as deep into the humanly unknowable as the Platonist Scheler. Was this the reason why Max Weber did not follow Rickert in this particular, although he was otherwise always willing to submit to his guidance?

[2] *Ideology and Utopia*, ed. 1952, 267.

without value, he asserts, because we do not know these verities and values in the concrete and so cannot decide, even on the basis of the Platonic-Schelerian creed, what is true and what is false in the world we live in, which is the only one accessible to us in experience. What is the use of such a yardstick (assuming it exists!) here below, if it is hidden away in the heavens above? 'How can we know in analysing history which of the entities proclaimed by various civilizations have been real, true entities? By what criteria can we judge that a certain civilization was mature enough to accomplish the "mission" of humanity as regards one or the other entity? If we really want to assign such rôles to all past epochs and civilizations, it is clearly not enough for us to have a valid, objective knowledge of our own entities; we must have supra-historical, super-human intuitive powers to identify all entities, or at least those which have emerged thus far in the course of history. Thus the historian of ideas in performing his essential intuition must twice transcend temporality: once when he identifies the eternal entities assigned to his own epoch, and for the second time when he interprets the past, trying to separate the genuine from the false, the real essence from the mere subjective appearance. This, however, amounts to the postulation of an absolute intuition of essences—at least of all essences thus far discovered—at each moment in history; or at least the postulation of the absolute character of the present moment.' [1] But such an absolute intuition of essences, such supra-historical, superhuman powers of identifying the eternal and separating it from the ephemeral, are precisely what we do not possess—that is the whole point of our predicament. And for that reason the metectic theory is bad in practice, even if it be good in principle (which Mannheim does not, of course, concede).

It cannot be denied that this argument has its force. We certainly cannot intuitively separate truth from error, when what is error *sub specie aeternitatis* appears in the guise of truth *sub specie temporis*, i.e. as relative truth: if we could, we should not be in the general human plight. Nevertheless, Mannheim overshoots the mark in his polemic against Scheler. Scheler does not assert that we are able, in a visionary manner as it were, to grasp the eternal essences at every moment or even at any moment. We must remember his decisive statement quoted above: 'To penetrate into the transcendent secrets of the *logos* is not given to one nation, one cultural circle, one or all cultural ages, but only to all together, including the future ones, in collective co-operation.' [2] His teaching is that every society, by the very peculiarity of its circumstances, conditions and constitution, is predisposed and enabled to perceive or comprehend another aspect of being, and hence that if we wish to have a more than partial or perspectival system of truth, we must learn to combine all such partial impressions into one vast

---

[1] *Essays on the Sociology of Knowledge*, 1952, 168.   [2] Cf. above, p. 330.

all-comprehensive picture. What Scheler suggests then, for purposes of positive investigation, as a practicable way out of the impasse of relativity, is the elaboration of a supra-temporal and supra-local synthesis of essential insights. Being a speculative thinker rather than a scholar, he did not elaborate his ideas on this head with sufficient detail or clarity. But this is a defect which it is hoped the fourth chapter of the present book has done something to remedy.

It is the pursuit of a general human synthesis of knowledge, then, to which this whole discussion leads us back. The metectic theory cannot indeed be proved correct—it contains an irreducible element of faith; but, like all faith, it can become an inspiration to us in the endeavour to rise superior to the human limitations imposed on us and to penetrate into the twilight regions within which our life is set. It may be true, as Merton maintains, that the concept of eternal essences is congenial only to the metaphysician, and wholly foreign to empirical research.[1] It may nevertheless be fruitful to consider the concrete insights resulting from empirical inquiry—and formulated perhaps in 'relationist' statements— at least provisionally and experimentally *as if* they were reflections and incarnations of transcendental absolutes, and to see where and how far such tactics will lead us. Assuredly they will lead us farther than pure pragmatism ever can, for the latter would incarcerate us in the tiny territory delimited by human practices and purposes, the petty prince-dom of utility. Humble no doubt we should be; but there is no point in being humbler than we need. Little as we are, we are large enough to conceive of verities finer than those that underlie our successful manipu-lation of the material world; but their pursuit must needs bring us up against the social determination of our thinking as an unwelcome boundary, a frustrating barrier. The social determination of thought, the historical and geographical specification of our mind, is, indeed, a fact, but like all that restricts us and reduces our measure, it is, or rather ought to be, a fact to be overcome. We can only hope to conquer it by pushing forward in the direction indicated by the neo-Platonic school— by widening our confined experience through the unprejudiced and sympathetic reception into it of the experiences of other, and at first alien, societies and cultures.

Such a universal summing-up is recommended (as we are more than happy to emphasize) not only by the metectic thinkers, though they have provided the firmest intellectual basis for it, but also, perhaps illogically, by some of the pragmatist ones, notably the arch-relativist Mannheim himself. Even Karl Marx, Mannheim's model in so many things, had already pushed in this direction. In his opinion—and this aspect of his system is all too little known—it is not only the class division of society which prevents men from reaching an adequate and objectively valid

[1] *Social Theory and Social Structure*, 1949, 232.

view of reality, but also the far more fundamental social institution of the division of labour, for that too confines, and so cripples, the human mind. In what was perhaps his most daring flight of imagination, Marx looks forward, in the dim and distant future, to a withering away even of this all-important feature of the 'pre-history' of the human race, and to the emergence of a complete man who would know the whole truth precisely because he was not restricted in his life and work and field of vision.[1]

In Durkheim we find the same idea, though it is, of course, elaborated in a different spirit. To begin with, he tells us, every society has indeed its own truth, 'is a particular subject, and consequently particularizes whatever it thinks of', but then the drift of development brings a progressive merging of distinct social units into one universal social life, which is, in a manner of speaking, the pre-ordained aim of all history, and by this substructural process a common human world-view with an irrefutable claim to general validity is prepared and may well be to some extent achieved. 'Really and truly human thought is not a primitive fact; it is the product of history; it is the ideal limit towards which we are constantly approaching.' [2]

While both these thinkers, in true pragmatist fashion, expect such universal conceptions of truth to be evolved in the sphere of practice, Mannheim moves much nearer to Scheler by laying their achievement, as a prime duty, on the shoulders of the theoretician and the intellectual, on the scholarly and philosophical mind. At this point, indeed, it may justly be said that extremes meet. For Mannheim, in spite of the fact that he is in principle an extreme pan-relativist, finds it psychologically quite impossible to abide quietly in his own pan-relativism. In one revealing passage he calls 'relativism with regard to scientific knowledge' a 'discouraging condition', and constantly casts about for an escape from the relativistic cul-de-sac. Not surprisingly, he finds only one way out: [3] the elaboration of a global synthesis of the competing

[1] On this in some respects most radical feature of the Marxian analysis, cf. Barth, *Wahrheit und Ideologie*, 1945, 71 *seq.*, esp. 122 *seq.* Lukacs, *Geschichte und Klassenbewusstsein*, 1923, emphasizes (cf. 153 and 155 *seq.*) that this concept of the 'complete man' links Marx with his great fellow-countrymen Schiller and Goethe. Goethe, in fact, says: 'Only all mankind together makes the true man' (*Dichtung und Wahrheit*, Bk. 9).

[2] *The Elementary Forms of the Religious Life*, Engl. ed., 1915, 1926 reprint, 444 *seq.* Cf. *ibid.*, the whole section IV of the 'Conclusion', and for a brief summary, Merton, *Social Theory and Social Structure*, 1949, 233. Cf. also Childe, *Society and Knowledge*, 1956, 104 *seq.*

[3] For the fact that another of the leading pan-relativists, namely Troeltsch, felt the same anguish in, and chose the same way out of, relativism, cf. Ziegenfuss, *Gesellschaftsphilosophie*, 1954, 33, and Lieber, *Wissen und Gesellschaft*, 1952, 108 *seq.* Znaniecki, too, recommends this solution of the 'dilemma of dogmatic certainty and sceptical doubt'. Cf. his *Social Rôle of the Man of Knowledge*, 1940, 197 *seq.*

perspectival world-views which contemporary life, and, beyond it, world history, have thrown up. 'The question is this,' he says: 'Is it possible for different styles of thought to be fused with one another and to undergo synthesis?' The answer, in spite of all his insistence on the limited validity of each particular world-view, is unhesitatingly affirmative: 'The course of historical development shows that such a synthesis is possible.'

Speculating about this possibility, groping for this sheet-anchor in the midst of his uncertainties, Mannheim is led to a position surprisingly close to that of his arch-antagonist Scheler.[1] 'One may admit', he writes, with more frankness than consistency, 'that human life is always something more than it was discovered to be in any historical period or under any given set of social conditions, and even that after these have been accounted for there still remains an eternal, spiritual realm beyond history, which is never quite subsumed under history itself and which puts meaning into history and into social experience.' The only question is how we can ever hope to approach this realm *beyond* history, since we are enclosed *in* history, and Mannheim asserts—what nobody, surely, can deny—that the only promising way open to us lies *through* history. 'May it not be possible', he writes in a passage that is perhaps unduly hesitant and diffident, 'that the ecstatic element in human experience which in the nature of the case is never directly revealed or expressed, and the meaning of which can never be fully communicated, can be discovered through the traces which it leaves on the path of history, and thus be disclosed to us?'[2]

One cannot imagine that Scheler would have had any serious objection to the sentiment, and even to the positive assertion, expressed in Mannheim's rhetorical question. Both would have accepted, with whatever differences of implication, Sprott's terse but felicitous formula: 'To look for . . . absolute validity, is to look for universal agreement.'[3] Mannheim, it is true, could never forget his quarrel with Scheler for very long. I want a 'dynamic relative synthesis', he wrote, not a 'super-temporal absolute one': 'A demand for an absolute, permanent synthesis would . . . mean a relapse into the static world-view of intellectualism.

[1] Also to that of Heinrich Rickert, in so far as the latter asserted that 'all the differing material value-attitudes are in the last analysis anchored in supra-historical, supra-personal, supra-psychological values which are absolutely valid, but only *formal—values whose progressive material realization is the historical process itself.*' Alexander von Schelting, *Max Webers Wissenschaftslehre*, 1934, 231. (Our italics.)

[2] *Ideology and Utopia*, Engl. ed. 1952, 237, 135, 82. Cf. also Kecskemeti in the introduction to Mannheim's *Essays on the Sociology of Knowledge*, 1952, 1 and 25; cf. further Mannheim's own text, *ibid.*, 171 *seq.*, 175, 178—three important passages showing Mannheim's nearness to, as well as his disagreements with, Scheler's position.

[3] *Science and Social Action*, 1954, 162.

In a realm in which everything is in the process of becoming, the only adequate synthesis would be a dynamic one, which is reformulated from time to time.' If this is meant as a thrust against Scheler, it is a singularly unfounded and aimless one. For Scheler, as we have seen, desiderated a synthesis of the essential insights of *all* generations, *including future ones*, and for this reason he, too, cannot be said to have demanded anything but a 'dynamic synthesis reformulated from time to time'.

No, however great the philosophical differences may have been, and still are, which divide the pragmatist from the metectic approach, both are agreed, and necessarily so, on the practical question as to what is to be done. Whether we accept the Platonic belief in the pre-existence of truths which merely *manifest* themselves *through* history, or whether we prefer the 'inverted Platonism' [1] of the historical school, to whom movement is more real than rest, becoming than being, so that truths are only *made in* history, it is in any case impossible to reach the more-than-historical otherwise than through the historical, the absolute through the relative, eternity through time; for time is the medium in which all our life, and hence all our mental life, is inescapably set. The ontological principles of the two schools may clash, but their research programmes coincide, and this is something for which we must be profoundly grateful. After having sought to open up a gap between Scheler's objective and his own, between a 'dynamic relative synthesis' and a 'supra-temporal absolute one', Mannheim himself is forced to close it again. 'Attempts at synthesis do not come into being unrelated to one another. . . . Each synthesis prepares the road for the next by summarizing the forces and views of its time. A certain progress towards an absolute synthesis in the utopian sense [i.e. towards a final synthesis] may be noted in that each [successive] synthesis attempts to arrive at a wider perspective than the previous one, and that the later ones incorporate the results of those that have gone before.' [2] If Mannheim means to emphasize in these sentences that a truly final and all-embracing synthesis is, practically speaking, an unattainable ideal, since it could not possibly be achieved before the last day, when man's progressive self-revelation in space and time has finally come to an end, and that the best we can hope for is a gradual advance towards that far-distant 'utopian' aim, he is merely formulating a conviction which Scheler also entertained, and which is expressed in some of his most moving passages, notably in *Vom Ewigen im Menschen*.

We find, then, that in the last analysis the pragmatist and the metectic theories concur in laying the same duty on the sociologist of knowledge:

---

[1] The expression is Nietzsche's who, like Mannheim, was an 'inverted Platonist' in ontology. Cf. Barth, *Wahrheit und Ideologie*, 1945, esp. 254 *seq.*

[2] *Loc. cit.*, 135 *seq.*

to widen the vision and wisdom of the culture to which he happens to belong by the sympathetic reception into it of the experiences of other, alien societies, divided from his own in space and time. Being more fully aware than any other type of scholar that human thought tends to be tied to the *hic* and *nunc*, to be fragmentary, relative, ephemeral and involved in the shifting and depressing conditions of human existence, —being, in short, unable to escape the realization that every mental horizon is limited and confined, he is all the more obliged to make his way to those uplands from whose summit there is more to be seen than a single culture, a single round and habit of life, and from which, perhaps, who knows, a glimpse may be caught of verities that are more than the products of a narrow valley or a passing day. This is the final task, the ideal end of the sociologist of knowledge: and it makes no difference to his obligation whether it is attainable or not. In this enterprise, as in all others in this mortal life, it is not given to us to know the issue: we must be satisfied, and more than that, if we may hope that we are travelling in the right direction.

INDEX

Absolutism, 136
Academic personnel, *see* University teachers
Adler, Georg, 321n.
Adler, Max, 120, 121, 122, 140, 146
Aesthetics, 128, 129, 130, 131, 157, 202, 234
Alberti, Leonbattista, 129
Alengry, Franck, 159
America, 19, 20, 24, 90, 117, 280, 305. *See also* Philosophy, American
Anaxagoras, 229
Ancien Régime, 3, 33
Anthropology, Philosophical, 141, 142, 196, 197, 198, 203, 204, 237, 238, 239, 240, 241, 314
Anthropology, Social, 287n.
Anticipations, 287–90
Antiquity, 117, 235, 266, 328
Antoni, Carlo, 68, 192n., 199, 206, 208n.
Apolline culture, 220
Aristocracy, 27, 42, 44, 51, 52, 58, 63, 65, 77, 78, 133, 134, 267, 268, 291, 296, 297, 302, 303. *See also* Class and classes
Aristotle and Aristotelianism, 31, 36n., 174
Aron, R., 53n., 74, 104n., 166n., 197n., 229n., 234n., 336n.
Art, 10, 18, 25, 26, 44, 93, 123, 124, 125, 130, 167, 169, 183n., 204, 225, 279, 286, 305, 318, 329, 330
Artisans, *see* Petty bourgeoisie
Artists, 25, 26, 31, 32, 44, 93, 123, 131, 167, 204, 283
Ascetics and Asceticism, 226, 306
Asia, 118
Association, 31, 38, 81, 204, 207, 284
Association of ideas, 39
Atheism and atheists, 202, 223
Atomism, *see* Individualism
Auden, W. H., 222
Augustine, St., 270
Austria, 67, 68, 302

Authoritarianism, 35n.
Axiological system, 16, 17, 18, 33, 34, 43, 44, 49, 50, 54, 66, 67, 70, 71, 72, 73, 74, 75, 76, 77, 78, 79, 86, 88, 91, 92, 93, 94, 95, 96, 97, 98, 102, 104n., 107, 108, 112, 113, 114, 115, 116, 118, 119, 121, 122, 123, 124, 125, 126, 127, 128, 129, 130, 131, 132, 133, 134, 135, 136, 137, 138, 139, 140, 144, 145, 153, 154, 155, 158, 164, 165, 166, 167, 176, 177, 178, 179, 180, 194, 201, 202, 205, 206, 244, 253, 272, 273, 274, 275, 276, 278, 285, 286, 287, 289, 295, 296, 298, 301, 308, 313, 314, 316, 332, 340n.

Bach, Carl Philipp Emanuel, 5
Bach, Johann Sebastian, 125
Bacon, Francis, 115, 116, 204
Ball, John, 84, 85, 86, 87, 89
Barth, Hans, 100n., 154n., 161n., 169n., 170n., 221n., 277n., 319n., 320n., 343n., 345n.
Barth, Paul, 228
Becker, H., 13, 205n., 214n., 233n., 265, 289n., 330n., 332
Beethoven, Ludwig van, 3, 4, 5, 6, 7, 25n., 26, 48, 123n., 204
Benedictines, The, 296, 297
Bentham, Jeremy, 7, 8, 24, 59, 183, 204, 280
Bergson, Henri, x, 187, 188, 314, 315, 319n.
Berkeley, George, *Bishop*, 215, 216
Berlioz, Hector, 32, 33
Berne, 89
Biography, 150, 214, 299
Bodin, Jean, 115
Bogdanov, Alexander, 229
Bohr, Niels, 160
Bolshevism, *see* Russia
Bonald, Louis Gabriel Ambroise, Vicomte de, 323

347

Index

Index

351

Index

Man, Doctrine of, *see* Anthropology, Philosophical

Mannheim, Karl, ix, x, 12, 13, 18n., 78, 101, 102, 103, 104, 105, 109, 111, 119, 121, 122, 126, 139, 148, 153, 154, 161, 164, 169, 170, 171, 172, 174, 180n., 181, 182, 187, 190, 194n., 201, 205, 227, 230, 231, 237n., 259, 261, 262, 263, 275, 276, 277, 287, 288, 289, 291, 297n., 300, 301, 302, 304, 306, 308, 315, 316, 317, 324, 325, 326, 327, 329, 330, 333, 334, 335, 336, 337, 338, 339, 340, 341, 342, 343, 344, 345

Maquet, J. J., 18n., 139n., 146n., 161n., 226n., 237n., 261n., 274n., 280n.

Marck, Siegfried, 332n.

Marcu, Valeriu, 321n.

Martin, Alfred von, 182n., 195n., 205, 206n., 236, 266, 267, 268, 269, 270, 271, 290n., 291, 297, 298, 304

Marx, Karl, ix, x, 12, 53, 80, 82, 90, 99, 100, 101, 104, 119, 120, 139, 140, 146, 147, 168, 169n., 174, 179, 181, 185, 187, 189, 190, 191, 227, 228, 229, 234, 235, 238, 250, 257, 259, 260, 261, 262, 263, 272, 273, 277, 278, 279, 290, 291, 293, 294, 295, 297, 298, 303, 305n., 308, 309, 313, 314, 315, 319n., 322, 323, 326, 327, 342, 343

Marxism, 53, 54, 58, 68, 75, 80, 90, 99, 100, 109, 110, 119, 120, 121, 143, 146, 147, 148, 161, 168, 169, 174, 176, 185, 186, 187, 188, 189, 224, 227, 228, 229, 230, 231, 234, 235, 257, 258, 259, 260, 261, 265, 278, 279, 289, 291, 296, 297, 307, 308, 309, 313, 315, 316, 343n.

Materialism, 77, 108, 119, 147, 148, 226, 229, 236, 238, 265, 310, 315, 334

Materialism, Historical, *see* Marxism

'Materialistic' theory, 219 *seq.*, 231, 232, 233, 236, 237, 238, 240, 242

Mathematics, 43, 115, 125, 161, 162, 167, 169, 182, 184, 192, 194, 314, 315

Mead, G. H., 241

Mechanism, 116, 205, 247, 249, 251, 261. *See also* Pan-mechanism

Mechanistic determinism, *see* Determinism, Mechanistic

Medicus, Fritz, 180

Meinecke, Friedrich, 69, 131n., 132n., 133, 134, 138n., 206n.

Mercantilism, 199

Merton, Robert K., 21n., 24, 25, 30, 35, 90, 106, 113, 122, 131n., 154, 155, 167n., 172n., 173, 174, 175n., 222, 224, 233, 234, 245, 246, 250, 254, 261n., 276n., 277n., 279, 280n., 281n., 294, 342, 343n.

Messianism, 186, 187, 189

Metaphysics, 19, 34, 35, 111, 123, 158, 159, 162, 163, 174, 175, 177, 197, 209, 225, 239, 240, 331, 334, 335, 340, 342

Metasociology, 197, 206, 210

'Metectic' theory, 328 *seq.*, 339, 340, 341, 342, 345

Methodology, 151, 168, 175, 184, 197, 204, 207, 209, 241, 242, 243, 254, 255

Microsociology of knowledge, 20, 21, 23, 26, 27, 28, 30, 31, 32, 33, 34, 35, 36, 37, 97

Middle Ages, 31, 32, 68, 74, 82, 84, 85, 86, 101, 114, 115, 117, 118, 127, 128, 130, 134, 157, 159, 161, 176, 202, 207, 235, 266, 267, 268, 269, 271, 288, 298, 302, 303, 304. *See also* Christianity; Church and churches

Middle class, *see* Bourgeoisie

Middle class, Lower, *see* Petty bourgeoisie

Mill, John Stuart, 7, 8, 11, 58, 59, 158

Millar, John, 198

Millenarianism, 186, 187, 263

Mills, Wright C., 106n., 175, 205, 327n., 335

Modern society, 74, 82, 117, 128, 138, 156, 158, 159, 201, 209, 226, 288, 296, 304. *See also* Western society and Western culture

Moleschott, Jakob, 219, 238

Mommsen, Wilhelm, 68

Monasteries, 32, 296, 297

Monism, 335

Montequieu, Charles, Baron de la Brède et de, x, 134, 135, 160, 203n., 216, 217, 221

Mozart, Wolfgang Amadeus, 3, 4, 26, 27, 32, 204, 283

Music, 3, 4, 5, 6, 7, 9, 10, 18, 26, 27, 32, 33, 123, 124, 125, 214, 218, 283. *See also* Counterpoint

Index

Myrdal, Gunnar, 55, 56, 57, 58, 59, 61, 62, 64, 66, 94, 97
Mysticism, *see* Contemplation

Nadel, S. F., 249n.
Naïve dogmatism, 15, 17, 93, 105, 110, 117, 120n., 127, 178, 191, 207
Napoleon, 68, 135, 178, 208
Nature, *see* Science
'Negativist' theory, 317 *seq.*, 334
Neo-Kantian school, x, 104
Neo-Platonic school, *see* Phenomenology
Newman, John Henry, *Cardinal*, 287
Newton, Sir Isaac, 165n., 173
Niebuhr, Barthold Georg, 67, 68
Nietzsche, Friedrich, ix, x, 8, 24, 44, 150, 151, 220, 221, 277, 317, 318, 319, 320, 321, 322, 323, 327, 332, 345n.
Nobility, *see* Aristocracy
Nominalism, 32, 38, 39, 40, 41, 81
Nomothetic sciences, 168, 194
Northrop, F. S. C., 274
Numbers, 161, 162, 163, 164, 315

Objectivity, *see* Prejudice; Truth
Occupation, 222, 224, 243
Ontology, 187, 190, 224, 225, 226, 254, 255, 258, 328, 340, 345n.
Organicism, 81, 101, 249, 251, 252, 253, 259, 262, 265, 266, 269, 283

Painting, 123, 124, 125, 158
Paley, William, 60
Pan-animism, 174
Panentheism, 334
Pan-ideologism, 101, 104, 105, 119, 135, 155, 158, 159, 321, 322. *See also* Ideology
Pan-mechanism, 117, 141, 174, 320. *See also* Mechanism
Pantheism, 35, 334
Pareto, Vilfredo, ix, x, 51, 52, 53, 80, 179, 183, 191, 192, 193, 194, 221, 233, 238, 239, 317, 318, 320, 321, 322, 323, 327
Pars pro toto fallacy, 156, 157, 158, 166, 180, 185, 194, 195n., 229
Parsons, Talcott, 139, 230n.
Parties, Political, 103, 276, 277, 304. *See also* Communism; Conservatism; Fascism; Labour Party; Socialism; Tories; Whigs

Pascal, Blaise, 141, 173, 177, 178, 337
Peasantry, 27, 58, 63, 64, 65, 83, 84, 89, 205, 223, 296, 305
Peirce, Charles Sanders, 327
Personality, 141, 142
Perspectivism, 122, 164. *See also* Axiological system; Relativity
Petty bourgeoisie, 27, 63, 64, 65, 84, 89, 133, 205, 223, 290, 302, 307. *See also* Class and classes
Phenomenology, 197, 258, 262, 342
Phillippe Égalité, Prince, 291
Philosophical anthropology, *see* Anthropology, Philosophical
Philosophy, 10, 18, 107, 130, 158, 167, 169, 180, 190, 203, 279, 284, 290, 310, 319, 334. *See also* Epistemology; Logic; Metaphysics; Naïve dogmatism; Nominalism; Phenomenology; Positivism; Pragmatism; Rationalism; Realism; Scholasticism; Sensualism; Utilitarianism; *and under individual names*
Philosophy, American, 19, 20
Philosophy, British, 7, 8, 9
Philosophy, German, 7, 8, 54
Philosophy, Medieval, 32
Physics, *see* Science
Physiocrats, The, 58, 63
Plato and Platonism, 35, 36n., 40, 41, 42, 43, 51, 52, 53, 188, 195, 220, 257, 265, 310, 324, 328, 330, 334, 340, 341, 345. *See also* Phenomenology
Plekhanov, Georgy, 228
Plessner, Helmut, 24n., 31, 205
Plotinus, 43
Poetry, 214
Political Parties, *see* Parties, Political
Positivism, 118, 167, 180, 261, 323, 330
Power politics, 69, 115, 129, 204
Praemonstratensians, The, 296
Pragmatism, 19, 20, 77, 118, 121, 137, 138, 327, 335, 338, 342
'Pragmatist' theory, 323 *seq.*, 329, 330, 331, 333, 334, 335, 339, 342, 343, 345
Prejudice, 15, 39, 57, 58, 59, 66, 67, 71, 72, 73, 75, 91n., 92, 93, 94, 102, 107, 118, 126, 127, 158, 186, 291, 323. *See also* Ideology
Price, Formation of, 207, 267
Primitive man and primitive thought, 38, 39, 96, 117, 118, 145, 156, 161, 162, 163, 164, 201, 233, 287, 309

Index

Turner, Frederick Jackson, 131
Typology, 206, 208n., 217, 227, 231, 259, 279

'Understanding' sociology, 141, 142, 143, 148
United States, *see* America
Universities, 20, 21, 22, 23, 30, 31, 32, 36, 300
University teachers and university teaching, 20, 23, 24, 30, 31, 32. *See also* Scholars and scholarship
Utilitarianism, 116, 117, 182, 183, 205. *See also* Philosophy
Utopias, 103, 139, 140, 262, 263, 287, 289, 316, 325, 326, 337, 345
Utraquists, The, 86

Values, Anarchy of, *see* Relativism
Values, System of, *see* Axiological system
Veblen, Thorstein, x, 36, 97, 234
Vico, Giambattista, x, 115, 160, 165, 328
Vierkandt, Alfred, 197
Villani, Giovanni, 290n.
Vinci, Leonardo da, 129
Vogt, Karl, 219, 238
Voltaire, François Marie Arouet de, 132, 133, 134, 135, 179

Wagner, Richard, 10, 32, 33
Walras, Léon, 183, 184, 207

Warynski, Stanislaw, 53, 54, 75, 109, 110, 111, 119, 120, 140n., 146, 147, 148, 179n., 187, 228n., 229, 230, 260, 297n., 309n., 321n., 322n.
Weber, Alfred, x, 104n., 166, 167, 168, 175n., 176n., 179, 181n., 192n., 198, 204n., 205, 225, 234n., 256, 259, 320n., 332, 333, 335
Weber, Max, ix, x, 25, 63, 104, 105, 112, 119, 122, 123, 127, 128, 156, 161, 168, 184, 185, 186, 192, 193, 194, 203, 205, 206, 218, 222, 223, 231, 239, 243, 246, 253, 256, 257, 258, 270, 271, 272, 275, 277, 291n., 298, 303, 306, 340n.
Western society and Western culture, 95, 117, 118, 157, 161, 176, 199, 200, 271, 332
Whigs, 68, 135, 136, 137. *See also* Parties, Political
Wilde, Oscar, 202
Wirth, Louis, 36
Wittfogel, K. A., 228
Women, 298
Working classes, *see* Proletariat
Wycliff, John, 86

Zeno, 314
Ziegenfuss, W., 195n., 244n., 282n., 338, 343n.
Znaniecki, Florian, 28, 29, 30, 31, 36, 327n., 343n.

356